MYCENAEANS
AND MINOANS

MYCENAEANS
AND
MINOANS

AEGEAN PREHISTORY IN THE LIGHT
OF THE LINEAR B TABLETS

SECOND EDITION,
SUBSTANTIALLY REVISED AND ENLARGED

LEONARD R. PALMER

*Professor of Comparative Philology
in the University of Oxford*

NEW YORK: ALFRED · A · KNOPF
MCMLXV

L. C. catalog card number: 64–19093

THIS IS A BORZOI BOOK,
PUBLISHED BY ALFRED A. KNOPF, INC.

SECOND EDITION, REVISED AND ENLARGED

First published 1961 in Great Britain.

Acknowledgements

Acknowledgements are due to the following for allowing the reproduction of certain material:

To the Trustees of the British Museum for reproduction of the Mycenae Slab of the Bull; to the British School at Athens for reproduction of one plate and five figures from volumes of the BSA Annual; to the Oxford University Press (Clarendon Press) for reproduction of two plates and two figures from SCRIPTA MINOA I; to Thames and Hudson Ltd. for reproduction of eleven plates from Spyridon Marinatos' CRETE AND MYCENAE; to *History Today* for reproduction of a figure from their May issue for 1957; to Mrs. Seton Lloyd for reproduction of her reconstruction drawing of the Late Bronze Age Shrine 'B' at Beycesultan; to Professor Blegen for reproduction of the photograph by Miss Alison Frantz of the Palace of Nestor; and to Mrs. L. Killick for reproduction of figures from her late husband Michael Ventris' unpublished work.

Thanks are also due to Mr. F. M. Blackwell for his help with photography and to Miss Christine Court for assistance in preparing the figures, plans and maps.

Mr. J. Raison supplied the photographs for plates 16 and 18, and the former is reproduced by kind permission of Dr. S. Alexiou, Director of the Museum of Heraklion.

Contents

7

Contents

Illustrations

PLATES

Illustrations

FIGURES IN THE TEXT

Illustrations

Preface to the Second Edition

The genesis of this book has been described in detail in the 'Biography of the Book'. Briefly, research both on the archaeological and the philological side raised doubts about the period of the Mycenaean occupation of the palace at Knossos and the date of its final destruction. The work presenting these arguments had already been sent to the press when the Knossos excavation documents came to light at Oxford, in the Italian book market, and in the excavation house at Knossos itself. Little more could be attempted in the first edition than to check Sir Arthur Evans's sole stratigraphic statement bearing on the date of the Linear B tablets. Now, after three years study of the primary sources it is clear that the results go far beyond the surmise of Professor Blegen and myself. The evidence revealed is so far-reaching in its consequences for Aegean prehistory and fraught with such grave personal implications that every effort must be made to achieve precision of factual statement. What Blegen asked for was the evidence obtained by excavation at Knossos. That evidence is contained abundantly in the excavation records. Its implications must be faced without regard for the convenience or inconvenience of the consequences. Such pre-occupations simply lead to a loss of intellectual integrity. With this in mind I have completely rewritten the second part of this book: it is now a separate work.

Chapter Six traces the history of the dispute about the relations of Minoans and Mycenaeans and poses the problem of Evans's reliability as a witness. It is Chapter Seven on 'Checking the Facts' which is the core of the presentation. It emerges with all clarity that Evans's sole stratigraphic key was wholly a work of his imagination. His own advocates have been compelled to admit that neither the tablets nor the pottery assembled at their various levels to form his elaborate 'decisive' stratigraphic picture were in fact found anywhere near that part of the palace, while the triple floor structure itself was transferred from a neighbouring room. Close scrutiny of the records showed that the inaccuracies of reporting extend to all parts of the palace and to all periods of its occupation including Middle Minoan and Early Minoan. The nodal points of Aegean prehistory which still figure as chronological indicators in the most recent accounts (e.g. *The Cambridge Ancient History*) are without foundation. Evans's famous 'système de classification' is shown not to have been based on secure excavation data. The inaccuracies are of all possible forms: adjustment, omission and invention. They began in the earliest reports and culminated in Evans's attack on Wace in his *Shaft Graves and Beehive Tombs of Mycenae*, which is built round a meticulously analysed and stratigraphically sited piece of evidence which is untrue. As for the problem, posed by Blegen, with which this study began, it now appears as a minor matter. The question is no longer whether the palace was destroyed at the end of the period Late Minoan III B but rather how many palaces had been constructed during the long period assigned to this ceramic phase — 1375–1150. What bears on this problem is the evidence secured by excavations which went unreported, particularly in 1923 (see p. 223).

It is understandable that the ruin of the long hallowed and canonical framework of Aegean archaeology should have produced shock effects. Controversy is salutary, but there are rules for scientific discussion. The opposition to the new evidence has taken on disquieting forms. I have examined the reactions of those who have taken the leading part in my Chapter Eight, 'The Conflict of Scholars'. They are of value in that they offer samples of the treatment of archaeological evidence by some of the most prominent practitioners. It will be seen that the pressure of the facts gradually forced the defenders into attacks on Evans himself. Finally, to justify the total rejection of Evans's own precise and detailed accounts, a piece of unpublished 'evidence' was produced by his advocate from the Ashmolean Museum. Investigation showed this to be an invention (see pp. 250 ff.).

Fortunately, for the general reader the issues are very simple: they concern the find positions of certain lumps of clay and other material objects. Was an Egyptian statuette found on the pavement or 70 centimetres below it? These are questions which require no expertise, but they are the stuff of which archaeology is made. This example is one of the nodal points of which I have spoken. It is on such matters that the general public is being misled. Archaeology, we are assured, is merely the application of common-sense, and I follow the practice of archaeologists in inviting the general reader to participate.

The first part of this book remains much as it was, but I have incorporated the results of recent important research into the Linear B tablets. Finally, in the last chapter I have ventured to offer some new workings bearing on the question of the language of the Linear A tablets.

L. R. PALMER

Postscript

The Preface to the first edition ended with a postscript reporting a recantation by Mr. M. S. F. Hood, Director of the British School of Archaeology at Athens. Mr. Hood is outstanding among British archaeologists for his detailed knowledge of the site of Knossos, and he has been among the most vigorous and influential defenders of Evans. Thus it marks an important step towards final agreement in this vexed question that in a paper submitted to the Mycenaean Seminar of the University of London on 30 September 1964 Mr. Hood admitted the main theses of this book, characterizing the so-called Reoccupation at Knossos as a myth invented by Evans and Mackenzie. Of more fundamental import is his recognition that several different pottery styles were in simultaneous use at Knossos at the time of the final destruction and that there is no evidence for their chronological separation. The catastrophic implications for prehistoric archaeology need no emphasizing (see pp. 303–6 and p. 320).

It should be acknowledged that Mr. Hood in so doing has shown exemplary detachment and scientific objectivity in a controversy inflamed by irrelevancies of personal reputation and inter-doctrinal rivalries.

MYCENAEANS
AND MINOANS

Biography of the Book

This may seem a strange title for an Introduction, but the fact is that this book claimed a will of its own, and eventually took a course and assumed a form contrary to the original plan and intentions of the author. Its life-history will serve simultaneously as apologia, summary, and guide through the labyrinth.

The book began with an invitation from the publishers to write an account for the general reader of the work on the Mycenaean Greek texts written in the Linear B script. This is the form of writing used by the Greeks of the Mycenaean age, whose decipherment by the late Michael Ventris marked a turning point in the study of the Late Bronze Age of the Aegean. I responded to this invitation all the more gladly because Linear B remains something of a mystery even to some professional classical scholars, with the consequence that ideas and results, reached tentatively in the infancy of this new branch of study, but later discarded, were beginning to find their way into general accounts of the Greek Bronze Age over the signature of authoritative names. Let it be freely confessed that at the beginning we all made mistakes in dealing with these bald counting-house dockets from the Mycenaean palaces, which give only the barest of hints at a form of Greek some five centuries earlier than any dialect of that tongue we had hitherto encountered. It was necessary to work out the best scientific method of coaxing the truth from these reluctant witnesses. After trial and error it proved that the safest way was to abandon the Greek lexicon and to try the way of pure analysis. In other words we repeated the experience of decipherers in other fields: the 'etymological' method of guessing at Greek words, long since discredited, had to give way to the 'combinatory' method, which attempts first to arrive at the meaning of the syllabically written words by contextual analysis before going on to the second step of equating these words with later words listed in the Greek lexicon of Liddell and Scott.

Provided at an early stage by Ventris, with his exemplary generosity, with much unpublished material, I began a systematic attempt to analyse the Linear B archives along these lines. Handwriting, size and shape of tablet, signs of cutting and breaking, the grouping of scattered texts into ordered series as the successive 'pages' of a book, arithmetical analysis of the quantities — all the results gradually accumulated by the patient labours of an international team were applied, and little by little the Mycenaean world began to take on an appearance less strange than that conjured up by the earlier method. A motley band of women described as 'headband makers, musicians and sweepers' turned out to be simply named after the villages from which they came. 'Absent carpenters', an entry of remarkable frequency, were petrified into a place-name of the pattern Newcastle-upon-Tyne. 'Female barley-reapers', of curiously mixed parentage, were found to be women attached to a temple establishment. Beneath this bright microscopic lamp 'kings', 'palaces', and 'Councils of Elders' all faded into insubstantiality and were consigned to a limbo reigned over by that short-lived Linear B character, 'Aigeus the Cretan', who turned out to be of greater importance when transformed into the description of a tripod: 'with goat's head handles, of Cretan workmanship'.

By the beginning of 1960 this re-examination was finished, and a work *The Interpretation of Mycenaean Greek Texts* was sent to press.

The task of summarizing the results for presentation to non-specialists in the first draft of this book proved far from easy. The many differences between this account and others which have appeared ruled out any simple categorical statement of my own results with the bland implication that the others are wrong and it is sufficient that I say so. Moreover, the message of these new documents concerns a wide circle beyond the limits of classical studies. The Bronze Age of Greece is one of the most formative periods of our civilization, and the results of investigation in this field have repercussions far outside the Aegean. The prehistory of much of Europe hinges on the correct interpretation of excavations in Greek lands. Consequently the reader had to be admitted to full partnership. The problems had to be stated, the material presented, and the workings shown, despite their difficulty. So I have not shunned the quotation of actual texts or the elucidation of the methods of analysis involved.

On reflection it seemed best to base the exposition on the finds made at Pylos, the site near Navarino in southern Greece where Professor C. W. Blegen in 1939 uncovered what he believed, rightly in my opinion, to be the palace of the Homeric King Nestor. Here was found the best preserved and the most coherent archive of documents written on clay tablets in the Linear B script. Without them the decipherment would hardly have been possible; without them it would have been difficult to make sense of the more fragmentary texts discovered by Sir Arthur Evans at Knossos in Crete at the beginning of the century. We begin, therefore, with Pylos and an historical account of the long scholarly controversy concerned with this place. It began in antiquity when Greek exponents of Homer tried to locate the places which figure in the stories of the Iliad and the Odyssey, and in particular 'sandy Pylos', where the aged King Nestor had his palace. This quarrel raged through the ages among Homeric philologues. In the late nineteenth century archaeologists brought their expertise to bear, only to make confusion worse confounded. For they split evenly, and the 'Greens' and 'Blues' of this ancient feud could each flourish an archaeological site to substantiate their claim. Our first chapter ends with an appeal by an archaeologist to the then undeciphered texts which held the decisive answer to the riddle.

Our second chapter is then perforce concerned with the dispute over the decipherment. The story of that remarkable achievement has already been told in moving terms by Michael Ventris's collaborator, Dr. J. Chadwick. But attacks still continue, sometimes in a disquieting form. Since the validity of the decipherment is basic to our whole enterprise, the question 'What constitutes a proof of any decipherment whatsoever?' has been considered in detail and the objections examined and assessed.

This essential preliminary completed, we return in the third chapter to the question which closed the first. The answer is

unequivocal: the texts show that the place where Professor
Blegen's palace is sited was called Pylos. To be more precise, we
have a fairly clear and detailed picture of the geography of the
territory controlled by this palace. Gratifyingly enough, its limits
coincide almost exactly with the extent of Pylian territory such as
we can piece together from the scattered references to this Mycenaean kingdom contained in the Homeric poems. We can see
that administratively its territory was divided into two provinces,
the Hither Province and the Further Province, the demarcation
being the cape which marks the southern point of the Messenian
peninsula, Cape Acritas. Pylos is the chief place of the Hither
Province. Still more gratifying, renewed archaeological exploration of the region mapped out in our analysis as the Further
Province has revealed important new Mycenaean sites.

Our geographical setting outlined, we turn in Chapter Four to
the Bronze Age society which lived there, to encounter a surprise.
The picture would have astonished Homer, on whose witness we
had previously to rely for the reconstruction of the Greek Heroic
Age, but not, I believe, Thucydides. The great historian, with his
penetrating vision, remarked that there were many features about
the way of life in early Greece which resembled the Orient of his
own day. In fact, the picture of the Mycenaean polity which has
gradually emerged from the combined labours of Linear B
scholars recalls the temple states of the Orient. A king who shares
his title 'Wanax' with a god is intimately linked with a goddess
simply called 'The Lady' or 'The Mistress'. This close association
shows itself in a variety of ways, in none more clearly or more
fundamentally than the texts dealing with land-tenure. For the
student of the structure of society there is no subject of greater
importance; and we are fortunate indeed that virtually a complete
land register, in two separate versions, has been preserved to us,
relating to what I believe was the King's estate at the holy town of
Pylos, where 'The Mistress' had her shrine. From these and other
similar texts we gather some idea of the various classes of land-
holders, among whom the 'servants (male and female) of the God'
are especially numerous.

But this is no mere offshoot of the Orient. The God-King or the
King-God is certainly paramount, but the *demos* also figures

prominently as a land-holding entity, leasing its lands and uphold-ing its rights *vis-à-vis* the palace in a case of disputed tenure.

The duality King-Mistress is particularly evident in the texts relating to bronze, for we have a great part of what must have been a census of the bronze-smiths of the Kingdom; it records those with allotted tasks, together with the amount of bronze issued, and also the bronze-smiths who are idle. It is here that we find the workers divided into those belonging to Potnia ('The Mistress') and the others, mentioned first, who presumably belonged to the royal establishment.

Yet another census concerns the cattle herds of both provinces of the kingdom. Here we find listed first the beasts of the king; then those belonging to a number of palace notabilities, whom we encounter elsewhere; and finally again the animals entered as belonging to Potnia. Gradually these dour archives reveal to us a complex administration with its queer titulature, practically nothing of which survived into later Greek, and many aspects of the economy. We need nothing to convince us of the importance of wheat, wine, oil and cattle in Mycenaean Greece. But one of the most welcome pieces of information gives some answer to a Bronze Age riddle: how did an intrinsically poor country like Greece manage to pay for its luxury imports? From the records of Pylos, Mycenae and Knossos we can now see the importance attached by all the palaces to the collection of aromatic substances for the manufacture of perfumed oil. The texts also give us interesting indications of the uses to which it was put. This dove-tails nicely with an archaeological fact of unique importance — the ubiquity of the stirrup-jar. Without undue distortion we may say that our picture of the extent of Mycenaean expansion and influence is little more than the distribution of this type of vessel on the archaeological map. The stirrup-jar is the *Leitfossil* of Mycenaean culture. We now know from the texts that they were used to con-tain perfumed oil.

Of no less interest is another set of facts of basic economic significance. It has proved possible to elucidate the grain ration scales, and it has become clear that a scheme of allocations ac-cording to social grade and function was in operation, a complex scheme common to both Pylos and Knossos. Again we are struck by the resemblance of the whole system to certain systems of the Orient which had been analysed by students of cuneiform texts. But this is not the only significant feature: the ratios of the corn-measures themselves are Mesopotamian in origin. They are dictated by the practical necessity of issuing a basic daily ration at monthly intervals (see pp. 118f). Moreover, the determination of these daily ration scales enables us to get some idea of the number of men and women the palace at Knossos was catering for; again by a lucky chance we have a number of texts recording the monthly allocation for certain dependent places, notably Phaestos in the south of Crete.

Finally the texts recording the things and substances offered to the gods, notably perfumed oil, enable us to give the precision of cult-titles, places, festivals and dates to the accounts of Mycenaean religion based hitherto on the dumb 'picture book' presented by the artefacts of Minoan and Mycenaean craftsmen. The result is gratifying to all concerned. It confirms in the main the deductions of the chief exponents in this delicate field of study. The Mycenaean religion shows itself profoundly under the influence of the Orient. For all the presence of Zeus, Hera, Artemis, Poseidon and Hermes, the views of Sir Arthur Evans and others that the Aegean, religiously speaking, was an offshoot of the Orient have been largely substantiated.

One simple physical fact about these clay tablets now focuses attention on a problem which has an undeniable fascination though authoritative cold water has diminished its historical pretensions. The records were originally inscribed on sun-dried clay which would soon have disintegrated. They present themselves to the scrutiny of twentieth century scholars only because they were unintentionally baked in the fire which finally destroyed the Palace of Nestor about 1200 B.C. They thus record the doings of the palace in the final months of Mycenaean civilization in those parts. Was it possible that the scribes and their masters were totally oblivious of their impending doom? This is the question to which we address ourselves in Chapter Five. We can answer it briefly: we see a society organizing itself with meticulous bureaucratic detail for its final ordeal. Women and children are gathered together into two main concentration areas, and arrangements are recorded for their supervision and provisioning. Bronze-smiths are allotted tasks, and it is recorded that officials are to yield up 'temple bronze' for armaments. Watchers are posted to guard an immense stretch of coast, a thinly spread line, with named officers and commanders. All this was clear by 1955–56. Further analysis has disclosed other facts of interest. The chain of watcher posts along the coast showed a great gap around the southern tip of the peninsula. We can now see, thanks to the analysis of what appeared to be a totally unrelated set of texts, that this gap is filled by the places where 'rowers' are recorded. Such complementarity shown by two different sets of texts can hardly be accidental, and I have ventured to conclude that these 'rower' texts reflect dimly the main concentration of the Pylian fleet in the area embracing the southern parts of the peninsula facing the Ionian Sea and the Gulf of Messenia, and that the complementary screen of coast watchers is the common-sense reaction of men faced with a sea-borne attack of unknown target area.

But this is not the only information which fits in here. Yet another set of texts is concerned with the allocation of craftsmen, especially bronze-smiths. Once again as minute analysis fitted the facts into place, it could be seen that these allocations affected the same area, and often the same places, as those recorded in the 'rower' texts. Here, too, a random coincidence seems excluded. We deduce that the craftsmen — bronze-smiths, chariot-wrights, 'sewers', masons, etc — are being posted to the military headquarters. Pylian society was facing its emergency with the clear rationality we associate with the Greek mind. Strategic concentration and organization of local defence units, with civil defence measures to protect the women and children housed in villages scattered over the open countryside against possible marauders — an evacuation in reverse. The last mentioned pieces in this complex jig-saw puzzle we have been able to put in place thanks to the detailed ration lists which this movement of population necessitated. It was arithmetical analysis of these lists which revealed the basic rationing system which was also found to apply to Knossos.

At this point my original undertaking to write the new story of Mycenaean society under the title 'Nestor of Pylos' seemed

Biography of the Book

virtually completed. All that remained was to compose a final synthesis, working these results into the accepted framework of prehistoric archaeology. It was at this point that the book took a new turn which necessitated the writing of a second part not envisaged in the original plan. It completely changed the character of the book. I had imagined that the final conspectus would not take much longer than a week, for once Ventris's decipherment had won acceptance, a clear picture of the Late Aegean Bronze age had achieved orthodoxy. But it gradually became clear that my results could not be fitted into this accepted framework.

This received opinion was given clear and cogent expression at the Eleventh International Congress of Historical Sciences held in Stockholm in August 1960. Among the reports submitted for discussion was one by Professor S. Dow of Harvard on 'The Greeks in the Bronze Age'. Its findings are that the Greeks entered Greece shortly after 2000 B.C. and introduced the Middle Helladic Culture. It was, however, not until Late Helladic times (beginning c. 1580 B.C.) that a concentration of power is to be observed centring around Mycenae. About 1480 B.C., according to Professor Dow, the Mycenaeans launched a successful invasion of Crete and ruled the island from the Palace of Knossos, where their period of dominance coincides with the Late Minoan II culture. The burning of this palace at the end of this period, c. 1400 B.C. is thought to mark the end of Minoan civilization. Professor Dow correctly summarizes archaeological opinion when he says that during the whole Late Minoan III period (c. 1400–1150) Crete was but a shadow of its former self, being isolated and quiet. In this, like all other Aegean specialists, he is following in the footsteps of Sir Arthur Evans, who called this the Period of Partial Reoccupation, when the denizens of the ruined palace were mere 'squatters'.

My own findings could hardly be a greater contrast. I have been forced to the conclusion that during this so-called 'squatter' period Knossos was in fact at the height of its power and that its Greek king controlled most of the island. Moreover, I now believe that many of the famous works of art, such as the Bull Relief Fresco, are also of this period, when the Greeks were in control. The steps which have led to this complete revolution in the accepted picture are set forth in Chapter Six. All that is necessary

24

to say here is that interpretation of the texts had convinced me by February 1960 that Sir Arthur Evans's dating of the Linear B tablets to the end of the Late Minoan II period, *c.* 1400 B.C., must be wrong. In particular my suspicions were focused precisely on his key stratigraphical statements concerning a little room called The Room of the Stirrup Jar. These doubts prompted a series of enquiries which revealed the existence in the archives of the Ashmolean Museum, Oxford, of important primary sources for the Knossos excavations, which had remained unexploited. The first to emerge was the Day Book of the Knossos excavations meticulously kept by Sir Arthur Evans's assistant and official recorder, Duncan Mackenzie. This document showed that the alleged clear stratification of the Room of the Stirrup Jar, on which my doubts had been concentrated, had not been observed at the time when the said room was excavated and the objects removed, thus destroying the evidence once and for all. The find objects were not in fact arranged in their neat and convincing stratigraphical pattern until the end of the fourth season, in 1903. The next document I examined confirmed this: it was Sir Arthur Evans's own notebook for the said year. He, like Mackenzie, had drawn a plan of the area, and they both agreed in siting the objects on the same level with no hint of a vertical section which later was to figure so prominently in the published discussions.

Chapter Six, which sets forth these doubts, the progress of the search and its culmination, was already in the press in its present form when another document of the first importance came to light. On returning from vacation at the beginning of September 1960 I was informed that more of the papers left to the Ashmolean by the late Sir John Myres had been brought up from the basement. Among them was the document for which I had been looking from the start of my enquiries. This was Sir Arthur Evans's own Handlist of the Linear B tablets, complete with drawings and indications of the find-places. It is a paste-up of his original notebooks which he had cut up and rearranged. In his first excavation report of 1900 Evans wrote: 'I have copied over nine hundred of these tablets which I hope carefully to revise with the aid of the originals on my return to Crete. . . . No effort will be spared to publish the whole collected material at the earliest possible moment. The

Oxford University Press (Clarendon Press) has undertaken the publication, and has already set in hand the preliminary work, including a Mycenaean Fount.' In fact over half a century was to elapse before the tablets were published. But from the snippets in the later paste-up it has proved possible to reconstruct Evans's notebook in what must have been its original form of 1900.

Study of this document brought complete confirmation of the doubts my researches had raised about Evans's chosen key to the stratigraphy of the tablets, to which he had lent emphasis by every device of typography. The heading of this important section of his monumental work reads thus: 'Hoard of Tablets referring to Painted Clay "Stirrup Vases" from Area above "Early Keep". Its Stratigraphical Relations.' The Handlist shows that there was only one such tablet and not a hoard; and that it was found 'Near Southwest Entrance' and not in the little Room of the Stirrup Jar lying to the west of the Northern Entrance Passage. I may add that a little later I found an unpublished commentary on the Knossos tablets by the late Sir John Myres, the literary executor of Sir Arthur Evans. He too places the said tablet 'near the southwest entrance'.

Throughout this investigation and discussion we have been at pains merely to record the documentary facts and to observe that the earlier and the later statements 'cannot be reconciled'. We stress again that the question of 'deliberate misrepresentation' is an irrelevance. Defenders of Evans, however, continue to insist publicly that the question of integrity is involved. If we are thus compelled to face it, then the problem will be most objectively considered as one aspect of the relationship between Volume Four of the *Palace of Minos* as a whole to the Handlist of 1900; for it was in this part of his work that Evans made his first extensive communication concerning the Linear B tablets to the world of scholarship thirty-five years after the discovery of the first tablets.

It may be said at once that throughout his exposition Evans makes intensive use of his Handlist, reproducing the drawings and quoting the texts by their HL number while discussing such minutiae as the variations in the shape of individual signs. Moreover he sometimes cut out the drawings and sent them to the press for making blocks for the figures. There are many instances where the drawings have been re-pasted along with pulls from the blocks.

Among the texts drawn in this original notebook of 1900 is the famous stirrup-vase tablet. The corresponding figure is *PoM* iv, fig. 719, p. 734. It is an exact replica *of the same size*. A tracing made of the figure fits exactly over the drawing. Now the drawing on the page of the Handlist is singled out by the word 'This written alongside, while the drawing above is distinguished by the note 'not this'. The stirrup-vase tablet is also marked off by four crosses drawn in red ink and below in the same red ink are written the words 'same size'. There can be little doubt that these are instructions to the press for making figure 719. Above the drawing written in ink in Evans's own hand stands his original indication of the find place: W. Area: Nr SW entrance. Thus while Evans was preparing the copy and assembling the facts which were to offer to his fellow scholars 'decisive evidence for relative dating of "stirrup Vase Tablets" '; while he was preparing to announce to the world of scholarship that the tablets in question were separated by a deposit 'about 20 cm thick' from the Late Minoan III stirrup-jars on the floor above, he had before his eyes his own record that the tablet in question was found in an entirely different part of the Palace. Hence there is a conflict of testimony relating to all the alleged facts about the 'stratigraphic relation of this deposit'.

Even so my comment takes the limited and prudent form that we had best ignore the data relating to the Room of the Stirrup-Jar. I have found that no doubt attaches to other detailed statements relating to finds of Linear B tablets. It is fortunate that, as the records now show, only a few miserable scraps of tablet were in fact found in the said room and that there was after all only one 'stirrup-jar tablet', the one we have just assigned to a different locality. It is surprising that Evans should so have singled out these scraps and this one stratigraphic statement. We must infer that this was the clearest case in his eyes. Yet only a few yards away is one of the most extensive and coherent of all tablet deposits, and unmistakably associated with, one may say entangled with, whole pots of clear late Reoccupation date. All the evidence, published and unpublished, harmonizes. No less clear

and acknowledged by Evans himself are the facts relating to the
four hundred and fifty tablets found within a space of ten metres
in the East Wing of the Palace, the so-called Domestic Quarter,
which Evans himself declared had remained in continuous occupation down to the end of Late Minoan III times, after the great
catastrophe dated to 1400 B.C. The Little Palace, some hundreds
of yards to the northwest of the main palace, offers evidence
which Evans himself originally found cogent, for here there was
no conflagration until the end of LM III. We are told in fact that
the wooden columns of this building still retained their flutings
which left their impression on the later plaster which set round
them. But without conflagration these sun-dried tablets and
sealings could not have survived. The facts in the important West
Wing, where were situated the Throne Room, the shrines and the
all-important magazines, are more confused. But fortunately the
unity of all the archives can be demonstrated by internal cross-
references.

To avoid friction due to misunderstanding we stress that
throughout Chapter Six our method has been to let Evans tell his
own story and to follow his own analyses. He discusses the various
artefacts drawn on these tablets and we accept his analysis without question simply in order to observe where the echoes of resemblance lie. It will be seen that once his key statement is
disregarded, all his arguments lead to the same conclusion, confirmed by the Day Book, that the tablets are of LM III date. The
same is true of his study of many of the works of art such as the
Bull Relief Fresco. Furthermore, by a curious irony, our new dating
restores to Evans the victory, awarded by almost universal
consent since 1952 to his main opponent in an archaeological
dispute which had for decades divided Aegean archaeologists
into opposing camps. A. J. B. Wace was the chief spokesman for
the 'mainlanders', who argued that the Late Minoan II palace of
Knossos had been the seat of Greek conquerors from the Mycenaean mainland. Once the language of these tablets was seen to
be Greek, Wace's thesis, tentatively propounded by him, attracted
a large following. But if the tablets are to be dated to *c.* 1150,
then Evan's stubbornly held views are shown to be right after
all.

Biography of the Book

There are other important consequences. The end of LM III Knossos is dated by archaeologists a half century or so later than the destruction of the Palace of Nestor at Pylos. This implies that the Knossos tablets, with their new dating, are somewhat later than those of Pylos. This purely archaeological conclusion is supported by observations of language and orthography. If the new date is right, then we must reopen the whole question of the history of the script. Serious doubt is cast on the idea that the Linear B script was evolved by Minoan scribes in Crete for their Greek masters in the fifteenth century or earlier. It would now seem more likely that the Greek invaders brought this form of script with them from the mainland. This would account better for a more important fact left unexplained by the previous theory: there is a totally different system of measurements of capacity from those of Linear A.

This brings us to the third important point where I would disagree with the accepted picture of the Greek Bronze Age. What evidence have we for associating the Greeks with the Middle Helladic invasion dated to *c.* 2000 B.C.? The Linear B texts are our first indubitable evidence for the presence of Greeks. If they are all to be dated to 1200 B.C. or later, then we are a long way from 2000 B.C. Now Professor Blegen has stressed that the whole history of the palace of Pylos was played out within the short period LH III B, i.e. 1300–1200 B.C. The rise of the palace at the beginning of this period marks, he believes, the arrival of a new dynasty, which legend suggests came from north of the isthmus of Corinth. Thus in the present state of knowledge we cannot safely go back further than 1300 B.C. for the use of Linear B at Pylos to write the Greek language. However, it would not be forcing the evidence overmuch if we say that the beginning of the Late Helladic period (*c.* 1580 B.C.) marks the arrival of the Greeks in Greece.

Who then brought the Middle Helladic culture to Greece? This is the subject of our ninth chapter. In the first place we follow the majority opinion among archaeologists about the affinities of this culture. They agree in the main in associating it with northwest Asia Minor; and more recent investigations show a distribution of its characteristic 'Grey Minyan' pottery as far south as the Maeander valley. If this is where the Middle Helladic folk came from, then they can hardly have been Greeks. There is not a shred of evidence for the use of the Greek language in those parts at that early date.

On the other hand, we have plenty of evidence for another Indo-European family of languages used throughout the second millennium in Asia Minor. These are the Anatolian languages, the best known of which is Hittite. But in the south and west, in the regions nearest to Crete, we find a closely related language, Luvian. Quite unexpectedly, while engaged in work in this field, I found some remarkable Luvian echoes in the Linear A texts. The possibility argued in Chapter Seven that the predecessors of the Greeks were Luvians from western Asia Minor should please both philologists and archaeologists. Before the decipherment the most important linguistic evidence for the pre-Greek people was place-names. Among these none figured more prominently in scholarly discussion than those of the type *Parnassos*. Now such names are particularly common in Luvian territory. Furthermore, Parnassos turns out to be a perfectly transparent word: it means 'belonging to the *parna*'. In the Luvian tongue *parna* means 'house' and in particular 'house of god', 'temple', a spread of meaning such as we observe in the German *Dom* 'cathedral', which is nothing more than the Latin word *domus*. Thus the Greek mountain name Parnassos not only has Asianic counterparts, as scholars had long observed; it also has an appropriate meaning in Luvian. While much remains to be done on the Linear A texts, which present the next important philological task in this area, as a working hypothesis I should propose to equate the archaeological 'Grey Minyan' folk with my philological 'Parnassos folk'. This would satisfactorily harmonize the results long reached through the study of pottery and place-names by two different disciplines. It would appear that Greece and Crete were twice invaded by Indo-European peoples during the second millennium B.C. in much the same way as our own island was first invaded by Celts and later by our Anglo-Saxon forebears. First came the Luvians, causing the Middle Helladic revolution; they were followed by the Greeks, who caused the less violent archaeological break at the beginning of Late Helladic. So far no archaeological evidence has come to light which suggests where they came from. That it was from the regions north of Greece seems, however, inescapable.

The book, in its drastically revised form, was already with the printers when the question of the credibility of the central witness was again raised in an acute form. It had been objected that if the Linear B tablets are all assigned to the late date, 1150 B.C., then there is a gap of some 400 years of apparent illiteracy in the history of the Knossian palace. This stimulated new enquiry, which is set forth in the inserted addendum pp. 250ff. From this it emerges that once again, precisely at two key points of the evidence, we observe retrospective adjustments of the observed facts. In the starkest case 'good painted pottery of the Palace style' has been altered into 'characteristic vessels of the Third Middle Minoan class'. Once again we choose the most objective presentation of the course of events. We say that our results are more compatible with the statements contained in the primary sources than with the second thoughts of later years. All scholars justly claim the right to re-interpret their primary facts in the light of later information and experience. But once the archaeologist has removed a given set of objects from the ground, he cannot retrospectively endow them with forms, or rearrange them in positions, more convenient to a favoured hypothesis.

If, in the absence of any decisive association of Palace Style LM II pottery with an undisturbed deposit of Linear B tablets, we regard the LM II dating as a pure hypothesis, then the drastic readjustments of the primary facts required to save the hypothesis are a measure of its validity. We state the course of our own investigation likewise in terms of the fundamental steps of any scientific inquiry whatsoever. First comes observation and analysis of the facts, leading to the framing of a hypothesis as a tentative explanation. In our case what serves as the hypothesis is Ventris's decipherment. From the hypothesis a scientist draws deductions which lead to the expectation of making verificatory observations. To do this experimental situations are devised or a suitable natural situation is awaited, such as an eclipse of the sun. In our case the deductions from the 'hypothesis' of the decipherment are the philological workings we have outlined. These cast doubt on a certain set of statements made by Sir Arthur Evans. The setting up of the experiment corresponds to our search for the missing documents. Then we make at the expected point the verificatory observations. It is necessary to stress once again that from this vast range of buildings and all the statements made about them in the excavation reports and Evans's huge work, we focused the experimental situation narrowly on the few pages devoted to this insignificant little room. It was precisely apropos of this that we found the statement which we had 'predicted'. No other statement relating to the Linear B tablets was challenged, and all are consistent both with the primary records and with our own findings.

Thus if we ignore these inadmissible retrospective adjustments in the physical positions of the objects found, if we keep to the statements of the primary sources — the Day Book, and the notebooks and Handlist of Evans himself — then the alleged gap between the two sorts of writing at Knossos disappears. Greeks using Linear B directly succeeded Luvians using Linear A. It is also satisfactory that we have been able to detect (see pp. 250f) some evidence for the use of Linear B at a date earlier than the very end of the long period LM III, to which the archaeologists allocate no less than 250 years.

Such was the life history of this book with its modest original plan and scope. The new philological wine had burst the old archaeological bottle. Yet its results were virtually the same as the conclusions reached in the meantime by the distinguished archaeologist to whom philologists owe the tablets from Pylos. We have accepted them gratefully from his hand and gone our own way of truth. After seven years of research we find ourselves at the same goal. For in the meantime Professor Blegen, who had so firmly supported Professor Wace in contending that the LM II palace was under the control of Greeks from the mainland, had for various reasons come to believe that the Throne Room was after all an LM III reconstruction and that the Knossos tablets formed part of an archive contemporary with those of Pylos and Mycenae.

For our part, what began as an attempt at 'high vulgarization', a general account of Linear B work within an accepted archaeological framework, has turned into a work of demolition and re-construction. This provoked a new dilemma relating to the format of the book. Should it now be provided with a complete apparatus of scholarly references? I have decided against it. The book abides by its original purpose. It is addressed to all interested in the history of the Aegean outside the narrow circle of Linear B specialists. Their demands I shall try to meet elsewhere: they will find the detailed arguments and the relevant scholarly references in my forthcoming book *The Interpretation of Mycenaean Greek Texts*,[1] and currently in the annual bibliography *Studies in Mycenaean Inscriptions and Dialect*.

I cannot disguise from myself that even so the book makes con-siderable demands on the reader. What I have tried to do is to set the facts before him and to trace step by step the procedures of analysis which have led to the results. Figures, plans, maps and tables illustrate the material, and the long captions repeat and summarize the arguments of the pages to which they refer. Finally I have added a chronological table for the guidance of those who share my initial unfamiliarity with the terminology of archaeological ceramic classification. On this table I have inserted the main historical conclusions and indicated by arrows the main currents of cultural influence and presumed invasions.

In the writing of this book my gratitude is owed to all those colleagues who have joined in exploring this exciting new world. First and foremost, to the man who made it possible, to Michael Ventris, pre-eminently endowed with gifts of intellect and charac-ter. The work *Documents in Mycenaean Greek* written together with his collaborator Dr. J. Chadwick, which was published soon after his tragic death, whatever reconstructions later researches have suggested, will always retain its monumental qualities as the 'First Palace' of Mycenaean philology. For a philologist to praise Carl W. Blegen as an archaeologist would be an impertin-ence. But like Ventris he wanted passionately to know what these tablets were saying. He has left nothing to be desired in the speed and precision of his reports from Pylos, and the tablets were made known to a small circle in advance of publication. For the privilege of being among them I owe him my thanks. It has been

[1] To be published by the Oxford University Press (Clarendon Press).

an especial pleasure that our linguistic work confirmed his brilliant insight of 1958. To Emmett L. Bennett, palaeographer-in-chief of Linear B studies, we owe the meticulous scholarly editions of the texts, which form the indispensable foundation for all students who have not had access to the original tablets.

I am indebted to the following for permission to reproduce material for the figures and plates: Professor C. W. Blegen, Mrs. L. Killick, The British School of Archaeology at Athens, the *Illustrated London News*, the Oxford University Press and Messrs. Thames and Hudson. I should also like to thank Dr. Ch. Karouzos, Director of the National Museum in Athens, and Dr. N. Platon, Director of the Archaeological Museum in Heraklion, for the generous facilities accorded for the study of the Linear B tablets in their care. In the Ashmolean Museum of my own university every assistance for the examination of the papers relating to the Knossos excavations was afforded by Mr. W. R. Hamilton, Keeper of Antiquities, and I am grateful to the Visitors for permission to publish material relevant to the milieu of the Linear B tablets.

Part I

PYLOS AND THE WORLD OF THE TABLETS

Chapter I

The Search for Pylos

The Bay of Navarino on the west coast of the Peloponnese, where today the Pacific and Orient liners call for the convenience of Greek emigrants to Australia, has in the long course of Greek history often been the scene of dramatic events. In 1827, three years after Byron had died for Hellas at Missolonghi, high policy, stepping warily after romantic ardour, stumbled from pacific blockade into the irregular destruction of the combined Turkish and Egyptian fleets. Thus Greece was liberated from her long thraldom to the Turk and restored to much the same territorial limits as she had occupied in the second millennium B.C. before, in the Late Bronze Age, an aggressive Mycenae had laid hands on Crete, Rhodes and Cyprus.

Navarino was also the scene of a famous incident of ancient history. The splendour of Mycenae, which Heinrich Schliemann, with simple trust in the poems of Homer and Greek heroic legend, had uncovered to the consternation of professional caution, was itself reduced to rubble and ashes *c.* 1200 B.C., some two centuries after it had embarked on its policy of expansionism. After a long Dark Age there emerged that Hellenic world, culminating in the Age of Pericles, in which our western culture is rooted. For all its splendid cultural and intellectual achievements it was a world riven by a chronic political antagonism, which itself was a legacy from the dark ages and the final agony of Mycenae. For there can be little doubt, as we shall see, that the destroyers of the Bronze Age culture of Greece were those barbarous hill-cousins of the Mycenaeans whom the later world knew as the Dorians. The Peloponnese, with the exception of the mountainous heartland of Arcadia, succumbed and became in later years the chief centre of Dorian power. Attica successfully beat off the invader and the memories lived on in legend. This age-old hostility between

The Search for Pylos

Dorian and Ionian was eventually to blaze up into that great civil war of ancient Greece known as the Peloponnesian War.

As described by the historian Thucydides this war presents itself as a classical struggle between a land and a sea power, between Sparta, the foremost Dorian power, and Athens, acknowledged leader, since the defeat of the Persians, of the Ionian world. In the course of her maritime strategy an Athenian fleet operating in the Ionian Sea established an offensive base at Pylos on the promontory commanding the north end of the Bay of Navarino which the Lacedaemonians called Coryphasion. The Spartans reacted vigorously, but the intervention of an Athenian fleet which had sailed south from Corphu trapped on the island of Sphacteria, which forms as it were an extension of the promontory of Pylos, over four hundred of the Spartan crack infantry together with their Helot batmen. The shock was such that the heads of the Lacedaemonian state came in person to the spot and arranged an armistice on terms which included the surrender of the whole Peloponnesian fleet. In the event the Athenians, on the urging of Cleon the tanner, overplayed their hand. The war was fought to a finish. But the Spartans did not long enjoy the fruits of victory. Before many years had passed an exhausted Greece had found unity and a peace of oppression in the embrace of the Macedonian conqueror.

Final victory has recently descended on yet another conflict centring on the Bay of Navarino. This had lasted some two and a half millennia. It had been a battle of the books, one aspect of the eternal Homeric problem. The question at issue was 'Where was Nestor's Pylos?' In the *Iliad* and the *Odyssey* Nestor appears as the king of an extensive territory in the western Peloponnese, ruler of 'sandy Pylos', who contributed one of the largest contingents of ships to the expedition against Troy. Full of years, he is in constant demand as a counsellor; yet his advice 'always platitudinous or unsuccessful', is constantly ignored. He has some claim to be called the Polonius of the *Iliad*.

Homer was the schoolbook of ancient Greece, and Greek scholars began to wrestle at an early date with the problems of exegesis. Among these problems were the locations of the numerous places mentioned in the two epics, many of which had ceased to exist by classical times. The controversy over Pylos had already become so notorious by the fifth century B.C. that it had been enshrined in a hexameter verse. That it was well known to Athenians is clear from the fact that Aristophanes could count on a laugh merely by quoting the first few words.

For the Greeks the simplest solution to the problem was to identify Nestor's Pylos with a town bearing the same name in their own day. Of these Pylos on Navarino Bay had the strongest claims. This was accepted without question by the credulous Pausanias, who wrote a guide book to Greece in the second century of our era. Remarking that 'the Lacedaemonian disaster has made Sphacteria known to all mankind', he explores Pylos on Coryphasion and reports the existence of a House of Nestor, in which there is a painting of the hero. Nestor's tomb is to be found inside the city and there is a cave where the cattle of Nestor, and of his father Neleus before him, were housed. Pausanias adds, however, that in his view most of Neleus' cattle were pastured across the border 'for the country of the Pylians is rather sandy and not capable of providing so much fodder for cattle'. A modern visitor to this rich and fertile part of the Peloponnese will immediately reflect that Pausanias is viewing the Messenian countryside with his mind's eye coloured by too much Homeric reading.

Strabo, the geographer of the Augustan age, is a 'homerizer' too, but one of a much more critical temper. He recalls that there are a number of towns called Pylos in the western Peloponnese. There is one in Elis, and another in Triphylia in addition to the more famous Messenian Pylos. Confronted with this dilemma, he quotes in full the hexameter to which Aristophanes alludes in *The Knights*,[1] from which we may conclude that the Athenian audience of the fifth century was prepared to be amused by the controversies of its learned men. Strabo based his rejection of the candidature of the Messenian Pylos on a reasoned analysis of the Homeric evidence. His case, refined in recent investigations, still seems to me unanswerable.

In the eleventh book of the *Iliad* Nestor begins one of his not infrequent recollections of the exploits of his youth with the formulaic 'If I were only as young and vigorous as when I . . .'. This time the subject is his first taste of battle.

[1] 'There is a Pylos before Pylos, and yet another Pylos.'

The Search for Pylos

'If only I were young and my strength still as firm as when a quarrel broke out between the Eleans and us over a cattle raid, when I killed Itymoneus. . . . We rounded up a rich booty, fifty herds of cows, as many flocks of sheep, as many herds of swine, as many herds of goats and one hundred and fifty bay horses, all mares, many with foals. And these we drove to Nelean Pylos to the town after night-fall. . . .'

Old Neleus's heart was gladdened by the success of his young son, and he divided the spoil among those of his people who had a claim against the Epeans. On the third day the Epeans took the field with all their forces and chariots.

'There is a city Thryoessa, a steep hill, far off on the Alpheus, on the border of sandy Pylos. Around it they mustered their forces eager to destroy it.' Athena brings the news to Pylos and Nestor joins the relieving force on foot, since his father had forbidden him to go and had hidden his horses.

'There is a river Minyeios, which flows into the sea near Arene. There we, the charioteers of the Pylians, awaited the divine dawn and the swarms of the foot soldiers streamed after us. From there in full force, arrayed in armour, we reached the holy stream of Alpheus during the day.' There they made sacrifice and slept beside the stream in full armour. Next day battle was joined and Zeus granted great victory to the Pylians. 'We pursued them through the vast plain killing and gathering the fine armour until we halted our horses at Bouprasion, rich in wheat, and the Rock of Olen and the hill called the Hill of Aleision. There Athena turned back the host. There I slew the last man and left him. But the Achaeans drove back their swift horses from Bouprasion to Pylos.'

Much may be conceded to poetic licence, but this appears to be a narrative of great topographical precision. Bouprasion and divine Elis, the Rock of Olen and Aleision are ascribed to the Epeans in the 'Catalogue'[1] of the Greek forces. The Alpheus marks the frontier between the domains of Nestor and the Epeans to the north who occupied present-day Elis. We note in particular that the cattle raided in their territory, including herds of swine,

[1] The 'Catalogue' is the name given to a geographical survey of Mycenaean Greece which is inserted in the second book of the *Iliad*. It is considered by some to reflect a tradition going back to the Mycenaean Age (See D. L. Page, *History and the Homeric Iliad*).

not remarkably swift moving animals, are driven back to Pylos at some time after nightfall on the day of their capture. The strategy of the Pylian counter-action to the punitive raid of the Epeans is carefully sketched. First their chariot-borne forces occupy a defensive position on the river Minyeius. After the arrival of the supporting infantry the full force moves on to the relief of the frontier fortress of Thryoessa ('Rush Town') on the Alpheus.

Strabo rightly asks how Nestor, after collecting so much booty including sheep and pigs, neither of which can travel fast or far, could complete a journey to Pylos on Coryphasion of more than a thousand furlongs, and how the mobilized troops of the Pylians could reach Thryoessa and the Alpheus on the third day. He therefore rejects the Messenian Pylos and identifies the town of Neleus and his son Nestor with the Triphylian Pylos, and the river Minyeius with the Anigrus which flows into the sea some twenty-five km south of the Alpheus.

Modern investigators, armed with all the formidable apparatus of organized scholarship, have done little more than refine Strabo's main arguments. Professor Wade-Gery in a recent article entitled 'What happened at Pylos?' has also concluded that the Pylos of this miniature epic in *Iliad* XI cannot be Navarino. 'The trouble is that Nestor's reminiscences — all of them I think — but most clearly this long passage in Book XI are . . . about a Pylos which was only a short distance south of the Alpheus — say within 10 or 20 miles of Olympia. . . . If you follow this on the map or on the ground itself, you will find that the battle must be in the plain of Olympia: the point guarded by the horsemen till daylight is the pass of Klidi, and Pylos is a few miles south of Klidi. It is all near Olympia. . . . There cannot be much doubt, I think, that in Book XI we have an authentic description of the Olympia country in prehistoric times' (see fig. 1).

It was to be expected that the new science of archaeology, having securely identified the palaces of Agamemnon at Mycenae and of Diomede at Tiryns, would address itself to the task of locating the capital of the Mycenaean kingdom of Nestor. The matter appeared to be clinched when Professor Dörpfeld, who had joined Germanic discipline and thoroughness to the amateur genius of Schliemann, in 1907 discovered on the acropolis of

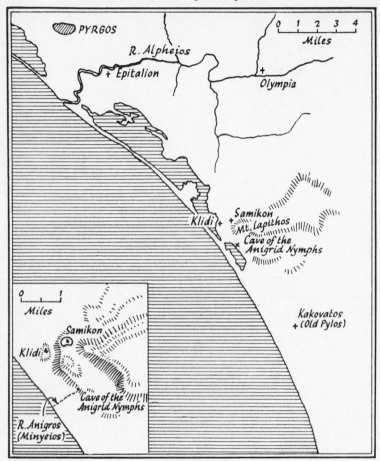

Fig. 1. The terrain of Nestor's Elean War. (After F. Bölte)

Kakovatos (fig. 1) the remains of a Mycenaean building and a
number of tholos tombs in the vicinity. Dörpfeld then devoted a
penetrating paper to the whole question and convinced himself
and many others that this was the Pylos of Nestor. Since that day
the equation Kakovatos-Pylos has figured constantly in reference
works of classical studies.

In 1912, however, and again in 1926, Mycenaean tombs were
also discovered near Coryphasion, and this gave some encouragement to those who still believed in the Messenian Pylos. They too
could appeal to Homer, but their case rested largely on the Nestor

of the *Odyssey* and in particular on the journeys of Telemachus from Ithaca to Pylos and from Pylos to Sparta in search of news of his father Odysseus, now ten years overdue after the fall of Troy.

Let us follow Homer's description of the latter journey first. Telemachus has been entertained by Nestor in Pylos and given what information he possessed about Odysseus. The time has come to move on to Sparta, where King Menelaus may have some news. At dawn Nestor gets up and goes to the polished stones before the door. His sons come forth from their chambers. The king organizes a feast for the goddess Athena. One son is sent to the plain to get an ox. Another is despatched to the ship of Telemachus to collect his companions. They come to the palace from the shore. The ox is brought, its horns are gilded; it is sacrificed and slaughtered. Telemachus is bathed and joins the feast. After these lengthy proceedings provender is made ready for the journey of Telemachus and his companion Peisistratus, the eldest son of Nestor. The chariot is yoked, the horses leave the steep fortress and hasten to the plain. All day long they shake the yoke. The sun set and the ways grew dark and they came to Pherae, to the house of Diocles, the son of Ortilochus, whom Alpheus begat. There they stayed the night.

Now there is little doubt that Pherae is identical with the classical town of that name near the modern Kalamata (see the discussion below on the extent of Pylian territory).

We must conclude, if we are intended by Homer to give any serious attention to time and space, that it would be wholly impossible to cover the distance from Triphylian Pylos to Pherae in what was left of the day after the above festivities. Dörpfeld, seeking an escape from this dilemma, seized on the fact that Ortilochus was the son of the river Alpheus. From this he drew the conclusion that the son's city must be near that river and so triumphantly conjured up another unknown Pherae more congenial to his theory. This he sited in Arcadia and brought Telemachus by an inland route past Megalopolis and so, skirting the great barrier of Taygetus, to 'hollow Sparta'. This simply will not do because, as we shall see below, there is a great deal of consistent evidence in Homer about the location of Pherae and the dynasty of Ortilochus.

It was open to Dörpfeld, however, to argue that the topographical evidence of the *Odyssey* was far from being as precise as that of Nestor's reminiscences in the *Iliad*. He could have drawn powerful support for this from the description of the next stage of Telemachus's journey from Pherae to Sparta.

'When the early-born rosy-fingered dawn appeared, they yoked the horses and mounted the chariot and drove through the gate of the echoing portico. And they whipped them into a run and the horses sped not unwilling. They came to a wheat-bearing plain and then set about completing their journey. For in such wise did the swift horses carry them on. The sun set and all the ways were darkened and they came to hollow Lacedaemon.' Here there is not the slightest hint that during the day the swift horses have negotiated the formidable barrier of the Taygetus range, which lies between Pherae and Sparta.

Dörpfeld, however, spurned this way out. Homer's accuracy was for him an essential prerequisite for another argument. This concerns his calculation of the distance from Ithaca to Pylos. We now go back to the beginning of Telemachus' journey. On Athena's prompting Telemachus has passed the word round to his chosen companions to gather at the ship at nightfall. They embark and Athena takes her seat in the stern beside Telemachus and sends them a following wind. All the night long and the dawn the ship cleaves its way. The sun climbed, leaving the lovely sea, to the brazen heaven that it might shine for gods and mortal men over the grain-giving earth, and they came to Pylos, the well-ordered citadel of Neleus, and found the Pylians making sacrifice on the shore of bulls, all black, to the Earth-Shaker.

The time taken is thus precisely from sunset to sunrise. In order to calculate the distance from Ithaca to Pylos we need to know first the time of year, which will determine the hours of darkness. Since, however, the Pylians are already in their sacrificial stations on the beach and the town is some distance inland, it will not be precisely at dawn that they arrived. This will offset the comparative shortness of the night after the spring equinox. Let us therefore say that the journey took roughly twelve hours. The only additional datum we require for our calculation is the speed of a Mycenaean ship propelled (1) by a favourable wind and (2) by

Athena sitting in the stern. Dörpfeld's argument is worth quoting in full. 'The voyage (of Telemachus from Ithaca) to Pylos . . . is accomplished by Telemachus in a single night. The distance from present-day Ithaca to the Messenian Pylos amounts to about 190 kilometres, and to the Triphylian about 130 kilometres. For the island of Leucas, in which I have located the Homeric Ithaca, these figures must be increased by about 30 km and thus amount to 220 and 160 respectively. Since a sailing ship with a favourable wind makes about 10 km per hour, it follows that the time taken for a voyage from Ithaca to Messenian Pylos will have been 19 or 22 hours, and to Triphylian Pylos 13 or 16 hours.' By thus reasoning from his premises Dörpfeld was able to satisfy himself and a large body of his fellow scholars that the Odyssean Pylos, like the Pylos of the *Iliad*, was to be identified with the Triphylian Pylos.

What causes some uneasiness is, of course, the assumption that the poet is thinking so precisely in terms of distance and speed for a heroic ship with Athena as a passenger. There is another possible approach which is less complicated and involves fewer unknowns. The reader should, however, be forewarned that it involves saddling the poet(s) of the *Odyssey* with consistency. I propose to question Nestor himself about the length of voyages in Mycenaean ships. In Book III Nestor describes to Telemachus his voyage home from Troy to Pylos after the capture of the city of Priam. Their first stage was Tenedos (fig. 2), where a dispute arose, and Nestor left for Lesbos. There they were in doubt whether they should sail straight across the open sea keeping the island of Psyra on their left or whether they should keep inshore past the windy promontory of Mimas and sail between Chios and the mainland. They prayed to the god for a sign, and he directed them to sail across the sea straight for Euboea. He sent a favourable wind and the ships swiftly traversed the fishy ways and put into Geraestus after nighfall. Geraestus is at the south-eastern end of Euboea (fig. 2) in the channel between that island and Andros. On the fourth day the comrades of Diomede reached Argos while Nestor made for Pylos. The poet evidently knows what he is about: we have here a clear and precise picture of Aegean navigational possibilities under favourable conditions. We do not know what port of Lesbos Nestor set sail from, but the distance

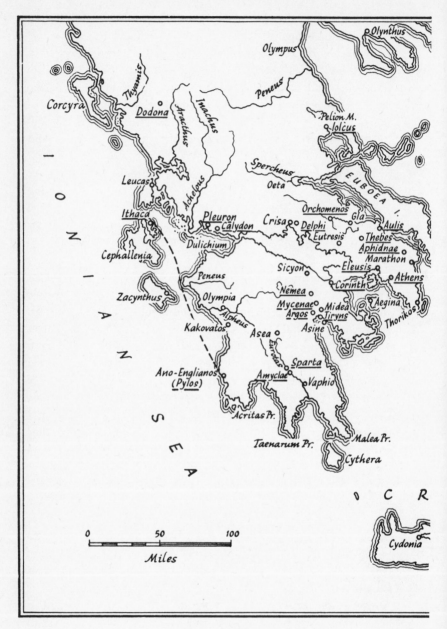

Fig. 2. Archaeological sites in the Aegean.

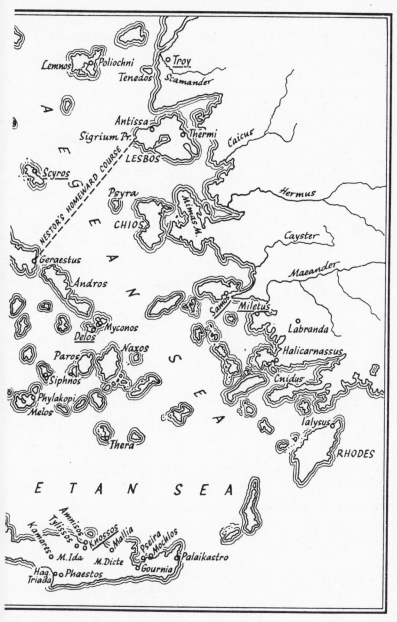

Lemnos
Poliochni
Troy
Tenedos
Scamander

Antissa
Sigrium Pr.
Thermi
Caicus
LESBOS

NESTOR'S HOMEWARD COURSE

Scyros

Psyra
Hermus
Mimas M.
CHIOS

Cayster

Geraestus
Maeander

Andros

Samos
Miletus
Labranda
Myconos
Delos
Halicarnassus
Paros
Naxos
Siphnos
Cnidus
Phylakopi
Melos

Ialysus

Thera
RHODES

E T A N   S E A

Amnisos
Tylissos
Knossos
Mallia
Kamares
Pseira
Mochlos
M. Ida
M. Dicte
Palaikastro
Haq.
Triada
Phaestos
Gournia

Names underlined are also centres of myth.

from the nearest point of Lesbos, Cape Sigrium, to Geraestus is roughly the same as from Ithaca to Navarino and somewhat longer if we imagine that Nestor's point of departure was Methymna on the north coast of Lesbos. The indications are that the time taken by Nestor's ships was the day and some unspecified part of the night as compared with Telemachus's night and some unspecified part of the day. Given this internal standard of epic voyaging, it would be special pleading to argue, with Dörpfeld, that the time and speed factors in Telemachus's journey rule out identification of Nestor's Pylos with a site near Navarino.

It remains true that until 1939 the weight of archaeological evidence was on the side of the German scholar. Kakovatos was still the most considerable Mycenaean site in the western Peloponnese, and it seemed reasonable to suppose that here was the capital of Mycenaean Pylos, although the other settlement near Coryphasion in all probability lay within its territory. There remained, however, a powerful and obstinate dissident minority. Among them was numbered the distinguished American archaeologist Professor C. W. Blegen of the University of Cincinnati.

In 1912 the Greek archaeologist Dr Kourouniotis had unearthed a fine bee-hive tomb ('tholos') only some two kilometres from the cliff of Coryphasion. Other discoveries of the same nature followed general exploration of this neighbourhood, and it appeared that these Mycenaean sepulchres had been constructed in a zone extending several kilometres 'more or less along the line of the modern highroad which connects modern Pylos with the village known as Chora' (fig. 13). The presence of so many royal tombs of the Mycenaean period made it 'perfectly clear that a capital of more than local importance had once stood somewhere along the northern border of the bay of Pylos'.

Arrangements were made for a joint Helleno-American expedition. Dr Kourouniotis entrusted the field work to Professor Blegen, and preliminary exploration of the district revealed at least six possibilities. The largest and most impressive of all the sites lay on a flat-topped elevation some 4 km from Coryphasion on the road to Chora commanding a superb view looking towards Coryphasion and the island of Sphacteria. Here trial trenches soon revealed a magnificent palace comparable in size and

character to those at Mycenae and Tiryns. By the end of that first
season of 1939 Blegen had little doubt that he had in fact found
the Palace of Nestor.

In his report of 1939 the distinguished archaeologist wrote: 'At
a moment when systematic excavation of the palace is only about to
begin it might seem indiscreet to advance categorical conclusions
regarding the identification of the site. The high interest of the
problem may serve as an excuse, however, if excuse be needed, for
discussing the matter at this stage ... the very limited range of
possibilities open, in any case, leaves little room for error. For
there surely can be no doubt that we have found the Pylos of
King Nestor, whose dominion extended over nine cities along the
western shore.

'Through the whole body of Hellenic tradition relating to the
Heroic Age a single dynasty of rulers is accredited with the over-
lordship of south-western Greece, and the most famous king of the
Neleid line, sage Nestor, is a peer and equal among the Achaean
leaders at Troy. Though presumably represented by subordinate
chieftains in his many towns, so far as the literary records tell, he
clearly had no rival of like standing anywhere in the district. His
royal residence might then confidently be envisaged as a palace,
built on a scale commensurate with that of the abodes of the other
Achaean kings, including Menelaus and even Agamemnon himself. It is just such a palace that has now been discovered at Ano
Englianos, the chief citadel of Western Messenia in Mycenaean
times.

'... Far better than Professor Dörpfeld's site at Kakovatos,
more than 50 km away (as the crow flies), our palace at Englianos
corresponds with the geographical indications given in the *Odyssey*;
and it agrees with the conservative voice of Greek tradition that
placed Nestor's domain in the immediate district of the homo-
nymous classical city and Bay. We venture therefore without
hesitation, even in these early phases of our investigation, to
identify the newly found palace at Ano Englianos as the home of
King Nestor, the Sandy Pylos of Homer and tradition.'

Other hostilities were soon to blanket this quarrel of the
moderns over ancient things. But in 1942 Mr W. A. McDonald,
who had assisted Blegen in the dig of 1939, reviewed the whole

problem in an article entitled 'Where did Nestor live?' He added
to arguments already adduced a telling one of human geography.
Nestor is stated to have contributed ninety ships to the expedition
against Troy, only ten less than Agamemnon himself, if we except
those the latter provided for the use of the inland Arcadians. 'It is
almost inconceivable', McDonald wrote, 'that they should have
failed to establish their naval base in the magnificent bay of
Navarino. It forms the only natural harbour along the entire west
coast of the Peloponnese, and it will be shown to have been
included in Pylian territory. If then the Pylian naval base was in
the bay of Navarino, their capital city would naturally be situated
nearby.'

This did not, however, satisfy the critics, and in 1959 there
appeared a volume of *Pauly-Wissowa*, the great and authoritative
encyclopaedia of classical studies, which by then had reached that
part of the alphabet which included 'Pylos'. The author of the
article, an authority on topographical questions of the Peloppon-
nese, contemptuously brushed aside McDonald's paper, and
propounded once again what is virtually the whole thesis of
Dörpfeld. It was evident that the question could not be settled to
everyone's satisfaction by the combination of literary analysis and
archaeological exploration. Though the weight of the archaeological
evidence was now decisively in favour of the Navarino site, the
clear topographical picture of the Pylian epic of *Iliad* XI could not
be reconciled with this. McDonald ended his paper with the
words: 'Perhaps the question of the site of Nestor's Pylos still
cannot be decided to the full satisfaction of all interested. If the
newly discovered tablets can be deciphered, they will almost
certainly settle it one way or the other.' These were prophetic
words, but meanwhile the confusion was symbolized by a comic
interlude which McDonald relates. 'An amusing incident occurred
during the trial excavation at Ano Englianos, when a local
policeman was sent to halt the work on the ground that our permit
allowed us to excavate only in the modern district of Pylos, while
we were actually digging in the modern district of Triphylia. So
perhaps after all scholarly differences will be reconciled and it will
be agreed that Nestor lived at the southern of the two sites in
question and yet in Triphylia.'

Chapter II

The Linear B Script and its Decipherment

The discovery of the first archive of written documents in a mainland site of Mycenaean Greece must rank as one of the greatest strokes of fortune in the history of archaeology. Professor Blegen is inclined to ascribe it to the piety he showed towards the Tree Goddess. In his preliminary survey of the site at Ano Englianos he wrote: 'The whole hill is now occupied by a venerable olive grove, the trees of which, according to the testimony of the owner, are unfailingly and remarkably productive. Seven trenches were laid out on the plateau ... *avoiding the olive trees.*' One of these trenches almost immediately revealed a flattish object. An inexperienced workman picked it up and wiped it clean with his hand. At one stroke he had endangered the writing on a clay tablet which had lasted for over three thousand years.[1] The delicate task of extracting these precious objects was then taken over by Mr McDonald himself, and Professor Blegen pays a warm tribute to him for his 'circumspection, perseverance and long suffering in spending so many days on his hands and knees in positions of extreme discomfort.'

The room in which the tablets were discovered came to be known as the 'Archives Room'. It was a narrow chamber some three by six metres in area in the south-eastern corner of the palace (see fig. 3). A clay bench ran around the three sides, and the tablets were found on this bench and scattered about on the floor. In all there were some 600 pieces. They were in a soggy condition, but after drying out became as hard as the contemporary pottery.

---

[1] The tablet when cleaned showed a text referring to 'rowers going to Pleuron' (see below, p. 145).

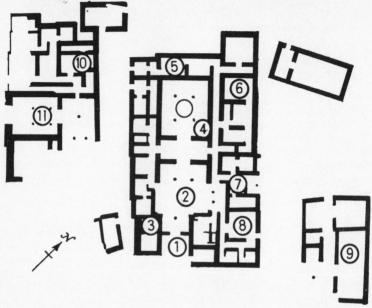

Fig. 3. Plan of the Palace of Nestor at Pylos. 1: Propylon;
2: Stoa and Aithousa; 3: Archives Room; 4: Megaron
(Throne Room) (some tablets); 5: Store Rooms for Oil etc.
(some tablets); 6: Room 48 (some tablets here); 7: Room 47
(some tablets); 8: Queen's Megaron; 9: Workshop (some
tablets); 10: Room 32 of Older Palace (some tablets);
11: Throne Room of earlier palace.

When the necessary cleansing had been carried out, the tablets
became easily legible and the script was at once recognized. Blegen
wrote in his excavation report of 1939:

'It can be stated at once that the documents are written in a form
of the Minoan script classified by Sir Arthur Evans as Linear B.
Most of the signs on our tablets are seen to be identical with signs
that occur on tablets of that class from Knossos, while the tablets
themselves are strikingly similar to their Knossian counterparts,
not only in composition and shape but in character as well. . . .

'In some other respects, too, our deposit of tablets bears a
remarkable resemblance to one found in the Palace of Minos at
Knossos, for in the southern corner of the room lying among

tablets on the floor, were recovered remains of some half dozen badly corroded, small hinges, perhaps the bronze fittings of a wooden box or chest in which documents were kept.'

Professor Blegen in speaking of the Linear B tablets of the Palace of Minos was referring to the sensational discoveries made by Sir Arthur Evans at Knossos in Crete at the beginning of the century. In 1876 Heinrich Schliemann, with fundamentalist faith in the stories of Homer, had used the bible of the Greeks to search for the buried cities and treasures of Mycenae and Troy and had found them. Yet in the brilliant civilization that had preceded by a thousand years the flowering of classical Greek culture there was one notable gap. Evans wrote:

'Amid all the varied objects obtained by Schliemann in the course of his excavation no single written document was brought to light. . . . Was this great early civilization then altogether dumb? Were the builders of the 'Treasury of Atreus', of the elaborate palace-citadels of Tiryns and Mycenae, the carvers of the Lions' Gate, so far below the level of their contemporaries not only in Egypt and Babylonia, but throughout the vast Anatolian and Syrian regions over which are scattered the inscribed monuments of the Hittite princes? Was it possible that such master-pieces as the intarsia designs of the daggers from the acropolis tombs at Mycenae, the intaglios of the signets, the living reliefs of the Vapheio vases, were the work of "Man before Writing"?

'Such a conclusion I could not bring myself to accept.'

In 1889 an object was presented to the Ashmolean Museum in Oxford, where Evans was Keeper, which gave him his first clue to the existence of writing in the prehistoric Aegean. It was a four-sided bead bearing characters which reminded him of Hieroglyphic Hittite. In subsequent visits to Greece Evans obtained more of these objects, and by 1893 he was able to communicate to the Hellenic Society his discovery of a native (i.e. Aegean) system of hieroglyphics distinct from the Egyptian and from the Hittite. All the objects bearing these characters were seemingly traceable to Crete. Evans now took up the search in that island. Great numbers of the inscribed relics were obtained. It became clear that the script had a history: the first stage of conventionalized pictographs (hieroglyphs) had been succeeded by another where the signs had been reduced to linear outlines with quasi-alphabetic values. The most remarkable example of this later stage came to light during the exploration of the cave on mount Dicte, where the mother goddess Rhea is said to have given birth to the Cretan Zeus. There Evans found a libation table bearing an inscription in the advanced type of the linear script. It was now clear to Evans that 'the great days of the island lay beyond history'.

The evident next step was systematic excavation. Evans had long been preparing to excavate the remains of the early civilization of the island. Legend pointed unequivocally to Knossos 'the city of Minos, the legendary site of the Palace wrought for him, with all the artistic wonders it contained, by his craftsman Daidalos, of the Dancing Place of Ariadne and of the Labyrinth itself'. Schliemann, too, had planned to excavate in Knossos but had refused to pay the exorbitant price demanded by the owners of the site. Evans encountered similar difficulties, but by skill and patience overcame them. He had already secured a share of the site by 1895; but six years were to elapse before he succeeded in purchasing the whole site from the co-proprietors who were 'Moslem Beys of an exceptionally intractable disposition'.

At last operations began in March 1900. The first clay tablet came to light on March 30. The succeeding days added more, and on April 5 a whole hoard of inscribed tablets were found in a bath-shaped vessel of terra-cotta. The tablets, some in perfect condition, were arranged in rows. From the fact that the tablets were embedded in charred wood Evans inferred that their immediate receptacle had been a wooden box.[1] Finds of such tablets were made in various parts of the Palace throughout the excavations. That they had remained undisturbed since the destruction was evident from one set in the Eighth Magazine, imperfectly baked, which was found in the original order with the totalling tablet at the bottom.

The overwhelming majority of these clay documents were inscribed in a linear script of a type different from that on the Dictean libation table. Evans called it 'Linear B' to distinguish it from the Linear A exemplified on the libation table. This class B had apparently been in vogue throughout the concluding period

[1] On the clay bath, see below p. 269.

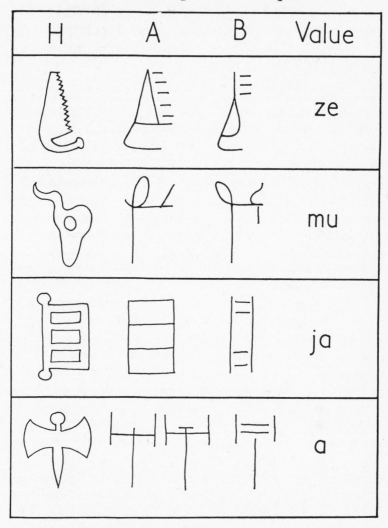

Fig. 4. The Development of the Aegean script. H=hiero-glyph, A=Linear A, B=Linear B.

of the Palace history, known as Late Minoan II (*c.* 1450–1400 B.C.).[1] In the course of the excavations it became clear that there was a historical relationship between the scripts of Crete. In the history of the Palace of Minos itself linear B had been preceded by

[1] See however Chapter VI.

two earlier types. One was the script designated Linear A, which
in its turn had superseded the still earlier one of conventionalized
pictorial aspect which reminded Evans of Egyptian hieroglyphs.
(For the three stages of the script see fig. 4.)

These abundant archives which the spade had so quickly
brought to light had fully justified the correctness of Evans's early
intuition that so brilliant a civilization could not have existed
without writing. The key to its identity and to the affinities of
'Minoan' with the other cultures of the Aegean and the Near East
lay in the language which was concealed in these clay tablets. It
was reasonable to hope and expect that early publication would
have made them available to the linguistic scholars who were
eagerly awaiting them. In fact, though Evans published a small
selection of the tablets from time to time, it was not until eleven
years after his death in 1941 and more than fifty years after their
first discovery that they were published in full, and then in an
edition which was far from meeting the demands of scholarship.

Meanwhile evidence for the use of the same script on the mainland of Greece had been slowly accumulating. Evans had written
in 1909:

'In spite of the negative results obtained by Schliemann at
Mycenae and Tiryns, all probability seems in favour of some form
of early writing having existed on the mainland side.'

A stirrup-vase with inscribed characters bearing some resemblance to certain Linear B signs had been found at Orchomenos
in Boeotia. Finds of similar inscribed vessels at Mycenae and
Tiryns were capped in 1921 by a haul of twenty-eight from a store
room in the Mycenaean palace at Thebes. A fine example was recovered later from the Mycenaean temple at Eleusis (fig. 28). These
finds had been, and are still, widely regarded as evidence that the
Minoan system of writing had been used widely on the mainland
of Greece. So we must anticipate our story and reveal that the
great majority of these inscriptions from these different sites
contain Cretan place-names which recur only in the Linear B
tablets from Knossos, and there can be little doubt that the vessels, which presumably contained oil (possibly perfumed), had
been exported from Crete.

It will now be clear that in fact Blegen's find, thirty-nine years after the emergence of the first tablets from the ruins of Knossos, was the first cogent evidence for the use of Linear B writing by a mainland administration. It remains to add that the British excavations during 1952–4 in the houses outside the walls of Mycenae at last conferred literacy on the greatest city of the Mycenaean age. The finds of Linear B tablets in these annexes of the palace (Professor Wace misleadingly called the chief of them 'the House of the Oil Merchant') made it plain that the failure of Schliemann to find such evidence in his earlier excavations of the citadel was due to chance or inadvertence. Wace was confident that the corpus of inscriptions would continue to grow. This hope was fulfilled when other fragments came to light in 1957 during road-widening operations at Mycenae, while the successive campaigns at Pylos have invariably yielded more or less important accretions of material. Only Mycenaean Attica remains obstinately dumb.

The tablets are of two main shapes. They take the form either of a rectangular page or of an elongated slip with wedge-shaped ends (figs. 8, 9). To make a tablet the scribe took a piece of moist clay and shaped it, pressing the surface to be inscribed on a flat surface. Finger prints are clearly visible on the backs of many of the tablets. The flat surface was then ruled off with varying numbers of incised lines. The entries are of two types. On the right side of the tablets we find the numerical entries of the '£ s d' type, in which signs (ideograms), often clearly representing objects such as chariots, wheels, swords, etc., are followed by numbers which reflect a decimal system. To the left of these numerical entries we find a text consisting of words separated by short vertical lines which function as word dividers. The long, narrow, 'palm leaf' type contain similar entries, but the text is arranged either in one or two lines, rarely more. We now know that such slips were some-times used to record preliminary arrangements which were later combined in page-shaped documents which formed sets like the leaves of a book (see pp. 100 ff. on the 'land register').

When the scribe had finished his tablet, he put it to dry in the sun. In normal circumstances this would have meant that the document would soon have disintegrated once it was exposed to the weather. Evans tells a story which reinforces this point. 'I had a disastrous experience of how easily moisture could affect the tablets when in this unbaked state. A group of four such which lay intact in their original order on the pavement of the room, held together by some indurated earth, were carefully cut out by me in one piece with their earthy matrix and transferred on a wooden tray to the old Turkish house in the glen below Kephala which served as headquarters. But a torrential storm coming on during the night, the rain-water poured in at several places owing to the bad state of the roof and unfortunately inundated the tray containing the group of tablets. When the mischief was discovered it was too late, and they had been already reduced to a pulpy mass.'

Evans might have recalled a story told by Pausanias about Messenia. After the death of Nestor came the invasion of the Dorians and the return of the Sons of Heracles, who drove the descendants of Nestor from Messenia. The Dorians assigned the territory of Argos to Temenus while Cresphontes asked them for Messenia. But this was disputed by the children of Aristodemus. Cresphontes suggested that the matter should be decided by lot, the arrangement being that the party whose lot came out of the urn first should have first choice of territory. But Cresphontes had come to an arrangement with Temenus, who put water in the urn and caused the lots to be made of clay. 'But the lot for the sons of Aristodemus he had made of sun-dried clay, and that for Cresphontes of clay baked in the fire. So the lot of the sons of Aristodemus disintegrated, and so Cresphontes, winning the lot, chose Messenia.'

The tablets once hardened in the sun were put into wooden boxes, which were tied with string and then sealed with lumps of clay, sometimes bearing brief inscriptions in the Linear B script to indicate the contents of the box and often the impression of engraved signets of beautiful workmanship (fig. 5).

The tablets have been preserved to us *in situ* because of their accidental baking in the fires which consumed the palaces in which they were found. This gives us a firm indication of their date. As Professor Blegen wrote in his first report: 'It is hardly conceivable that so large a collection of rather fragile documents could have been kept together for centuries in an open apartment of a building actively occupied.' Since the destruction of the palace of Pylos cannot have occurred before 1200 in round figures, the

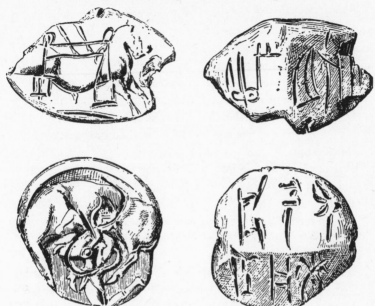

Fig. 5. Inscribed sealings from Knossos.

tablets cannot have been written long before that date. That in fact they were written in the final year of the Mycenaean power in western Messenia we now know from the contents of the tablets. They contain indications of time in the form of the names of months and the expressions 'this year' 'last year', and 'next year'. It is evident that what we have recovered are records of current transactions. Comparison of two sets of texts, one of the palm-leaf type and the other of the page variety, showed that the latter were a sort of fair-copy of the first. In 1954 I wrote: 'In Pylos there is evidence that shortly before the end came the scribes were busy in the archives room at the routine task of making con-solidated records from earlier provisional jottings.' New texts published in 1956 brought a striking confirmation of how short a time intervened between the making of this copy and the final catastrophe. The scribes after making a large tablet often found that they had left quite a usable piece of 'blank paper'. They would then score a line across the tablet and break off the unused piece for later use. Professor E. L. Bennett, in a renewed and thorough study (1956) of the now nearly complete document, was able to find the blank piece cut from one of the page tablets of the fair-copy. Internal analysis suggested to me that this was in fact the final page of the document. The blank piece which fitted the bottom of this tablet was preserved still uninscribed. Bennett rightly concluded that this tablet, and by inference the rest of these texts, were copied very shortly before the palace's destruction. We thus possess some of the last records inscribed in the Mycenaean age of Greece.

Even before the script was deciphered and the language diagnosed it was evident to Sir Arthur Evans from the ideograms alone that the 'great majority of the clay documents of Class B contained business records, such as accounts and inventories, and in nearly all cases are associated with numbers. The objects referred to by these lists are in most cases easily recognizable from the pictorial representations appended to the different entries. . . .

'We see here implements and weapons, chariots and their parts, and the cuirasses of royal charioteers, ingots, and the scales in which the Minoan talents were weighed, precious vessels and others apparently containing various liquid products, granaries or storehouses on piles, and different kinds of cereals, the saffron flowers used for dies, several kinds of trees, domestic animals, including horses and swine, and crook signs which seem to indicate sheep or goats.'

From the numerical entries which figure on practically every tablet it was clear that a decimal system was in vogue and that signs were used for units up to 10,000. But the conventionalized

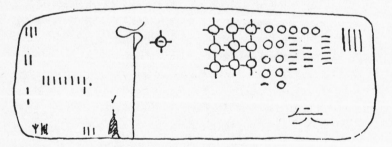

Fig. 6. The Linear B decimal notation. The number reads
10,000 + 9,000 + 1300 + 160 + 4.

pictograms of the ideographic system could tell us nothing about the underlying language any more than '£ *s d*', etc. would be a clue to English. Such a system is in fact of universal applicability. Evans believed that no linguistic change was involved in the transition from Linear A to B. 'The occurrence in both of similar sign-groups seems at any rate to prove that the language itself of those who used the one or the other script was essentially the same. It looks then, as if the introduction of Class B at Knossos may have been the result of a dynastic revolution. . . . There was no real ethnic break, and the general continuity of the Minoan culture remained unaffected. . . . The bureaucratic methods of control here visible are themselves the outcome of a long inheritance of dynastic organization.'

Evans ventured no guess at the possible affinities of the Minoan language. That it was Greek never entered his head. Even in 1939 Blegen, for his part, was 'almost certain' that the language of his tablets was 'Minoan', and this despite the fact that they were apparently[1] some two hundred years later than the bulk of the Knossian hoards and found by him in a palace which Blegen believed was certainly occupied by the Greek dynasty of the Neleids.

Nor did the possibility that the Linear B tablets concealed the Greek language occur to Michael Ventris. As a schoolboy at Stowe his imagination had been fired by a lecture given by Sir Arthur Evans on the occasion of the fiftieth anniversary of the British School of Archaeology at Athens (see p. 176). This brilliantly endowed man, whose decipherment was eventually to win the almost immediate approval of international scholarship, guessed that the language was related to Etruscan. The guess was a reasonable one for a language diagnosed as 'pre-Greek', since although Etruscan is still a largely unsolved problem, the balance of the probabilities seems to favour the idea that this people came from the Aegean, and an inscription in a language evidently related to Etruscan was known from the island of Lemnos.

This wrong diagnosis was maintained by Ventris right up to the final stages of his decipherment. It figures in the so-called 'Mid-Century Report' (see p. 168), which records what could be deduced

---

[1] See pp. 173 ff. on the date of the Knossos tablets.

by the most eminent living authorities from the archaeological and other evidence available at the time preceding the decipherment of the script. The remarkable fact stands out that not one of the scholars concerned suggested that the language could be Greek (see further below, pp. 168 ff.). Ventris's final solution is a notable example of the triumph of logical deduction by a powerful intellect over its own preconceptions.

The story of the decipherment of the Linear B script has been lucidly and movingly told by his friend and linguistic collaborator Dr John Chadwick of the University of Cambridge. Since, however, opposition continues and agnosticism is still widespread among professional classical scholars, who maintain that there is still no strict 'proof' that the decipherment is correct, an evalua tion of the decipherment must precede an account of the light thrown by the new texts on the Heroic Age of Greece.

Those who demand a 'proof' of the decipherment must state what they consider a proof to be. How is any decipherment 'proved'?

The answer to this question results from the nature of language. An example from English will make the basic principle clear. Suppose we have a sentence in an unknown script representing a language which from the archaeological data we suspect to be English: 'If anyone should damage this monument, may the DOGS of the GOD xxx eat him up'. Because the three-sign group G–O–D occurs constantly in front of sign-groups which link up on our monument with figures of gods, we identify it tentatively as the English word *god*. But if our hypothesis that the language is English is correct, we find ourselves committed to the proposition that the same three signs D–O–G in the reverse order must occur in 'dog' contexts. Not merely this, but G–O and D–O must yield common verbs. This is the crux of the problem: each language from the decipherer's point of view is a *unique* pattern of a limited number of signs. English written in the Roman alphabet may be defined as that language in which the sign-group 7–15–4 = 'god', when reversed, (4–15–7) conveys the meaning 'dog', where 7–15 means 'go' 4–15 means 'do' and 7–15–15–4 means 'good'. If we consider that the whole vocabulary of our language as contained in the *Oxford English Dictionary* is represented as a patterning of twenty-six basic signs, it is easy to see that the decipherer after a few guesses finds himself enmeshed in a network of cross-relationships which are unique to the English language. The above pattern does not hold good even in a closely related language like German, where the corresponding words are *Gott, Hund, gehen, machen, gut*. Each language is a *uniquely* complicated lock. There is only one key, and the test of its rightness is that it should open the door. Such is the complexity of the sounds (and in script the corresponding letters) that diagnosis becomes certain once a comparatively small number of such cross-relationships have been established. The test is an empirical one. We may conclude from the D–O–G/G–O–D relationship alone that the language is English. Any objector will simply be invited to go out and bring evidence from any language in the world which exhibits such a relationship between the two words for 'god' and 'dog'. If he is successful, we shall confront him with another pair, and this time he will have to bring back evidence *within the same rival language* for a similar relationship.

Nearly all the classical decipherments of the last century used this procedure. Their identifications were guesses at probable place-names or proper names. Signs identified in the 'first guesses' were tested by their occurrence in other probable words. Champollion, the decipherer of the Egyptian hieroglyphs, first guessed the name *Ptolemaios*, and then proceeded to *Kleopatra, Alexandros*, etc. Grotefend, who solved the riddle of the Persian cuneiform, tried his luck with 'Dareios, the Great King, King of Kings'. Hieroglyph Hittite inscriptions have been found on monuments in various centres of the neo-Hittite kingdoms of south-eastern Anatolia and North Syria, notably at Carchemish on the Euphrates (fig. 45). Texts from this city contain a frequently recurring sign-group distinguished by the CITY or COUNTRY determinative. It was attractive to identify it as *ka-ra-ka-me-s*. For inscriptions found at Gurguma decipherers looked for a word beginning with a repeated sign, just as for English, if we had occasion to suspect the mention of King GEORGE, we should look for a word in the titulature which began and ended with the same pair of signs and should pick it out all the more easily if we had already identified the word G–O–D.

The Linear B Script and its Decipherment

Ventris employed the same commonsense procedures: his first values emerged from guesses at the common expected Cretan place-names, Knossos, Amnisos, etc. The last name was picked out because it began with a sign of high frequency, and it is a fact that in all languages written syllabically *A*– has a high frequency in the initial syllable. That the script was a syllabary had already been deduced by Evans from the number of signs.

What gave Ventris's decipherment its especial elegance was his use of a principle discovered by the American scholar Alice Kober. This gifted lady, who did not live to see the final decipherment, pointed out that if an inflexional language like Latin is written syllabically, then a series like *dominus, domini, domino, dominorum* will appear with the first two signs constant but with an alternation in the end of the word. Thus even in its undeciphered state the language will have a visual declension. The words will be seen as it were to wag their tails and can be arranged in tail-wagging classes. Moreover, the signs which alternate in the final position will share the same consonant (in our example N–). Not only this, but in words of the same 'declension' the final signs will share the same vowel: *dominus: servus, domini: servi, domino: servo.* Ventris applied this principle systematically, and even before beginning his 'guesses' had been able to establish a complex pattern of interrelationships between the signs of the syllabary. The consequence was that when he started to guess the Cretan geographical names he found himself committed to no fewer than thirty-one values of the syllabary (fig. 7a) containing some sixty-five signs of frequent occurrence. It was not until he started applying these values systematically to the texts that he found them exhibiting Greek inflexions. This fact is of more profound significance to the philologist than mere identifications of vocabulary. The occurrence of *pot, robe, table* in English does not serve to identify it with French. This, as we shall see, is the basic flaw in recent attempts to identify the language of the Linear A tablets (see pp. 327 ff.). What Ventris found in abundance was Greek words *exhibiting Greek inflexions*. By a providential find, which came to his knowledge after the communication of the decipherment to the circle of international specialists, it became possible to test the decipherment and to offer a 'proof' based on the above principles.

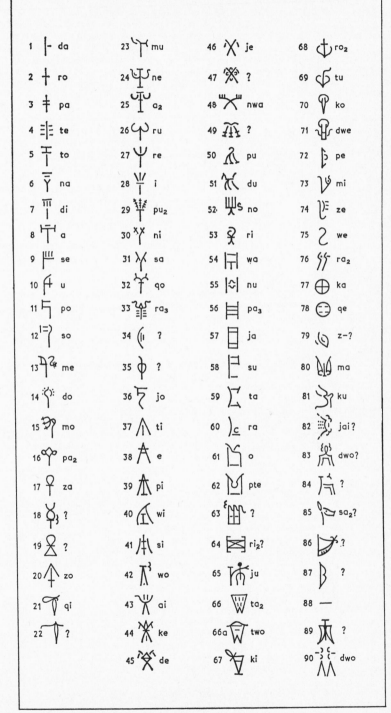

Fig. 7 a. Table of phonetic signs of the Linear B syllabary.

People and Animals

100 A–		MAN
101 A–		MAN^C
102 A–		WOMAN
103 B–		MAN^B
104 Cn		DEER
105 CaS–		HORSE
105^a Ca		HE–ASS
105^c Ca		FOAL
106^a C–D–		RAM
106^b C–D–		EWE
Cn		SHEEP + TA
*21		SHEEP
*75		YEARLING ?
107^a C–		HE–GOAT
107^b C–Mc		SHE–GOAT
*22		GOAT
108^a C–		BOAR
108^b C–		SOW
		PIG + SI
		PIG + KA
*85 C–		PIG
109^a C–		OX/BULL
109^b C–		COW
C–		OX + SI
*23 C–		OX

Units of measurement

110		Volume
111		Volume
112		Dry

Units of measurement (cont.)

113		Liquid
114		Weight
*21		Weight
*2		Weight
115		Weight
116		Weight
117		Weight
118		TALENT
*72 G–		Bunch?
*74 S–		Pair
*15		Single
*61		Deficit

By dry measure

120 E–F–		WHEAT
121 /–		BARLEY
122 F–U–		OLIVES
F		OLIVES + A
F		OLIVES + TI
*30 F–		FIGS
*65 F–		FLOUR
123 G–Un		CONDIMENT
G–		Coriander
*70 G–		Coriander
*31 G–		Sesame
*81 G–		Cumin
*9 G–		Celery
*80 G–		Fennel
*124 G–		Cyperus
125 F–		Cyperus ?

Dry measure continued

126 F–		Cyperus + KU
*34		MONTH
127 Un		Fruit ?
128 G–		Safflower

By liquid measure

130 F–		OIL + WE
G–		OIL + A
131 Fs U		WINE
		MUST ?
132 Un		?
133 Un		Unguent
134 Un		Linseed Oil ?
135 Fs Gg		HONEY
Gg		Amphora of Honey
*13 Un		Honey ?

By weight

140 J–		BRONZE
141 Kn		GOLD
142 Mc		?
*53 Ma		Linseed ?
*44 Ma		?
*61 Ma		An Aromatic
*33 Np		SAFFRON
143 La		?

By weight or in units

*31 N–		?
145 L–O–		WOOL / Aromatic
146 M–		?

Counted in Units

No.	Meaning
150 Mc	?
151 Mc	?
152 M	?
153 Un	?
154 On	?
155 G-	A container
156 Un	CHEESE
157 Un	An aromatic
158 Ld	A bag
159 L-	CLOTH
L-	CLOTH + PA
L-	CLOTH + TE
L-	CLOTH + ZO
L-	CLOTH + PU
L-	CLOTH + KU
160 La	?
161 L-	Description of Cloth: MI+PU2?
162 Sc	CORSLET
Sc	TUNIC + QE
L	TUNIC + KI
L	TUNIC + RI
163 Sh	CORSLET (set)
164 L	A kind of cloth ?
165 Sc	INGOT ?
166 Oa	INGOT + WE
167 Oa	INGOT + PE
168 Pp	Adze? + SE

No.	Meaning
169 Pa	?
170 Cn	?
171 G Sn	?
172 U	? + KE
173 Mn U	?
174 Gv	Seedling ?
175 Gv	FIG TREE
176 Gv	OLIVE TREE
177 U	?
178 U	?
179 U	?
180 U	?
181 U	Thong ?
182 U	?
183 U	?
184 U	?
185 Ws	?
186 Wa	?
187 Xa	cf. 130 ?
188	=*61 ?

Vessels

No.	Meaning
200 K Ta	BOILING PAN
201 Ta	TRIPOD
202 Ta	JAR
203 Ta	WINE JAR ?
204 Ta	EWER
205 K Tn	JUG
206 Tn	HYDRIA
207 K	TRIPOD AMPHORA
208 Tn	BOWL
209 Uc Tn	AMPHORA
210 Uc	STIRRUP JAR
211 K	WATER BOWL?
212 Uc Tn	WATER JAR ?
213 Uc	COOKING BOWL

Furniture

No.	Meaning
220 Ta	FOOTSTOOL

Weapons

No.	Meaning
230 R	SPEAR
231 R	ARROW
232 Ta	DOUBLE AXE?
233 Ra	SWORD

Chariots

No.	Meaning
240 Sc	WHEELED CHARIOT
241 Sd Se	WHEEL-LESS CHARIOT
242 SF Sg	CHARIOT FRAME
243 Sa So	WHEEL
Sa	WHEEL + TE

Fig. 7 b and c. Table of ideograms of the Linear B script.

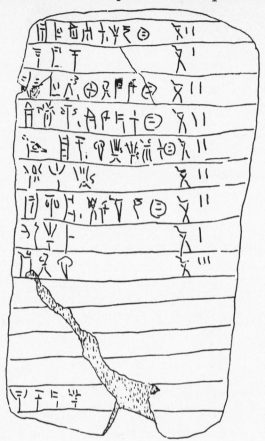

Fig. 8. List of men from Mycenae. Where there are two words opposite the entry MAN 2, *the second word always ends with the 'currant-bun' sign, which represents the enclitic word 'and'.*

I propose to consider this tablet with some care since the 'proof' it provides is so cogent that the opposition has latterly suggested that Ventris had secret knowledge of it before his decipherment. This 'hypothesis' it will be necessary to consider later on.

From texts of a pattern like that illustrated in fig. 8 it was possible to deduce the function of one sign which is attached to the end of words. In this particular instance the document is distinguished by the MAN ideogram. The entries take the form

Fig. 9. The Tripod tablet from Pylos discovered after the communication of the decipherment. In the last three entries the sole change in the ideogram entry is the number of handles. This correlates with the sole change in the text, the last word indicating the number of handles. The word for 'four' begins with the 'currant-bun' sign.

either of a single group followed by the entry MAN 1 or two sign groups followed by MAN 2. It was reasonably concluded that these were men's names. What is evident is that in every entry of the type MAN 2 the second group ends with the 'currant-bun' sign no. 78. The repetition of this phenomenon in a variety of texts imposes the conclusion that this appended sign represents the enclitic word for 'and'. Now in 1952, when Blegen resumed the excavations which had been interrupted by the war, he recovered a further haul of tablets. Among these was the famous Tripod tablet illustrated in fig. 9. Attention is drawn to the last three entries, which are particularly favourable to interpretation, since the syllabic text varies only in the last word and the ideogram varies only in the number of the handles drawn. The correlation is apparent. The final word correlated with the three-handled pot begins with the signs 37–53; but precisely this group begins the first word of line 1, which stands against the ideogram representing a TRIPOD. This is some encouragement to the belief that this group of syllables represents the numeral 'three'. Now in the entries relating to the four-handled pot the final word begins with our 'currant-bun' sign. We deduce that the word for 'four' begins with this syllable. But we are already committed to the fact that this sign when appended to the second of two words means 'and'. We can thus, without assigning a value to the sign in question, attempt a diagnosis of the language by applying our GOD/DOG principle. Here we have a language where the enclitic word for 'and' is also the first syllable of the word for 'four'. This is true of some Indo-European languages including Greek. Now the tablets in question were found in a site of the Peloponnese at a date when it had been universally agreed Greeks had long been established there. Thus our diagnostic spark discharges into a rich mixture of already established linguistic probabilities. Without assigning a phonetic value, simply from observing the behaviour of a single sign, it is possible to diagnose the language in all probability as Greek.

The next step which will confirm it is the observation of inflexions. Here again we can proceed first simply by visual observations without recourse to decipherment. The last three entries relate to a single pot and will presumably be in the singular.

The one immediately preceding lists two pots. The first word is increased by a syllable (no. 38), which is also attached to the other words of this text. Here we have a clear visual example of a grammatical inflexion and agreement. The same is true of the previous entries. The first line relates to a single tripod but the second to two. The first word again increases by a syllable in correlation with the number two of the ideogram entry.

This text enables us to treat Ventris's decipherment as a complex set of 'predictions' relating to the behaviour of a set of signs. This has the advantage that we can admit all the objections brought against his methods and his extremely elastic use of spelling rules which link the syllabic words with Greek. I propose to go even further than his critics and assume that he assigned his values by taking them out of a hat. Let us pin down the decipherer to his predictions. He has told us:

(1) that the language of this tablet is Greek and that consequently in the presence of an ideogram unequivocally recognizable as a TRIPOD we must expect the Greek word *tripos*;

(2) this word will be spelt *ti-ri-po*;

(3) this will be rendered by sign-groups 37–53–11;

(4) since the language is Greek, the inflexions of this language will reveal themselves as modifications, substitutions and additions to the end of the word. In particular the dual and plural of the word in question will be respectively *tripode/ tripodes*;

(5) this inflexion will be revealed by the addition of a single sign to the singular form, and in particular by the addition of sign 45.

Now it is true that precisely this complex set of predictions was exhibited by the tablet in our illustration. Our destructive criticism of Ventris's methods, however, leaves us no alternative but to ascribe these correlations to chance. This random 'success' of the prediction admits to some extent of mathematical formulation, but it will be preferable to use a visual aid to bring home the nature of the probabilities involved.

Let us suppose we have a roulette wheel with 88 compartments, instead of the normal 37, to represent the syllabic values. The table supervisor has before him the picture of a tripod with a word

The Linear B Script and its Decipherment

written on it in a language unknown to us. We are first required to guess the language and hence the word and then play roulette *en plein* against the Bank simply by putting our stake on one of the 88 numbers which we predict will turn up for the first syllable. The game continues until we have reached the number of syllables corresponding to the word on the card. This means that we must also predict the word-divider which marks the end of the word in the Linear B script. We can allow for this by adding a number zero to the wheel, an extra chance which becomes operative at any stage of the game after the first stake. In order, therefore, to predict correctly the sequence actually on the card, after the preliminary hazard of guessing the language, we must succeed in a chance of one in 88 at the first step and one in 89 at each of three succeeding steps, the final 'success' being our stake on zero (= the word-divider). If the bank pays us according to the strict probabilities, our initial stake will have increased by $87 \times 88 \times 88 \times 88$.

The game now proceeds, and the card is subtly altered merely by substituting the figure 2 for 1 after the tripod. We are now faced with the problem of choosing a piece of grammatical machinery, namely the expression of the dual or the plural in the unknown language: no change? substitution of one or more signs of the singular form? prefix? infix? suffix? combination of these procedures? Of all the manifold possibilities a peep at the card reveals that we are required to predict the addition of a single sign, and in particular number 45 of the syllabary. Success in this vital point of grammatical procedure cannot be expressed mathematically, and we must leave its assessment to the collective common sense of the scholarly world. But this apart, the chances against the successful random prediction of the series 37–53–11–45–0 are sufficiently formidable for international opinion to have preferred to applaud the success of the decipherment by the young Englishman rather than to believe in his phenomenal luck.

The attack came from a fellow countryman, and one who had been the teacher of Ventris's linguistic collaborator, Mr Chadwick, at Cambridge. In his first attempt to destroy the evidence of the tripod tablet Professor Beattie at a crucial stage of his argument made twelve mistakes in reading the signs in half a page. When this was corrected by a number of scholars, the attack took a more distressing turn. The evidence of this key text was unassailable, as was its authenticity. It remained to attack Ventris's integrity. In an article published in an East German periodical Professor Beattie analysed the alleged progress of the decipherment and came to the conclusion that Ventris 'somehow obtained the text of the larger portion of Ta 641 [this is the tripod tablet] almost as soon as it was unearthed'. Subsequently 'he composed Worknote 20, and since he desired to make the proof appear independent of Ta 641, he backdated it, somewhat frivolously, to 1 June.' Professor Beattie reaches the following verdict: 'I am bound to conclude that the Worknote was written with full knowledge of the text of the "tripod" tablet and with the purpose of proving the decipherment of the key-words in it.'

Professor Blegen's devastating reply showed that such unauthorized access to a tablet was quite out of the question. In any case they could not be read until they had been cleaned. This had long been known to those familiar with the documents in question. Blegen himself had written: 'All the tablets when found were coated with a heavy lime accretion, rather hard and very adhesive, which in most cases permitted little or no trace of the writing to appear.'

Professor Beattie was not deterred. In an article in the *Glasgow Herald* of May 29, 1959, entitled 'Comparison with Piltdown Hoax' he returned to the charge. The decipherment is branded as 'a concoction, clever but fallacious.' In 'foisting the decipherment on the public' . . . 'some of his ruses are childish' . . . 'Much more serious is his concealment of evidence. He also used texts that were not known to everyone and this too he failed to reveal.' Finally we read:

'There are only two possible explanations of this fantastic business. Either the tripod-tablet itself was found long before June 4, 1952, or another tablet very like it was found at an earlier date and not disclosed. Since the archaeologist who found the known tablet insists that he cannot be mistaken on this point, it is preferable to believe that another tablet was the source of Ventris's information in 1951. Since Linear B tablets in general are very repetitive, it is by no means unlikely that there should have been more than one tripod-tablet. It is impossible to say who

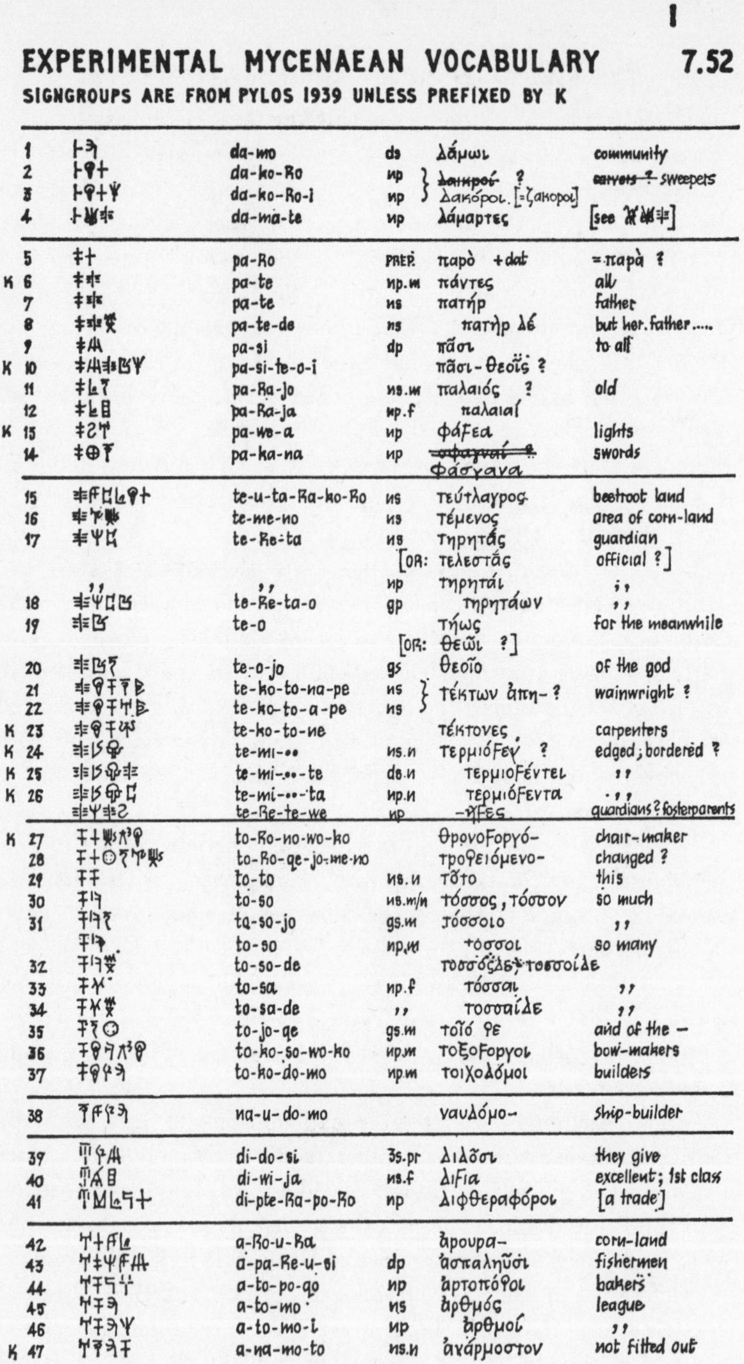

EXPERIMENTAL MYCENAEAN VOCABULARY 7.52

SIGNGROUPS ARE FROM PYLOS 1939 UNLESS PREFIXED BY K

#		transliteration		Greek	meaning
1		da-mo	ds	δάμωι	community
2		da-ko-Ro	np	δαικρού ?	~~carvers~~ ? sweepers
3		da-ko-Ro-i	np	δακόροι [=ζακοροι]	
4		da-ma-te	np	λάμαρτες	[see ...]
5		pa-Ro	PREP.	παρά +dat	=παρά ?
K 6		pa-te	np.m	πάντες	all
7		pa-te	ns	πατήρ	father
8		pa-te-de	ns	πατήρ δέ	but her. father.....
9		pa-si	dp	πᾶσι	to all
K 10		pa-si-te-o-i		πᾶσι-θεοῖς ?	
11		pa-Ra-jo	ns.m	παλαιός ?	old
12		pa-Ra-ja	np.f	παλαιαί	
K 13		pa-we-a	np	φάϜεα	lights
14		pa-ka-na	np	~~φαργανά~~ ? φάσγανα	swords
15		te-u-ta-Ra-ko-Ro	ns	τεύτλαγρος	beetroot land
16		te-me-no	ns	τέμενος	area of corn-land
17		te-Re-ta	ns	τηρητάς	guardian
				[OR: τελεστάς	official ?]
18		te-Re-ta-o	np / gp	τηρητάι / τηρητάων	,,
19		te-o		τήως	for the meanwhile
				[OR: θεῶι ?]	
20		te-o-jo	gs	θεοῖο	of the god
21		te-ko-to-na-pe	ns	τέκτων ἀπη- ?	wainwright ?
22		te-ko-to-a-pe	ns		
K 23		te-ko-to-ne		τέκτονες	carpenters
K 24		te-mi-**	ns.n	τερμιόϜεν ?	edged; bordered ?
K 25		te-mi-**-te	ds.n	τερμιόϜεντει	,,
K 26		te-mi-**-ta	np.n	τερμιόϜεντα	,,
		te-Re-te-we	np	-ηϜες	guardians? fosterparents
K 27		to-Ro-no-wo-ko		θρονοϜοργό-	chair-maker
28		to-Ro-qe-jo-me-no		τροφειόμενο-	changed ?
29		to-to	ns.n	τότο	this
30		to-so	ns.m/n	τόσσος, τόσσον	so much
31		ta-so-jo	gs.m	τόσσοιο	,,
		to-so	np.m	+όσσοι	so many
32		to-so-de		τοσσόϊδε+τοσσοίδε	,,
33		to-sa	np.f	τόσσαι	,,
34		to-sa-de	,,	τοσσαίδε	,,
35		to-jo-qe	gs.m	τοῖο ϙε	and of the —
36		to-ko-so-wo-ko	np.m	τοξοϜοργοι	bow-makers
37		to-ko-do-mo	np.m	τοιχοδόμοι	builders
38		na-u-do-mo		ναυδόμο—	ship-builder
39		di-do-si	3s.pr	διδόσι	they give
40		di-wi-ja	ns.f	διϜja	excellent; 1st class
41		di-pte-Ra-po-Ro	np	διφθεραφόροι	[a trade]
42		a-Ro-u-Ra		ἀρουρα—	corn-land
43		a-pa-Re-u-si	dp	ἀσπαλῆϜσι	fishermen
44		a-to-po-qo	np	ἀρτοπόϙοι	bakers
45		a-to-mo	ns	ἀρθμός	league
46		a-to-mo-i	np	ἀρθμοί	,,
K 47		a-na-mo-to	ns.n	ἀνάρμοστον	not fitted out

FIG. 10(a)

Fig. 10. First page and the 'grid' from M. Ventris's 'Experimental Mycenaean Vocabulary', the first communication (circulated privately in July 1952) of the decipherment.

EXPERIMENTAL SYLLABARY

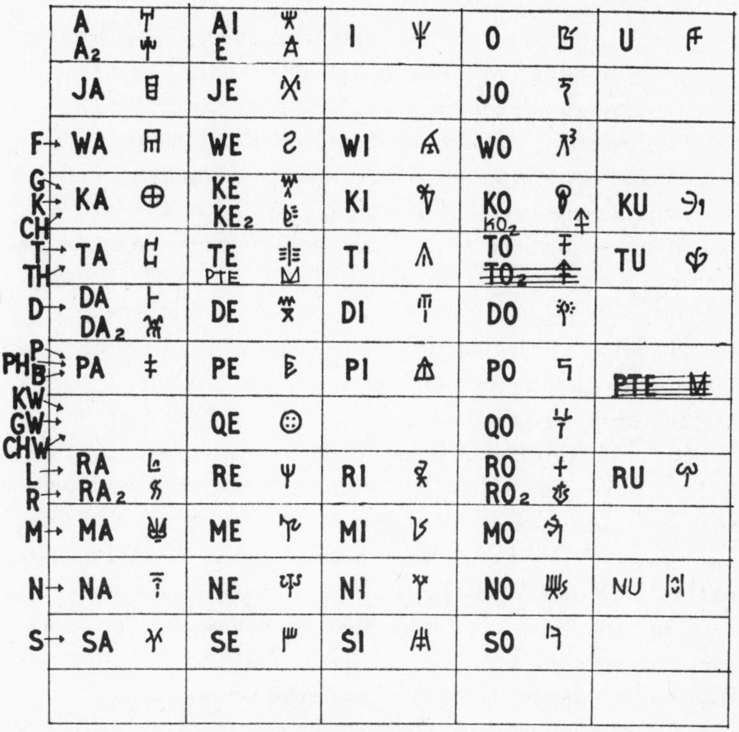

	A A₂	AI E	I	O	U
	A / **A₂**	**AI** / **E**	**I**	**O**	**U**
	JA	**JE**		**JO**	
F→	**WA**	**WE**	**WI**	**WO**	
G / K / CH→	**KA**	**KE** / **KE₂**	**KI**	**KO** / KO₂	**KU**
T / TH→	**TA**	**TE** PTE	**TI**	**TO** / TO₂	**TU**
D→	**DA** / **DA₂**	**DE**	**DI**	**DO**	
PH / P / B→	**PA**	**PE**	**PI**	**PO**	~~PTE~~
KW / GW / CHW→		**QE**		**QO**	
L / R→	**RA** / **RA₂**	**RE**	**RI**	**RO** / RO₂	**RU**
M→	**MA**	**ME**	**MI**	**MO**	
N→	**NA**	**NE**	**NI**	**NO**	NU
S→	**SA**	**SE**	**SI**	**SO**	

FIG. 10(b)

can have found the tablet or how Ventris obtained a copy of it; but the evidence of its key-words in the "Worknotes" is unmistakable.'

Thus Professor Beattie from his analysis of Ventris's privately circulated analyses, which began in 1951, infers the existence of a duplicate tripod tablet which the excavator has not published and presumably never saw. How this completely unknown young man succeeded in persuading some member of the American excavation team is left to the imagination. At all events the readers of this provincial newspaper are told: 'In addition to being wrong, the decipherment is in effect a fake — as serious in its own way as the Piltdown skull.'

Professor Beattie asks 'Why if the results are so poor, did any sensible person ever accept them? The answer is simple. Few classical scholars knew much about decipherment or even about the prehistoric phases of the Greek language.' However, such was my own estimate of the probabilities involved that *ti-ri-po* TRIPOD 1 and *ti-ri-po-de* TRIPOD 2 was enough for me, and I was among the first to acknowledge the success of the decipherment. Others may be more exacting, but comparatively few successes of this kind should convince all those who make clear to themselves the simple mathematics involved. The continuing success of the excavators in finding new texts enables us, however, to ignore the doubt cast on the tripod tablet as a verification of a prediction.

In 1954 Professor Blegen unearthed a tablet at Pylos bearing the ideogram which had already been identified as olive oil. It followed a sentence consisting of a number of syllabic groups in the Linear B script. Most of the signs had been identified by Ventris in 1952; others had been added by various scholars in the general discussion which followed publication. The sentence of the new tablet was at once clear to all who had an elementary knowledge of Greek: 'Kokalos gave so much oil to Eumedes: OLIVE OIL 18 units.' Now both the individuals named were known from previous texts, and they were both described by a word which Ventris had long before identified as an occupational description, 'unguent-boilers'. This led to yet another text which read 'How Alxoitas gave Thyestes the unguent-boiler spices for him to boil in the unguent'. This introductory sentence was followed by entries relating to the aromatic herbs in question. Of these coriander and cyperus had already been identified by Ventris in the original circular sent round in July 1952 (see fig. 10). But some of the ingredients presented a puzzle which may serve to underline the difference between decipherment and interpretation.

As we have said, comparatively few certain identifications will suffice to prove the correctness of a decipherment. The interpretation of documents which give only rough hints at a form of Greek some four or five centuries older than Homer is a different matter and it may take years of patient analysis and experiment. We are in precisely this position with the texts of another recently deciphered language — hieroglyph Hittite (see pp. 327 ff). Now among the ingredients described as for boiling in the unguent are wine and honey. At first I supposed that there had been some mistake about the identification of the ideograms. But on reading the literature about the manufacture of unguents in antiquity I came across the passage '. . . the Greek and Latin authors mention many other (perfumes), such as henna flowers, the *root of the iris*, *honey and wine*'. This not only removed my misgivings about the entry but cleared up an adjacent one which had been rendered nonsensically 'root (?) 6 Kg of wool'. It was now possible that the entry related to the root of some plant and the ideogram had been confused with the very similar one for wool. Later on it was discovered that these two ideograms differ as regards their measurement. wool is measured more roughly than the aromatics destined for unguents and ritual purposes, and the latter entries present sub-units of weight ignored in entries relating to wool.[1] By a sort of chain reaction this led to closer observation of the records concerned with the aromatics, and this again proved of great importance for our picture of Mycenaean religion (see below, p. 131 on Eleuthia).

The final sentence in the new text contained a word which could not be identified with one known from later Greek sources. But here we were fortunate beyond reasonable hope. The word also occurred in a tablet from Knossos which depicted vessels of various kinds from which it was evident that this unknown word designated a vessel which is particularly characteristic of the Mycenaean age — the stirrup-jar (see fig. 28) in which perfumed olive oil was presumably exported. Thus the meaning of the final sentence was in harmony with the general context indicated by the introductory sentence. 'From *I-pe-se-wa* stirrup jars: 38.'

In the preceding paragraphs the decipherment has been applied not to isolated words but to a whole group of texts dealing with a particular technical activity containing long sentences which must exhibit the grammatical peculiarities of Greek. They also illustrate the difficulties which we are bound to encounter in dealing with the records of a bronze-age civilization which was divided from the later Hellenic world by a dark age of some centuries.

The progress of the excavations in 1957 faced both the decipherment and the interpreters with a test at which they might well

---

[1] J. Killen has argued that the 'root' may be part of the wool rich in lanolin.

quail considering the hazards involved. The tripod tablet discussed above turned out to be one of a whole series containing an inventory of household goods. It will be discussed below (p. 160). In 1952 one of the tablets was still incomplete and only the two ends had been published. The circumstances in which the missing centre piece came to light may be described in Professor Blegen's own words, 'Elsewhere in the palace only a few minor test pits

Fig. 11. The 'Missing Link'. The two end pieces of this Pylos tablet were published in 1955; the centre piece was discovered in 1957 after the publication of translations of the two end pieces.

were dug. One trial was made to the south-east of the Archives Annex in an attempt to find the piece missing between tablets Ta 709 and 712. This essay was unsuccessful. Subsequently when we reopened the earth-filled trench left by the looters, who long ago carried off the stone blocks of the wall between the Propylon and the Archives Rooms, we had better luck. The much-sought missing fragment was actually recovered along with some 28 other pieces.' The whole tablet was communicated by Miss M. Lang in a paper entitled 'The Missing Link' (see fig. 11). Meanwhile the two end-pieces had been separately translated by various scholars, including myself. We now had to face the fact that the translation of the missing centre piece had to fit what we had previously committed ourselves to.

It was evident from the ideograms that the text dealt with cooking utensils. The words immediately preceding the gap in the second line had been translated by myself, divergently from the others, as 'shovels, brush, fire-tongs and fire-rake', and I summed up this group of objects as 'the minor appurtenances of the hearth'. It would hardly be possible to commit oneself more precisely to a context. So it was some relief to find that the word which now appeared immediately after on the missing piece was the Greek word for 'hearth'! Not merely this, but the words which the scribe had entered following after *e-ka-ra* 'hearth' on the right-hand end-piece were now seen to be a description of the hearth. I had also ventured a translation of these words. Moreover, it so happens that such portable Mycenaean hearths were remarkably conservative in their decoration; and so the 'predicted' translation had to satisfy the severest of tests. In the first place the adjectives had to agree with what now appeared as a feminine singular noun. Worse still, the description had to be appropriate to Mycenaean hearths. It turned out that there was a satisfactory grammatical agreement between noun and adjectives and in particular one, diagnosed as a compound adjective, followed the Greek rule of having no separate feminine form. As for the meaning of this adjective, I had diagnosed it as some part of the support of a table and proposed a translation as 'with splay-legs.' The 'missing link' now showed that it alternated with another adjective which I had previously suggested meant 'with uprights'. The archaeological background of the translation was now examined by specialists. The verdict runs: 'Surviving hearths are distinguished by splayed and straight legs.' Finally there remained a pair of words which occurred constantly at the end of descriptions of artefacts. This position in the formulae had suggested to me that the word represented some accessorial element of Mycenaean decoration. Another such word had already been identified independently by Ventris and myself as 'decorated with spirals'. For statistical reasons I had hazarded the guess that the word now under discussion meant 'decorated with rosettes'. We can now see that one of the hearths in this inventory bears this description. Again the verdict of archaeology was favourable. Evans in his great *Palace of Minos* had already commented on the remarkable conservatism in the decoration of the hearth which he ascribed to its religious value. It is the decoration shown in fig. 12 called by archaeologists either 'flame pattern' or 'notched plume' with rosettes in between.

It will be evident that the 'missing link', recovered in 1957, has shown that both the decipherment and the interpretations based on Ventris's values pass the most exacting test yet devised. We

The Linear B Script and its Decipherment

Fig. 12. A portable table of offerings from Knossos showing the traditional decoration of 'notched plume' and rosettes.

conclude that the values for the signs are correct and that the messages on the tablets are in Greek. The Heroic Age of Greece is no longer illiterate. I quote with full agreement the verdict of a leading authority in the field of Mycenaean archaeology and pre-history. Professor Fritz Schachermeyr of Vienna in a recent appraisal of the decipherment has written: 'All doubts may be set at rest and we may without further ado designate the decipher-ment of Linear B as one of the most brilliant scholarly achieve-ments of all time.' A quotation from the standard work in English on Homeric archaeology will indicate how great an advance in our knowledge has been occasioned by the decipherment. Miss H. L. Lorimer in her masterly *Homer and the Monuments* wrote: 'The Bronze Age of Greece is at present unilluminated by any con-temporary record. . . . Blegen's excavations near the site of the classical Pylos brought to light a Mycenaean palace in which some 600 inscribed clay tablets were found. Though they are still un-published, much work has been done on squeezes taken from them and the result is wholly unfavourable to any hope that the language of the inscriptions might be Greek.' The date of Miss Lorimer's book is 1950.

Chapter III

The Land of the Pylians

We may now revert to the problem with which our book began and the concluding remarks of W. McDonald in his article of 1942: 'Perhaps the question of the site of Nestor's Pylos still cannot be decided to the full satisfaction of all interested. If the newly discovered tablets can be deciphered, they will almost certainly settle it one way or the other.' Thanks to Michael Ventris we are now in that happy position. It may be said at once that the question is settled. The name Pylos figures repeatedly in these texts, and there can be little doubt that this was the name of the region in which the palace of Ano Englianos stood. Below it will be argued that Pylos was in fact the 'capital' of one of the two provinces into which this Mycenaean kingdom was divided.

The new facts provide classical scholars with a salutary opportunity for self-examination and a critique of our scholarly methods. For we are now well placed to judge what could be achieved by analysis and assessment of the evidence available to us before the decipherment. This comprised the geographical indications culled from the Homeric epic, the statements of ancient authorities such as Strabo, and the place names of classical Greece. By a curious, and some may think, fortunate chance an authoritative survey of the problem was written just before the decipherment became known, though it was not published until 1959. This was the article on 'Pylos' in *Pauly-Wissowa*, the encyclopaedia of classical antiquity to which we referred above (p. 50). On the Homeric Pylos the author had written: 'That Pylos was originally the entrance to the lower world and that it was only later that it was localized in the western Peloponnese as a place-name admits of no doubt. . . . The transformation of Neleus from a god of the dead into an earthly hero and the localization of his realm Pylos on earth belong together.' One of the props of this pretty hypothesis is the etymological interpretation of the name Neleus as 'The pitiless one'. On this we shall have more to say below when discussing the dynastic name of the Neleids.

Meanwhile the facts of the decipherment and the resulting interpretations had been gaining ground, and the volume of the encyclopaedia contains in its addenda some further remarks by the author of the article on Pylos. They read: 'In the clay tablets of Ano Englianos the name Pylos is of frequent occurrence, apparently referring to the Palace, although that is not certain. . . . But the fact that the name Pylos is now attested here too for the Mycenaean Age makes no difference to the case.' It remains to add that the same author in 1954 engaged in an intensive search to find the Triphylian town which figures so largely in his case for siting Nestor's Pylos there. The final words of his report, however, read: 'Thus the search for this historic Pylos remained still without success.'

But if we may concede to Professor Blegen that he has found near Navarino the Pylos of the Mycenaean age which lay behind the later legends preserved in the Homeric poems, this does not alter the fact that this location cannot be reconciled with the Pylos of the Nestorian reminiscences in the *Iliad*. On the other hand the Messenian Pylos best fits the admittedly vaguer indications of the *Odyssey* and the journeys of Telemachus. So we find ourselves willy-nilly in the ranks of those who deny the single authorship of the two great Greek epics.

If the later poem can pride itself on the more accurate memory of the site of a Mycenaean town, the *Iliad* gives us some clear indications of the extent of Pylian territory in Mycenaean times. We may begin with the famous offer of Agamemnon to make restitution for his insult to Achilles.

'I wish to make amends and to give requital beyond count. Among you all I shall name the glorious gifts. Seven tripods, untouched by the fire and ten talents of gold; twenty gleaming cauldrons and ten horses, strong of frame, prize-winners who have gained trophies by their swift running. . . . And I will give seven women skilled in handicrafts, women of Lesbos, who surpass in beauty the tribes of women. These I will give him and along with them shall be the girl I took from him, the daughter of Briseus.

'And if we come back to Achaean Argos, most fertile of lands, he shall be my son-in-law. . . . Three daughers have I in my well-found hall, Chrysothemis, Laodike and Iphianassa. Of these let him lead to the house of Peleus the one who pleases him, without bride-gifts. And I will add a dower beyond all a man ever gave to his daughter. I shall give him populous cities: Cardamyle and Enope, and grassy Hira and sacred Pherae, and Antheia with its deep meadows and lovely Aipeia and vine-clad Pedasos, all near the sea, next to sandy Pylos.'

This was amends handsome indeed, but it was not enough. An insult to heroic honour could not be measured in the currency of metal, horses and women. The passage is rich in information about life and customs in the Heroic Age of Greece and in fuel for scholarly controversy. At this point our concern is merely with the seven cities which were to form the major part of the dowry proffered by king Agamemnon. Their location inevitably attracted the attention of ancient commentators on Homer. The geographer Strabo, in dealing with this part of Greece, after working his way down the west coast of Messenia as far as Cape Akritas (fig. 13) suddenly jumps to the far side of the Gulf of Messenia and works his way back round the coast as far as Akritas again. In so doing he discusses the location of the seven cities. Starting with that part of Cape Taenarum which is called 'The Windows', from the numerous sea-caves found there, he mentions a list of places beginning with Oetylos, a city assigned in the 'Catalogue'[1] to Menelaus, brother of Agamemnon and king of Sparta. The third and fourth places enumerated by Strabo are Cardamyle and Pherae, which are among Homer's Seven. The former, Strabo tells us, is situated on a strong rock and the latter on the river Nedon, which flows through Laconia (fig. 13). It is apropos of Pherae that Strabo gives us an interesting piece of information. This city, he tells us, borders on Thouria and Gerena. Now Nestor is constantly referred to as 'Gerenian Nestor' although his town and domains lie on the west coast of Messenia. This surprising localization of the aged king of Pylos tallies with another indication we gather casually from the Odyssey.

[1] See p. 40 n. 1.

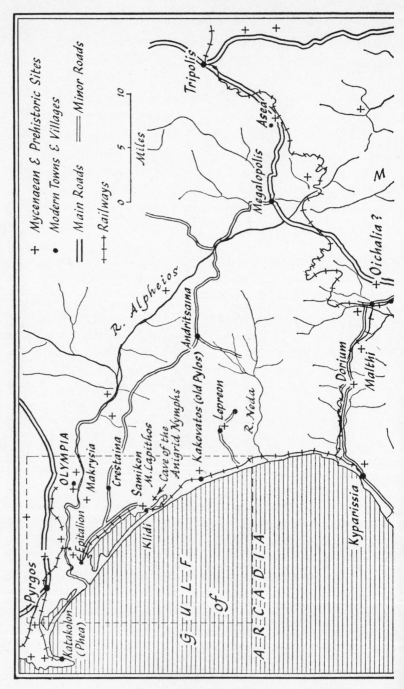

Fig. 13. Map of Mycenaean Messenia. Prehistoric sites

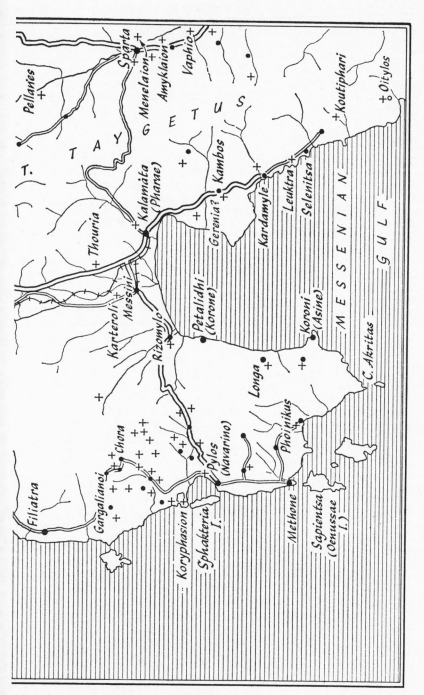

after R. Hope-Simpson and W. McDonald.

Athena puts it into Penelope's head to go and fetch the bow and quiver 'which Iphitus, the son of Eurytus, had once given him as a present when he met him in Lacedaemon and they had come together in Messene in the house of Ortilochus.' Odysseus, we are told, had gone there to make a claim because Messenian men had carried off from Ithaca three hundred sheep together with their shepherds, whereas Iphitus had been looking for some mares which had strayed from his own territory of Oechalia. At the time of this meeting Odysseus had been a mere stripling and he had gone on this errand on the instructions of his father and the other Elders. But by the time of the Trojan War Ortilochus of Pherae had been succeeded by his son Diocles, whose two sons, Crethon and Orsilochus, were slain by Aeneas before Troy. It was this Diocles, son of Ortilochus, who acted as host to Telemachus and Pisistratus on their journey from Pylos to Sparta.

From all this we are now in a position to state that Pherae was in Messene, which was a district of Lacedaemon bordering on Oechalia. At the time of the Trojan War it was in the possession of Diocles, son of Ortilochus, 'whom Alpheus begat'. Yet Agamemnon proposed to include this city and its territory in the dowry he was proffering to Achilles. The position is all the more puzzling because Agamemnon's own domains lie north of Mycenae along the Gulf of Corinth, Corinth itself being numbered among those subject to him. The territory assigned to his brother Menelaus lies in 'hollow Lacedaemon', but it extends around the coast westwards as far as Oetylus, which as we have said, is the first place mentioned by Strabo in the Gulf of Messenia. The Seven cities of the dowry thus occupy a strip of coastal territory extending at least as far as Pherae, which is most plausibly located at or near the modern Kalamata. Nothing in Homer justifies the extension of this territory beyond the river Nedon or the Pamisus, for the locations suggested by Strabo and Pausanias for the other places are sheer guesswork.

Since, then, we are told that these cities lie 'next to[1] sandy

[1] As a curiosity of scholarship we may mention the view that the word I have translated 'next to' really means 'the outermost part of (sandy Pylos)'. Agamemnon is speaking to Nestor about the terms of the reconciliation, and this interpretation would have us believe that Agamemnon, without as much as a 'by your leave', tells Nestor to pass on to Achilles the proposal to slice off a large part of Nestor's territory in the interests of peace and harmony among the Greeks.

Pylos', we must imagine Nestor's domains as extending roughly as far as the Nedon. The northern frontier of Pylos lay, as we have seen from Nestor's reminiscences, on the river Alpheus. Other incidental references in the poems confirm the picture. Thus when Aeneas kills the two sons of Diocles of Pherae, the poet adds that they were descended from the river Alpheus, *which flows broad through the land of the Pylians.* The epic thus represents Nestor as king of a large domain extending far beyond the boundaries of the historical Messenia. This fact had already been emphasized by the Swedish scholar M. P. Nilsson in his discussion of the problem in his book *The Mycenaean Origins of Greek Mythology.* 'It is comprehensible that scholars have thought according to the usual geographical units and have identified the dominion of Pylos with the historical province of Messenia in general, perhaps with the addition of Triphylia. But this has in my opinion vitiated the problem. The boundaries were not the same in the Mycenaean age as the historical age.'

Once again our new documentary evidence offers us the opportunity of sitting in judgement on the methods and results of traditional classical scholarship. We have abundant material since the tablets deal in the main with the registering and movement of commodities and personnel in connexion with a large number of tributary places. However, two major difficulties impede the exploitation of this geographical information contained in the tablets. The first is the ambiguity of the script, which makes it difficult to be certain that we have correctly identified the name itself. The second is that place-names tend to recur in various localities of Greece as they do in other countries (e.g. *Newport* and the like). A case in point is the place *ko-ri-to*, which is reasonably identified as *Korinthos.* But this Pylian dependency can hardly be the famous Corinth of later times. Again, we can see that *re-u-ko-to-ro* is an important place in the Pylian world, and again there can be little doubt that this word is to be read *Leuktron.* But Leuktra occurs widely as a place-name in later times, and it would appear that our town is not to be identified with any of them. Again, the 'Catalogue' lists a Helos among the dominions of both Nestor and Menelaus. Such a repetition is not surprising since the word simply means 'swamp' or 'water meadow'. In early work

87

on the Pylian place-names these considerations were incautiously neglected, and the resulting picture showed names scattered all over the Peloponnese. Worse still, the King of Pylos was credited with slaves from as far afield as Miletus in Asia Minor and Lemnos. It became necessary to devise methods of diminishing these ambiguities.

Most important is to operate with clusters of names which tend to occur together in the tablets. Another is to establish some kind of order in the entries from which we can deduce the geographical relationships. We can then, instead of operating with isolated identifications, apply the clusters to the later map as a complex pattern. In this way any given 'fix' is immediately subject to a series of confirmatory tests.

The material proved easy to treat in this way for the scribes observe an amazing degree of consistency in listing the series of places. From the start it was noted that one set of 'Nine' occurs repeatedly in a constant order, and they evidently represent the main tributary places of Pylos. Another set of 'Seven' also occurs, but the order varies to some extent. At a later stage of the analysis it became clear that these two sets of places are referred to as the places 'This side of *Ai-ko-ra*' and 'The far side of *Ai-ko-ra*'. Thus the 'Nine' and the 'Seven' constitute a 'Hither Province' and a 'Further Province', the dividing landmark being the as yet unidentified *Ai-ko-ra*. If we now turn to the Nine places of the Hither Province,[1] so named from the point of view of the capital Pylos, it will be seen that the fourth of the Nine (see fig. 14) is a place *Pa-ki-ja-nes*, on which we have a good deal of information. It appears to have been the holy city of Pylos, the seat of the goddess Potnia ('The Mistress'), where there was a large estate apparently belonging to the Wanax, the King of Pylos. The arrangements on this estate and the relationship of the king to the Goddess will occupy us later. But evidently *Pa-ki-ja-nes* will have been at no great distance from Pylos itself, which thus lies, satisfactorily enough, roughly in the centre of its own Hither Province. The constant order of the Nine places implies a geographical order. At all events, at one extremity we have the two

---

[1] See map fig. 13 and lists fig. 14.

The Land of the Pylians

places *Pi-jai*[1] and *Me-ta-pa*, in that order, with *Ri-jo* occupying the other extremity, it being a further proviso that when we have passed the last place we are in the Further Province.

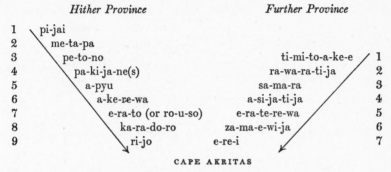

	Hither Province		Further Province	
1	pi-jai			
2	me-ta-pa			
3	pe-to-no		ti-mi-to-a-ke-e	1
4	pa-ki-ja-ne(s)		ra-wa-ra-ti-ja	2
5	a-pyu		sa-ma-ra	3
6	a-ke-re-wa		a-si-ja-ti-ja	4
7	e-ra-to (or ro-u-so)		e-ra-te-re-wa	5
8	ka-ra-do-ro		za-ma-e-wi-ja	6
9	ri-jo		e-re-i	7

CAPE AKRITAS

Fig. 14. The geographical lay-out of Mycenaean Pylos. Schematic arrangement of the 'Nine' and the 'Seven' places of the Hither and the Further Provinces.

We can now, in accordance with the above stated principle, apply this complex pattern to the later map. We find to the north of Pylos just beyond the Alpheus a place Phea, and there is evidence for a place Metapa in the neighbourhood of Olympia on the Alpheus. At the other extremity on the far side of Pylos we find that Rhion is the name in later times for the region round Cape Akritas. This satisfies our further proviso, for the promontory functions as a satisfactory landmark dividing the two provinces, especially where communications are largely by sea, as they are in Greece. Our pattern of resemblance presents itself thus:

> Linear B: *pi-jai*   *me-ta-pa*   *PU-RO*   *ri-jo*
> Later map: Phea(i)   Metapa   Pylos   Rhion.

But we are not yet finished with the deductions generated by our analysis. When we pass beyond *Ri-jo*, we are in the territory of the Seven. Thus we are forced to the conclusion that the places of the Further Province lie within the Gulf of Messenia. Further information and analysis next showed that the palace scribes when listing these places started at the farther extremity of the

[1] This sign is still under discussion, but since the other suggestion *Pisa* is in the same northern area, the general geographical relationships are not affected.

Further Province and worked their way back to the demarcation point at Cape Akritas. This happens to be precisely the way the geographer Strabo described this region over a thousand years later (see above). An important consequence flows from this. If the scribes have to list a given sequence of places in their geographical order starting down the west coast of Messenia, once they have rounded Cape Akritas the succeeding places belonging to the Further Province should appear *in the reverse order of the Seven*. This enables us to make a most complex test on the order we have deduced for the Nine and the Seven and also for their geographical location.

By a great stroke of fortune we have precisely such a set of texts. They are concerned with the stations of 'rowers'. Since they have reference to the arrangements reflecting the final emergency of Pylos, they will be best discussed below (Chapter V). But it may be said at once that as the scribe works his way along the coast the stations of the Hither Province are listed according to the proper order of the Nine. But when we have passed *Ri-jo*, the places now appear in the *reverse order* of the Seven, as we deduced. As will be shown below, this is a fact of great interest for the location of the Pylian forces in the final crisis, but in the present context what concerns us is the striking verification of the arrangement of the places of the Hither Province and the Further Province. Since there are indications that the first place of the Seven, which is also geographically the most remote from Pylos, was not far from the River Nedon (fig. 13), the Pylian Kingdom will have extended from this point round south-westwards past Cape Akritas and then up the coast beyond the Alpheus as far as Phea(i). This is all the more satisfactory because, as we have seen, it corresponds precisely to the Epic picture of Nestor's domains. The Alpheus flows through the land of the Pylians.

No less satisfactory was the verdict of the archaeologists on these deductions. In the summer of 1959 Professor W. McDonald, who had assisted Professor Blegen in the 1939 excavations at Pylos, in company with Mr Hope-Simpson, explored the area indicated by me as the likely location of the Further Province. Not only were two important Mycenaean sites located but traces were found of an ancient road leading from Pylos to the Gulf of

Messenia (fig. 13). Thus there can be little doubt that the Pylian domains extended as far as the River Nedon. On the other hand there is no evidence that it included the eastern shores of the Gulf of Messenia which a poet of the *Iliad* regards as being in the gift of Agamemnon, 'next to sandy Pylos'.

Some classical scholars have recently maintained the extreme view that Homer had little memory of the Mycenaean age, so it will be of interest to consider a little more closely some of the names he mentions in the land of the Pylians. The most northerly of the Nine places of the Hither Province we have diagnosed as *pi-jai* and identified this syllabic name as *Phiai*, which in its turn has been equated with Phea(i). Two passages in Homer are relevant. For the first we are again indebted to one of Nestor's reminiscences. 'If only I were young again as when the Pylians gathered together and fought the Arcadians on the swift-flowing Keladon, by the walls of Pheia on the stream of Iardanos.' Another mention of the same place seems to recur in the description of Telemachus's return voyage from Pylos to Ithaca. 'They went past Crounoi ("The Springs") and the fair-flowing Chalcis. The sun set and all the ways were shadowed. But the ship made for Pheai urged on by the wind of Zeus, and then sailed past divine Elis, where the Epeans hold sway.' From this passage we can see that Pheai is a prominent land-mark for voyages along the west coast of the Peloponnese and that after passing it north-bound the voyager found himself skirting the territory of Elis, the land of the Epeans, whom we have already encountered in Nestor's tale of the cattle raid as the northern neighbours of the Pylians. Phea(i) will thus have been a frontier town. A Phea is mentioned often by later authors and there is general agreement that it was the port of Olympia at the base of the promontory of Ichthys (see fig. 13). However, it is typical of the difficulties which beset scholars in this field that Pheai in the above passage of the Odyssey is actually an emendation; but the probabilities in its favour have been such that it is read in all modern editions.

If we now turn to the other arm of the equation, we shall find scholars disputing about the reading of the second syllable of the Pylian name. I believe that these doubts have been largely set at rest by new evidence. Here, however, are the facts on which we must pronounce judgement. Traditional classical scholarship had decided that the text of Homer contained a reference to a Pheai at the northern extremity of the Pylian kingdom. A Linear B scholar at the beginning of 1954 proposed a value *jai* for sign *82. This produced a place-name *pi-jai*. Later new information came to hand which suggested siting this place at the northern extremity of the Further Province with *Me-ta-pa* immediately to the south. Rejection of the identification carries with it the implication that the convergence of two wholly separate lines of research is due to accident.

We now carry out other tests on the place-name material. A Helos is listed among the towns of Nestor's kingdom in the 'Catalogue', without any clues to its whereabouts. The archives of Pylos, however, include a place *E-re-e*, or *E-re-i*, which is identified as Helos in the locative case; it is the last of the Seven places of the Further Province which lie within the Gulf of Messenia. According to our deductions the places of each province are enumerated starting from the furthest points and each list ends at the demarcation point represented by Cape Akritas. This means that *Ri-jo* (Rhion), the last of the Nine, and *E-re-e* (Helos), the last of the Seven, are adjacent and that the latter will lie next to the promontory just within the Gulf of Messenia. It so happens that an ancient source followed by Pliny sites Helos next to Cape Akritas. Admittedly such sources are more than suspect, but at least we can say that our findings are consistent with such later information as we possess.

The 'Catalogue' also lists Cyparisseis and Aipu among Nestor's towns. The former has always been identified with the later Cyparissia, north of Pylos and just south of the river Cyparisseis. A place *Ku-pa-ri-so* is mentioned in the Linear B archives, and the coast defence document which will be discussed below links it with certain other places in a way which leaves little room for doubt that it was situated in much the same area as the classical town. For Aipu the 'Catalogue' offers no clue as to its location. Here, too, it will be well to trace in detail the line of the investigation. Ventris's decipherment yielded the name of the place as *A-*29*. In 1953 I was able to suggest that the value for the unread sign was *pu₂*. Further analysis produced a refinement. It appeared that the syllabary made a general distinction between plain consonants and similar sounds followed by a *y* sound. We make a similar distinction in the first consonants of *coo* and *cue*. The latter type of sound (*ky*) philologists call 'palatalized'. It became clear that our pu_2 was in fact such a palatalized sound, *pyu*, so that the name was really *A-PYU*. In later Greek such palatalized sounds tend to produce an intrusive *i* in the preceding syllable. All this made it difficult to resist equating the Linear B place-name *A-pyu* with the later Aipu. But where was it? Here again we can profit by the orderliness of the Pylian scribes. It is listed in the Nine places of the Hither Province after the holy city of *Pa-ki-ja-nes*. This, we concluded could not be very far from Pylos itself. Thus Aipu will have lain immediately to the south of the Pylian capital.

We now return to *Ku-pa-ri-so*, tentatively and temptingly equated with *Cyparissia*. It will be necessary now to anticipate some findings which emerge from the coast defence document discussed in Chapter V. There we shall find men of *Ku-pa-ri-so* linked with others called *O-ka-rai*. This last name immediately evokes the Oechalia we encountered in the story of Odysseus' mission to seek indemnity for the cattle stolen by the Messenians. In Messene he met Iphitus, the son of Eurytus, whose territory was next to Messene. Now Eurytus was king of Oechalia, and we know again from the 'Catalogue' that he was also a neighbour of Nestor. The entry listing the latter's towns reads at this point '. . . and Dorion, where the Muses meeting Thamyris the Thracian, stopped him from his song as he came from Oechalia, from Eurytus of Oechalia.' This king figures in one of the adventures of Heracles. Thwarted in his passion for Iole, daughter of Eurytus, Heracles hurled Iphitus, who again was looking for some lost cattle, from the walls of Tiryns. For this crime he sought purification from Neleus of Pylos. Rebuffed, he made war on Neleus and killed all his sons except Nestor. It was during this period of Pylian weakness that they had been subject to the raids by the Epeans which provoked the first warlike exploit of the young Nestor, recounted in the 'Pylian epic' we have already discussed.

An Oechalia is also attributed to Thessaly and Euboea, but the general geographical pattern of this group of legends is reasonably clear. They are sited in the Peloponnese. We recall once again that

Messene was the territory of Pherae and formed part of Lacedae-mon. If we follow the route of the present-day railway from Kala-mata through the upper Messenian plain, we shall pass through the domains of ancient Oechalia and again emerge into Pylian territory at Dorion and eventually reach the sea on the western coast at the mouth of the river Cyparisseis just a little north of Cyparissia (fig. 13). In a later chapter we shall have occasion to consider whether it is reasonable to find in this locality a detach-ment of Oechalae figuring as coastal watchers.

It will, however, be convenient to remind ourselves at this point of the uncertainties which beset the investigator in this field. The ambiguities of the script make suspect any isolated resemblances to later place and ethnic names. Credence will increase if we can operate with clusters which exhibit a coherent geographical pattern. The reasoning involved is similar to that in the notorious *Ahhiyawa* question, which turns on the alleged mention of Achaeans in the Hittite cuneiform texts. None of the equations adduced can be said to be above reproach: *Milawanda* = Miletus, *Ahhiyawa* = Achaea, *Alaksandus* = Alexandros and so on. Dr. Gurney has recently written; 'All these identifications are in themselves tentative and uncertain; but as remarked by the late Sir John Myres, when a considerable number of identifications of this kind can be made and the places in question form a connected group, the effect is cumulative and the likelihood of coincidence diminished. We therefore present these equations as plausible. . . .' It is true to say that 'there is now general agreement among scholars that the name Ahhiyawa represents in some way the Achaioi of Homeric epic.'

We ourselves are in a much more favourable situation. The places mentioned occur together in a single text and the geo-graphic coherence is guaranteed by the fact that they are grouped in a single sector of a coast defence document and that the document as a whole seems to proceed from north to south accord-ing to the order of the Nine places of the Further Province.

Seeing that the degree of credibility depends on the cumulative effect, to assist judgement in this question, which is of consider-able interest to historians of the Mycenaean age and to students of the Homeric epic, I list the Linear B place-names which have

The Land of the Pylians

plain echoes in the later records and traditions. *Pi-jai* = Pheai, *Me-ta-pa* = Metapa, *A-pyu* = Aipu, *Ri-jo* = Rhion, *E-re-e* (locative) = Helos, *Ku-pa-ri-so* = Cyparissia. If to these identifications we add the general picture of the extent of the Pylian territory, as culled from the tablets, and its virtual identity with the Homeric account, it would be hypercritical to resist the conclusion that the bardic tradition preserved a fair notion of the geography and quite a few of the actual place-names of Mycenaean Pylos. There remains the fact that the *Iliad* unequivocally situates Pylos itself not far south of the Alpheus. It has often been suggested that there may have been two towns of the same name within the territory of Nestor and that the memory of the northerly one has been preserved in the *Iliad*.

If we consult once again the archives of the palace of Nestor, we find that in fact there are two places called Pylos. One is the chief place of the Hither Province. The other Pylos is situated in the Further Province, the capital of which is *Re-u-ko-to-ro* = Leuktron. It is mentioned in cattle inventories; and the general arrangement and the fact that it is called 'Pylos-in- *Ra-wa-ra-ti-ja*' shows that it is situated in the district farthest but one in the Further Province (p. 89). We shall meet it again as one of the places where women and children were concentrated in the arrangements connected with the final emergency. This site, well within the Messenian Gulf, (see list p. 89 and fig. 13) is wholly wrong for the presumed Pylos near the Alpheus, but it is at least evidence for the existence of this famous place-name elsewhere than at Navarino even in Mycenaean Messenia.

We end with a brief consideration of another attempt to find the northern Pylos in our texts. In the cattle inventories a cattle station *Ma-to-ro-pu-ro* is mentioned. One scholar jumped to the conclusion that this represented *Matropylos*, and proclaimed that he had identified the 'Mother city of Pylos'. However, the text in question simply lists herdsmen and beasts absent from the territory of *E-ra-te-re-wa*(*i*), which is the fifth in the Seven places of the Further Province. Against the name *Ma-to-ro-pu-ro* we read the entry: RAM 1. This solitary beast is the sole evidence for the alleged metropolis of Pylos. Perhaps it would be as well to end the chapter on this salutary note of warning.

Chapter IV

The World of the Tablets

Before the decipherment of Linear B, which enabled us to read contemporary records of Bronze Age Greece, we were dependent for our knowledge of Mycenaean institutions and social life on the *Iliad* and *Odyssey*. These poems, written in the eighth and seventh centuries B.C. respectively, do not picture the contemporary world of the poets but describe a more or less remote past. But how remote? Ostensibly the background of the poems belongs to the Age of Heroes, to the world of Agamemnon and his associates, say the thirteenth century B.C. Palace bards must have begun to celebrate the exploits of the great Mycenaean kings and lords soon after the Sack of Troy, and an unbroken tradition of oral poetry linked Homer with those first unknown lays of the Heroic Age of Greece. Can we be sure that no distortion of the picture took place in those five or six centuries of bardic transmission which separated 'Homer' from the events he purports to describe? Certainly the spade of the archaeologist has verified the existence of the palaces where Homer's heroes lived, and Professor Martin Nilsson showed that the Mycenaean sites thus revealed correspond in importance to the main centres of Greek heroic legends and myths. However, in a recent, stimulating, and richly informative book Dr M. I. Finley has challenged the long held view that the picture which emerges from Homer can be attributed to the late Bronze Age of Mycenae. We must distinguish, he argues, the Heroic Age depicted in the Greek epic from the Mycenaean Age of the archaeological finds. Claiming a 'historian's licence', he would pin down the world of Odysseus to the tenth and ninth centuries B.C. As for Homer, 'On the whole he knew where the Mycenaean civilization flourished, and his heroes lived in great Bronze Age palaces unknown in Homer's day. And that is virtually all he knew about Mycenaean times. . . .'

The World of the Tablets

The study of the texts reveals that the truth lies between this revolutionary notion and the traditional picture based on Homer. Certainly there is much in this complex, bureaucratically controlled society that recalls the temple economies of the contemporary Orient. Yet curiously enough it was the abundant new information on land tenure, a subject to which Dr Finley has devoted much attention, that showed a social structure which in its main lines is reconcilable with that of Homer's Heroic Age and wholly different from the Orient.

1. THE SOCIAL STRUCTURE

That the society of the Heroic Age of Greece was feudal in form has often been asserted and as often denied. By feudal we mean, of course, that the bonds of society were 'baronial' in nature: in other words that land was held of an overlord in return for an obligation to render military service. The word *baron* in its original sense carries this implication. A baron, according to an attractive interpretation, is a 'man of the service', the underlying word being connected with the verb 'bear'. The 'burden' undertaken is that of 'service'. Homer provides a significant pointer to such obligations in the behaviour of Echepolus of Sicyon (west of Corinth on the Corinthian Gulf), who when called upon to join the expedition against Troy gave Agamemnon instead a fine mare named Aithe ('Blazing'), which Menelaus yoked to his chariot when competing in the funeral games of Patroclus. Sicyon was one of the cities ascribed to Agamemnon in the 'Catalogue', which lists the contributions, measured in terms of ships, made by the various Greek potentates to the expedition against Troy. Then there was the case of Euchenor of Corinth. His father was a seer and had foretold that his son would either die of disease if he stayed at home or be killed in battle if he went to Troy. So he joined the expedition, thus 'avoiding a grievous fine and loathesome disease'. His father's prophecy was fulfilled when he was struck by the spear of Paris 'beneath the jaws and the ears'. The mention of a technical word for a legal penalty (*thōē*) as an alternative to military service implies an obligation to an overlord, and Corinth like Sicyon is listed among the cities of Agamemnon.

97

The World of the Tablets

The key to the feudal mode of organization is land tenure. Agriculture was the basis of ancient society and the structure of power should be reflected in the arrangements governing the ownership and the use of land. Sir William Ridgeway long ago made a close study of the references to land tenure scattered in the Greek epic and constructed a picture of Homeric land tenure. For instance, the elaborate description of the Shield which Hephaestus, the craftsman god, was commissioned to make for Achilles in preparation for his final duel with Hector includes vignettes of Greek society. One panel of the shield described by the poet depicts the large cattle grazing in the water meadows, while the sheep are on the upland pastures. The description of the shield suggests that the arable land of the typical 'heroic' community was divided between the large open field of the commune, on which many plough teams operate simultaneously, and the personal holding of the 'king' (*basileus*), who stands and supervises the gathering of the harvest.

Again, when the Trojans and Greeks are locked in close struggle over the wall enclosing the Greek ships drawn up on the Trojan shore, the poet compares the scene with a quarrel between 'two men who in a common field on each side of the boundary stones with measuring rods in their hands dispute about their share in a small plot.' Boundary stones are mentioned in another passage of the *Iliad* when Odysseus and Diomede set a trap for the Trojan Dolon ('Trickster'), who passes them as they lie in wait. They let him get as far ahead 'as the boundary marks of mules are wont to be, which surpass oxen in drawing the plough over the deep fallow'. These 'marks' imply a division of the fallow, and the distance between them must have been conventionally established, otherwise it could not be referred to as a standard of measurement.

From such occasional hints Ridgeway and others pieced together a picture of 'heroic' land tenure. Much land and indeed whole cities were dedicated to the gods and priests were men of great wealth. One of them provided Odysseus with seven talents of gold and also with the wonderful wine which was the undoing of the Cyclops. The king and the war captains received personal allocations of land called 'cuts' (*temenos*), a word which survived later only with a religious connotation. Yet all these deductions

from the scanty and ambiguous Homeric evidence have been disputed, and it could be asserted that the Homeric picture may
merely be that of Greece after the collapse of the Mycenaean
world and the ensuing Age of Migrations.

By a great piece of good fortune we can now by-pass many of
these interpretational difficulties and disputed points. We now
have much more detailed information about the complex land
tenure system of the last years of the Mycenaean Age than,
for instance, about seventh-century Sparta. Perhaps the most
important documents for the historian which were contained in
the Archive Room at Pylos are those dealing with land holding.
Much work was needed on these particularly difficult texts before
they became reasonably clear. But the general picture which has
emerged enables us to sit in judgement on the various accounts of
'heroic' land tenure based on the study of Homer. The palm must
unquestionably be awarded to Sir William Ridgeway. His picture
approximates most closely to that which we shall now describe.

The chief categories of land-holders at Pylos are set forth in a
document which consists of two tablets. The first entry relates to
the *Wanax*, the King. He is credited with a *temenos*, literally a
'cut', measured as thirty units of seed corn. A *temenos* is registered
in the next line against the *Lawagetas*, literally the 'Leader of the
War-Host', for the word *lawos* 'folk' in Homer has the narrower
meaning 'the body of warriors'. The scribe now leaves a blank line
after these two *temenos* entries to show that they are *sui generis*.
The following entry relates to *telestai*, a word about which there
has been some dispute, but which, I shall argue, means 'service
men'. There are three of them and the seed corn entry is thirty
units, so that they each have as much land in this place as the
Lawagetas himself, whose allocation is ten units. Next we have an
entry for the *damos*, the 'commune' (see p. 103) and then an obscure
reference to 'deserted' or 'uninhabited' land which may have been
set aside for cult purposes.

The document is continued on the second tablet, which is in the
same hand. It refers to one who seems to have been a great noble,
Echelawon by name. Ventris and Chadwick identified him with
the King. However, once it became clear, thanks to the work of
Professor E. L. Bennett, that these two tablets formed a single

document, such identification was ruled out. The beginning of the tablet is slightly mutilated, but it seems reasonably clear that at the place in question Echelawon had two arable plots and two pieces of land planted with trees. The seed corn allocation is 94 measures. What is of importance is that his arable is referred to by the term *ki-ti-me-na* and not *temenos*.

This technical word recurs in the most complex document we possess relating to land holding. It concerns the holy place *Pa-ki-ja-nes*, which we have sited close to Pylos itself and where there was an important shrine of the goddess Potnia, 'The Lady, the Mistress'. Two versions survive of this register. The first consists mainly of a number of tablets of the elongated 'palm-leaf' type, each of which records the provisional 'proposals' for given individuals. In the later version these individual proposals are consolidated in a 'book' consisting of a series of tablets of the oblong 'page' type. It was naturally of importance to be able to establish the correct order of the 'pages' in the book. After careful examination of the tablets in Athens in the spring of 1959 it proved possible to deduce the original order, and this threw a flood of light on the nature and grouping of the entries in the register.

The document falls into two halves. The first is concerned with land called *ki-ti-me-na* and the second with holdings of *ke-ke-me-na* land. At first these two terms were regarded as synonymous, but it soon became clear that the first type of land was always held from a named individual of the *telestas* class whereas the *ke-ke-me-na* type is always held 'from the *damos*'. We have already seen that Echelawon's huge holding was also designated *ki-ti-me-na*. So far from being equivalent terms, the distinction between *ki-ti-me-na* and *ke-ke-me-na* represents a fundamental cleavage in Mycenaean society. As we shall see, the *telestai* are men in royal service and they presumably held their land of the King. The etymological analysis of *ki-ti-me-na* will occupy us below, but what delimits the meaning of the word is its opposition to *ke-ke-me-na* land, which being held of the *damos* I shall call 'common land'. The details of the register will be discussed later. What is of importance is that some entries suggest that the main estate of the King was at *Pa-ki-ja-nes*, where he is closely associated with the goddess Potnia. This has an interesting Homeric echo. It is characteristic of the casual nature of the Homeric evidence that we learn of such an arrangement only incidentally in the course of Nausicaa's conversation with Odysseus. The girl modestly explains that it will excite unfavourable comment if she accompanies him in person and she proceeds to describe the way to the town of the Scherians. 'You will find a lovely poplar grove of Athena near the road. In it a spring flows and about it is a meadow. There is the *temenos* of my father and his fruitful orchard.' In this way we learn that Alcinous, Wanax of Scheria and father of Nausicaa, had his *temenos* closely conjoined with the precincts of Athena. The link of the royal *temenos* with his religious functions appears clearly even in post-Homeric times. Herodotus records that when the constitution of Cyrene was reformed on the advice of Delphi, king Battus was allowed to keep his '*temenea* and his priesthoods'.

A *temenos* of the 'War-leader' also appears clearly in a number of Homeric passages. Thus Meleager ('He who cares for the chase') was offered a *temenos* to persuade him to take part in the fighting against the Curetes. The military aspect of the War-leader's *temenos* is explicitly stressed by Sarpedon, the Lycian, in addressing his comrade-in-arms Glaucus. 'Why do the Lycians honour us and why do we enjoy a large *temenos* beside the banks of the Xanthus river? . . . For that reason we must take our stand in the front ranks of the Lycians. . . .'

Now there is another smaller register in the Pylian archives and a number of its entries strongly suggest that it is concerned with the estate of the Lawagetas. Notable among the tenants is one who is described as 'the Charioteer of the Lawagetas' and a number of others are dubbed *lawagesioi*, that is 'belonging to the Lawagetas'. Two separate lines of enquiry indicate that the land recorded in this set of texts was at a place called *Ti-no*. On the back of one of the tablets the scribe has tallied the amount of seed corn. It is some 130 measures as against 170 or so measures recorded for the estate at *Pa-ki-ja-nes*. On the front of the tablet showing the tallying there is a puzzling entry which indicates that one of the most prominent tenants had a holding in respect of 'a horse'. The holding is large, and at first it was supposed that the man in question held this land by way of upkeep for a war-horse. But this was not very convincing. New light was thrown on this problem when a text came to hand which recorded the issue of quantities of cyperus to *I-qo* ('Horse'). Cyperus is an aromatic plant used in the making of perfumes and in offerings to divinities. It could no longer be supposed that this was any ordinary horse. The recipient *I-qo* was evidently the name of a god. Below we shall discuss the evidence bearing on the god Hippos. At all events such a god is congenial company for a Mycenaean War-leader, on whose land we find the Charioteer of the War-leader. It may well be that the noble horse depicted on the seal from the Little Palace at Knossos (p. 195) represents this god of the Mycenaean warriors and is more than a mere indication of cargo as Evans suggested. Here then are the facts relating to the Wanax and the Lawagetas which our study has elicited from the Pylian texts:

Wanax:　　*temenos:* estate at *Pa-ki-ja-nes: wa-na-ka-te-ro* holders: 170 units: goddess Potnia.

Lawagetas:　*temenos:* estate at *Ti-no: ra-wa-ke-si-jo* holders: 130 units: god Hippos.

We now return to the great land register of *Pa-ki-ja-nes* with its division into two parts contrasting *ki-ti-me-na* land with *ke-ke-me-na. ki-ti-me-na* land, as we have said, is leased from *telestai.* This word means literally 'men of the *telos*', and *telos* is a noun connected with the root meaning 'lift'. Its basic meaning is 'what is lifted, burden', but it has the derived meanings 'charge, due, obligation' and the like. Suggestions have been made that these men were 'initiation priests', but this will not bear examination. In the first place the *telestai* include a fuller, a potter, and a shepherd. Moreover, when the pages of the register were put in their proper order, it could be seen that the document grouped the holders according to function. The *telestai* were not grouped with the cult functionaries. This was confirmed by yet another observation. Another set of tablets summarizes the entries of the register and gives the total amount of seed corn involved. The groupings here are the same as those of the register. Again the *telestai* do not appear along with the cult personnel.

No less cogent was an observation made apropos of the other

sort of land. After listing the *ki-ti-me-na* land of the *telestai*, 'service men', the register goes on to record in its second part the *ke-ke-me-na* land held from the *damos*. The first entries of this second part relate to personalities some of whom we know as *telestai*. What is important is that now they are no longer given this description but receive a new appellation — '*ktoina* holders' (*ktoina* is a word which survived later in the dialect of Rhodes and signified a division of land with predominantly religious connexions). From this it was clear that the *telestai* were designated as such only in respect of their holdings of *ki-ti-me-na* land. In other words *telestas* is a tenure-bound status word. A *telestas* owed *telos* to the Wanax (the king) presumably in return for his holding of *ki-ti-me-na* land.

We have said that this class of *telestai* includes men designated shepherd, fuller and potter. However, the size of their holdings suggests that these terms are not to be taken in their literal sense any more than words like 'Steward', 'Constable', etc. in our own medieval terminology. The 'shepherd' will have been the Master of the Royal herds, the 'potter' the Master of the Royal Potteries and the 'fuller' perhaps the Master of the Cloth.

That the Mycenaean polity was no absolute despotism of the Oriental type is clear from the character of the *damos* or 'commune'. The *damos*, from which so much of the land here recorded was held, wâs no subservient and downtrodden body. This emerges clearly from a pair of texts recording a case of disputed tenure. The earlier version runs 'The priestess declares that the god has an *e-to-ni-jo* (this being the term for a large religious holding), but the *ktoina*-holder says that she has leases of *ke-ke-me-na* plots.' We have said that the term '*ktoina*-holder' designates a person of *telestas* status in respect of his holding of *damos* land. What is significant is that in the later consolidated document the protest by the *ktoina*-holder is taken up by the *damos*. The version now reads '. . . but the *damos* says that she has leases of *ke-ke-me-na* plots.' Here the *damos* acts as a collective, as it also does when making certain deliveries for religious purposes. A protest in the name of the *damos* implies an organ to deliberate and speak on its behalf, as indeed the leases 'from the damos' also do. What is of interest is that the protest is duly recorded in the palace register.

In this entry, then, we see enshrined an acknowledgement of the vested rights of the commune. This is not the *damos* of the *Iliad*, where Odysseus beats a man of the *damos* for venturing to raise his voice in the assembly. But doubtless in the field the commoner would be well advised not to run foul of the princely warriors. There are some indications that the bulk of the land was held by the *damos* and that their holdings are only reflected in the palace archives in so far as palace folk had some concern in them.

It remains to review briefly the other classes of tenants on the *damos* land. After the '*ktoina*-holders' we find entries relating to a type of holding designated *ka-ma*. With such land we find constantly references to three kinds of obligation. The words have been difficult to identify but I have argued that the three obligations are to occupy, to render services, or to pay. After the *ka-ma* holding the register goes on to record the most numerous holdings: these are by persons designated 'slave of the god', both men and women. Then follow the entries relating to the slaves of the prominent cult personages and finally the priestess, the priest and other officiants. We summarize the main classes of holders and the type of land which they hold and lease to others.

Wanax:	*temenos*
Lawagetas:	*temenos*
Echelawon:	*ko-to-na ki-ti-me-na*
telestai:	*ko-to-na ki-ti-me-na*
damos:	*ko-to-na ke̦-ke-me-na*

The distinction between the two technical terms for the two sorts of land is clear in that they refer to *telestas* and *damos* land respectively. There is no difficulty about the etymological identification of *ki-ti-me-na*: it is the participle *ktimena* from a verb whose range of meaning centres about 'win from the waste, set in order, settle'. A rough English equivalent would be 'assart land'. *ke-ke-me-na* has proved more difficult, although it clearly means 'common land'. I have brought the verb into connexion with the Greek word *koinos* 'common' and analysed the Mycenaean word as the participle of a verb *kei* with the original meaning 'split, share'. Thus *ke-ke-me-na* means literally 'share-land'. It is of interest that we find terms for the common land having precisely this significance in other languages. In Old English we have *gedalland* and in Welsh *rhandir*. Hittite has a closely resemblant term in *takšannaš*, literally 'joint land', this also being apparently the word for the 'village land' as opposed to land held from the palace.

These purely philological analyses harmonize with the results reached by students of early land tenure systems in Western Europe. Geographers had independently commented on the importance of the institution of the 'share-land' in early European society. It lies beyond the scope of this book to consider whether this resemblance is due to independent evolution in the societies concerned or whether there is a historical connexion between them. But in view of statements to the contrary it must be insisted that the picture of Mycenaean society sketched above has emerged entirely from analysis of the texts. It was not based on an 'Indo-European hypothesis', and imposed from without on the texts.

Apart from craftsmen and slaves, whom we shall consider below, the tablets contain only incidental references to the great nobles, a class whose existence we should have to suppose even in the absence of direct reference. It will be convenient to discuss them when considering the military arrangements connected with the final crisis of Pylos. We may, however, note the fact that they are often given the resounding combination of name and father's name typical of the Homeric epic. 'Alectryon, son of Eteocles' is a splendid figure to conjure from the baked clay of the Pylian archives. That these nobles do not figure in the land-registers is easily understood. They doubtless possessed their own estates, and the palace had no occasion to refer to them. We recall again that the 'Nine' and the 'Seven' places of the two provinces are palace-tributary. Though scattered over the whole kingdom, they do not necessarily encompass all the available territory. They may have been in the nature of 'royal vills', although extensive enough to include numerous cattle stations (see below).

2. ADMINISTRATION

How did the king of Pylos retain control of the affairs of his extensive territory? The picture which has gradually emerged from a close analysis of the archives is one of a meticulous and efficient bureaucracy. Each of the sixteen tributary localities was in the charge of an official named the *ko-re-tēr*. This is one of the many words for Mycenaean technicalities which did not survive into post-Mycenaean times. Let us call him the 'district officer'. I prefer this to 'mayor' because one Knossos text draws a distinction between the district *O-du-ru-wi-jo* in the charge of the *ko-re-tēr* and the town *O-du-ru-we* with officials called *u-wo-qe-we*. This last word I have explained as meaning 'overseers'. A junior official is also recorded for each of the sixteen tributary localities. This is the *pro-ko-re-tēr*, a compound noun constructed like *pro-consul*. This man I shall call the 'assistant district officer'.

The lay-out of one Pylos text connects each of the two provinces with the name of a prominent personality, who may well be the provincial governor. For the Hither Province it is *Da-mo-ko-ro*, who in some texts is referred to as **85-ke-wa*, while in another he bears his full style **85-ke-wa Da-mo-ko-ro*. There has been some difference of opinion about the interpretation of the second word of his full style, but I regarded *Da-mo-ko-ro* as the rendering, in perfect accordance with the accepted spelling conventions (this is not in dispute), of the name *Damoklos*. New evidence, however, supports the view that *da-mo-ko-ro* is the title of an official. It is significant that his title alone serves to identify him: he is *the Da-mo-ko-ro*.

There are a number of references to another official called the *du-ma*. Again we are dependent on the lay-out of the same Pylian text for the possibility (it is no more than a hint) that the *du-ma* was the second-in-command of the Province. Deliveries of bronze and gold recorded against these various worthies give some indication of their relative standing. Noteworthy is that both *Te-po-se-u* and the *Da-mo-ko-ro*, our supposed 'provincial governors', stand to most *ko-re-teres* on the 'gold standard' in the ratio 12:6 or 12:5. As for the *ko-re-ter* and the *pro-ko-re-ter*, their relative gold rating is 6 (or 5):3 whereas on the bronze standard their relative importance is of the order 8:3 or, in four places, 11:3.

There remains the question of the *pa₂-si-re-u*. In the early stages of the decipherment this was hastily identified with the later term *basileus*, and since then 'kings' and 'palaces' have figured largely in works on Linear B. One pa_2-si-re-u however occurs in the gold list: his contribution is on the lowest scale, that is equivalent to that of the po-ro-ko-re-$tēr$, our 'assistant district officer'. The functions of the pa_2-si-re-u will be more conveniently discussed below apropos of the Mycenaean economy but we anticipate to the extent of saying that such persons appear only in connexion with the working of metal.

Many of the sets of tablets record, as we have said, assessments and deliveries of various materials and commodities from the provincial districts to the palace. One tablet gives the break-down of the total for one place into the individual assessments. Here we see that the bronze-smith is assessed at one unit, the (two?) shepherds at two units, the cowherds at two units, a master bronze-smith (known from another tablet to be in charge of thirty-one smiths) at four units, whereas no fewer than twenty-four units are entered against the ko-re-ter.

Details of these stocks, incomings and outgoings were communicated to the palace, and the records give us the names of some of the chief palace administrators. Most prominent is A-ko-so-ta, which may stand for the name $Alxoitas$. One tablet records the grain he 'saw' on a tour of inspection of localities lying to the south of Pylos in the Hither Province. Another states that he had 'received' amounts of an unidentified nature; yet another that he had 'given' materials to an unguent-boiler (see below); ivory is another material associated with his name. But it is above all in the great cattle inventories that he is prominent (see below).

The administrative chain of command may be represented thus:

The Palace Bureau (*Alxoitas*)

The Hither Province	The Further Province
85-ke-wa Da-mo-ko-ro	*Te-po-se-u*
Du-ni-jo du-ma	*? ? du-ma*
Nine Districts each	Seven Districts each
with a *ko-re-ter* and	with a *ko-re-ter* and a
a *po-ro-ko-re-ter*	*po-ro-ko-re-ter*

The tentative nature of this construction should be stressed. It is built up from a number of scattered indications. The general outline is given in a single tablet where many of the entries are fragmentary; yet the general lay-out shows *Da-mo-ko-ro* and *Te-po-se-u* 'in parallel' in their respective paragraphs, each of which is devoted to entries relating to one of the two provinces. *Te-po-se-u* also occurs in the gold tablet, where the amount entered against him is on the highest level. In the same gold tablet *85-ke-wa* appears in the next entry but one, with an identical amount of the metal. He also figures in a list of notables and there his name is adjacent to *Du-ni-jo* the *du-ma*. Finally *85-ke-wa Da-mo-ko-ro* appears with his full style in the inventory of furniture which will be discussed below. There the diagnosis of the two components of his name will assume unexpected importance.

3. THE MYCENAEAN ECONOMY

The chief staple agricultural products of the Mediterranean world, wheat, olive oil and wine naturally figure prominently in our texts. As for animal husbandry, we have preserved to us a good part of what appears to have been a cattle census covering the whole Pylian kingdom. What was not realized at first is that the surviving tablets can be grouped into sets, each one of which begins with a heading containing the name of one of the sixteen tributary places; the heading appears to mean simply 'herds of *X*'. The order of entry is significant. The top tablet of each set lists sheep and goats without indication of 'ownership'. The owner who requires no explicit mention is doubtless the King. The succeeding tablets list smaller numbers of beasts against the names (in the genitive case) of a limited number of well-known personalities, one of them being our 'Lord High Steward', Alxoitas. Others have plain connexions with cult. In these inventories there are tens of thousands of sheep and goats, comparatively few pigs and no larger cattle. In fact bulls, oxen, and cows appear only in contexts which suggest offerings. At Knossos the larger cattle appear to be so rare that they are listed by their names, such as *Aiwolos* 'Dapple', *Kelainos* 'Dusky', *Stomargos* 'Chatterbox', *Xouthos* 'Ginger' and so on.

These Knossos tablets belonged to the Great Deposit of Tablets discovered in the northern entrance passage (see pp. 227 ff.). Others of this hoard appear to give a census of the cattle place by place. We choose by way of interest the register for the place *Wa-to*. The figures read RAMS 60, EWES, 270, HE-GOATS 49, SHE-GOATS 130, BOARS 17, SOWS 41, BULLS 2, COWS 4. Another place has 952 sheep, 365 goats, 81 pigs, but only 2 bulls and 10 cows.

Other cattle inventories reveal that the Greek King of Knossos possessed vast herds scattered all over the island. As in Pylos most of these beasts have no indication of 'owner', and here, too, we should surely conclude that where there is no specific record of owner, these cattle are royal possessions. Again, as in Pylos, animals are recorded along with a limited number of names in the genitive case. These will be the palace notabilities of Knossos corresponding to their Pylian counterparts. This is one of the many close resemblances between the administrations of Pylos and Knossos.

Some herds of Knossos are recorded as 'belonging to Potnia', one of the chief divinities. We have a similar indication for Pylos. This leads to a consideration of the religious aspects of the organization of economic life in Mycenaean Greece. We have already alluded to the affairs of the great estate at *Pa-ki-ja-nes*, the seat of the goddess Potnia ('The Mistress'), and the fact that most of the holders are cult personnel. We may now turn to the documents connected with the working of bronze.

These form one of the larger sets at Pylos, and each text lists the bronze allocations to smiths at the chief tributary places, some of which appear in pairs, a fact which reflects adjacency. What is of the greatest interest is that in a number of these records, after the names of the individual smiths and their allocations have been registered, there follows just before the total, and sometimes divided by a blank line, the name of a *pa₂-si-re-u* with no bronze entry against him. Still more significant is that certain of these texts have a second paragraph headed 'bronze-smiths belonging to Potnia', followed by similar details of allocation. All the evidence indicates that the *pa₂-si-re-u* is an official responsible for the *secular* bronze-smiths in a particular place. There are no contexts for this title and the derived *pa₂-si-re-wi-ja* other than craftsmen, and metallurgy in particular. Nothing justifies the rendering 'King' (*basileus*).

The role of the temple in the organization of this side of My-

cenaean industry is vividly illuminated by a text which records
amounts of bronze against all the sixteen tributary localities. This
document with its orderliness gives us what may be called the
'canonical' order of the Nine and the Seven places of the Hither
and Further Provinces respectively. A long introductory sentence
explains the purpose of the record. It reads: 'How the *ko-re-tē-res*
and the *du-ma-tes*, and the *pro-ko-re-tē-res* and the 'Key-bearers',
and the *opi-su-koi* and the *opi-ka-pewes* are to give temple bronze
(as) points for spears and arrows'. In the early stages of the decipherment there was some doubt whether the word *na-wi-jo*
meant 'ship's bronze' or 'temple bronze'. However, it is now clear
that the 'keybearer' occurs in that part of the land register of
Pa-ki-ja-nes which concerns the cult personnel (see p. 102), so that
there can be now little doubt that 'temple' bronze is the correct
choice.

We turn now to a text (fig. 19) of the greatest interest, which we
shall have to consider repeatedly at various stages of our argument. This lists amounts of barley against various classes of craftsmen. At this point all we need to note is that it begins with several
entries of the type: man's name in the genitive followed by the
word pa_2-*si-re-wi-ja*. At an early stage scholars jumped to the conclusion that this meant 'the palace of X', and this notion continues
to figure in many works of vulgarization. However, further information and closer analysis have shown that many of the personalities concerned reappear in texts from the palace workshop.
Still more interesting is that a text recording the personnel
allocations to these men has paragraph headings containing the
word Potnia. Below under Religion we shall have to consider the
identity of the *Potnia Iqeia*, who is one of the divinities concerned.
In yet another context we shall have to assess the significance of
the fact that the place *Po-ti-ja-ke-i*, one of the 'rower' stations, is
concerned with the supply of personnel. Further, apropos of the
amounts of barley recorded, we shall argue that the text under
discussion may well be a daily wage-sheet. What clearly emerges is
that pa_2-*si-re-wi-ja* is caught up in a craftsman context and that
the persons so designated have a supervisory-managerial function.
The amounts of barley recorded are so trivial that the suggestion
that these are deliveries to 'palaces' will not bear examination.

Other texts which link up with it again show the 'Potnia' aspects of the economic organization at Pylos.

Connected with the *pa₂-si-re-wi-ja* text is another which has assumed an unwarranted importance in the current picture of Mycenaean society in that it is thought to contain evidence for the institution of the Gerousia ('Council of Elders') in Mycenaean Pylos. The tablet records groups of men who are assigned to units designated the *ke-ro-si-ja* of *X*, where *X* is a man's name in the genitive case. In early work on the text the word was crudely identified simply by applying the spelling rules to the Greek lexicon — the long discredited 'etymological method'. This produced the word *gerousia*. This could not fail to interest historians of Greece, and the interpretation is accepted and repeated in virtually all surveys of the evidence of the tablets known to me.

Again detailed analysis has shown that this idea is chimerical. Three of the four men credited with a *ke-ro-si-ja* recur in the 'bronze' tablets. Their dossiers showed that the first two are both from the place *E-ni-pa-te-we*, which is linked with *A-ke-re-wa*, the sixth place of the 'Nine' of the Hither Province. Moreover the second of the two men is listed among the 'Potnia' smiths: he is connected with the temple side of the organization. The last entry on the tablet under discussion ascribes a *ke-ro-si-ja* to *A-pi-qo-ta*. This man's dossier records him as a *pa₂-si-re-u* in charge of secular smiths at *A-pe-ke-e*. Thus there is no doubt that all these quite separate lines of enquiry lead to the same theme of 'bronze working'. The *ke-ro-si-ja*, on this evidence, cannot be a 'council of elders'. The word evidently has reference to a craftsman unit under the charge of a master bronze-smith. The significance of the geographical locations of these craftsmen will appear below in our discussion of the arrangements to meet the final emergency of Pylos.

The connexion of the goddess Potnia with bronze-smiths leads naturally to consideration of the part played by slavery in Mycenaean kingdoms. It will be convenient to delay for a moment analysis of the inventories of women and children, who can hardly be anything but slaves, although doubts have been voiced. Instead I begin with a curious text which was much misunderstood in the early stages. It concerns the place *Me-ta-pa*, which is the second most northerly place of the Hither Province (list, p. 89). It lists

111

women, and there is a heading which explains the purpose of the list. Here, too, the words are strange to post-Mycenaean Greek, and rash etymological attempts to make up Greek words led to translations such as 'barley-reapers'. However, analysis shows that one of the key terms, *ke-ri-mi-ja*, occurs in connexion with cloth manufacture, and that the other, *ki-ri-te-wi-ja*, appears in that part of the land-register concerned with cult personnel immediately after the priestess. The entry is in the plural, so that the *ki-ri-te-wi-ja*, whose land holding is collectively recorded, will have been a corporation of women connected with cult. The heading will thus have the summary meaning: 'Clothworkers of Metapa: *ki-ri-te-wi-ja* of *Do-qe-ja*'. There can be little doubt that *Do-qe-ja* is the name of the divinity to which these women are attached. The detailed entries throw a colourful light on the family life of these women, since the details concern their parentage. Their attachment to the Goddess is apparently determined by the relation of one of the parents to the goddess. Thus the entries read:

'The father is a slave of *Do-qe-ja*, but the mother is from *Ku-te-re-wes*' (the latter is likely to be a place near *Metapa* and not the island of Kythera, as others have supposed. Strabo records a river *Kythērios* in the Pisatis, and this lies near our location of *Metapa*).

'The father is a slave of *Do-qe-ja*, but the mother is a slave of *Diwia*' (here there is a conflict of divine interests, decided in favour of the father's part in the matter).'

The last two entries again reveal the activity of the bronze-smiths in temple life. They both read: 'The mother is a slave of *Do-qe-ja*, but the father is a bronze-smith'. Here the relation of the daughters to the Goddess is determined by the status of the mother. What is of interest is the reference to the father so anonymously as a 'a bronze-smith'. Their presence in the temple organization is consistent with the references to 'Potnia' bronze-smiths. It would doubtless be possible to read the simplicities of a comfortable monogamy into these facts, but the conclusion does not impose itself. The obvious analogies are to be found in the temple estates of the Near East.

It has always been a puzzle to know what so unproductive a country as Greece had to offer in exchange for the luxury goods for which the remains from the Mycenaean Age offer such striking

evidence. Gold and ivory, to mention only the most obvious, must
have been procured from abroad. Viking raids will hardly account
for more than sporadic hauls. Archaeology has had one important
pointer. This is the ubiquity of the stirrup-jar, which vastly out-
numbers all other types of Mycenaean vessels in the eastern
Aegean and in Egypt. The conclusion has been rightly drawn that
these pots were not imported for their own sakes but for their
contents. Their structure suggests that they contained olive oil,
and its particular function is pointed by their frequent occurrence
in tombs. The most attractive suggestion has been that this
stirrup-jar was the forerunner of the later *lekythos*. This was a
container for oil, and especially perfumed oil or unguents, frequently burnt or buried with the dead.

We can now add considerable precision to this suggestion. In
the first place we know that the Mycenaean name for the stirrup-
jar was *ka-ra-re-u*, and thanks to the survival of a Cretan word for
an oil vessel *khlaros* it is tempting, with Professor Householder, to
interpret the Linear B word as *khlareus*, for such pot names are
often distinguished by the ending *-eus*: *amphiphoreus* 'amphora' is a
case in point. What is more, the Mycenaean word occurs in a text
recording the issue of oil to an unguent-boiler. It has been discussed above (p. 77). This brought the stirrup-jar into an unguent context.

Now another text from the 1939 finds also contained as we saw
(p. 77), a reference to an 'unguent-boiler'. The introductory
sentence reads: 'How Alxoitas gave to Thyestes the unguent-
boiler spices for boiling in the unguent'. The detailed entries
referred to amounts of coriander, ginger-grass, and, mysteriously
enough, wine and honey. These strange ingredients, as we saw,
cast doubt on the interpretation. But it so happens that Theo-
phrastus in describing the manufacture of unguents mentions that
perfumers use wine and honey, however strange this may seem to
us. Many of the Pylian texts deal with materials required for
perfumes and unguents. The full extent of this palace interest in
unguent making is still *sub judice*, but repeated tests made by the
present writer on one of the most comprehensive returns in the
whole Pylian inventory have shown that all the substances listed
have predominantly 'spice' contexts.

The World of the Tablets

New evidence was forthcoming from Mycenae, where the excavations of Professor Wace from 1952 onwards yielded tablets from houses outside the walls which were concerned with the issue of 'spices' to a number of persons. The substances are coriander (this is easily the most plentiful) red and white safflower, pennyroyal, ginger-grass, cumin, fennel, mint, sesame, and celery. Many stirrup-jars were also found. Professor Marinatos and I have independently studied the facts from different angles. We both came to the conclusion that Professor Wace was mistaken in believing this house to be the house of an 'oil merchant'. It seems most probable that this house just outside the walls was an annexe of the Palace concerned with the making of unguents. That it was the unguent kitchen is consistent with the fact that Wace discovered an arrangement for heating jars in one corner. From ancient descriptions we know that the aromatic substances were gently heated in the oil. The oil vessel had no direct contact with the fire, for this could have led to burning and spoiling of the perfume. Instead the vessel was stood in a kind of *bain marie*.

The realization that this house is not a 'private' house but a palace annexe has important consequences for our ideas of the literacy of the Mycenaean world. Believing that this was the residence of a private merchant, Wace further concluded that there was widespread literacy. This induced in him the further belief that so intelligent a people as the Greeks would never have lost the boon of writing once they had possessed it. Consequently he could not bring himself to believe that there had been a dark age of illiteracy between the Mycenaean Age and the introduction of the Phoenician alphabet. However, the only evidence we possess connects the use of the Linear B script solely with the palace administrations.

At all events we now have written evidence connecting the stirrup-jars with the manufacture of perfumes and unguents. Such contents are perfectly in accord with the tomb contexts which are so prominent. The large numbers found in the area of Mycenaean influence together with the evident interest of the palaces in the collection of the necessary ingredients and their processing shows that the Mycenaean world possessed an economic resource of unsuspected importance.

Modern readers may be inclined to underestimate the importance of such trade. A few quotations from the work of Professor R. J. Forbes, who has specialized in the technology of the ancient world, are illuminating. In his discussion of 'cosmetic arts' this authority stresses the Egyptian acceptance 'as an obvious fact that ointments and aromatic oils were necessary for all classes.' After alluding to their distribution by priests, a fact which has echoes also in the Pylos tablets, Professor Forbes discusses rations of ointment in the Egyptian army and also records that labourers in the Theban necropolis even went on strike because the food was bad and 'we have no ointment'. In Mesopotamia, too, the same relationship is observable between religion, magic and medicine on the one side, and unguents on the other.

Finally we may mention the discovery that most of the inscribed stirrup-jars found at the chief Mycenaean sites on the Greek mainland bear place-names known only from the Knossos tablets. This must surely mean that they were imported from Crete. The question arises what was the interest of the mainland in importing such products from Crete when they were busy manufacturing them from their own staple products. As we have seen, there was no lack of oil in the Peloponnese and the records reflect the collection of the aromatic substances for blending with the basic vehicle. The answer may suggest itself when we come to study the unguent texts with a religious background. That Crete was an important centre of religion in early times was already clear from the Homeric Hymn to Apollo, which pictures the foundation of Delphi by priests from Crete. The finding of one such inscribed vessel bearing a Cretan place-name at Eleusis may have greater significance than we had supposed. The designation *WA* written on it, if we are right in supposing that this is an abbreviation for the word *wanakteron* found on a similar Theban jar, will also appear in a new light when the religious meaning of *Wanax* has been elucidated.

4. SHEEP, WOOL, AND TEXTILES

One of the puzzling features of Wace's 'House of the Oil Merchant' at Mycenae was that the Linear B texts found in it dealt largely with wool and personnel engaged in its processing, such as fullers. The neighbouring perfume texts may also have been connected, for it is known that perfumes were used to impart a pleasant odour to clothes. Wool is, of course, unlikely to appear in the archaeological record of burnt buildings. However, a recent study by John Killen of the Knossos tablets referring to sheep has thrown new light on the importance of wool growing in Mycenaean Crete.

Evans himself had noted that this great hoard of tablets (see above p. 109) recorded flocks which mostly numbered one hundred. He called them the 'percentage tablets'. But most of the animals listed were males. Evidently the tablets could not reflect a census of natural breeding flocks for we should expect a preponderance of ewes. Mr Killen, drawing on the analogy of medieval practices in this country, provided an illuminating answer to the problem. Wool flocks may consist predominantly of castrated males (wethers), and control of the shepherds is facilitated by giving them a fixed round number of sheep for which they have to account. The tablets enable us to see how the authorities at Knossos secured administrative control of flocks over a great part of Crete. I propose to study these texts in a contextual framework reconstructed from ancient references to sheep and wool growing.

In Roman republican times sheep farming on a large scale was a source of great wealth, and the arrangements made have continued down to our own day. What governed the life of the shepherds and their flocks was the climate: in summer the sheep were grazed on the highland pastures but they moved to the more protected lowlands for the winter. This is the system known as transhumance. To facilitate these seasonal migrations the state maintained tracks (*calles*) linking the winter and summer grazing grounds. These were under the supervision of state officials, and in 59 B.C. it was proposed to thwart Caesar's ambitions by allotting him as his 'province' the care of the *silvae callesque* 'woodland pastures and cattle tracks', for which, of course, he would require no army.

This whole system began, as the historian Pelham pointed out, when the wealthier Roman citizens, enriched by war, created large estates by absorbing small-holdings. They also tended to monopolize the large stretches of 'rough ground' suitable for summer pasture. In this way a large-scale sheep breeding industry was created requiring much capital and elaborate organization. References to it occur in Varro's treatise, in dialogue form, on agriculture. He refers to the great distances between the winter and summer pastures. He also discusses the ideal number of sheep that a single shepherd can take care of. One speaker allots a round hundred to each shepherd, and this is said to be the practice in Epirus, but another contributor to the discussion thinks eighty is a high enough number.

In the Knossos tablets, too, we can now see that one hundred is the normal number, although there are numerous exceptions, some flocks being as high as 400. The census recorded in the tablets appears to have taken place in the spring before the flocks moved off to their summer grazing grounds. The animals are listed according to sex and age. Wethers predominate, as we have seen. As for the age classes, Killen has shown that there are references to sub-classes 'this year's', 'last year's', 'young', 'old' and 'missing'. Of particular interest are the classes of lambs: these are listed with their mothers and divided into two classes 'this year's' and 'last year's'. This description throws indirect light on the Mycenaean calendar. There are in fact two crops of lambs, and Columella, a Roman writer on agriculture, informs us that the first mating took place in the third week of April and the second about July. In cuneiform sources, too, we get references to the two crops of lambs, but there they are referred to as 'summer' and 'winter' lambs. The Knossian lambs still registered with their mothers and designated 'last year's' were presumably not a year old but still immature: they were in fact the earlier crop of lambs. From the designation it would follow that the beginning of the Mycenaean calendar year fell between the two crops of lambs.

From the texts it is also possible to work out the yield of wool per sheep. In the mixed flocks it required four animals to produce one unit of wool. Now an archaeological fact comes to our assistance in giving a precise absolute value of weight. We can now see that much of the textile administration at Knossos was concentrated above the west magazines of the palace, particularly above Magazine XV. Evans found in this magazine a stone weight in the form of an octopus, and here again the find place, suggesting a connexion with the textile administration, finds an echo in cuneiform documents. There we hear that the weight used in measuring wool was a special heavy wool stone. Evans gave the weight of his octopus weight as 29 kilograms, and he compared this to half the Babylonian 'heavy talent'. On this basis scholars had already calculated the weight of the Mycenaean talent (see next section), and we may anticipate the results here. Each animal of the mixed flocks yielded ·75 kg i.e. 1·6 lb of wool. Now it is known that a wether fleece weighs considerably more than a ewe fleece. Another set of data offered a possible way of calculating the respective yields from the two sexes. The tablets in question were those dealing with ewes and lambs, and it was noticed that the ratio of animals to wool was 10 : 1 as opposed to 4 : 1 for the mixed flocks. What was overlooked was that the immature lambs were unlikely to have contributed anything to the wool crop. Once they were ignored it could be seen that the ratio ewes : wool was regularly 5 : 1. In other words the yield per ewe was ·6 kg. Now the mixed flocks vary greatly in their composition, with different proportions of wethers, ewes, 'last year's' and 'old' sheep. Obviously, in view of the difference of fleece weights, only very rough administrative justice could be done to the responsible shepherd, whose burden would increase as the number of wethers diminished. If we assume that the yield from the mixed flocks is the mean between a wether fleece and a ewe fleece, since this average fleece weighed ·75 kg and the ewe fleece weighed ·6, it would follow that the wether fleece weighed ·9 kg. Thus the ratio ewe fleece : wether fleece was 2 : 3. The English figures indicate a proportion 3 : 4 or 5 : 8–10. The yields are astonishingly close to those of medieval sheep keepers.

We next consider the processing. Both men and women were engaged in the manufacture of cloth. One interesting fact is that the men appear to have worked in pairs. One tablet lists single pieces of cloth against pairs of men's names, and a sealing drawn in Evans's notebook but unpublished suggests that two such men delivered a piece of cloth to the palace with the sealing attached. On the piece of clay were inscribed the two names and also the word *pa-wo=pharwos* 'woollen cloth'. This links up with an illustration from an Egyptian tomb which shows two men sitting side by side at a vertical loom. This is stated to be a new type of loom which appears in the paintings of the New Kingdom from *c.* 1580. 'On this loom, for the first time, the weavers are almost all men!'

Women appear in the texts of the west magazines particularly in connexion with the apprentice system. The women and children listed appear to be 'in school'. Two main classes of children are distinguished, 'bigger' and 'smaller', and appropriately the latter are not yet in the textile 'school'. There are other class indications and here we note a curious fact: the abbreviated indications appear to be the same as those for the age classes in the sheep tablets. Quite obviously such indications as 'last year' cannot refer to the real age of the women. But here again cuneiform sources offer a clue. Female slaves and their children formed the personnel of the wool factories, and one list distinguishes between those previously present and newly acquired slaves. If we apply this hint to the classes distinguished in the Knossos tablets, it looks as though these women were looked upon in much the same way as the flocks of sheep which provided the raw material, and the state of the 'flock' of women year by year was surveyed on much the same administrative lines. Just as the sheep are assigned to 'owners', so we find women too listed as the property of the palace notabilities.

It is in the same west magazines that we find ration texts, and it is reasonable to suppose that they refer to the same personnel. As we shall see below it is possible to arrive at some kind of estimate of the number of women maintained by the palace authorities in different Cretan places including Phaestos.

The wool was made up into cloths of different types carrying obscure technical names but evidently of different weight. When finished they were made up into sets of five units and stored in what looks like a bag, possibly of leather, screwed together at the top. The set of tablets recording them was also found in Magazine XV.

All the information we have drawn on so far has come from Knossos. At Pylos we also have texts relating to flocks of sheep and herds of goats. But so far little or nothing has been preserved relating to the manufacture of cloth. However, that this is due to the accident of survival is indicated by some of the entries in the tablets relating to the 'evacuated' women and children. While most of the groups carry descriptions of location (i.e. of the village from which they come), there is a coherent set of terms which link up with textiles. The evidence from Knossos and Pylos may be harmonized if we suppose that skilled slaves were maintained in establishments in dependent townships. Some of the women are described as 'belonging to Potnia', and this recalls the similar bronze workers. Here again we have an indication of the importance of the temple economy in Bronze Age Greece.

Finally, we may consider the economic importance of wool and textiles in the Mycenaean world. When I suggested that the House of the Oil Merchant at Mycenae ought to be rechristened in view of the fact that the tablets deal so largely with wool, it was pointed out that little trace of wool would be left in a burnt house. Now Killen's important study has revealed to us the economic significance of the Knossian sheep flocks. We may add this to the evidence already discussed for the importance of perfumed oil carried in Mycenaean stirrup-jars. It may well be that the economic puzzle posed by the Mycenaean balance of payments is due to an inevitable gap in the archaeological record. Perhaps the Mycenaean world was in this respect much like medieval England. R. W. Southern has written (*The Making of the Middle Ages*): 'But just as it was that England's coal made this country an industrial area in the nineteenth century, so it was the large-scale production of wool and manufacture of cloth which made western Europe an important export area in the Middle Ages. ... the cloth industry was the basic industry of the Middle Ages.'

5. Rations, Weights and Measures

Long before the decipherment it was clear that the quantitative entries on the right hand side of the tablets were based on a system of weights and measures. We have already referred to E. L. Bennett's fundamental study of these facts. For the weights the finding of an octopus weight of some twenty-nine kilograms at Knossos and the close approximation to this amount of the bronze ingots from Hagia Triada had suggested to Evans that the

Fig. 15. Two tablets from sets recording a muster of women and children. The bottom tablet lists the personnel and a TA (female supervisor). The top tablet is the corresponding one from the second set, which also records the rations in equal amounts of wheat and figs.

Mycenaean 'talent' was close to the Babylonian light talent. The determination of the volumetric series was however distorted by uncertain premisses until it became possible to solve the puzzle represented by the rations.

Here we must turn to the inventory of the Pylian women and children, of which two versions have survived. The occasion of this inventory will occupy us again below when we discuss the war emergency arrangements. For the present it will suffice to say that one series simply lists the women, girls and boys together with mysterious entities represented by the syllabic ideograms DA and TA (fig. 15). All kinds of guesses were made at these. Their true nature did not reveal itself until a simple arithmetical analysis of the rations recorded in the second set was made by the present writer. Equal amounts of wheat and figs were recorded on each

		Weight Series			
Symbol	 ⟁	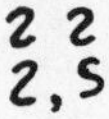 2 2 2, 5	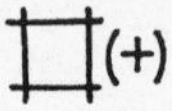 ⊓(+)	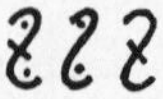 ₹₹₹	 ۹ ۶
Fraction of preceding		$\frac{1}{30}$	$\frac{1}{4}$	$\frac{1}{12}$?	$\frac{1}{6}$ or less
Fraction of whole	1	$\frac{1}{30}$	$\frac{1}{120}$	$\frac{1}{1440}$	$\frac{1}{8640}$
Absolute value	29 Kg.	967 gr.	242 gr.	20·2 gr.	3·36 gr. or less

		Dry Measure			
Symbol	None	T	◁,ℂ,Ϝ	⌣	
Fraction of preceding	—	$\frac{1}{10}$	$\frac{1}{6}$	$\frac{1}{4}$	
Fraction of whole	1	$\frac{1}{10}$	$\frac{1}{60}$	$\frac{1}{240}$	
Absolute value (approx)	60 L.	6 L.	1 L.	$\frac{1}{4}$ L.	

		Wet Measure			
Symbol	None	↗,↑	◁,ℂ,Ϝ	⌣	
Fraction of preceding	—	$\frac{1}{3}$	$\frac{1}{6}$	$\frac{1}{4}$	
Fraction of whole	1	$\frac{1}{3}$	$\frac{1}{18}$	$\frac{1}{72}$	
Absolute value (approx)	18 L.	6	1 L.	$\frac{1}{4}$ L.	

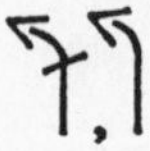

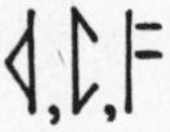

Fig. 16. Table of the Weights and Measures of the Linear B script.

text, the total amount varying proportionately to the numbers involved. It was clear to Ventris and Chadwick from the simpler groupings that a woman received two of the second largest units of the volumetric series (fig. 16), and that each child received one such unit. Thus one text simply lists two women and one girl, without DA and TA. The ration entered is five units ($2 \times 2 + 1 = 5$). But this simple arithmetical picture was quite exceptional. In the great majority of the texts there was a discrepancy between the expected ration and the actual ration recorded. An arithmetical analysis of the data showed the following correlations. When DA and TA were present, the surplus was seven units. When they were absent, the surplus was nil. The preliminary conclusion imposed itself that DA and TA were two consumer entities. Then texts which showed only a TA had a surplus of two units. All that was required to complete the circle of proof was a text which recorded only a DA. There was one such clear case: the surplus was five! Thus a TA accompanying the groups of women and children has a ration on the level of a woman and a DA two and a half times as much. Was TA a woman slave-supervisor and DA a corresponding man? There was at least one text which recorded a lone woman: she was accompanied by a TA.

A small group of aberrant texts still offered difficulty. Here the surplus was nine units: in other words this suggested the presence of an extrâ TA. All these texts listed very large contingents, for which it would be reasonable to supply an extra woman supervisor. The Knossos texts provided the confirmation. Here too we find women and children listed accompanied by DA and TA, but a number of them show DA 1 TA 2 when the numbers recorded are high.

The next step in this investigation proved to be of unsuspected importance. If DA is a man and his ration is five units of the stated size, it would be of interest to know for what period this ration was intended. By a great stroke of fortune the Knossos archives contained a monthly ration statement (fig. 17) relating to 18 men and 8 boys. On the rations we had deduced the expected total should have been 98 units. What the scribe actually entered was $97\frac{1}{2}$! This discrepancy was not a matter of rounding up. The official concerned had gone to the trouble of calculating to a de-

Fig. 17. A monthly ration statement from Knossos. The top line reads MAN 18 BOY 8; *the bottom line* si-to (=*grain*) MONTH 1 BARLEY 9/7/3. *The barley ration is half that calculated for the free man.*

gree of accuracy involving the next lower unit. So meticulous a measurement involving only a few litres in the total monthly ration of a largish group demands some explanation. Ration texts from Mesopotamian societies shows that these distinctions were made according to the age class of the children. Now the Knossian documents distinguish carefully between larger and smaller children. So the missing amount, which is precisely half a child's ration for a whole month, may be accounted for by supposing that one of the boys was a 'smaller' boy, who got only half a 'larger' child's ration. However, what is important is the determination of the man's monthly ration at five of the second largest units in the above series. Again the significance of this was not realized until this figure was converted into the next lowest unit (fig. 16), which is one sixth of the unit which has so far formed the basis of our calculations. The man's monthly ration of wheat is thirty of the third lowest unit of the series. In other words this last unit is the key to the whole system: it represents the standard daily ration of wheat for a man. This fact, once established, linked up with facts known from later Greece and from other ancient societies.

In classical Greece the basic daily ration of wheat was one *choenix*, a unit which varied somewhat in size in different systems but which we may conveniently equate with one litre. Now wheat has a greater nutritional value than barley; consequently two *choenices* of barley were reckoned as the equivalent of one *choenix* of wheat.[1] That this conversion ratio also held good for Mycenaean

[1] Professor Moritz has suggested a better reason to account for the two-to-one ratio than the supposed smaller nutritional value. Barley may have been measured in the husk and so weight for weight occupied a larger volume. At all events the same ratio holds good for the classical period.

*Fig. 18. Knossos tablets recording monthly wheat state-
ments. The three lines of the second tablet refer to 'women
of Knossos', 'women of Amnisos', and 'women of Phaestos'.*

Greece is clear from a number of facts. In the first place we have a
Pylos tablet recording a group of men and their rations. On the
front of the tablet the amount is entered in wheat. On the back
there is written a kind of endorsement in barley: the sum is complex but to the nearest fraction it is exactly double the amount of
wheat entered on the front. Again, in Pylos rations are recorded
in exactly equal amounts of wheat and figs. A number of Knossos
documents, however, record rations involving *barley* and figs. In

the majority of cases the barley is twice the amount of figs. Again we have a reflexion of the two-to-one conversion rate.

We have a number of monthly ration statements from Knossos, and the scales we have established enable us to calculate the number of persons being catered for by the palace in the places referred to. On a single text the rations for the 'men of Lyktos', the 'men of Tylissos' and the 'men of Lato' are entered. The figures work out at 493 men in Lyktos, 522 in Tylissos and 61 in Lato. The sole tablet relating to women's rations is tantalizing. It starts with 'women of Knossos', with a minor entry relating to the *ki-ri-te-wi-ja*, whom we have encountered also in Pylos as a corporation of religious women. The subsequent entries relate to the 'women of Amnisos' and 'women of Phaestos'. Unfortunately the numerical entries are broken, and all we can say is that the numbers catered for in all these places lie between 500 and 1,000, say an average of 750. Administratively it is of interest to see the central control of rations issued at places so far apart. We should not suppose, of course, that the grain itself was transported from Knossos, for it will doubtless have been stored in royal granaries close to the place of harvesting. But the texts show clearly that the King of Knossos was in firm control of most of Crete, and of Phaestos in particular. It surely implies that some lieutenant of the King was resident in Phaestos, and his residence is presumably to be located in one of the buildings excavated there.

The scale of rations at Pylos for men, women and children exhibits, as we have said, the proportions $5 : 2 : 1$ (with $\frac{1}{2}$ for the smaller child?). There are analogies for similar allocations from other ancient societies. Particularly interesting are the figures from Nuzi in Mesopotamia, where the man-boy ratio is $6 : 1$ and the woman's allocation was only twice that of a child, not even daughters of the royal house rising above the level of a slave's, which was three times the child's ration and half the free man's allocation. The resemblances do not stop here. From Pylos, too, we have evidence that the slave's ration was half of the standard. This is clear from the figures contained in the barley texts and particularly from the troublesome *pa₂-si-re-wi-ja* tablet, to which we must now again return (fig. 19).

Little attention has been paid to the numerical entries in the

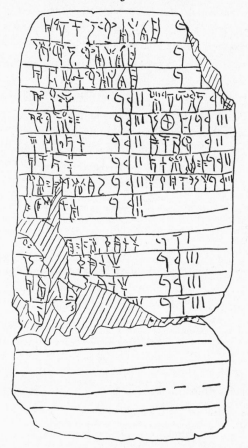

*Fig. 19. A Pylos tablet with barley entries on different
scales. The bottom four entries below the blank line refer to
'slaves' on scale 1. The four lines above refer to craftsmen
on scale 2, the next line above has entries on scale 3. The
top three entries are on scale 6+, and the men concerned
appear to have the title pa₂-si-re-u.*

long-sustained efforts to diagnose the types of men who figure in
this puzzling document. Yet it is at once clear that the 'slaves' in
the final paragraph receive one unit of barley apiece. In other words
this is half the standard man's daily ration of one 'choenix' of
wheat or two of barley. But many of the preceding entries relate

to skilled craftsmen, for some of the words are clearly trade designations such as 'bakers', and all may be diagnosed as belonging to the same semantic sphere. All these receive the expected two 'choenices' of barley. Some wholly mysterious entities had been the subject of wild guesswork such as 'supervisors of sowing' and 'supervisors of honey', which hardly fitted into the evident craftsman context. It was again simple arithmetic which provided a clue.

The first step was to reduce all the entries in this rather forbidding series of barley texts to the 'choenix' unit. At once some remarkable facts emerged. There was one text recording barley as sent to certain shrines or issued to cult personnel. What is peculiar was that all the amounts are multiples of three, and in particular one identifiable individual receives the basic amount of three 'choenices'. The thought at once suggests itself that this was the daily allowance for cult personnel. Again Knossos provided some confirmation. Among the earliest texts recovered by Evans in the first few days of his excavations were some recording the issue of oil and other commodities to shrines and divinities. One set in particular records in a fixed order barley, figs, along with other comestibles. In all cases the amounts of barley and figs are multiples of three. Could this fact be used to diagnose the mysterious persons on the pa_2-si-re-wi-ja text, who also enjoyed allocations on 'scale 3'? If the me-ri-du-ma-te were temple functionaries, this would certainly fit the information we possess about the allocation of men from 'Potnia' quarters. It is unfortunate that the pa_2-si-re-wi-ja entries at the top of the tablet are broken, but enough survives to show that the allocation was $6+$.

Yet another set of the barley texts, when reduced to the 'choenix' unit, revealed that all the amounts were multiples of five. Here, too, some of the personalities could be identified, and it was clear that they belonged to an exalted social class, one of them being possibly identifiable with *Du-ni-jo* the *du-ma*, (an official who, we have suggested, acted as second-in-command of the administration in the Hither Province). There are many complexities, but the general system which emerges from the BARLEY texts appears to be one of daily payments measured in barley on scales which vary according to skill and social status.

Such a system is by no means unparalleled. Professor J. Černy has shown that in Egypt of the same period as the Pylos tablets the basis of the workmen's food and wages alike was corn and that as a rule the payments were made monthly. What is of interest is that the simple worker received 5½ *khar* of grain per month, whereas the foreman of the 'crew' received 7½ *khar*. The ratio of 3 : 2 is exactly that between the skilled workers of our *pa₂-si-re-wi-ja* text and the temple officials whose titles we cannot identify in terms of later Greek.

The Measures of Capacity

We have seen above that the third largest unit of the Mycenaean series for the measurement of dry volume was the hinge of the system, in that it represents the man's standard daily ration of wheat. We tentatively equated it with the later *choenix*. There is an additional reason for believing that this equation is valid. The later *choenix* was divided into four 'cups' (*kotylae*). Our Mycenaean 'choenix' is similarly divided into four, and this sub-unit is represented by a sign which has the appearance of a handleless cup. Further cogency is given to the equation by calculating the size of the major Mycenaean unit, which is sixty times the 'choenix'. The Attic *choenix* is believed to have contained 0·9 lt., the Aeginetan *choenix* which was in use in the Peloponnese being somewhat larger. If we take a mean value as approximately 1 lt., the Mycenaean major unit will have been *c.* 60 lt. This value lies between the Attic major unit, the *medimnos*, and the Spartan ('Pheidonian') *medimnos*, but it lies much closer to the latter (62 lt.). What is of greater significance, however, is this ratio 60 : 1 as between the major Mycenaean measure of dry volume and the unit which represents the daily ration of wheat.

Of great historical interest is the close similarity of the Mycenaean system of capacity measures to the Mesopotamian. H. Lewy has stressed the importance of the monthly ration figure in the genesis of the sexagesimal system. A large number of texts reveal, she writes, the importance of the quantity of 30 *qû* of grain for the inhabitants of Babylonia and Assyria. It is evidently a great practical convenience, if rations are calculated and issued monthly, to have a measure which is exactly 30 times that representing the daily ration of grain. There is further evidence that

30 such units was the slave's monthly ration, whereas persons of higher social standing received twice that amount, boys being allowed one third of the slave's ration. It was practical convenience in issuing monthly rations which doubtless occasioned the intrusion of a unit representing 30 *qû* into the one-time purely decimal Sumerian system. Later still in the Sumero-Babylonian sources another unit appears containing 60 *qû*. In practical terms this means that a unit based on the slave's 30 per month was replaced by one based on the free man's 60 per month. It is this system which now finds its distant echo in Mycenaean Greece. By what intermediaries this form of the Mesopotamian system reached Greece must remain a matter of speculation. A possible pointer is that the word *medimnos* has an Indo-European root *med* 'measure' and an Indo-European suffix -*mnos*; but it has proved difficult to account for the vowel in terms of native Greek development. Between Mycenaean Greece and the world of Mesopotamia in the second millennium lay the Anatolia of the Hittites and their linguistic cousins. The relations of this world to Mycenae we propose to consider in the final chapter.

One point we must stress again. These measures are peculiar to Linear B. Linear A has a different system. Since we shall see growing reason to regard Linear B as an intruder into Crete from the mainland, this implies that the system of measurements and their symbols were likewise evolved on the mainland. Did the Greeks of the Late Helladic Period inherit the system from their Middle Helladic predecessors? Or was it a creation of the Mycenaean Greek civilization, which we shall date from the sixteenth century? If the latter, then we cannot avoid the conclusion that its relations with the Orient were closer than has been suspected from the archaeological finds. At all events the measures with their peculiar ratios and the system of social rationing speak for themselves. That the system was ultimately derived from the Mesopotamian world is hardly open to doubt.

6. THE MYCENAEAN RELIGION

We now have the most concrete information on Mycenaean cult and gods. This is derived from documents which record the issue of supplies for cult purposes. At Knossos these were among the very first tablets discovered by Sir Arthur Evans. In particular the tablet which received the number one in his Handlist has some entries of an uncanny appositeness to his search. It is one of a series accounting for the issue of oil to various shrines and divinities. This first tablet is headed with a date giving the month. The first two entries read: 'To Dictaean Zeus OIL, To the Daidaleion OIL.' Scholars had, of course, been long familiar with Zeus whose shrine and birth place was on Mount Dicte. But Daedalus was merely the legendary craftsman of Minos, who built inter alia the Labyrinth and the 'dancing place of Ariadne'. Another tablet yielded the combination 'The Lady of Athana, Enyalios, Poseidon'. Still more remarkable was the tablet recording a jar of honey to 'The Lady of Labyrinthos'. The last word is spelt with initial d for l, a well-known phenomenon in Aegean-Anatolian linguistics; I take it to be the name of a cult place, for we have a number of such designations, 'the Potnia of X', where X is a place-name. It is difficult to dissociate cult this title from the later myth about the labyrinth, but our text must be interpreted within the frame of the Linear B evidence as a whole. This gives no encouragement to any view of $da\text{-}pu_2\text{-}ri\text{-}to\text{-}jo$ except as a place-name. The same is true of $a\text{-}ta\text{-}na\text{-}po\text{-}ti\text{-}ni\text{-}ja$. It was tempting, of course, to read this as Lady Athena, but the clear parallels make it advisable to resist the temptation and diagnose $a\text{-}ta\text{-}na$ likewise as a cult place and presumably in Crete, where there is evidence for this place-name, which was, of course, not confined to the famous Athens.

Another Cretan divinity was Eileithyia, the goddess of child-birth, who had a sacred cave at Amnisos on the coast north of Knossos. It is mentioned by Odysseus himself when, in his guise of Cretan, he tells his false tale to Penelope. He declares that he once saw Odysseus when he was driven south to Crete on his way to Troy. 'He anchored in Amnisos, where there is a cave of Eile-ithyia.' So it was satisfactory to find a jar of honey recorded with the words $A\text{-}mi\text{-}ni\text{-}so$ $E\text{-}re\text{-}u\text{-}ti\text{-}ja$. It is worth noting that the name of the goddess is spelt in a way which reflects the form found in later times on an inscription from Messenia: Eleuthia. Other commodities are listed in texts featuring Eleuthia. One of these is the puzzling substance indicated by the syllabic ideogram *MA*, which was for long confused with WOOL until it was pointed out that this is an ingredient of unguent boiling. It is evidently some aromatic substance used in offerings to the gods.

The religious picture which emerges from the Pylos tablets is strangely different though there are points of resemblance. Gratifying is the confirmation given to the deductions about Peloponnesian religion long ago voiced by the great Hellenist Wilamowitz. He based his conclusions on the actual cults attested for the Peloponnese in classical times. Everywhere Poseidon is prominent and Olympian Zeus pales in comparison. 'What have these hole-and-corner cults to say as against the Poseidon of Laconia and Arcadia? Is it permissible to project Homeric Zeus back into the most ancient times? This would be a *petitio principii*.' The Pylos tablets have corroborated this conclusion for Mycenaean Messenia. In an important tablet, recording the offering of gold vessels, women and men to a number of divinities, one side deals with the town (*wastu*) of Pylos, and the first shrine mentioned is the *Posidaion*. The offerings recorded are two women and a gold cup. In Mycenaean BULL compositions LEAF PLANT is a frequent accessorial motive, and trees are prominent in the BULL scenes on the famous gold cup from Vaphio. So it is of interest to note that the scribe has written a sort of marginal note after the ideograms. This I have interpreted as a description of the ornamentation of the cup: 'decorated with bulls . . . and leaf ornament.' Other divinities and their offerings follow. Among them we have detected the Dove, Iphimedeia, Diwia, and Hermes. Last of all we find the mention of the shrine of Zeus together with three divinities. The first two are Zeus and Hera. The third is puzzling. It appears to be '*di-ri-mi-jo*, the son of Zeus'. But what is beyond doubt is the mention of Zeus and Hera and that they receive a less grand type of vessel than Poseidon, who has pride of place.

Poseidon figures largely in other texts connected with land-holding and deliveries. Thus we can add to the supremacy of Poseidon in Hellenic Laconia and Arcadia his predominance in the Messenia of the Linear B tablets. This weakens a thesis advanced by Nilsson which has commanded widespread support. This is that the figure of Zeus as king of the gods was the creation

132

of the Mycenaean world which rearranged the divine world on the model of their own 'great house' society. On the contrary, we can now see the force of the dictum of the historian Ephorus who observed 'The Peloponnese in olden days seems to have been the dwelling place of Poseidon and the land was considered as sacred to him'.

The other side of the tablet we are considering is, in fact, the beginning of the text, since it is headed with the name of a month, which I have interpreted as 'Navigation Month' (see below). This part of the text is concerned with the holy place *Pa-ki-ja-nes*, the site of the estate discussed above. The shrine mentioned is that of Potnia. She too receives a gold cup and a woman. The associated deities are rather mysterious. There is a feminine counterpart of Poseidon named Posidaeia. The last line has two recipients and the words have been interpreted as 'Clan Ancestor' and 'House Lord'. If there is anything in this suggestion, then the Clan and the House concerned can hardly be anything else than the Royal Clan and House. *Wanax*, as we have seen, is closely associated with Potnia and the place *Pa-ki-ja-nes*.

The significance of the close association of the Pylian *Wanax* with *Potnia* (literally 'The Mistress', 'Lady') was not fully realized until the discovery of a new hoard of tablets at Pylos in the campaign of 1955. Professor Blegen was exploring a room in the palace which proved to contain large storage jars (*pithoi*). In association with these vessels he found tablets bearing the ideogram long before diagnosed as OLIVE OIL. Similar tablets were recovered from another store room close by (fig. 3). Copies of the tablets were in due course made available, first to Professor Bennett who was to edit them, and soon afterwards to Ventris and Chadwick. I owed my first knowledge of them to the kind intervention of Professor Blegen in June 1957. On January 15, 1958 Mr Chadwick and myself submitted to a private meeting of the Linear B Seminar of the Institute of Classical Studies, London wholly independent studies of these texts. Professor Bennett's own edition was sent to press on March 1, 1958, but it may be considered also as independent. What is of importance for the critics of the decipherment is that all three versions agreed in diagnosing the texts as concerned with the issue of perfumed oil and unguent for cult purposes. The oil was described in terms of its perfume such as 'rose perfume', 'cyperus perfume', etc. Again, all three studies distinguished the following categories of entry: (1) divine recipients in the dative case; (2) destinations characterized by the suffix *-de* (as in later *Athenasde* 'to Athens'); (3) dates in the form of month names. These were precisely the categories already detected in the corresponding Knossos texts. Bennett and I agreed in adding another important type of entry. These were the names of festivals, the study of which opened up interesting vistas of the remoter affinities of Mycenaean religion. But before going on to discuss the considerable divergences of detailed interpretation the overall agreement in the general diagnosis by all three scholars should be stressed.

Of the recipient deities recorded in the Olive Oil texts Poseidon, Potnia, The Divine Mother, and others quite simply 'The Gods' (perhaps dual) were immediately apparent. What occasioned some dispute, still unresolved, were entries relating to *Wa-na-so-i*, which was related to another mysterious entry *wa-na-se-wi-ja*. This last word had already occurred in a Linear B text, and agreement had been reached that it was derived from *Wanassa*, the archaic Greek word for 'queen'. This word continued to be used in post-Mycenaean times as the cult title for a Cypriot mother-goddess of the Astarte type to whom the Cypriot kings acted as priest. There was also agreement among all scholars concerned that 'two queens' would be *Wanasso* in Mycenaean. A photograph of one of the new tablets was published in the *Illustrated London News*: it bore the inscription *wa-no-so-i. po-se-da-o-ne*. Without knowledge of the other texts I had hazarded the guess that the first word was a misspelling for *wa-na-so-i*, and that the text recorded offerings to 'The Two Queens (and) Poseidon'. Now students of Greek religion had long known of 'Two Mistresses' in the religion of Arcadia, where the language and religion of the Mycenaean Age persisted into classical times. Moreover, the leading authority on Greek religion and Mycenaean religion in particular had stressed the close association of the 'Two Mistresses' with Poseidon. This was encouraging.

As a result of enquiry into the contemporary languages of Anatolia and particularly the western and southern parts, with which the Mycenaeans were in the closest contact, I had become aware that 'Queen' was a widespread title of the Mother Goddess, and further that the Young God, her son and consort who dies and is resurrected, in many languages bore the title 'The King', 'The Lord', or 'The Ruler' (e.g. Adonis). A number of pointers suggested that if *Wanassa* was the Greek equivalent of 'The Queen', then her son-consort was likely to be called *Wanax*. In a lecture on 'Language and Prehistory' given before the Hellenic Society on March 15, 1957 I hazarded the prediction that this title might be expected to appear in Linear B texts. The objection was made, rightly, that I had manipulated the evidence to the extent of emending *wa-no-so-i* to *wa-na-so-i*, although such a spelling alternation could be paralleled. However, some three months later Professor Blegen made available to me a transcript of all the new evidence. The objection was disposed of: the 'emended' version *wa-na-so-i* occurred a number of times. Better still, there were some examples of the entry *Wa-na-ka-te* 'to the Wanax'. Of the greatest significance was the text *Wa-na-ka-te Wa-na-so-i* 'To the King (and) the Two Queens'. Here we had a combination which could be tested in two ways. We could verify it by asking the archaeologists whether there was any pictorial evidence for such a tableau, and enquiring of the students of religion whether later Greece, and especially Arcadia, presented a combination of a young god with two Mother Goddesses.

The questions were in reality rhetorical. In the first place the famous ivory statuette found at Mycenae by Professor Wace depicting two women and a child had immediately been brought into relationship with the later combinations of the type Demeter, the corn-goddess, plus her daughter-double Kore ('the virgin'= Persephone, goddess of the underworld) together with Triptolemus, the young god of Eleusis, of whom an Athenian, a priest of the Mysteries, once said: 'we are told that Triptolemos our ancestor . . . gave a gift of the seed of Demeter's fruit to the Peloponnese before all other lands'. The figure from Mycenae is widely regarded as a most beautiful representation of the Mycenaean 'divine family'. But there is other evidence of a more schematic kind. A number of terracotta figures are known which show two women joined together like Siamese twins and with a child seated on their common shoulder. These too have been interpreted as representations of Twin Goddesses with Young God. Thus there was a welcome harmony between the straightforward philological interpretation of the texts and the contemporary evidence from the Mycenaean world on the one hand and that of later Greek religion on the other. What is heartening, too, is that the lines of the linguistic analysis were laid down before the discovery of the new texts. The key word *wa-na-se-wi-ja* had been analysed as a derivative of *Wanassa* in 1955, and the Mycenaean grammars already contained the statement that nouns of this class had their dual in -*o*. All that was necessary was to apply these 'predictions' to the new texts. The harmonious picture of Mycenaean religion which has emerged constitutes a test of the predictions.

Still more exacting and revealing was another early guess that the word *po-ro-wi-to-jo*, which stood alone at the head of the offering text (p. 133), was a month name. That the syllables stood for the genitive of *Plowistos* 'Navigation Month' I had suggested in 1954; it was presumably so-called because it marked the resumption of navigation after the winter months. The full purport of this in relation to the new religious texts has only recently been realized. It will be necessary to consider a little more closely the festival names which Bennett and I had detected in the Olive Oil tablets.

The most remarkable of these was 'The Spreading of the Couch', for there is widespread evidence from the Orient that such a festival formed the culmination of the Spring Festival; this was the Sacred Marriage between the Mother Goddess and her risen Son, the rite which symbolizes and promotes the renewed fertility of the earth. This convergence of detailed interpretation by two scholars is encouraging. What now brought matters a stage further was a contribution by Professor W. K. C. Guthrie apropos of an entry *Di-pi-si-jo-i*. The ending clearly was dative plural and hence the word referred to recipients of an offering. I had identified the word as *Dipsioi* 'The Thirsty Ones' and supposed they might be representative of parched nature. Guthrie, however, while accepting the identification of the word, showed that the Greek connotations of 'the thirsty ones' suggested rather that they were 'the dead'. This proved a most important determination.

For besides this dative there was a derived form *di-pi-si-je-wi-jo*, which was likely to be the name of the corresponding festival. Now 'The Festival of the Dead' recalls the Athenian 'All Souls Day', which was the third day of a complex series of festivals known as the Anthesteria. We were now offered a welcome opportunity for a test of the most complex character. The successive festivals of the Anthesteria could be compared with the data on this set of the Linear B tablets, to the interpretation of which we were now firmly committed.

The first day was 'The Opening of the Pithoi (jars)', the broaching of the new wine. One of our tablets bears a date formula which had already been interpreted 'New Wine'. The second day of the Anthesteria was taken up by a Sacred Marriage (*hieros gamos*) between Dionysus and the wife of Archon Basileus, the Athenian official on whom the religious duties of the King had devolved. This had long been regarded as a symbolization of the 'Young God-Queen' marriage rite. This corresponded satisfactorily to our 'Spreading of the Couch' festival. After the sacred wedding followed drinking and revelry, which as elsewhere doubtless symbolized the blessings and bounty which the wedding rite was intended to procure. Here, too, the texts had an appropriate festival name: *Xenwia* 'The Banquet'. Finally the last day was devoted to the festival of the dead. This gave rise to the saying 'Be off Dead Spirits (*Kēres*); the Anthesteria are over'. With our 'Festival of the Thirsty (Dead)' the cycle of evidence appeared to be complete. There was an astounding degree of correspondence between the new Mycenaean data, as previously interpreted, and the Anthesteria, which through Guthrie's important suggestion had now been brought into the picture.

There was one further step. This was the name of the month and its proposed interpretation. *po-ro-wi-to* now presented itself in a number of the new texts. This offered no difficulty to our long-established diagnosis of it as the name of a month. But what we were now committed to was that the 'Festival of the Dead' took place in this month, and further that this was the month of the 'resumption of navigation'. One sentence from the standard handbook on Greek religion by Professor Nilsson of Lund should suffice for the verification. We read apropos of the Anthesteria:

137

The World of the Tablets

'The Epiphany of Dionysus in the spring became the festival of the resumption of navigation. . . .' In view of the suggestions being made by a critic of the decipherment that there are grounds for suspecting collusion and 'Piltdown' fraud, it may be pointed out that my analysis of *po-ro-wi-to-jo* on the 1939 tablet as 'Navigation Month' is recorded in the Minutes of the Linear B Seminar of the Institute of Classical Studies, London for May 26, 1954, one year before the excavation of the Olive Oil tablets.

This is still not the end of the matter. The *Anthesteria* at Athens concerned 'Dionysus in the Marshes'. We can now see a new significance in this title; for Nilsson has stressed how the Peloponnesian group of associated deities The Two Mistresses, Poseidon and Artemis (whom I would equate with Potnia) are closely connected with marshes and underground water. Poseidon in particular is not merely the god of the sea but also of springs and underground water in general. Some new information enables us to make a new approach to the problem of his name.

The eminent philologist Paul Kretschmer had long ago proposed an analysis of the name which is widely accepted. He pointed out that the *-ōn* is merely the Greek characterizing suffix, which can be attached to names in general, like *Kleon*, *Platon* and so on. That this is so is shown by the fact that it does not figure in the name of the shrine: *Posidaion*. The name itself Kretschmer analysed as *Posei-Dās*, in which the first element is the vocative case of the Greek word *posis*, originally meaning 'lord, master' but used poetically for 'husband'. The second element he identified as the word for 'earth' that we also encounter in the divine name *Dāmāter*, which is self-evidently 'Earth-Mother'. Thus the whole name means 'O! Husband of the Earth'. Such fossilized vocatives recur in divine names. The best known example is *Jū-piter*, which is the exact equivalent of *Zeu pater* in Greek. In the oblique cases of *Iupiter* the second element is not used of course: *Iouem*, *Iouis* etc. Kretschmer's Viennese colleague, the ancient historian Fritz Schachermeyr, added a most acute observation. He pointed out that the word order in *Posei-Dās* 'Lord of the Earth' is un-Greek and recalls the German *Vater Unser*, where the foreign word order is due to translation from the Latin *Pater Noster*. Schachermeyr therefore concluded that the model for *Posei-Dās* was a

138

pre-Greek religious title, and that it is a 'calque', an unidiomatic literal rendering, of a kind often found in the translation of religious texts. New evidence from Anatolia and the Near East has further illuminated the problem and greatly increased the probability that Kretschmer's analysis was correct.

On the Syrian coast opposite Cyprus lies the ancient town of Ugarit, where the Mycenaeans established an emporium. Texts recovered during the French excavation there were rapidly deciphered and shown to be written in a Semitic language. The documents from a temple library have given us some idea of the religion, cult and myths of the Canaanite people who lived in this region. We hear particularly of the fertility god *Aliyan Ba'al*, who in his guise of god of the underworld, and of the underground waters in particular, bears the title *Ba'al Arṣ* 'Lord of the Earth'. If we now explore the vast territories stretching to the north and east of Ugarit, we shall come across repeated echoes of this same title in the religious culture area of which Ugarit formed a part. In northern Mesopotamia the Hurrians had their centre. During the course of the second millennium this people expanded their power and moved south and west, and they had a profound influence on the Hittite empire. In their language, too, the name of the god who interests us is *Irbitiga*, again 'Lord of the Earth'. At the beginning of the second millennium an Indo-European people, the Hittites, moved into north-east Anatolia, presumably from the regions lying to the north of the Caucasus. This was the people who were to become the dominant power in Anatolia and to rank with the great powers of Babylon and Egypt. In the Hittite lands proper, in the north-east, the indigenous pre-Hittite 'substratum' population spoke the language known as Hattic. They too, as has been recently shown by Mr Macqueen, knew a god of the underground waters, and they called him *Wurunkatte*, literally 'Earth-King'. But the source and fount for this title in its many translated forms is presumably to be found in the ancient civilization of Lower Mesopotamia, of Sumer-Akkad. In Sumerian too we encounter a god of the E.A, the underground world of water, and he bore the name EN.KI literally 'Lord (of the) Earth'. The following is the geographical distribution of the above cult-titles schematically represented:

The World of the Tablets

Wurunkatte (Hattic)
Irbitiga (Hurrian)
Posei-dá-ōn (Mycenaean) *Ba'al Ars* (Canaanite) EN.KI (Sumerian)

Many classical scholars feel reluctance to look into the light that comes from the east, but it would hardly be 'cautious' to assert that it is an accident that the Greek name for the god of the underground waters, as interpreted by Kretschmer-Schachermeyr, is the exact correspondent of the oriental titles we have assembled, the nearest of which lies no further away than the coast opposite Mycenaean Cyprus.

The fact that *Posei-Das* is a literal translation contrary to Greek word order, like the German *Vater Unser* from *Pater Noster*, argues a bilingual 'missionary' situation and thus reflects a religious movement from the Orient into Mycenaean Greece. This conclusion is all the more welcome in that it coincides with what we may call the received opinion about the affinities of the religion of the Minoan-Mycenaean world. The great majority of scholars from Sir Arthur Evans on have insisted that the religion of Minoan Crete was an offshoot of the tenacious vegetation-cult of the ancient Near East. One further step may now be taken. We see that the Greek dialect into which the 'Lord of the Earth' was translated as *Posei-Das-* used *dā* as its word for 'earth'. Which dialect was it? Long ago Wilamowitz had analysed the Cypriot word for the nymphs as *en-da-ides* 'those who are in the earth' and concluded that *dā* is the Cypriot word for 'earth'. It recurs in *Dā-māter* 'Earth Mother'. Thus another line of investigation has led us to the conclusion that the 'Lord of the Earth' and the 'Earth Mother' were first clothed in Hellenic dress in the island where the Mycenaeans most closely impinged on the religious culture area of Mesopotamia. It was in Cyprus, we recall that *Wanassa* 'The Queen' still reigned supreme down to late antiquity. It was in that island that the kings of Paphos acted as her priests carrying on the tradition evinced in the close connexion of the Mycenaean *Wanax* with the 'Mistress' of the Pylian lands. Professor Guthrie recalls some striking evidence for the tenacity of these religious beliefs. He quotes from D. G. Hogarth's book *A Wandering scholar in the Levant*. 'In honour of the Maid of Bethlehem the peasants of Kuklia (in Cyprus) anointed lately,

140

and probably still anoint each year, the great corner stones of the ruined temple of the Paphian Goddess. As Aphrodite was supplicated once with cryptic rites, so is Mary entreated still by Moslems as well as Christians, with incantations and passings through perforated stones to remove the curse of barrenness from Cypriot women, or increase the manhood of Cypriot men.' Guthrie notes further (after Frazer's *Golden Bough*) that the Virgin is worshipped there under the title of Panaghia Aphroditessa.

Now that the new texts have increased our confidence in the diagnosis of these scholars, it is legitimate to use the ritual texts from the Oriental cradle land of this religion to paint a backcloth against which we may set the hitherto dumb religious tableau we can see on the artefacts from the Minoan and Mycenaean worlds.

A Sumerian hymn often quoted in discussions of the New Year Festival is that addressed to the Goddess Ishtar. Written for use in the cult of Idin-Dagan, a king of the first half of the second millennium, it depicts him as an embodiment of Tammuz, 'The Son', embraced by the Mother-Goddess, who is referred to as 'The Queen'.

> *At the festival of the New Year . . .*
> *For My Queen a couch I have laid.*
> *My Queen upon her couch goes to repose.*
>
> *. . . . . . .*
>
> *She embraces her beloved husband*
>
> *. . . . . . .*
>
> *The King like the Sun-god*
> *Plenty, happiness and abundance before him prosper*
> *A feast of good things they set before him.*

Here we find the themes of the 'Spreading of the Couch' and 'The Banquet' we have detected in the Pylian documents. But we have still not exhausted the riches of these storeroom dockets.

There is no mistaking the horsiness of Poseidon in the Peloponnese. He was called Hippios, and in horse guise he mated with a horse-headed goddess, who on occasion is known as *Medusa*, literally 'the Queen'. Euripides even introduces on to the stage, as a *deus ex machina*, a goddess Hippo. From all this scholars had deduced that behind Poseidon Hippios there lurked a more ancient god Hippos. Apropos of the estate of the *Lawagetas* we have mentioned the offering of cyperus to *I-QO*, and also the land held 'in respect of *I-QO*'. This is likely to be the very god Hippos (in the Mycenaean spelling) which had been suspected from previous analysis of religious data.

We also recall the seal impression found by Sir Arthur Evans in the Little Palace (fig. 22). In view of the frequency of the religious motifs on such sealings, which have long been one of our main source books for Minoan-Mycenaean religion, it is at least equally probable that this magnificent beast is not merely an indication of the cargo but a representation of the god Hippos, whose presence on the Commander's estate is a clue to his martial propensities. The sealing I should interpret as a Mycenaean 'Viking ship' under the protection of Hippos. A further thought obtrudes itself, which we immediately brand as an idle speculation. If the great exploits of the Mycenaean warriors in the Aegean were carried out under the aegis of Hippos, if in fact Troy was successfully attacked 'with Hippos', is this the religious reality which lies behind the legend of the Trojan horse?

If we now cast our eyes back over the divine pantheon which has gradually emerged from the enveloping clay, we shall find nothing that need alarm the students of the 'picture-book' of Minoan-Mycenaean religion. Poseidon, The Horse God, The Two Queens and the Young God, and Potnia ('The Mistress') correspond to the main figures already detected by scholars before the decipherment. We may add the negative trait of the comparative unimportance of Zeus and Hera. Nor will the Dove Goddess surprise those who have followed the gradual unfolding of Sir Arthur Evans's picture of Minoan religion. Even his 'Two Handmaidens', who regularly accompany the Mother Goddess, have their clear counterpart in the *Amphipoloi*, 'The Handmaidens', of the Pylian Olive Oil tablets. In Crete Dictaean Zeus and Eleuthia at Amnisos are exactly right. As for the Daidaleion and, still more, the Lady of Labyrinthos, one can sympathize with the Italian scholar who at a recent international congress of classical studies exclaimed 'È troppo bello!'.

Chapter V

The Last Days of Pylos

W e now turn from this new and strange picture of the Mycenaean world to face an insistent historical question. What happened at Pylos? The tablets are witnesses, no longer dumb, to the last days of Pylos: they were preserved because they were unintentionally baked in the fire that destroyed the palace. We have seen evidence that shortly before the end came the scribes had been busy in the archives room at the routine task of making a consolidated register from earlier provisional dockets containing proposals for land holdings. More significant still is the fact, noted above, that the blank part cut from the final 'page' of the register was found still uninscribed. The evident context of destruction will prompt the historian to ask whether these records show any awareness of the impending catastrophe. The answer is unequivocal: a sense of emergency pervades the whole archive for all its sober and matter-of-fact appearance.

Unmistakable is the note sounded in the tablet recording 'temple bronze' for making into points for spears and arrows. But the most direct and dramatic testimony was to come from tablets characterized by the MAN ideogram. One of these was recovered in the campaign of 1939 and had lain in the vaults of the Bank of Greece during the German occupation. It had been singled out by an Italian scholar as being complete gibberish despite his acceptance of the decipherment. However, at an early stage close analysis had suggested to me that it represented military dispositions. The entries seemed to be set out in an orderly way. The tablet first named a military unit distinguished by the name of its commander in the genitive singular. Then followed a place-name, which I took

143

to be the HQ of the unit in question. This entry was in its turn followed by a group of proper names which I suggested were the 'officers'. The last entry in the paragraph gave the number of men and their station. At intervals after successive paragraphs of this structure there came an entry 'And with them is the *e-qe-ta X*'. *X* was the name of a man: what was significant was that he receives the full 'heroic' style of name and father's name, like 'Ajax son of Telamon'. From this I concluded that he was a grandee. The word *e-qe-ta* was identified as meaning 'Companion' and brought into connexion with the 'companions' of the king known from Homer, from Macedonian society and, further afield, from the Germanic world. I suggested, therefore, that here we had the Mycenaean equivalent of the *comes* 'the Count', and representative of the king in the field.

All this received further illumination from the renewed dig of 1952, when other parts of the same document were recovered. All important was the first tablet with its introductory explanatory sentence: 'How the watchers are guarding the coastal regions'. Here was the confirmation of the diagnosis based on the solitary tablet secured in 1939. It could be seen that the complete document records such dispositions from the area of *Me-ta-pa*, the second most northerly of the places of the Hither Province, round the coast as far as *Ti-mi-to-a-ke-i*, the first and farthest place of the Further Province. Some of the troops stationed at the last place are stated to be bound for *Nedon*, a name that can hardly be dissociated from the river Nedon, which flows south-west from Mount Taygetos and runs into the sea near Kalamata (see fig. 13).

Closer study of the dispositions showed a curious gap. The last tablet of the series jumps from *Ka-ra-do-ro* ('The Ravine'), the last but one of the Hither Province, just north of *Ri-jo* (our 'Cape Province'), to *za-e-to-ro*, which according to our analysis (see below) is well within the Messenian Gulf, while the next HQ mentioned is *Ti-mi-to-a-ke-i* on the furthest confines of the Further Province of the kingdom. This yawning gap in the defensive screen was explicable only on the assumption that the series was incomplete; but this was hard to reconcile with the order of the entries on the tablet we have just discussed. The explanation of the gap did not become apparent until very recently, when closer analysis of a quite different set of tablets recording dispositions of 'rowers' was undertaken.

There are three of these tablets. The first states baldly 'Rowers going to Pleuron', and the entries add up precisely to thirty, which is presumably a ship's complement. The places supplying them recur in the other two tablets, which supply valuable information. The heading of the first of these is broken, but the word *e-re-ta* 'rowers' is clearly visible. The entries take the form of a place-name followed by the number of men. What is particularly valuable about this text is that it clearly follows a geographical order round the coast and so offers the most searching series of tests for our deduced order of places in the two provinces. Here are the entries:

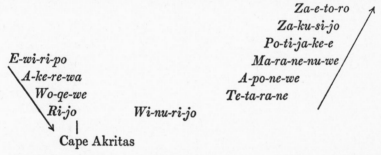

We begin with the first place, which can be certainly identified as Euripus. Now Ventris and Chadwick had correctly deduced that this must be a place where there was an appreciable current, and by elimination they were led to the channel between the island of Sapientsa (fig. 13) and the mainland. The next place mentioned was *A-ke-re-wa*, which according to our deductions (p. 89) was situated in the Hither Province two stages south of the holy place *Pa-ki-ja-nes*, which we have reasonably placed close to Pylos itself. Thus our deduced locations show a satisfactory consistency with the first 'fix' of Euripus. But we now find ourselves firmly bound in a chain of deductions. The string of rower stations leads to *Ri-jo*, the last of the Hither Province, and we are irrevocably committed by our analyses to a further conclusion. The places listed after this must lie within the Messenian Gulf. It so happens that by good luck other tablets provide enough information to verify these deductions. We can see that certain of the rower stations after *Ri-jo* are in fact connected with places which occur

in the list of the 'Seven' of the Further Province. Better still they
are listed in the reverse order of the Seven, which again was a
consequence of our presumed order of listing in each case from
the farther extremity to the dividing point at Cape Akritas (see
p. 89). What is of the greatest interest is that the last of the 'rower'
stations is *Za-e-to-ro*. This, as we saw, was on the further side of
the great gap in the screen of 'watchers' which yawns between
Ka-ra-do-ro and *Za-e-to-ro*. This is a fact of the greatest interest
and significance. The complementarity of the 'watcher' stations
and the 'rower' stations cannot be due to accident. It is inconceivable that two different scribes, dealing with wholly separate
and unconnected matters, should by chance have listed strings of
places in such a way that the second fills the gap left by the first.
It will be evident that these two sets of documents record two
aspects of one and the same set of dispositions. Naturally the
places where there is a mustering of ships (and for what other
purpose would the palace record these large numbers of rowers?)
would not require the services of watchers to guard the coastal
areas. We can hardly avoid the conclusion that the screen of
'Watchers' spread thinly over the immense stretch of coast from
Me-ta-pa in the north to *Ti-mi-to-a-ke-i* near Kalamata is merely
a complement to the main concentration of forces, to which the
'rower' tablets offer such precious clues. That the rower stations
embrace Southern Messenia on both sides of Rhion, the 'Cape
Province', cannot fail to intrigue naval strategists.

The other tablet concerned with rowers helps to fill in this
general picture of the dispositions. It records rowers 'absent from
Ro-o-wa'. This place occurs constantly in maritime contexts, and
there can be little doubt that it was an important naval station,
perhaps the main one of Mycenaean Pylos, as Ventris and Chadwick had already suggested. It also figures in the 'watcher' series,
and all the indications we have point to its having rather a northerly location. However, what is particularly important about this
text is that 'absent rowers' are first mentioned in connexion with
Echelawon and the *Lawagetas*. These men we have already found
associated on the land text discussed above (p. 100) and they were
undoubtedly among the most exalted personages of the kingdom.
Since other entries of this text list men at other stations known to

us from the other rower texts, this is precious testimony for the association of the two men, and particularly of the War-Leader, with these dispositions. The text is mutilated, but what is clear is that the scribe is concerned to record where these 'absent rowers are stationed. The word which occurs after the War-Leader and *Ekhelawon* (and also after one *Me-nu-wa*) is obscure, but I am inclined to think that it is a place-name. If this can be substantiated, then it is of the greatest importance as giving the station of the War-Leader and Echelawon when these rower dispositions were recorded. The word is spelt *a-pe-e-ke*, and it is probably identical with a place which is elsewhere spelt either *a-pe-ke-e* or *a-pe-ke-i-jo*. There are many places with this type of double name, and it is clear that they are of the pattern *Newcastle-upon-Tyne*. That is to say a name which recurs in several localities is more closely identified by adding the name of its district. Thus *A-pe* will have been in the district *Ke-e*; this district name also occurs in the adjectival form *Ke-i-jo*.

Again we are fortunate in having information which enables us to fix the location of this district. As we shall see from the series recording the location of the women and children, *Ke-e* is in the Further Province, and this is further supported by one of the rower stations. *Po-ti-ja-ke-e* (see list above) is again one of the double place-names: it consists of *Po-ti-ja* plus the district name *Ke-e*. Better still, yet another text lists this place next to *Ra-wa-ra-ti-ja*, and this in the 'canonical' order of the 'Bronze' tablet (p. 110) is listed as the second of the Seven places of the Further Province next to *Ti-mi-to-a-ke-i*, which we site close to the river Nedon. Thus our analysis suggests that the 'War-Leader' at the time when the tablet was written had his HQ at *a-pe-e-ke* (*a-pe-ke-e*?) well within the Messenian Gulf.

These clues, delicate and fragile though they are, are precious enough. Before turning to yet another aspect of these arrangements it must be insisted that rejection of the deduction concerning the HQ would not affect our conclusions about the order and location of the 'rowers' and their relation to the stations of the 'watchers'. These are quite separate investigations, and stand by themselves. We repeat: it can hardly be an accident that the rowers fill the gap observed in the chain of the 'watchers'.

147

Further enlightenment on the war-emergency arrangements came unexpectedly from quite a different study. I was interested in establishing the ration scales and their relation to the various groups of craftsmen listed in these complex texts (see p. 125ff). To lay a firm foundation of fact it was first necessary to compile the dossiers of the persons mentioned by indexing the texts. In this detailed work it gradually became clear that one group of places recurred so often that this could not be due to chance. *The places were all in the same general area as the rower stations.* One of these texts, distinguished by the word *ke-ro-si-ja*, has already been discussed above (p. 111). Here we are interested only in the locations of the men concerned. Of the men credited with a *ke-ro-si-ja* the first two are both from the place *E-ni-pa-te-we*, and this is near *A-ke-re-wa*. Moreover the second of these two men is listed among the 'Potnia' smiths; that is to say he is connected with the temple organization. The last entry on our text ascribes a *ke-ro-si-ja* to one *A-pi-qo-ta*. This man's dossier records him as a *pa₂-si-re-u* (see p. 111) in charge of secular bronze-smiths at *A-pe-ke-e*. Thus all three lines of enquiry evoke the same theme 'bronze-working'. More important in the present connexion is that they lead to the places mentioned in the geographical area of the rowers.

The mention of a *pa₂-si-re-u* brings us back once again to the difficult *pa₂-si-re-wi-ja* text, the craftsman context of which has been already established (p. 127). What now interests us are the geographical indications. A new text from the palace workshop, recovered in 1957, has shown that the persons who are credited in the *pa₂-si-re-wi-ja* text with 'slaves' receive men in the new text. What is significant is that these allocations are recorded in paragraphs headed *Potnia Iqeia* and *Po-ti-a-ke-i-ja Potnia*.[1] Thus these men will have come from the temple establishments of the 'Mistresses' in question. But it is the place mentioned which is significant in this context. For *Po-ti-ja-ke-e*, as we saw, was one of the 'rower' stations. Yet another fragmentary tablet can now be put in its correct place in the jigsaw puzzle. It is headed *I-qe-* [and it also mentions the personalities of the *pa₂-si-re-wi-ja* text,

---

[1] The precise form of the first word is in doubt, but it is clearly some form of the place-name *Po-ti-a-ke-e*.

including the first person recorded, one *A-ki-to*. Again the indications are convergent as to location and consistent as to subject. The conclusion is plain: we are dealing with postings of craftsmen, especially bronze-smiths, in the area of the rower stations.

The evidence at this stage of the investigation continued to pile up. There was a pair of texts written in the same hand and both headed by a simple prepositional phrase: 'Along with *X*'. Again every dossier which could be compiled for the persons listed led to bronze-smith contexts. In the case of the first tablet the person in charge, *A-ta-o*, was known from a 'bronze' tablet to be at *A-pe-ke-e*! Moreover, the first man listed as being 'with *A-ta-o*' was also listed after him in the next line of the same 'bronze' tablet. Thus there could be no doubt about the identity of the two men, who are listed adjacently in the same order in both tablets. All other 'clicks' were consistent. Particularly noteworthy was the fact that smiths in *A-ta-o*'s company were from *A-ke-re-wa* and the near-by place *Ro-u-so*: *A-ke-re-wa* is a 'rower' station. The other text produced fewer echoes, but it actually has an entry 'with the bronze-smiths', so that again there is no doubt about the consistency of the contexts, which in any case is assured by the identity of the 'hand' and the parallelism of the lay-out in this pair of texts. The sole personnel 'click', moreover, leads to yet another text which lists master bronze-smiths. They include one who has a *pa₂-si-re-wi-ja* in the text we have so often had occasion to study. Thus the circle is complete. It remains to add that a geographical pointer in this last text locates the person concerned at *Ka-ra-do-ro*. Once more we are in southern Messenia and at a station of 'rowers'.

It would be possible to pile up further detailed evidence of this kind which has resulted simply from meticulous indexing of the available material. It would merely serve to confirm the general picture which has emerged. The main concentration of 'rowers' (and would it be 'incautious' to imply the Pylian fleet?) was in Southern Messenia and units of craftsmen were being detailed to the same general area. Perhaps it would not be over-bold to entertain the notion that these bronze-smiths were to be employed as armourers. But we must not forget that the *pa₂-si-re-wi-ja* texts list various types of craftsmen, including 'bakers' and others whose sphere of activity is 'chariots'. The total impression is that these scattered texts reflect the assembly of artificers assigned to military duties.

We may now add another text which records 'masons going to build'. Some of the men are recorded at Pylos and Leuktron, these being, as we have seen, the 'capitals' of the Hither and the Further Provinces respectively. The other masons are 'bound for *Me-te-to* and *Sa-ma-ra*'. The first of these places is in the Hither Province near *Ro-u-so*, which appears to lie a little to the north of *Ri-jo*. That is to say it lies in the most southerly part of the Hither Province. *Sa-ma-ra*, in the 'canonical' order of the Seven, lies to the south of *Ra-wa-ra-ti-ja*. So it cannot be far from *Po-ti-ja-ke-e*, and this place recurs both in the dispositions of the rowers and the associated bronze-smiths. Ventris and Chadwick had already suggested that these 'masons' might have been detailed for work on fortifications. Our detailed analysis has supported this guess.

It remains to add that the rations recorded for this group of masons on the normal scale discussed above would last the twelve men listed for precisely twenty days. Since the participle is in the future tense, this figure must represent an estimate by the palace administration of the probable time required. The round figure of twenty days is suggestive. It is known that the Greeks divided their month into periods of ten days.

There is one other small point of detail in this 'masons' text which deserves attention. A ration of wine is recorded in addition to wheat. The proportion of wheat to wine is 4 : 3, when reduced to 'choenices' (=litres). It so happens that we have another pair of texts which list allocations of barley and wine respectively. There, too, we find the ratio 4 : 3. This coincidence of ratio with entirely different sets of figures can hardly be an accident. It enables us to say that the Mycenaean craftsman received as his basic daily allowance one 'choenix' (roughly one litre) of wheat and three-quarters of a litre of wine. We may compare this with the allowance negotiated with the Athenians for the Spartan élite troops trapped on Sphacteria in the Peloponnesian War. They received two *choenices* of barley and only two 'cups' (*kotylae*), that is half a *choenix*, of wine. Their Helot servants had to content themselves, like Mycenaean slaves, with half this amount. Thus the allowance of wine made to the Mycenaean worker was about half as much again as the half-choenix negotiated for the Spartans.

We are by no means finished with the echoes which the 'rower' tablets evoke from the Pylian archives. One group of forty rowers (a number which recurs and is likely to be the complement of a warship) is described as *Da-mi-ni-jo*. This is an adjective from a place with a name like *Damnos*. This entry links up with one from an entirely different set of tablets, one of which records women called *Da-mi-ni-ja*, which is the corresponding feminine form. We have already had occasion to study these texts in connexion with the rations. There are three sets. What we may call set *A* simply lists the women, children and their locations, together with the male and female supervisors indicated by the ideograms DA and TA. Set *B* repeats the same data, though there are some modifications of detail, and records in addition the monthly ration allocations (fig. 15). Set *C* lists men who are described as *ko-wo* of the various groups of women. We may consider this last set now.

Some of these *ko-wo* texts have glosses. The one relating to the 'young men' (this must be the meaning of the word here; the Greek word *korwos* can mean either 'boy' or 'youth of military age') of the *Da-mi-ni-ja* carries a note which is best translated 'willing to row'. Yet another text of this set refers to the *korwoi* of the women *Ti-nwa-ti-ja* and the gloss written above refers to 'rowers at *A-pu-ne-we*'. This links up with the rower station *A-po-ne-we*, which is on the far side of *Ri-jo* and hence in the Further Province. Some scholars have denied the connexion between the two because of the slight difference of spelling, but there are plenty of parallels for the interchange of *u* and *o*, and in any case the two 'rower' references in these texts surely provide mutual support. There can be no doubt about the connexion between the *Da-mi-ni-ja* and the *Da-mi-ni-jo*. So it would be attributing too much to coincidence to assert that the other 'rower' reference in these same texts has an otherwise completely unknown Greek verb (this has been asserted) which happens to counterfeit the name of another 'rower' station.

We now turn to the consideration of Lists *A* and *B* which deal with the women and children. Thanks to E. L. Bennett's fundamental study of these texts we know that two scribes were responsible for set *A*. One of these men listed the women stationed at different places within the Hither Province, the other scribe those in the Further Province. In set *B* the same facts are recorded, but this time the monthly rations are entered on the scales discussed above. Two facts are significant. One is that there are many discrepancies of detail about the composition of the groups. This suggests a fluid situation, and this impression is strengthened by the occasional notes entered in set *C*, for instance, that '*X* did not arrive'. Another curious fact is that set *B* records rations only for the groups in the Hither Province. Now the majority of these are centred on Pylos, whereas the main concentration place for the Further Province is *Re-u-ko-to-ro*=Leuktron. It seems probable, therefore, that groups stationed in the Further Province received their rations from Leuktron, which may well have been the 'capital' of that province. This further implies that there was a palace there and it was there that the records pertaining to missing ration allocations were kept. The important Mycenaean site discovered by Professor McDonald and Mr. Hope-Simpson at Rizomylo (fig. 13) may well be *Re-u-ko-to-ro*. It lies on the road linking Pylos with the Further Province, and it would be reasonable to suppose that the two 'capitals' were so linked.

Most of the designations applied to the women can be interpreted as derivatives from names of places: e.g. 'women of Adrastus', 'women of Cnidus', 'women of Cythera', 'women of Milatus', 'women of Carystus', 'women of Rhamnus' and so on. In the earlier stages of the decipherment and interpretation these names were hastily identified with names far from Pylos, such as Miletus and Cnidus in Asia Minor, Chios and Lemnos and so on. However, names like these may have occurred widely in Greece and the Aegean. A Miletus is known also from Crete, while both Corinthus and even Amnisus occur in the Pylian tablets in contexts which leave little room for doubt that they are to be sought in Pylian territory. While most of the designations of the women, as we have said, are derived from place-names, there is a small nucleus of occupational descriptions which recur elsewhere in connexion with cloth-making. Others again are simply called 'handmaidens' (*amphipoloi*). One curious group is labelled 'surplus', a Greek word which is best taken in this context as 'miscellaneous'. This category carries a note written above the line which I have interpreted as meaning 'wage-earners and ancillaries'. Regardless of the correctness of these details of interpretation, the picture which emerges is one of the concentration of the women from the various villages of the kingdom into two areas adjacent to its two main centres: Pylos, the seat of the palace, and Leuktron, the 'capital' of the Further Province, with minor groupings elsewhere. We have noted the connexions with the rower tablets.

It remains to add another text which shows that some women and children were being assigned emergency tasks. It lists three groups of women, also known from the above sets, together with their children, who now are simply lumped together without the distinction of sex observed in the detailed inventory. The tablet is headed by a single word 'grain pourers' (*sitokhowoi*). The entry has been compared by Dr F. Tritsch with arrangements made in preparation for the siege of Plataea at the outbreak of the Peloponnesian War, when the non-military population was evacuated and only one hundred and ten women retained as *sitopoioi* 'breadmakers'. The number of 'grain pouring' women and children of the Pylian text is ninety.

The overall picture of emergency which is evoked by all this detailed study is unmistakable. Inevitably voices of doubt and 'caution' have been raised, but such caution may be dispelled by closer acquaintance with the facts. We have said, and now repeat, that the archive is permeated with this sense of emergency. We give one illustration of how it penetrates to the most unlikely corners.

A long series of texts records the assessment of Pylian villages for the delivery of some commodity the nature of which has been in doubt. Every now and again there is a note saying that such and such a group of men 'have' a certain number of units of the commodity in question. It was evident from the first examination of these texts that these groups were the same men who reappeared in the 'watcher' texts. A Swiss scholar, Dr H. Mühlestein, then noted that the number of units of the commodity recorded as 'had' was the same as the number of men in the corresponding

'watcher' groups. Thus it was evident that each man had been
issued with one unit of this substance apiece. This ruled out the
previous suggestion that this substance was 'flax'; for what would
these men on guard duty be doing with a unit of flax apiece? The
only other possibility for the substance in question was 'linseed'.
But could this be conceivably an emergency ration? By a most
extraordinary coincidence one of the few references we have in
classical literature to linseed is in connexion with the Spartans
trapped on Sphacteria. Thucydides records the desperate attempts
made by the Spartans to bring supplies to their soldiers. 'Under-
water swimmers swam through the harbour towing after them, by
means of a cord, bags containing poppyseed mixed with honey and
pounded linseed. At first they eluded discovery but then watch
was kept for them. In every way both sides were up to tricks, the
one trying to send in provisions and the other out to foil them.'

Thus alerted and organized, the Pylians awaited the attack
from the sea. The ruin of the palace and the fire that preserved the
archives to our own times are eloquent testimony that the attack
was successful. Pylos was blotted from the face of the earth and
its site was never again occupied by human habitations. The scene
must have been such as Homer painted:

'As when the smoke rising from a city reaches the bright sky far
from an island that foemen beset, and the day long they contend
in grievous strife from their city wall. At sundown the beacon fires
blaze in rows and the glare reaches aloft for their neighbours to
see in the hope that they will come in their ships and ward off
their doom.'

2. The Dorian Invasion?

The destruction of the Palace of Nestor at the end of the
Bronze Age of Greece was no isolated incident. The power and
influence of Mycenae had spread throughout the Eastern
Mediterranean during the fourteenth and the first half of the
thirteenth centuries. Then signs of insecurity begin to make
themselves apparent. The fortifications of Mycenae and Tiryns
were strengthened and remodelled so as to protect and secure
access to water supplies. Archaeologists have also thought to
observe symptoms of a decay in techniques, and regional ex-

clusiveness begins to impair the essential cultural unity which marked the hey-day of Mycenae. The Bronze Age of Greece ends with the storming and firing of all the major strongholds of Mycenaean power.

The agony of Greece at this time was part of a catastrophe that afflicted much of the Aegean and the Near East at the turn of the thirteenth to the twelfth century. The empire of the Hittites was swept away, and the onrush of the invaders by land and sea was checked only at the gates of Egypt when Rameses III hurled back the Peoples of the Sea. To which people can we attribute the over-throw of Mycenaean power in Greece? Professor Blegen began his dramatic excavation report of 1939 with the following passage.

'The Dorian Invasion, whatever its source and however it ran its course, has left a broad gash, like a fire-scar in a mountain forest, cutting through the archaeological panorama of ancient Greek history. Many towns and settlements that flourished in the preceding Heroic Age were henceforth abandoned or declined to a state of insignificance. Even some of the great and noted strong-holds sank into virtual oblivion, and the places where they had stood were lost from the view of men.'

Here Professor Blegen is not speaking solely as an archaeologist. The data provided by the excavated sites present simply a picture of destruction. The pottery of the following sub-Mycenaean period offers no positive clues to the identity of the aggressor or to the wholly different pattern of facts and distribution of peoples which the Greece of Hellenic times presents. That the Dorians were responsible is suggested in the first place by a study of the distribution of the Hellenic dialects and secondly by folk-memory.

A map showing the dialects of Greece in classical times (fig. 20) presents a strange appearance. In the centre of the Peloponnese, in the mountain fastness of Arcadia we have, as it were, a dialect island entirely surrounded by dialects of the Doric type. These Dorian dialects occupy Crete and the intervening islands as far as Rhodes. But virtually identical with the isolated Arcadian is the dialect of Cyprus. Philologists had concluded back in the last century that this distribution could be explained only by supposing that dialects of the Arcadian type had once extended to the coast of the Peloponnese and that Greeks of this type of speech had gone off to colonize Cyprus before they were overwhelmed and cut off by the invasion of the Dorians. As we have seen, this 'retrodicted' dialect, Arcado-Cypriot, is virtually identical with the

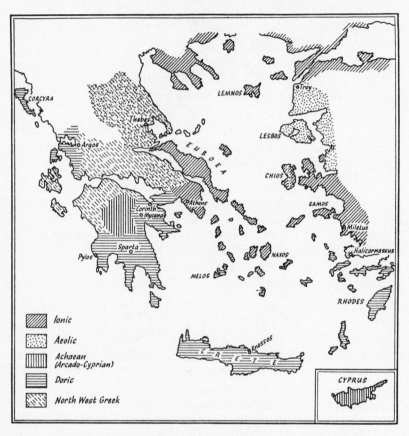

Fig. 20. The Distribution of the Greek dialects in Classical times.

one which we find in the Linear B tablets of the Peloponnese and Knossos. The Dorian dialects form a close unity with those on the northern side of the Gulf of Corinth which we call Northwest Greek. This dialect has also coloured to a great extent the dialects of Thessaly and Boeotia, which go together with that of Lesbos and the adjacent parts of Asia Minor. Thessalian,

156

The Last Days of Pylos

Boeotian and Lesbian together form the Aeolic group; Aeolic has much in common with the pre-Dorian dialects of the Peloponnese (Arcado-Cypriot). There has been much discussion of these complex dialect interrelations, but I adhere to the view that in Mycenaean times a group of dialects, the ancestors of the later Aeolic and Arcado-Cypriot, were spoken in the Mycenaean kingdoms of Thessaly, Boetia and the Peloponnese and that the Peloponnese was settled by immigrants from the northern kingdoms. We know nothing directly about the dialect of Attica at this time, but in my view other evidence points to the existence of a distinct dialect in this area even at this early date. The disruption of this linguistic picture of the Mycenaean age was due to the incursion of the Dorians. Only this historical postulate can account for the patterning and distribution of the Doric dialects in later times.

We could at a pinch suppose that the destruction was due to the action of unknown aggressors X, and that the Dorians later merely took advantage of this situation of weakness to infiltrate from their previous abodes somewhere in the north-western regions. This would be a classical example of the use of a superfluous hypothesis. In fact Greek folk memory is unusually clear and consistent on the subject of the coming of the Dorians. The legends relating to those movements are connected with 'The Return of the Sons of Heracles'.

We may now ask 'What happened afterwards?' To answer this question we must turn to Athens. Like Mycenae and Tiryns the Acropolis, the site of a Mycenaean palace, 'the well-built house of Erechtheus', had been the scene of feverish refortification in the latter part of the thirteenth century B.C. A squatters' quarter outside the walls was hastily abandoned and, to guard against the possibility of an interruption to the water supplies lying outside the walls, a shaft was sunk to the depth of 120 feet below the level of the acropolis. Professor Broneer has shown that the construction of the stairway in timber work, soon liable to rot, argues hurried preparations to meet an emergency. In fact after no very long time the stairs collapsed and the shaft was never used again. It is evident that Athens weathered the storm.

To fill in the picture we must again turn to legend. It was a proud boast of the Athenians that their land had never been conquered. The onslaught of the invading Dorian tribes was met in the valley of the Ilissos, and success was assured by the voluntary sacrifice of their king Codrus. A curious feature of this traditional tale is that king Codrus was no Athenian, but one of the Neleid dynasty, who had come as a refugee from Pylos. It is no accident that the Athenians revered his ancestor Neleus and his consort Basile (The Queen) in a joint sanctuary near the acropolis. That Athens was a gathering ground and a rallying point for Mycenaean refugees in the troubled period of the Dorian invasion has received some slight confirmation from a new Pylos tablet.

This has to be considered along with other evidence which has suggested a new answer to a long-standing puzzle presented by Greek heroic names. When an invading people succeeds in establishing itself as a warrior aristocracy in a conquered country, we should expect to find the largest proportion of their own native names among the earliest generation. As time passes these will gradually be diluted with foreign names from the subjugated population as the result of marriage with indigenous women. Such is the case with the Gaulish invaders of Galatia in Asia Minor. Scholars have long been puzzled to note that the reverse is apparently true for Heroic Greece. Thus Atreus has not been analysable as an Indo-European name, whereas Agamemnon ('he who abides fast') and Menelaus ('he who stays the war-host') are perfectly transparent. However, it must be stressed that present opinion in the matter of these proper names is merely a confession of failure. No one has been able to point to Aegean or Anatolian names with the ending -*eus* or full names of which Atreus and all the rest could be naturalizations. What scholars have said is that given certain principles of analysis they still cannot take *Neleus* and the like to pieces and arrive at Indo-European components. This is the sole line of enquiry which has led to the doctrine that these names are non-Greek and therefore Pre-Greek. However, it has proved possible to suggest a way out of this impasse.

We are now in a position to see that the names in -*eus* are nothing more than abbreviated forms of full names, much as we say *Nicky* for *Nicholas*. Now many Greek names are agent nouns, such as *Men-tōr*, *Ak-tōr*, *Hek-tōr*, *Kas-tōr*. Here -*tōr* is simply the agent suffix which we also meet in Latin words like *actor*. The same verbs also occur in compound names, of a type which is found among most Indo-European peoples. Thus we have *Mene-lāwos*, *Age-lāwos*, *Eche-lāwos* and so on, where *lāwos* means 'folk, warriors'. Now *Nes-tōr* plainly belongs to this type of agent nouns functioning as names. The verb *nes* occurs in Greek in the sense 'return safely', but proper names often preserve a more archaic sense; and the evidence of other related languages shows that this verb once had the meaning 'save, rescue'. Thus parallel to the series *Mene-lawos* we can expect a name *Nese-lawos* ('he who saves the folk'). This name, however, was obscured in Greek by a sound change: an -*s*- in Greek became an aspirate and then was lost in between vowels. A plain example of this change is the word for 'seven', *hepta*, corresponding to Latin *septem*. Thus our name should appear in Greek as *Ne(h)elawos*. This name is now actually attested in a Pylos tablet. But these names were often abbreviated and then received the ending -*eus*. In the dialect of the region from which Nestor's father came the shortened form of the name would be *Nēleus*. We may add that it is common in Greek naming habits for the son to receive a name containing merely a part of his father's name. Thus all fits perfectly and Nestor's father Neleus had after all a good Indo-European name, half of which he duly bequeathed to the son who succeeded him as King of Pylos.

It is of interest to our theme to pursue further the fortunes of this dynastic name. If carried to Athens the name *Ne(h)e-lawos*, according to all the rules, which are well established, would assume the form *Neileōs*. It is precisely a name of this form which is given in the legends to a son of King Codrus, the Pylian saviour of Athens. It was this *Neileōs* who led the Greeks overseas to found the colony of Miletus on the seaboard of Asia Minor. The new evidence that this very name was actually in use in Mycenaean Pylos encourages the belief that some historical reality lies at the heart of the foundation legend with its Pylian connexions.

The evidence presented thus forms a coherent pattern. In the sixteenth century a dynasty of chariot lords appears in Mycenae in the Shaft Grave Period. By the end of the fifteenth century Mycenae had established its supremacy. Knossos fell and during the next century and a half the influence of Mycenae spread widely in the eastern Mediterranean. A period of uncertainty then set in, marked by a preoccupation with defence. After 1200 B.C. came collapse and widespread destruction, which may be attributed most reasonably to those Greek tribes known later as the Dorians. This invasion, as Professor Wade-Gery has emphasized, split the Greek world into two hostile camps, the Dorian and the Ionian (in which Attica is included of course). It is this antagonism which stamps the Hellenic world of post-Mycenaean times and culminated in the Peloponnesian war. The traditions of Mycenae lived on in unconquered Athens and were transplanted to the new colonial world of Ionia. But Pylos also sent its contingents direct, if we may believe the early poet Mimnermus of Colophon, who sings of the time 'when we left Pylos and came by ship to lovely Asia'. So two streams of Mycenaean memory fed the poetic spring of Ionian Homer. How much detail was faithfully preserved in the glacial flow of bardic tradition has been brilliantly illuminated by the opening of the archives of the Mycenaean palaces. It remains true, however, that no account of Mycenaean civilization based on Homer resembles the temple organization of the priest-king which has gradually taken shape from the patient analysis of the Linear B tablets.

3. EPILOGUE: A MYCENAEAN TOMB INVENTORY

The *Iliad* ends with a funeral: its closing words are: 'In this way were they busied with the funeral of horse-taming Hector.' Our account of the archives of Pylos may also fittingly conclude with a set of tablets which I believe is an inventory of the royal tomb. It should be said at once that this interpretation has been disputed and also that the dispute is merely about one word. What is not in doubt or controversy is that the document is an inventory of household effects and of the greatest importance and interest to archaeologists. It begins with cooking vessels and the appurtenances of the hearth and then moves on to tables, chairs and footstools. There can be no doubt that the whole set of objects is connected with preparations for a feast. The gorgeous character of this furniture will emerge from the translation given below. From this it will be clear that no archaeological finds from Greek lands had given us any idea that furniture of this luxuriousness adorned the palaces of the Mycenaean kings. The nearest parallel is offered by the tomb of Tutankhamen.

The document in question consists of thirteen tablets and, as usual, the scribe has told us in the introductory sentence which begins the first tablet on what occasion the document was written. There were two rival versions of this sentence and they agreed in all details except for the last word. Since it has turned out that I was wrong in my analysis, the point may be elaborated in order to bring out the uncertainties which beset the interpretation of the Linear B texts. The word on which all else turns in the translation of the key sentence describing the circumstance when the objects were listed is *da-mo-ko-ro*. No word corresponding to this group of syllables is to be found in the lexicon of post-Mycenaean Greek, and the first step must be to diagnose the word category. This is done by listing the words which occur in corresponding positions in other texts, and it so happens that we have a text in two paragraphs which are repetitive. The word in the second paragraph which corresponded to *da-mo-ko-ro* was *te-po-se-u*, and this was known to be a proper name. The conclusion was that *da-mo-ko-ro* belonged to the same word class. Now a second test was made. When the syllabic groups were applied to the dictionary of proper names known from later times, the only 'click' was *Damoklos*, a shortened form of *Damoklewes*. On the evidence available in 1955 the probabilities lay in taking *da-mo-ko-ro* as a proper name. Ventris (with the adhesion of Chadwick), however, guessed the word to be the title of a Mycenaean functionary, but they could bring no evidence for this. Recently a young Belgian scholar, J. P. Olivier, while working at Knossos, succeeded in joining two scraps of tablet. The resulting text showed that *da-mo-ko-ro* was in parallel with a word known to be the title of an official — the *du-ma* (see p. 106). This reduced the area of uncertainty to the key verb *te-ke*, which is agreed to stand for *thēke*. Unfortunately this is a verb of wide meaning in Greek, and in the context as now established it may be translated either 'appointed' or 'buried'. Ventris and Chadwick translated the key sentence as follows: 'Thus P. made inspection on the occasion when the king appointed Sigewas to be a *damo-koros*.' Their general interpretation was that the document is the inventory of a gorgeous reception room. However, there were some queer things. One of the tripod cauldrons on the hearth is described as 'one tripod cauldron of Cretan workmanship, burnt away at the legs, useless'. This seems an odd item to figure in a luxurious reception room at a grand feast of investiture. Moreover, one of the tablets records swords and, I believe, double-axes and gold necklaces. This whole tablet again offered difficulties, and in *Documents in Mycenaean Greek* (p. 348) the authors admit that the entry hardly fits into the other tablets in the series.

There remains the other possible meaning of the Greek verb: 'buried'. If this is chosen, most of the material difficulties disappear. Damaged items constantly appear, for instance, in later temple inventories: they are preserved because of their sacred character. More significant is that swords and necklaces are a common part of tomb furniture; but most telling is the presence of double-axes, for this object is believed to have been the symbol of the goddess who presided over the dead. The tomb hypothesis would also explain the curious disparity in the numbers of tables, chairs and footstools listed in the inventory: 10 tables, 5 chairs and 14 footstools. There seems to be no reason to believe that the set of tablets is incomplete, and a curious scene is conjured up if these are really the furnishings of a luxurious reception room. One may wonder who were the privileged guests at this feast held to celebrate the installation of the *da-mo-mo-ro*. Who sat on the five chairs at the ten tables, doubtless with a footstool apiece, while the food was cooking in the useless tripod cauldron with its burnt away legs?

Common sense still continues to favour the interpretation of the verb *te-ke* as 'buried'. *85-ke-wa* the *da-mo-ko-ro* is no less mortal than *85-ke-wa Damoklos*. I still prefer to believe that the inventory records what was inspected when the King buried *85-ke-wa* the *Da-mo-ko-ro*. It is significant that on the above-mentioned text the title alone is sufficient to identify the man: he is *the Da-mo-ko-ro*, and other texts testify to the importance of this personage (see p. 100). The introductory sentence should thus read: 'What *Pu-ke-qi-ri* saw when the Wanax buried *85-ke-wa* the *Da-mo-ko-ro*.'

The Last Days of Pylos

A translation of the whole text follows. Many of the details of the decoration are obscure but the renderings here suggested will not be far wrong.

One jug, decorated with Mother Goddess, bull's head(s), and shell pattern.
One jug, decorated with chariot scene and throng of soldiers.
One jug, decorated with Mother Goddess, women, bull's head(s), and spiral pattern.

Three boiling pans, with spiral pattern. Two jars with filters(?). One ladle. Six shovels. One brush. Two firetongs. One fire-rake. One portable hearth, with splay legs, footed. One portable hearth, with upright legs, decorated with flame-pattern and rosettes. One tripod cauldron, of Cretan workmanship, with lynx-head (? ? ?) protomes. One tripod cauldron, of Cretan workmanship, with a *keiris* bird (? ? ?) on it.

Two tripod cauldrons, of Cretan workmanship, with goat's head protomes. One tripod cauldron, with one foot, with ear-shaped handles. One tripod cauldron, of Cretan workmanship, with the legs burnt off. Three urns. One jar, large, with four handles. Two jars, large, with three handles. One jar, small, with four handles. One jar, small, with three handles. One jar, small, with no handles.

One table, of stone and crystal, inlaid with undulations[1] of cyanus, tin (? ? ?) and gold, with nine feet. One table, of stone (and some other material), inlaid with ivory, worked with rosettes and helmets. One table, of stone, splay-legged, with nine feet, the feet and the support of ivory worked with spirals.

One table, of stone, with supports of ebony and ivory, splay legged, with nine feet, worked with spirals. One table, of ivory, with marble shaft, decorated with feather pattern, with six feet, worked with spirals. One table, of ebony, with ivory supports, splay-legged, with nine feet, decorated with shell pattern.

[1] Another translation, also possible, reads 'aquamarines'. The word means literally 'sea-water'.

The Last Days of Pylos

One table, of ebony, with ivory supports, splay-legged, with nine feet, decorated with shell pattern. One table, of (some kind of material) and ivory, splay-legged. One table of (some kind of material) and ivory, with marble shaft. Two tables, of yew wood, splay-legged, with box-wood shaft, with nine feet, decorated with spiral pattern, inlaid with tin (???).

One chair, of ebony with golden birds on the back (or sides?), and a footstool inlaid with ivory rosettes. One chair, of ebony, with back (or sides?) of ivory worked with a pair of stag's (?) heads and the figure of a man and heifers. One footstool, of ebony, inlaid with ivory rosettes.

One chair, of ebony, with back (sides?) inlaid with ivory. One chair, of ebony, with the back (sides?) of ivory, with stag's (?) heads and with human figures. One footstool, of ebony, inlaid with ivory human figures and lions.

One chair, of crystal, inlaid with cyanus, tin (?) and gold, the back (sides?) inlaid with golden human figures and a pair of stag's (?) heads and golden bull's heads and with golden palm trees (or palmettes) and with palm trees (or palmettes) of cyanus. One footstool, inlaid with cyanus and tin (?) and gold, with golden struts.

One footstool, inlaid with ivory rosettes and spiral and flower bud (???). Three footstools inlaid with ivory rosettes, and flame-pattern and a spiral. One footstool, inlaid with ivory rosettes and flame-pattern. One footstool inlaid with ivory rosettes and flame-pattern. One footstool inlaid with ivory rosettes.

One footstool, inlaid with ivory man, horse, polypod and palmette. One footstool, inlaid with ivory lion's heads and flame pattern. One footstool, inlaid with ivory flower buds (???).

The last text of this set (it must be emphasized that all were written by the same man and they were found together) at first sight falls right out of this framework of household equipment. All students of the text agree that it lists a pair of swords. An unhappy suggestion of my own, made within a few days of re-

164

ceiving the first copies of the texts in 1953, has received a warmer welcome than it deserved. I thought that the next item on the tablet referred to the rivets on the sword, and I translated 'with golden rivets round the hilt'. But it is extremely unlikely that the taker of the inventory would have listed the two rivets as separate items. Moreover, our greater understanding of the syllabary (my suggestion was made in December 1953) now makes it difficult to take the key word in the sense 'rivets'. I have recently reconsidered the whole problem and come to the conclusion that this tablet lists, in addition to the two swords, two golden necklaces and a pair of double axes.

All these items are at home in Mycenaean tombs. Swords need no elucidation. Apropos of a tomb at Knossos, the Chieftain's Grave, Sir Arthur Evans has written (*PoM*, iv, 861 f.) that 'with the skeleton itself had been placed the relics most distinctive of his rank and military profession — his gold necklace, his long and his short sword. That gold necklaces, like the torques of Gaulish warriors, served as a sign of rank or distinction may be gathered from more than one pictorial and sculptural record'. As for the double-axe, it is familiar as a religious symbol to all students of the Mycenaean-Minoan world, and it is likely that it stands for the Mother Goddess, whose cult name was Wanassa, The Queen. We may now note a curious echo. The inventory begins with libation jugs. Their decoration is said to be either Wanassa or Chariot Scene. Thus the libation jugs, which occupy pride of place in the inventory, echo with their decoration the symbolism of double-axes (= Mother Goddess) on the one hand, and swords plus gold necklaces (= Warrior) on the other. Thus this text which offered such difficulties to the reception room hypothesis fits smoothly into a tomb inventory.

It is not known on what occasion this Mycenaean lord met his death in those final months of Pylos's existence. That the King himself officiates is significant. Archaeologists have unearthed scores of Mycenaean tombs. The most magnificent are, of course, the famous tholoi of Mycenae, dominated by the huge Treasury of Atreus. That these great tombs were once equipped in a style worthy of golden Mycenae cannot be doubted. The plundering of tomb robbers throughout the ages has, however, left only a few

SUMMARY OF EMERGENCY DISPOSITIONS AT PYLOS

Watchers	Rowers	Bronze-smiths etc.	Women and Children
HITHER PROVINCE I HQ of Klymenos near *Me-ta-pa*. Count Alektryon son of Eteocles. 110 men.			ME-TA-PA
II HQ of Statiboeus at *To-wa* (?). 60 men.			
III HQ of Tros at *Ro-o-wa*. 110 men.			
IV HQ of *Ke-wo-nos*. Count Loukios son of Kyrsamenos. 80(+) men.			
V HQ of *Ma-re-u* at *O-wi-to-no* (probably near Kyparissia). 50 men.			O-WI-TO-NO
VI HQ of Nedwatas. Count Kerkios. Count *Ai-ko-tas*. 80 men.			**PYLOS**
VII HQ of Warpalos at *Ne-wo-ki-to* (north of *A-ke-re-wa*). Count Pherephonios Areios. Count Diwieus. Man entry defective. 20 +	E-WI-RI-PO		
VIII HQ of Dunios at *A-ke-re-wa*. Count *Di-ko-na-ro* son of Adrastos. Count Pleuronios. Count *Ka-e-sa-menos* of *A-pu$_x$-ka*. 80 men.	A-KE-RE-WA WO-QE-WE	A-KE-RE-WA RO-U-SO	RO-U-SO
IX HQ of *A-ki-nos*, south of *A-ke-re-wa*. 110 + men.		KA-RA-DO-RO ME-TE-TO	
	RI-JO		
FURTHER PROVINCE	WI-NU-RI-JO TE-TA-RA-NE A-PO-NE-WE MA-RA-NE-NU-WE PO-TI-JA-KE-E ZA]-KU-SI-JO	SA-MA-RA PO-TI-JA-KE-E	KE-E PYLOS-IN-
Contingent at *Za-e-to-ro*	ZA-E-TO-RO	 A-PE-KE-E	RA-WA-RA-TI-JA
X HQ of Erkhomenatas at *Ti-mi-to-a-ke-i*			**LEUKTRON**

miserable fragments of all the treasure once stored there for the honour and delectation of the dead. Professor G. E. Mylonas has written (*Ancient Mycenae*, p. 87): 'We wish it were possible for us to visualize the burial ritual held in this magnificent grave, to recover its interior as it was when the body of the last king was deposited on its floor or in the side chamber, and a solid wall was built across the *stomion*. But the contents of the grave were gone before the time of Pausanias, and all we have left is the varied pictures our imagination can provide as it is stimulated by the impressive and massive architectural remains.'

If our interpretation is right, then the archives of the Palace of Nestor have provided us with what may serve as an archaeological report on an unplundered royal tomb.

Part II

KNOSSOS AND AEGEAN HISTORY

In the following chapters it will be shown how gradual penetration of the Linear B texts and study of the Knossos excavation documents sapped confidence in the accepted accounts of Aegean history during the Late Bronze Age. For guidance in the tangle of archaeological hypotheses the following table may prove useful. It sets forth the relations between the two main cultures: the Minoan civilisation of Crete and the Helladic civilization of the Greek Mainland. The Late Helladic period is also known as Mycenaean. All dates are approximate and vary widely from author to author.[1] For my own revised account see pp. 360-1.

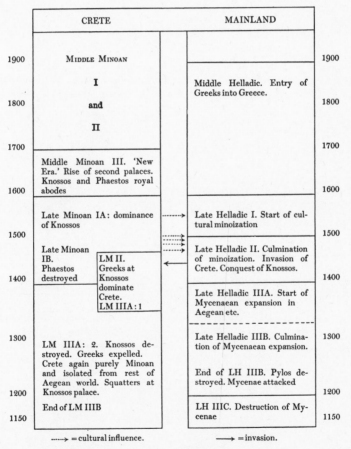

	CRETE	MAINLAND	
1900	MIDDLE MINOAN		1900
	I	Middle Helladic. Entry of Greeks into Greece.	
1800	and		1800
	II		
1700			1700
1600	Middle Minoan III. 'New Era.' Rise of second palaces. Knossos and Phaestos royal abodes		1600
1500	Late Minoan IA: dominance of Knossos	Late Helladic I. Start of cultural minoization	1500
1400	Late Minoan IB. Phaestos destroyed / LM II. Greeks at Knossos dominate Crete. LM IIIA:1	Late Helladic II. Culmination of minoization. Invasion of Crete. Conquest of Knossos.	1400
		Late Helladic IIIA. Start of Mycenaean expansion in Aegean etc.	
1300	LM IIIA: 2. Knossos destroyed. Greeks expelled. Crete again purely Minoan and isolated from rest of Aegean world. Squatters at Knossos palace.	Late Helladic IIIB. Culmination of Mycenaean expansion.	1300
		End of LH IIIB. Pylos destroyed. Mycenae attacked	
1200			1200
	End of LM IIIB	LH IIIC. Destruction of Mycenae	
1150			1150

------> = cultural influence.   ⟶ = invasion.

[1] Thus the Swedish scholar Paul Åström, like the Italian D. Levi, has argued that the beginning of Middle Minoan should be lowered by two hundred years.

Chapter VI

Crete and the Mainland

1. MINOANS AND GREEKS

The precise location of Mycenaean Pylos, though of absorbing interest to Homeric scholars, cannot be regarded as a matter of any great historical importance. Again, while the glimpses we catch of Pylian society in the last months of its existence as it ordered its affairs to meet the final attack have their fascination, they add nothing but human colour to the already established historical fact that the Palace of Nestor was destroyed at much the same time as other major Mycenaean sites. More shattering was the impact of the decipherment on a major problem which had long bitterly divided Aegean archaeologists. It presents itself almost as a conflict of scholarly vested interests. Heinrich Schliemann, it will be recalled, had put his trust in Homer and found the objects of his dreams: the site of Troy and the palace of the King of Mycenae who had organized and led the expedition which destroyed Troy. The Mycenaean civilization that gradually took archaeological shape through the labours of Schliemann and his many successors conjured up a rival some twenty-five years after its first discovery. It was in 1900 that Arthur Evans, firm in his belief that so glorious a civilization could not be illiterate, followed Homer's guidance and the trail of the inscribed seal-stones to Crete. His astonishing discoveries at Knossos in the first four seasons of his dig revealed an altogether new world, of an artistic refinement far surpassing that of the Shaft Graves. As the soil yielded its treasures Arthur Evans became more and more convinced that Mycenae was a mere provincial outpost, 'a transmarine offshoot', of an island empire ruled over by a Cretan king whose memory lived on in the legends about Minos. The word 'Mycenaean' itself gradually faded from his writings and was replaced by 'Minoan' even with reference to the culture of the mainland.

When the excavations at Knossos had reached their conclusion, it was clear that the hill of Kephala had been occupied by human settlements since Neolithic times. In the following Bronze Age three main layers could be distinguished, which Evans dubbed Early,[1] Middle and Late Minoan. This was a fundamental archaeological insight, and it was found applicable to the sites of the Cyclades and also the mainland (see Chronological Table, p. 360). The palace of the early period took the form of a group of blocks, and it was not until the period Evans called Middle Minoan III B (1700 b.c.) that the 'Palace of Minos' took its final shape as a complex building around a central court. Thereafter minor modifications were made and reconstructions necessitated by earthquake and other damage, but the palace remained essentially in the form assumed in the 'new era' of MM III B until what Evans believed to be its final destruction at the end of Late Minoan II (*c.* 1400 b.c.).

There was, however, ample evidence from close at hand that life still went on at Knossos in much the same way, although at a lower level of wealth, even after the 'final' destruction of the great palace. Some six hundred metres to the north of Knossos on the road to the sea a hill called Zafer Papoura begins to rise. There in 1904 Evans located a cemetery belonging to the Minoan town. In all some hundred tombs were excavated, and with few exceptions the contents belonged to the age succeeding the fall of the palace which is called by archaeologists Late Minoan III. During this period of the Minoan town Evans believed that there had also been an extensive reoccupation of the palace by 'squatters'. But, as he himself wrote, 'the tombs at Zafer Papoura show that even this blow (the destruction of the palace) did not seriously break the continuity of local culture.'

To this he could add evidence from the south of Crete. Close to Phaestos, where the Minoan palace vies with Knossos in its magnificence and surpasses it in the grandeur of its situation, Italian excavators had unearthed near the church of Hagia

[1] On Early Minoan, see now pp. 281-83 ff.

Triada ('Holy Trinity') a building which might have been a royal summer residence. Though of smaller dimensions, it was rich in artistic and other treasures. In particular it was here that the biggest hoard of Linear A tablets was found. It is considered probable that this palace, like that of Knossos, was built early in Middle Minoan III and was also destroyed at the end of LM I B (this is contemporary with Knossian 'LM II', which is the designation for a type of pottery peculiar to Knossos).[1] However, in the following period a building of the mainland type of megaron was constructed at Phaestos above the ruins of the previous palace. Still more remarkable was the discovery of the famous painted sarcophagus [Plate 12] 'in an unmixed LM III A deposit'. Evans firmly believed that all the evidence went to show that there was a revival of purely Minoan culture after the widespread destruction at the end of the Knossian LM II. He was certain that 'there is no room for a foreign settlement as yet in Crete'. In all these excavations 'we have a story of the ups and downs of insular life and of internecine struggles like those that ruined the later cities of Crete, but with no general line of cleavage such as might have resulted from a foreign invasion. There is no break. . . . The unity of civilization is such as almost to impose the conclusion that there was continuity of race.'

The spirit of the place entered into Evans; he seemed to put on the mask of the priest-king and seat himself on the gypsum throne in the Throne Room. Schliemann's great Mycenaean culture became 'the mainland branch of the Minoan culture at Mycenae'; Mycenaean was only a provincial variant of the same 'Minoan' civilization, and he refers to a subject race of Hellenic stock.

Evans's Knossocentric views had already hardened by 1912, which is the date of the paper from which we have taken our

---

[1] This fact is unchallenged among archaeologists. In the Chronological Table the above facts relating to Late Minoan I B would best be represented thus:

	Crete
1500	LM I B
1450	LM II
	Knossos
1400	only

175

quotations, and they were maintained by him until the end of his life. A summary restatement can be read in the lecture 'The Minoan World', which he gave on the occasion of the exhibition held in connexion with the fiftieth anniversary of the British School at Athens. Inevitably he referred to the discovery of clay documents illustrating the evolution of a highly developed linear script. It was a version of this lecture which was heard by the schoolboy Michael Ventris.

Long before this, however, evidence from excavations on the mainland had been refractory, and heretical views maintaining the independence of 'Helladic' culture begun to be expressed. Among these champions of the mainland was Mr A. J. B. Wace, then Director of the British School at Athens. Events may be left to speak for themselves. 'Disagreement with Evans contributed to Wace's retirement from the direction of the British School at Athens in 1923[1] and to his temporary exclusion from archaeology in the field' (*Documents in Mycenaean Greek*, p. 14). Wace persisted in his views and in 1939 he published, conjointly with C. W. Blegen, a reasoned statement of the facts which ran counter to the orthodox belief that Crete exercised a dominion over the Greek mainland down to the end of the Late Minoan period *c.* 1400 B.C.

Wace argued thus: 'If we went merely on the evidence of pottery and other artefacts we might maintain in the absence of historical documents that there was an Athenian domination of Etruria. The pattern of archaeological facts in the Aegean would be better explained if we imagine that the mainland and Crete were separate powers, the former merely adopting the outward trappings of a higher civilization. In Late Minoan II mainland power had advanced so much that it established control over Crete. This would account for the extremely mainland character of the Palace style. The destruction of the palace at the end of Late Minoan II (*c.* 1400) was then attributable to a native Cretan revolt over the Mycenaean overlords. This would account for the fact that in the subsequent period (LM III) Crete again has little connexion with the mainland but becomes again markedly Minoan.'

This view, though fairly stated by Pendlebury in his *Archaeology of Crete* (1939), was decisively rejected by him. For him

[1] For Evans's unreported excavations in 1923, see pp. 223–27.

archaeology is in perfect accord with the legends. Minos dominated the mainland and exacted cruel tribute from it. The story of Theseus mirrors dimly the successful revolt of the Mycenaean subjects. The sudden mainland influence on the Knossian 'Palace style' of LM II is explained away as resembling rather the Germanization of palace circles in England after Queen Victoria's marriage. It was not until the end of LM II that the blow fell.

'And in the last decade of the fifteenth century on a spring day, when a strong South wind was blowing which carried the flames of the burning beams almost horizontally northwards, Knossos fell.'

'The final scene takes place in the most dramatic room ever excavated — the Throne Room. It was found in a state of complete confusion. A great oil jar lay overturned in one corner, ritual vessels were in the act of being used when the disaster came. It looks as if the king had been hurried here to undergo too late some late ceremony in the hopes of saving the people. Theseus and the Minotaur! Dare we believe that he wore the mask of a bull?'

'Such imaginings may not be suitable to archaeology, but with this possibility in mind, I defy anyone to enter the Throne Room without a strange thrill.'

'Crete had fallen and henceforth she was to be a mere satellite of the world centring round Greece, gradually drawing nearer until she was absorbed in the general Hellenic culture which she herself had done so much to found.'

. . .'Where does the Achaean domination of Crete come? In Homer Idomeneus is King of Crete and vassal of Agamemnon. . . .

'It is possible to put forward a tentative theory that after letting Crete alone for some hundred and fifty years the mainlanders, with the rise of the new Dynasty at Mycenae, decided to bring it into the empire, which probably implied little more than the granting of the fief to some condottiere who made his home at Knossos[1] and concocted himself a pedigree reaching from the old royal family of Minos. It was in no sense an act of colonization.'

Such was the historical interpretation sustained in 1939 in the most authoritative handbook of Cretan archaeology. It should be added that Wace's contrary view received little support in the

---

[1] On the failure to unearth any Mycenaean residence at Knossos for this condottiere, see pp. 269 ff.

archaeological literature right down to the eve of the decipherment. In her *Homer and the Monuments* of 1950 Miss H. L. Lorimer observes that the relations between Crete and Greece in the period of the earliest *tholoi* are obscure. . . . But she holds that a militant Cretan dynasty established itself at Knossos leading to an efflux of refugees to the mainland from the devastated cities. Mycenae welcomed them. . . . 'With an ambitious trade policy (she) might fear Knossos as a rival and be glad to admit her enemies, especially if they did not come empty handed. . . .'

'. . . The "Minos" who in the latter half of the fifteenth century appears to have ruled all Crete doubtless kept a jealous and watchful eye on his formidable neighbour. . . .'

Thus though the facts are acknowledged to be obscure, the interpretation favoured is wholly in the spirit of Evans.

2. MID-CENTURY REPORT

We owe it to Ventris's extraordinary energy and enterprise that we have on record expressions of opinion by leading authorities on Aegean questions just before the decipherment. In 1949 he sent out a questionnaire on matters relating to Linear B and its archaeological background. The replies it elicited he embodied in a work published privately entitled *The Languages of the Minoan and Mycenaean Civilizations*. Distributed in 1950, it is known to initiates as 'Mid-Century Report'.

G. P. Carratelli of Florence found 'no reason to think that the language spoken in Crete in the period of Linear A texts was replaced by another during the brief period in which Knossos alone resisted the general decay of the Cretan centres on the eve of the Achaean invasion. The LM II phase peculiar to Knossos does not represent an interruption in the development of Cretan culture. . . .'

He argues from 'the recognition, shared by all, of the continuity of the Minoan cultural phases' to the 'identity of language in the two phases which these documents (Linear A and B) represent.'

As for the mainland, 'it seems possible to conclude now with relative certainty . . . that the *lingua aulica*, the language of administration of the official cults was identical with that which resounded in the Cretan palaces.' He compared the use of Latin in the middle ages.

E. Grumach, who was to become a bitter opponent of the decipherment, wrote 'general historical considerations make it improbable that it (the Minoan B language) belongs to the Indo-European language family'. . . .

'I do not believe that there is the slightest evidence for assuming that the language of the B tablets is not identical with that of A.' For Sir John Myres of Oxford the mainland use of Minoan B simply 'reflected Cretan cultural intercourse. . . .'

E. Peruzzi of Florence showed great caution but wrote: 'I am willing to say, however, that the Linear B language is closely related to that of Linear A.'

Fritz Schachermeyr of Vienna also regarded 'the use of the Minoan script and language of the Mycenaean mainland as a *cultural influence*. I think it very probable that Minoan scribes, themselves actually born in Crete, were employed as officials or as slaves in the offices of Mycenaean palaces and were responsible for carrying out the whole clerical work for their Mycenaean masters.

'It was not until after the second destruction of the palace at the end of LM II *c.* 1400 that it was conquered by the Achaeans from the mainland and partially settled by them.'

It remains to add that Wace himself had become more circumspect. In an article which actually appeared in 1953 after the publication of the decipherment, entitled 'The history of Greece in the third and second millennium B.C.', he was content to say: 'Perhaps then a mainland Dynasty had gained power at Knossos. Could the Palace period at Knossos in LM II have flourished under mainland rulers? Such a situation would help to explain Idomeneus's later position as a vassal of Agamemnon. This view is, however, still *sub judice*, and we must maintain an open mind towards it, though we can admit that there is some evidence in its favour. Further research on the Pylos tablets and the Knossian tablets may throw more light on the subject. . . . The future too may well bring discoveries of similar tablets at Mycenae or some other mainland site.' This hope was soon fulfilled by the excavations of Wace himself at Mycenae.

It is not in any spirit of malice that we have thus brought into the light the considered opinions of leading authorities on the eve of the decipherment. On the contrary, the world of scholarship, so often accused of stubborn and even malicious resistance to new truths, may here hold up its head. It should be recorded with pride that, with the exception of E. Grumach, all the professional scholars who had so firmly committed themselves on the eve of the decipherment, promptly acknowledged the achievement of the brilliant amateur and swallowed their discomfiture. But the lesson we must read is essential for our final chapter on the origin of the Greeks and the date of their first entry into their historical habitat. An unexampled wealth of material resources and brilliant intellectual gifts for three-quarters of a century had been concentrated on the problems of the prehistory of Greece and the Aegean. Yet it had proved impossible to secure a clear, agreed answer to the simplest of questions concerning the relationship between the powers of Crete and Greece. Above all, a change of ruling class and the domination of Crete by lords of Greek speech had apparently occurred without decisive clues in the material culture which it is the business of the archaeologist to recover. The basic principle of interpretation was firmly stated by Arthur Evans in one sentence: '*There is no break*'. Consequently, he concluded, there could be no foreign intrusion. This is a basic fact and a fundamental assumption that we meet throughout the archaeological literature: 'The unity of the whole civilization is such as almost to impose the conclusion that there was continuity of race.'

From a leading German authority in this field we welcome, for the important lesson it carries, a frank admission. In his excellent picture book *Kreta Mykene Troia* F. Matz writes: 'The discovery that the Linear B tablets of Knossos were written in Greek is surprising because in the archaeological finds from this period of Crete there is an unbroken continuity. On the whole, therefore, the change of government or dynasty in Crete took place without the use of force. At any rate the new masters continued the material culture along exactly the same lines as their predecessors.' The realization that historical and political events of this fundamental character can take place without any interruption in the continuity of the material culture is, of course, not strange to archaeologists and prehistorians.

Fritz Schachermeyr in his contribution to the 'Mid-Century Report' had written: 'It is a great mistake to assume that historical events are always reflected in the archaeological record of stylistic phases. Many historical upheavals occurred without leaving any such traces behind them.'

The mass discomfiture of the experts should have burnt the lesson deep into the consciousness of the prehistorians. Yet we shall observe with melancholy that the almost universally held opinion concerning the origin of the Greeks rests on this discredited principle — 'no archaeological break — no intrusion of new people'.

3. THE RENEWAL OF DOUBT

Mr Chadwick has justly written that Ventris's proof that the masters of Knossos spoke Greek came as an electrifying shock to almost all who had studied the question. How devastating the impact was may be gathered from the opinions we have just quoted from 'Mid-Century Report'. The triumph of a scholar who, like A. J. B. Wace, had held unorthodox views and had suffered some persecution for upholding them appeals to the little man in all of us. Yet we must now record that a protest has been entered and that there are growing grounds for disqualification.

In the first place it must be observed that Evans's picture of the state of Knossos at the time when the flourishing Mycenaean palaces of the Greek mainland were in a position to launch the war against Troy (say the middle of the thirteenth century) is wholly at variance with Homer. Idomeneus is stated to be king of Knossos and to rule over much of Crete including Phaestos; he contributed eighty ships, only ten less than Nestor of Pylos. Homer had led Schliemann to Troy, Mycenae and Tiryns; he was undoubtedly right about an important palace attributed to Nestor in western Messenia. Was he so utterly wrong about Knossos? For it would be hardly possible to imagine a greater contrast between Homer's Knossos and that imagined by Evans. The picture of decadence, isolation and stagnation is briefly stated by Pendlebury (*AoC*, p. 239): 'Once her wealth had gone and her power was broken, Minoan Crete offered no attractions to the mainlander.' Rich colouring is added to this bare outline sketch by the same author in the *Handbook to the Palace of Minos*, which guides tourists round the ruins and reconstructions of

Knossos. 'For centuries the palace lay deserted except for the ghosts of its departed glory mournfully wandering down the empty mouldering stairways. . . . With that wild spring day[1] at the beginning of the fourteenth century B.C. something went out of the world which the world will never see again: something grotesque perhaps, something fantastic and cruel, but something also very lovely.'

It is a strange fact that Aegean archaeologists, whose great discoveries are in the last resort traceable to Homer, have unquestioningly rejected the epic account and preferred Evans's. Even Wace, Evans's most stubborn and fearless opponent, remained so much under his ban, that he involved himself in contradiction on this very point. Believing that the LM II palace at Knossos housed Mycenaean dynasts, he accepted their downfall and expulsion in 1400 B.C., attributing the event to a revolt by native Cretans against the intruding overlords. That Knossos then passed back into the hands of the Minoans and relapsed into a quiet backwater Wace did not dispute. Yet he could still write in 1953 and tacitly reaffirm in 1956 that a Mainland dynasty at Knossos in LM II would explain Idomeneus's position as a vassal of Agamemnon at a period which is, archaeologically speaking, Late Minoan III B — the age of the Minoan squatters who had chased out the Greeks in 1400 B.C., when Crete had become again 'markedly Minoan'.

The authenticity of Homer's picture of Mycenaean Crete in the Late Helladic III B period has been powerfully and trenchantly defended by D. L. Page, Regius Professor of Greek at Cambridge, in his recent book *History and the Homeric Iliad*. Page goes so far as to argue that the Homeric 'Catalogue of Ships' goes back to an authentic Mycenaean source. Be that as it may, the Iliad in its present form is unthinkable without the Cretans Idomeneus and Meriones. It is evident that no scholar who believes in the general correctness of Homer's picture of Mycenaean principalities in the age of Agamemnon and Nestor can also give credence against Homer to Evans's 'squatterdom'.

The general historical picture of the Aegean at this time is no

[1] That the fire took place in the spring is deduced from the evidence that a strong south wind was blowing (see below p. 296).

less puzzling. After the destruction of Mycenaean Knossos, it is still tenaciously believed by the great majority of British Aegean specialists, the Mycenaean potentates of the mainland went from strength to strength. Under the leadership, perhaps even the domination, of the mighty kings of Mycenae they extended their power to the eastern Mediterranean and even established a footing on the Anatolian coast at Miletus. In Crete itself an imposing megaron of the mainland type built above the ruins of the Minoan palace at Hagia Triada close to Phaestos testifies to successful intrusion and establishment in the south of the island. They built a complex palace at Phylakopi on the island of Melos, roughly half-way between Crete and the southern tip of Attica (see fig. 2). Still more remarkable, a fine Mycenaean megaron has recently been traced by the Greek archaeologist N. Platon at Tylissos a short distance west of Knossos (see fig. 2), which is described by D. Levi as approaching in size that of Hagia Triada. Yet during these centuries of power and expansion which extended to Crete itself, they feared to touch Knossos, defended only by 'squatters', who had given such offence by chasing out the powerful Mycenaean dynasts of LM II, (1450–1400). Yet one impressive archaeological argument was against Wace. The architectural expression of a Mycenaean ruler is the megaron. He had argued that the Throne Room reflects those of the mainland; but no megaron[1] had apparently been detected. Wace had evidently not noticed an article published by Evans in *The Times* in 1907, announcing the discovery of a mainland megaron in the south west part of the palace (see p. 269).

The pattern of settlement itself in Crete cannot be reconciled with the evidence of the tablets. Pendlebury insists that the west part of Crete was not settled until the Late Minoan III period after the great disaster. 'The disaster at the end of the previous period had broken the spirit of the Minoans . . . With the destruction of the great centres and palaces the concentration of power ceased. Perhaps the ruling caste was wiped out. At all events the map clearly shows the tendency for the population to scatter. Particularly noteworthy is the extension of habitation in the West. Thrown back on to their own resources, . . . the Minoans were

[1] For a typical mainland megaron plan see Plate 2 (Pylos), and fig. 3.

forced to exploit and tame the wild country West of Ida.' Pendlebury notes that these new settlements in the west are in commanding positions. A leading German authority, F. Matz, repeated this in 1950 in his standard work on Aegean archaeology.

Much the same picture is painted in the most recent book known to me,[1] while Professor Kirsten, who had excavated during the war, submitted similar conclusions to the First Cretological Congress held at Heraklion in Crete in September 1961. Kirsten emphasized that not only were Aptara and Cydonia first settled in LM III times, but that the typology of settlement was different from the Minoan: the new settlers were Mycenaean Greeks and they chose commanding sites on hill-tops. It will be evident that archaeologists who insist that Cydonia and Aptara were first settled at a date subsequent to the destruction of the Palace of Minos cannot maintain that documents relating to men and beasts in these two places date from a period before their foundation. Yet the Knossos tablets do in fact refer repeatedly to Cydonia and Aptara. There is a way out: these sites are not the same as the Cydonia and Aptara of later times. To this we should object that in that case we must suppose that the Knossos, Amnisos, Tylissos and Phaestos of the tablets are also duplicates. The other escape route, which some archaeologists prefer, is that the apparent blank in the west is due to the accident of discovery. Excavation, they say, may yet prove the picture preferred by Pendlebury, Matz, and Kirsten to be wrong. Still, at the time of writing, Desborough (1964) has reaffirmed the general accuracy of Pendlebury's account (see below, p. 317). Thus as matters stand the objection is merely an expression of hope; in the present state of knowledge tablets in Greek which refer to Cydonia and Aptara cannot antedate the foundation of those places but must belong to the LM III period of Crete, which we might call Creto-Mycenaean. At all events it is the period of Evans's Knossian squatterdom.

4. ARCHAEOLOGY AND PHILOLOGY

While philologists and archaeologists must go their separate

[1] V. R. d'A. Desborough, *The Last Mycenaeans and their Successors*, 1964 (see below p. 317).

1. Coryphasion, from the north. In the foreground the tholos tomb believed in antiquity to be the tomb of Thrasymedes, son of Nestor.

Reproduced from *Crete and Mycenae* by Spyridon Marinatos, published by Harry N. Abrams, Inc.

2. The Palace of Nestor seen from the northwest looking towards the sea, with Sphacteria top left. The Throne Room has its circular central hearth framed by four columns. (See p. 49.)

3. Nest of Linear B tablets found in 1900 on the floor of the Eighth Magazine in the Palace of Minos. The tablets are in their original order with the totalling tablet at the bottom.

4. Offering table (reconstructed) from the Dictaean cave in Crete. Its Linear A inscription contains a word which can be read as Luvian *Ja-sa-sa-ra-me, 'My Lady.' (See pp. 54 and 331.)

5. Palace of Phaestos looking north from the Central Court with Mount Ida in the background. (See p. 174.) Reproduced from *Crete and Mycenae* by Spyridon Marinatos, published by Harry N. Abrams, Inc.

6. The Palace of Minos at Knossos seen from the east. In the front, partly obscured by trees, is the Domestic Quarter (East Wing) of the palace. On the far side of the Central Court the reconstructed parts, from right to left, are (1) the Bull Relief of the Northern Entrance Passage, (2) the Anteroom to the Throne Room, (3) the Room of the Column Bases giving access to the Room of the Tall Pithos and the Temple Repositories, (4) South Propylon.

Reproduced from *Crete and Mycenae* by Spyridon Marinatos, published by Harry N. Abrams, Inc.

7. The Northern Entrance Passage of the Palace of Minos at Knossos looking south towards the Central Court. Left, the North Pillar Hall, and right, the reconstructed portico with the Bull Relief. Here was found the Great Deposit of Linear B tablets together with a hoard of intact couple-amphorae of Late Minoan III date. Beyond this point to the right lie the Room of the Saffron Gatherer Fresco and the Room of the Stirrup Jars.

Reproduced from *Crete and Mycenae* by Spyridon Marinatos, published by Harry N. Abrams, Inc.

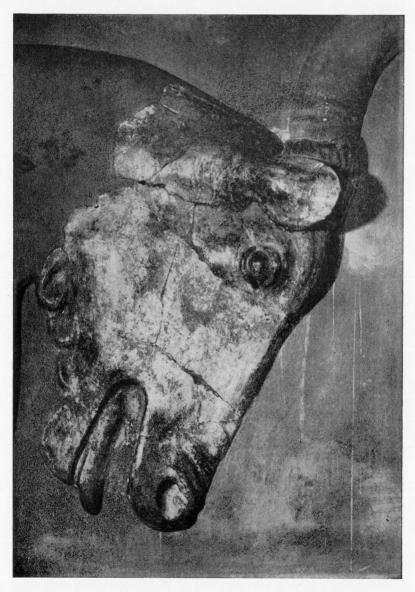

8. Head of a bull in coloured stucco relief from the Northern Entrance
Passage at Knossos. Dated by some scholars to Middle Minoan III, ca.
1600 B.C., but actually found one metre above the Great Deposit of tablets
with their accompanying Late Minoan III B couple-amphorae.

Reproduced from *Crete and Mycenae* by Spyridon Marinatos, published by
Harry N. Abrams, Inc.

9. Fragment of a relief of a bull, with olive tree behind, from the façade of the 'Treasury of Atreus' at Mycenae. Equated stylistically by Sir Arthur Evans with the Bull Relief from Knossos. Dated by Professor Mylonas to ca. 1250 B.C.

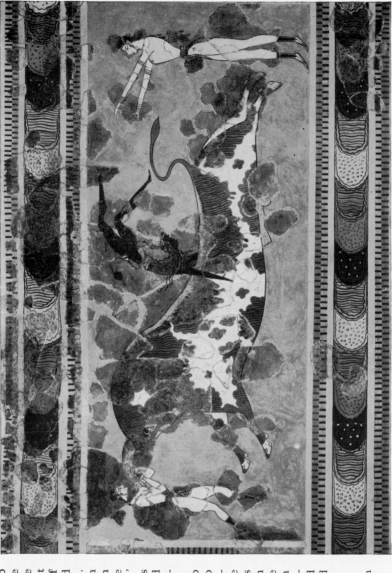

10. The Toreador Fresco from the Court of the Stone Spout in the Domestic Quarter (east wing) of the Palace of Minos. Commonly dated to shortly after 1500 B.C. Actually found at a high level in the court, which was in use during the 'Reoccupation Period' and contained late walls (removed in 1902) and correspondingly late pottery.

The court gives access to the School Room, also used during the 'Reoccupation Period,' where Late Minoan III sherds were found underneath the threshold. Above the 'reoccupied' School Room was the Lapidary's Workshop with unfinished stone amphorae found close to the surface.

Reproduced from *Crete and Mycenae* by Spyridon Marinatos, published by Harry N. Abrams, Inc.

11. The Throne Room of the Palace of Minos at Knossos showing the Griffin Fresco above a marbled dado. Dated by Sir Arthur Evans to Late Minoan II (1450–1400 B.C.). A Late Minoan II sherd is reported from beneath the threshold of the ante-room and another of Late Minoan III date from beneath a floor-slab of the ante-room. (See p. 261.)

Reproduced from *Crete and Mycenae* by Spyridon Marinatos, published by Harry N. Abrams, Inc.

12. Sarcophagus from Hagia Triada near Phaestos, painted in fresco technique. Found in an unmixed Late Minoan III A deposit. Left, women bringing offerings to a shrine marked by double axes surmounted by a bird. Right, men bringing offerings to a shrine or tomb. The figure standing at a lower level before the building is variously interpreted as the dead man or as a god symbolized by the tree. (See p. 175.)

Reproduced from *Crete and Mycenae* by Spyrid. Marinatos and M. Hirmer.

13. Ivory found in 1939 under the supporting wall of a Greek temple erected over the Mycenaean palace at Mycenae. Believed to represent the Divine Triad of the Mycenaeans called *Wanasso* (The Two Queens) and *Wanax* (The King). (See p. 135.)

Reproduced from *Crete and Mycenae* by Spyridon Marinatos, published by Harry N. Abrams, Inc.

14. Faience figure of the Snake Goddess from the Temple Repositories at Knossos. Height 29.5 cm. Middle Minoan III, ca. 1600 B.C.

Reproduced from *Crete and Mycenae* by Spyridon Marinatos, published by Harry N. Abrams, Inc.

15. Three-handled amphora with papyrus decoration. Height 70 cm.
From the Palace of Minos at Knossos. Typical of the 'Palace Style'
of Late Minoan II.

Reproduced from *Crete and Mycenae* by Spyridon Marinatos, published by
Harry N. Abrams, Inc.

16. Typical pottery of the Mycenaean ('Reoccupation,' Postpalatial) period in Crete. The three upper shelves are from Knossos and the lower shelf from Phaestos. The vessel at the extreme right top shelf is the 'pilgrim flask,' found in the Throne Room Corridor. Next to it are two stirrup jars; the one on the left was found on the South Front but figured in Evans's 'decisive stratigraphy' from the Room of the Stirrup Jars. (See p. 262.)

17. Detail (reconstructed) from the Boar-hunt Fresco from the Mycenaean Palace at Tiryns, showing the 'dual type' of chariot which was the
standard form in Late Helladic III.

18. The scene of the unreported excavation of 1923 at Knossos. (See pp. 223 ff., Plate 19 and Figs. 33 and 34.)

1. Pavement of the Central Court.
2. South Wall of the Room of the Lotus Lamp built over steps descending to floor 3.
3. Floor of gypsum slabs 80 cm. below Central Court. Patched with plaster of Mainland-'reoccupation' type, it was ca. 37 cm. deeper than the plaster floor uncovered in 1900. The Miniature frescoes and other finds of 1900 were found above the latest floor.
4. Deep 'prison' underlying floor level 3 containing Late Minoan III sherds.
5. Limestone block belonging to the 'reoccupation' wall.
6. Re-used gypsum door-jamb forming end block of 'reoccupation' wall. Fragments of a Late Minoan II B pithos were found on the west side 32 cm. below the level of floor 3.
7. Doorway. The 'reoccupation' plaster of floor 3 continued down through the doorway and north into the Room of the Saffron Gatherer. Evans sited on this lower floor the fresco actually found above the clay floor 60 cm. higher and two architectural phases later.
8. Bull Relief Portico (reconstructed by Evans).

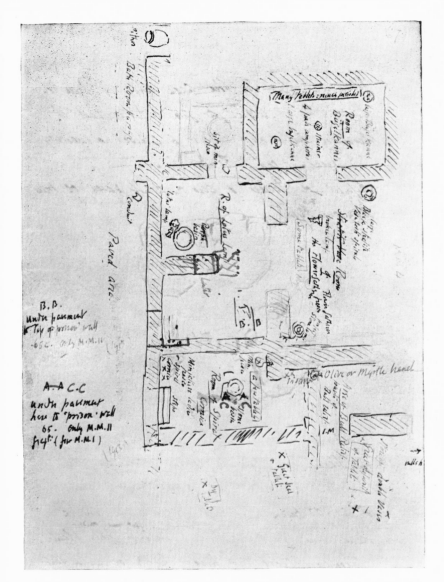

19. Sketch plan (dated May 4) from Evans's 1900 notebook relating to finds
in the Room of the Saffron Gatherer and the Room of the Stirrup Jars with
adjoining areas. Points to be noted: (1) 'Many tablets: much perished' on
floor alongside the Bügelkanne (stirrup jar); (2) 'Some tablets 1 m. down
May 3' alongside the Flower Gatherer fresco and other finds in this room
(see p. 225); (3) 'Great Deposit of Tablets' alongside 'Store of double vases'
in Northern Entrance Passage; (4) the partition wall in the Room of the
Lotus Lamp has been revised and the word 'later' written against it; this
is the 'reoccupation wall' (see p. 224 and Plate 18, 5).

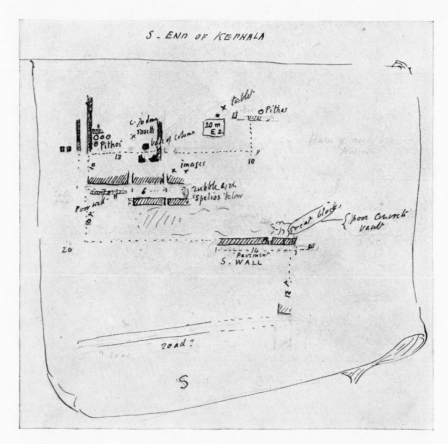

20. Plan of the South Propylaeum area from Evans's 1900 notebook. Points to be noted: (1) 'c. 70 down rosette'; this is the carved stone decoration which Evans later sited 70 cm. below the Middle Minoan III B floor in his polemic against Wace (see pp. 263 ff.); (2) 'Tablet' close to 'Pithos'; this is the unreported Pithos 6 alongside the clay bath filled with Linear B tablets (see Fig. 39a).

Crete and the Mainland

ways and the convergence of their results will be all the more impressive if reached in entire independence, there are fields where both sets of scholars may, and must, walk hand in hand. Such are the tablets which depict artefacts and carry descriptive texts. Since prehistory is essentially pot-based history, it will be appropriate to begin with tablets which list vases.

Stirrup-Jars

I take first the most characteristic vessel of the Mycenaean civilization: the so-called stirrup-jar. Its form may be seen in Plate 16 top centre. This is the type of vessel on which the archaeological accounts of the Mycenaean civilization of the fourteenth and thirteenth centuries largely depend. In fact it is no exaggeration to say that the present picture of Mycenaean expansion during this period (1400–1200) is little more than a distribution map of the find-places of this type of vessel. Now Evans insisted again and again that stirrup-jars became common only after the destruction of the Palace of Minos *c.* 1400 B.C. He wrote: 'at Knossos and elsewhere during the very flourishing Palace Period clay vessels of this form are almost wholly wanting, though the type occurs in the clay inventories of the Knossian Palace. On the other hand, in the age of comparative decadence (LM III) such vessels became common.' The same story is told by D. Mackenzie, who was Evans's chief of staff and whose pottery analyses formed the basis of Evans's communications: 'The Bügelkanne [= stirrup-jar], which is rare in the great days of the palace, is characteristic of this third period [when the palace is only partially inhabited and probably is no longer a royal residence].' In 1905 Evans submitted his famous 'système de classification' to an international congress at Athens: here, too, the contrast between LM II and the 'reoccupation' is marked by the appearance in great quantities of stirrup-jars in the age of decadence. Finally, Evans's later assistant Pendlebury, in his standard work on *The Archaeology of Crete* (p. 243 f.), when discussing LM III pottery includes the stirrup-jar among the new shapes that appear after the destruction in 1400 B.C. Evans stated categorically in the excavation report of 1902: 'Hitherto *no single example* of such a vessel had been brought to light in the Palace itself. Such vessels, indeed, had

185

occurred in sufficient abundance on the site, but *always* of a decadent style and often exhibiting coarse octopus designs — dating from the subsequent period of Partial Habitation' [my italics].

The excavators leave us in no possible doubt about their observations and findings: stirrup-jars are overwhelmingly characteristic of the post-destruction (sometimes called post-palatial) period of Knossos. They are virtually absent from their ceramic accounts of the Late Minoan II period. It is symptomatic that Evans's defenders find themselves compelled to challenge him on this fundamental point. Men not yet born in 1902 now intervene to say in his defence that Evans-Mackenzie-Pendlebury were wrong on a central point of their ceramic accounts: stirrup-jars, they insist, were common in LM II. Why is this so? Once again we encounter the evidence of the Linear B tablets. It so happens that one tablet fragment alone lists no fewer than 1800 stirrup-jars (fig. 33).

Let us suppose that by an extraordinary chance this fragmentary text was a complete record of all the stirrup-jars stored in the palace at the time when it was written, in the final months of 'Linear B Knossos' (I use this term to avoid the question-begging LM II or LM III). The LM II period, according to present accounts, lasted some fifty years, so that simple multiplication would suggest that something like 90,000 stirrup-jars had during this period been made, stored and used in the palace. It is on the survival of pots whole or fragmentary that archaeologists reconstruct their prehistorical pictures. Here we have a type of vessel which is above all characteristic of the Mycenaean world. We know from the clay inventories that in the last months of its existence stirrup-jars were present in great quantities. Let us match the two sets of facts, the purely archaeological findings of Evans-Mackenzie-Pendlebury and ask the question: into which ceramic picture, as drawn by the excavators, do the tablets fit? Into LM II with a virtual absence of stirrup-jars, or into LM III, when this vessel makes its appearance in large quantities? There can be only one answer. This is why the defenders of Evans are obliged to challenge the excavators on this fundamental point. But Evans showed himself fully aware of the difficulty. His answer was that in LM II the palace folk were so wealthy that the vessels were made of bronze and these were naturally plundered when the palace was sacked. The imagination boggles at the 1,800 bronze stirrup-jars listed on a single tablet. What is worse is that no archaeologist has ever seen a bronze stirrup-jar. What then was Evans's evidence for such artefacts? In a grave of the Knossian cemetery on Zafer Papoura a clay stirrup-vase was found. The ornamentation recalled metal work. To quote the *ipsissima verba*, 'It is only from the reflection of metal technique on this vase that we know that metal stirrup-vases existed at Knossos.' The contradiction between tablets and the 'LM II period' is evident. The Linear B users possessed stirrup-jars in abundance. The LM II dynasts, on Evans's own repeated and emphatic testimony, had few if any. The succinct phrase of his *système de classification* leaves no room for doubt.

The Palace Style

If Evans's Late Minoan II period was characterized negatively by an absence of stirrup-jars, its positive mark is the pottery style known as the Palace Style (see Plate 15). Evans's statements about the occurrence and distribution of Late Minoan II pottery likewise prompt serious doubts. We recall that in the Linear B period Knossos had tight administrative control of much of the island including Phaestos. We have seen how the palace archives contain documents relating to ration distributions in different centres. Above all, the palace bureaucrats had minute knowledge of the state and composition of the flocks of sheep in the care of hundreds of shepherds throughout the island. Such meticulous control is conceivable only if there were resident representatives in these different centres in close and constant communication with the palace of Knossos. Now if there is any basis in the claim of archaeology to detect prehistoric social and political organisations from the analysis and distribution of pottery, this tight organisation of Late Minoan II Crete should be reflected in a corresponding distribution over the island sites of the same type of dominant pottery as that which characterizes the 'LM II palace'. On this point again Evans and his lieutenants and adherents leave us in no doubt: Late Minoan II pottery is practically confined to

Knossos, apart from a small number of 'imported' pieces. Above all, 'LM II' is not found at Phaestos, the second major site of the island, which on the evidence of the tablets was firmly under Knossian control in the 'Linear B period'. Thus, if our archaeological colleagues insist that the tablets are to be assigned to the 'LM II period', and this style of pottery is virtually confined to Knossos, it would follow that they must give up their claim to be able to base valid prehistorical conclusions on ceramic observations and analyses. Once again sherd-based history would appear as a delusion. If, however, we seek a period when there is a pottery style common to the whole island, we get the same answer as emerged from our study of the stirrup-jars: Late Minoan III B.

Difficulties arise not merely with the distribution of Late Minoan II in Crete as a whole, but even on the site of the palace. What is meant by a 'LM II palace'? This descriptive term implies that the building as excavated yielded pottery which was predominantly of the type classified as Late Minoan II. At the time of its final burning and destruction, Evans implied, this vast labyrinthine complex occupying an area of some six acres was stocked with pottery of this description. Moreover, in the upper stories were the offices that contained the Linear B archives. As a consequence of the fire these boxes of tablets fell into the basement spaces, where they lodged with the pottery which is the archaeologists' clue to their date. The site remained largely undisturbed[1] until it was excavated by Evans, coherent deposits of tablets being found with remains of their containers and often with the sealings alongside, quite close to the surface before excavation. But let us grant the operation of forces of disturbance, natural and human. Such interference will not have distinguished between the lumps of clay in the ground which are sherds and those which are tablets baked by the fire. In other words, if the tablets were in fact originally stored in a building stocked with LM II pottery, then the distribution of LM II tablets over the site should largely coincide with that of LM II sherds. Was this the case? We have

[1] Evans insisted that the site had been undisturbed. Only a few inches of soil covered the top of the throne in the Throne Room. Evans stated that not a plough could have passed over it, not even trees could have grown, for their roots would have caused damage.

an important statement by the excavators which reveals that in the first season the distributions of tablets and LM II sherds were mutually exclusive.

In 1900 excavation began in what proved to be the South Propylaeum (Fig. 39), and after a campaign lasting some nine weeks the west side of the palace and the Northern Entrance with the rooms to the west had been cleared. Of the magazines, nos. I–VIII had been uncovered. Tablets had been found in virtually every room: they numbered close on a thousand pieces. What of LM II (Palace Style) pottery? I quote: 'Thus the pottery found on the floors in the more central region of the Palace all belongs to the mature Knossian period. . . . Already in the first year of excavation some fine fragments in this grand Palace style were found in the Eighth, Ninth, and Tenth Magazines . . . and in the second year in the great angle outside the Eighth Magazine'. This extract from the fundamental article on the pottery of Knossos by Evans's assistant Duncan Mackenzie contains one inaccuracy: Magazines IX and X were not dug until 1901. Thus we have the admission that the only LM II pottery found with the first season's tablets lay in Magazine VIII. What was the state of this magazine before Evans arrived on the scene? I quote again, this time from the excavation report for 1900. 'We had been previously informed that a native Mahometan, digging here for stone, had come upon some mysterious Kaselles, and at the bottom of a hole dug here by him some remains of stone cists were visible between intervening stone pillars that lay immediately below the pavement.' In other words, a deep hole had been dug in the Eighth Magazine before Evans began his excavation. It had penetrated through the paved floor of the magazine, revealing the cists, built-in chests, which had formed part of the arrangements *in the previous phase* of the building before they were covered up by the pavement. Let us now reflect on what happens to the upcast when a deep hole is dug. Evidently, the last shovelfuls will lie uppermost. Evans makes it clear that the LM II sherds found in 1900 lay at a high level and partly over the west wall in the court outside. Such then is the purely archaeological evidence for the distribution of tablets and sherds over the extensive area dug in 1900. Great quantities of inscribed tablets in undisturbed deposits over the whole area; a few LM II sherds only in Magazine VIII, where there had been a deep disturbance by a native Mahometan. Can we believe that the forces of disturbance had been selectively operative over the long period between 1400 B.C. and A.D. 1900? Is it credible that they had removed all the LM II pots, whole and fragmentary, from the soil, leaving in undisturbed coherent deposits the other lumps of clay, the tablets, which must have been massively associated with LM II pots if this was indeed a 'Late Minoan II palace', for that is the sole meaning of the description in terms of observed archaeological data?[1]

No less puzzling are the international implications of ascribing a date of 1400 B.C. to the 'Palace Style'. I choose an example from a site for which there is a good popular account: *A Forgotten Kingdom* by Sir Leonard Woolley. The site uncovered at Tell Atchana proved to be the ruins of an ancient city named Alalakh. Lying on an important trade route in north Syria, 'it bears on the development of that Cretan art which astonished us in the palace of Minos at Knossos . . .' An interesting case is discussed on p. 156: it is worth quoting in extenso.[2] 'But at Alalakh in Level II we find a whole range of vessels of the same shapes and the same fabric as the normal Nuzu pots but with a design which is not Eastern at all but palpably borrowed from the art of Crete (p. 16a). It is always the same design basically, with very slight modifications and it is remarkably like what we see on vases of the 'Palace' style from Knossos, *but the difficulty is that those are older than the Alalakh vases by about a hundred and fifty years.* Had the Alalakh potter employed a number of different Cretan patterns the problem of how the time gap was bridged would have been almost insoluble, since neither country has produced any intermediate link — *indeed we know that in Crete the fashion had died out completely after* 1400 B.C.; but the general similarity of all the Alalakh pieces does suggest that all are derived from a single original. I cannot but think that a fine Cretan vase had been preserved at Alalakh, probably in the temple treasury, possibly in a private collection, and in the Level II period, a working potter saw and was struck by the unusual design and copied it on his own

---

[1] See below on the search for burnt sherds from this part of the palace.
[2] My attention was drawn to it by D. N. Lee.

pots, believing that the current craze for Aegean art would ensure
a ready sale. In this he was right and the single model available
had to be reproduced *en masse*; it was clear that no self-respecting
gentleman of Alalakh could afford to be without one, and in the
richer houses we even found sets of what, since the style is
peculiar to the Amq, we named 'Atchana ware' [Italics mine].

This is an illuminating passage, a working model of the
archaeological virtues and vices we shall encounter throughout
this investigation. It brings home how important it is to make a
firm distinction between observed facts and inference. What
Woolley found was a mass of pottery dated by him to c. 1250 B.C.
with an unmistakable resemblance to the Palace Style of Knossos.
It does not occur to him to reopen the question of the 'dating' of
this Knossian style. He accepts unquestioningly Evans's dogma
that this style died out completely after 1400 B.C. As a consequence,
he has to devise a hypothesis to account for the gap of one and a
half centuries. His imaginary account of the potter wide awake to
the commercial possibilities of the 'prevailing craze' for Aegean
objets d'art may serve as a type specimen. Again and again we
shall meet with stories of this kind devised to explain away awkward
constellations of fact. Note particularly the intervention of the
disappointed plunderers who carried boxes of tablets into the
Northern Entrance Passage at Knossos and confused the archaeological record by mixing them up with great quantities of Late
Minoan III B pots (see below p. 229).

Now Evans himself had been perplexed by another very curious
circumstance of his 'Late Minoan II' palace. It contained hardly
anything in the way of ordinary small domestic pottery. 'That on
the Palace site itself there was a dearth of smaller vessels contemporary with the fine palatial fabrics . . . must largely be accounted
for by the very affluence of its occupants, who doubtless made a
large use of metal vessels.' Once again, as with the missing stirrup-
jars, Evans seeks to make good a mysterious gap in his basic
ceramic evidence by a hypothesis: the required vessels had once
been there but they had been stolen. Yet a contemporary dig at
Knossos contained the hint of a solution. In 1900 Mr F. B. Welch,
discussing the pottery found in the houses at Knossos which were
excavated while Evans was engaged on the palace site (which he

had bought and was reserved to him), wrote: 'Along with this finer and more delicate ware a number of fragments turned up, representing a very coarse Mycenaean technique: they were chiefly pieces of large *pithoi* [jars] and *Bügelkanne* [stirrup-jars] with spiral, vegetable and octopod designs, freely drawn in poor, thin brown varnish on a reddish or buff-coloured surface. *This was evidently the coarse household stuff, which existed side by side with the more delicate ware.*' The thought obtrudes itself: is this the answer to Evans's odd 'LM II palace' containing only fine pottery but mysteriously lacking both stirrup-jars and common household stuff? A great abundance of stirrup-jars and common pottery was in fact found by Evans on the site. Was it contemporary with the finer ware which he alone considered fit for his grand palace folk? This is a solution on the lines of the emperor's clothes. Yet the possibility that several different styles might have been in simultaneous use has already occurred to certain eminent Aegean archaeologists. The matter will be discussed below under 'The Dilemma of Archaeology' (p. 302). Meanwhile it will suffice to note Evans's perplexity and the far-fetched nature of the hypotheses he had to devise to explain the gaps in his ceramic picture: bronze stirrup-jars and smaller household vessels stolen by plunderers.

It is not merely the study of pottery that raises difficulties with the current prehistorical accounts. Evans also studied other artefacts depicted on the Linear B tablets of Knossos. In the following sections I propose simply to follow his own exposition without criticism and simply to note where the echoes of resemblance lie. Again and again we shall see that Evans's own comparisons point to the mainland and other areas at a time later than the supposed destruction of the Palace of Minos.

The Chariot

We may begin with the chariot tablets, found at an early stage of the excavations in 1900, which depict items of military equipment: a chariot, horse and corselet. We have abundant pictorial representations for the war-chariot which was in use at the time when the destruction and burning of the Palace preserved to posterity this valuable first-hand evidence. The chariot depicted

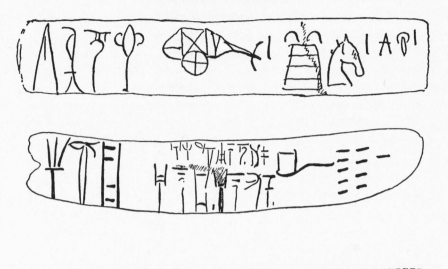

Fig. 21. Knossos tablets depicting military equipment including chariots and corslets.

(fig. 21) was closely studied by Evans himself. It is of the type which he called 'dual'. By this he meant that to the rectangular outline of the box or body there is added a curved annexe or 'heel', sometimes depicted with a central bar. The wheels have four spokes and the axle lies beneath the centre of the body. The pole is a projection from the bottom of the floor and its extremity is attached by some kind of stay, perhaps acting as a spring or shock absorber, to the top of the body; pole and stay are joined at intervals by thongs or the like. Evans is insistent that this type makes its first appearance in our tablets. He did not know that they were written in Greek; it is thus associated with the *Greek* occupation of the Palace of Minos. Other authorities (e.g. H. L. Lorimer) have noted that this 'dual chariot', wherever it may have been invented, is the standard form on the mainland in My-cenaean III (=Late Helladic III), that is the period following the destruction of the Knossian palace. Moreover, this strange form of chariot body also figures regularly on the Mycenaean vases of Cyprus: *the type was thus common to and confined to the Mycenaean Greek world* (Lorimer). Thus if Evans's dating were right, we should have to suppose that this type of war vehicle appears first in Crete and spread to the Mycenaean mainland and thence was carried to Cyprus. But has Crete a terrain which would prompt the use and development of this engine of war? We quote the words of Sir Arthur himself: 'There were few districts of Crete where, even in the height of summer, chariot driving could have been really practicable without the existence of a made track.'

He also wrote: 'The concentration of war-chariots by the lord of Knossos could only be construed as a threat to mainland power, and the fleet might transport both horses and chariots'. One may wonder where was the terrain on which these crack troops of the Knossian armoured brigade acquired their expertise. Pendlebury in fact devotes barely two lines of his book to the subject: 'The chariot probably came in with the horse in LM I–II, but Crete was too rough for the regular use.' Yet the archives make it plain that the lords of Knossos possessed such equipment in abundance. We see then that the war chariot is as revolutionary an intrusion into Crete as the Throne Room itself (see pp. 257 ff.). Typologically its affinities are with Late Helladic III.[1]

The Horse

Doubts crowd more thickly when we turn to the horse which drew the chariot. A series of tablets represent warrants for the supply of a pair of coats-of-mail, a chariot, and usually a pair of horses (fig. 21). The standard ideogram for the horse shows an animal with its mane dressed in three tufts. Where does this peculiarity recur? Evans himself comments. 'It so happens that a find of remarkable interest apparently reflects the transport of horses to the island.'

In 1905 Evans, pursuing the course of the Minoan highway leading west from the Palace (fig. 30), came across a building which eventually came to be known as the 'Little Palace', though Evans first dubbed it the 'House of the Fetish Shrine'. It was in this building that a seal-impression of exceptional interest came

[1] On the Arsenal see below p. 274.

to light (fig. 22). It represented a one-masted sailing ship, and superimposed was the figure of a noble horse, with its mane done up in three tufts. Now in our calculus of resemblances so remark-able a detail cannot be overlooked. Indeed in his excavation report for the 1905 season Evans immediately seized on the significance of this peculiarity. 'A noteworthy feature in the present example, as on the horses of the tablets and the frescoes, is the binding up of the mane in a series of tufts. . . .'

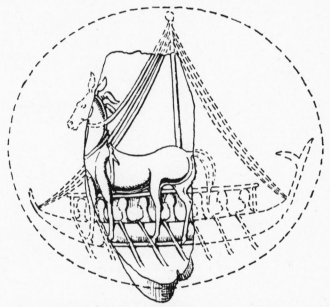

Fig. 22. Sealing from the Little Palace at Knossos of Late Minoan III date. The horse may represent the god Hippos.

'The exact correspondence between the dressing of the mane here shown and that of the horses on the fragmentary frescoes found in the Megaron of the Palace of Mycenae may be taken as a fair indication that we have to do with the same stock.' Thirty years later there is a significant change of wording. In the *Palace of Minos* (1935) the same facts are discussed: 'These knots of hair are well illustrated on the painted fragment showing a horse's head from the "Men's Megaron" at Mycenae . . . , and another good example occurs in the case of a similar head on a fragment of the stag-hunting fresco from Tiryns. . . . This method of gathering up the horse's mane into separate tufts must be regarded as a distinctively *Minoan* fashion. It reappears on the Cypro-Minoan "kraters" from Enkomi.'

The facts are thus exactly parallel with those relating to the dual chariot of Late Helladic III. They point to mainland and to 'colonial' Mycenaean of Cyprus. Evans's substitution of the word 'Minoan' is symptomatic. It implies the priority of Crete over the

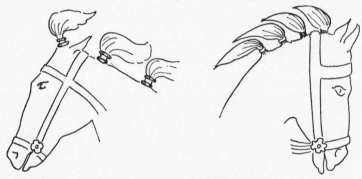

Fig. 23. Horses' heads from mainland frescoes: l. Mens's Megaron, Mycenae; r. Hunting fresco, Tiryns.

mainland in this matter of horses as well as the chariots associated with them. Yet elsewhere Evans writes: 'The evidence of the Grave *Stelae* at Mycenae, on which chariots and horses appear for the first time in Aegean lands, tends to show that the use of the horse in this connexion was earlier diffused on the mainland side, where the Argolid Plain offered more special facilities than in Crete itself.' Nevertheless the same paragraph ends with the observation that the horse depicted on a sword blade from one of the Shaft Graves 'give a magnificent idea of this Minoan breed'. Pending our enquiry into the stratification of the tablets, we simply note that the affinities of both chariots and horses are unequivocally with mainland Greece of the Late Helladic III period and with the settlements in Cyprus. Nor can there be serious doubt that horses and chariots were intrusions into Crete, which, as Evans himself declares, offers no suitable terrain.

The Coat-of-Mail

We now turn to the corslet associated on the tablets with the chariots and horse. The elucidation of this problem has had unexpected repercussions. It will be found to affect not only the chronological question which engages us at the moment and the relationship between Minoan Crete and the mainland. Homeric scholarship will also not go unscathed. It will be both kind and expedient to let the scholars tell their own tale as the rising sun of Linear B cast its light on these gropings in the dark.

Sir Arthur Evans saw immediately that the second object on the above tablets (fig. 21) was clearly a corslet or breast-plate of a simple form. The ideogram suggested to him that it consisted of horizontal plates of metal, probably backed by leather, covering the body and suspended from the shoulders by curved pieces, doubtless also of bronze. Evans deduced that the material concerned was bronze from a curious fact which is observable on these 'knight's equipment' tablets, as he designated them. In some of the entries the CORSLET ideogram has been erased and an ingot sign substituted. In others the ingot sign is inserted after the chariot, or it may be written as a sort of endorsement on the back of the tablet. Another point which he made was that in the best drawn ideograms there are five rows of such plates, and in no case more than six. Evans now sought for illustrative material and pointed out that the corslets worn by the Egyptian soldiers of Rameses II in his campaigns against the Hittites early in the thirteenth century were precisely of this type, showing five rows of plates and shoulder pieces. He did not fail to note that these illustrations are over a century later than his presumed date for the Knossos tablets.

Certain mercenaries employed by the Egyptians such as the Shardana (often identified with the people who eventually gave their name to Sardinia) wore very similar types of corslet.[1] Evans summed up his analysis with the truly prophetic words 'In any case

[1] Miss D. H. Gray of Oxford, in a recent survey of the archaeological background to the Linear B texts, makes a similar observation. 'A waist-length corslet is not known on the monuments as early as 1400, but it is found about 1200 among the invaders of Egypt and in Cyprus, and the corslets of the Warrior Vase and Stele, bronze-studded rather than plated, worn by foot-soldiers, have the same shape and proportions.'

we may assume a leather tunic below, to which metal bands were applied. The number of the curved bands was, in this case five. . . .'

This was as far as analysis could go until the decipherment was achieved. Yet at first sight we were no better off. In the Knossos tablets the word standing alongside the corslet ideogram was *qe-ro₂*, and the sign representing the first syllable of this word is sometimes 'surcharged' on the ideogram (fig. 24c) in accordance

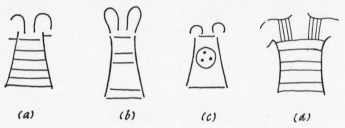

(a)   *(b)*   *(c)*   *(d)*

Fig. 24. Corslet ideograms from the Knossos tablets: (a, b) showing rows of plates, (c) with surcharged sign QE = qe-ro₂ pair of coats-of-mail, (d) Egyptian corslet of time of Rameses II (after Sir Arthur Evans).

with scribal practice (for instance, *A* is often written on the AMPHORA ideogram). But no corresponding word was known from later Greek. This is not surprising; technical words like *hauberk* tend to become obsolete once the piece of equipment they denote has gone out of use. There was, however, one curious detail: the *qe-ro₂* in a set were always two in number. There the matter had to rest until the publication in 1955 of the Linear B tablets recovered by Professor Blegen at Pylos in 1952. These included a group describing suits of armour. Here we were more fortunate: on one of these the scribe used the word *thorakes*, which is the normal Greek for 'corslets'. What is more, he listed them as so many 'pairs'. Here was the explanation of the two *qe-ro₂*: *qe-ro₂* was a two-piece object. Corslets are also listed as 'pairs' in cuneiform inventories.

Of still greater interest is the fact that the Pylian scribe in recording the individual suits normally adopted the following formula: '20 large *X*, 10 small *X*, 4 *X* of the helmet, 2 cheek-pieces'. The word I have transcribed as *X* was also unknown in later Greek (it is *o-pa-wo-ta*); but the fact that they are found both on the corslet and the helmet and that 4 go to make up a helmet makes it clear that these must be plates of some resistant material. The fact that four cover the helmet and 20 + 10 are sufficient to cover back and front of the two-piece corslet gives some rough indication of their size. Most interpreters agree in translating the word *o-pa-wo-ta* as 'plates'.

At this point new evidence was forthcoming. Some tablets which had been mislaid in Knossos made their belated appearance and were published by J. Chadwick. It could now be seen that the Knossos scribes used much the same formula in their detailed descriptions of armour. They too ended their descriptions with '4 *o-pa-wo-ta* of the helmet and 2 cheek-pieces'. But unlike the Pylian scribes they put in the word for helmet immediately preceding: this was *korus*, the later Greek word for the helmet. In their specifications of the main item they also added valuable information. Before the *o-pa-wo-ta* (the number is unluckily missing) they insert '*qe-ro*$_2$ 2, shoulder-pieces 2'. This is an astonishing and gratifying confirmation of Evans's diagnosis. His words may in fact function as an adequate translation.

We may now play back these results on to the facts contained in the Pylian archives. A two-piece corslet contains 20 larger and 10 smaller plates 'arranged in bands'. This gives us 2(10 + 5). The number 5 for the smaller plates springs to the eye in view of Evans's diagnosis. It becomes immediately obvious that there are five rows, just as Evans had noted, and that each row has a central smaller plate flanked by two larger plates arranged thus:

The plates were presumably sewn on to a leather backing, and this was an effective way of covering a curved surface and achieving flexibility, for there would have been a hinging effect where the two larger plates joined or overlapped the central smaller plate.

We can now again confront the facts from Pylos and Knossos and assess their relationship in terms of similarity. Apart from the parallel formulae and their identity in respect of the 'four *o-pa-wo-ta* of the helmet and two cheek-pieces', we must seize on the fact that the standard corslet ideogram of Knossos with its five rows tallies with what we have deduced from the number of plates in the corresponding Pylian inventories. If the two archives are dated respectively to the beginning and the end of the Mycenaean power curve, then we must conclude that throughout these two eventful centuries of military enterprise protective armour remained virtually unchanged. The record of man's inventiveness in time of war, and in particular the development of the Mycenaean sword, would lead us to expect considerable differences between the corslets of the fifteenth and the twelfth centuries B.C.[1]

Swords

We turn now to swords. The drawings on the tablets (fig. 25) are of two types. One is schematically drawn (*a*) and represents a triangular blade with a central rib prolonged into the hilt, which terminates with a pommel. The more elaborate drawings (*b*) show a less pronounced pommel; above the hilt is a rounded guard and the blade gradually widens to a kind of shoulder, whence it narrows rapidly to a point. The Knossian swords are called by the Homeric word *phasganon*, and a recurrent formula states that they are 'joined with rivets', with again a Homeric word *desmos* in the sense 'rivet'. The swords with the closest resemblance to these are not far to seek. They are found in tombs located in the cemetery of Zafer Papoura to the north of the Palace (see fig. 26). The bulk of the tombs belonged to the post-palatial age when the Palace was in ruins or was at most partially inhabited. In the main, therefore, the remains here brought to light illustrate the Third Late Minoan Period. The number of weapons found was

[1] The dangers of arguing from archaeological silence are shown by the recent discovery of a fine corslet in a Mycenaean chamber tomb at Dendra south-east of Mycenae. There is an excellent photograph in J. Alsop's *From the Silent Earth* p. 255. This suit of armour is wholly different from those described in the tablets. The main piece is in two parts hinging at one side; there is a kind of metal cape fitting over the shoulders, and a skirt consisting of three bands of metal. Nothing in this outfit corresponds to the 10 smaller and 20 larger *o-pa-wo-ta*. Technically the Dendra corslet is a more sophisticated piece of equipment. It is much earlier in date than the tablets, according to the excavators. We might suppose that such a corslet belonged to one of the aristocracy or the elite of warriors while the simpler outfits recorded in the tablets were issued to ordinary soldiers and chariot drivers.

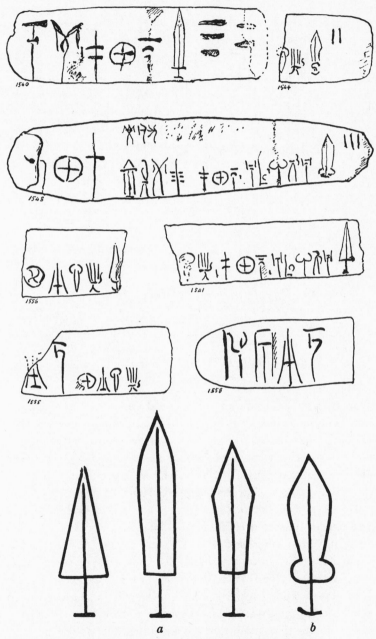

Fig. 25 a, b. Knossos sword tablets and ideograms.

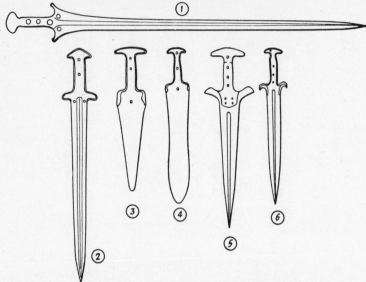

*Fig. 26. Types of Aegean swords: (1) the long 'horned'
type (LM II and earlier), (2) LH III A: 2 — III B, (3)
from Knossos, LM III A: 2, (4) the 'leaf-shaped' type,
LH III A: 2 — LH III C, (5) 'horned' dagger from end of
LM II (?), (6) LH III C (after Sir Arthur Evans and A.
Furumark).*

proportionately considerable: out of sixty intact interments there
were obtained nineteen bronze weapons, including two long
swords and six short swords. Now one of these swords (3) is singled
out by Evans as belonging to a class of short swords and daggers
extremely characteristic of the very latest Mycenaean culture. It
is the type, of triangular shape, depicted on the Linear B tablets.

Evans then goes on to discuss still more striking evidence for its
comparatively late date. These were two short swords found in a
tomb at Muliana in East Crete (4). Evans insists that they are late
examples of their class 'as the blade shows a slight tendency to
increase in breadth towards the extremity. In Crete, as in mainland Greece and in Cyprus, the iron swords of the succeeding
Geometrical Age are copied from this class.' Now this peculiar and
characteristic shape is much the same as that depicted on the more
carefully drawn examples from the Linear B tablets. This did not

escape Pendlebury, who in his standard handbook of 1939 repeated Evans's facts and conclusions, but added the significant
footnote: 'This shape seems to go back to LM II as it appears on
the Sword Tablets from Knossos.' In other words, the swords on
the Linear B tablets, if assigned to LM II, are nearly a quarter of a
millennium out of phase with the actual archaeological finds.

So far we have been dealing with doubts suggested by Evans's
own stylistic analyses of the artefacts. It was the growing penetration and understanding of the Linear B texts themselves which
gradually sapped confidence in the received opinion about Late
Minoan III Knossos and Crete. By 1955 my own researches had
reached the point when I felt that I must challenge the alleged two
hundred year gap between the archives of Pylos and Knossos.
Summarizing a lecture given in Oxford in 1955 I wrote (1956):
'Was the fall of "Achaean" power in Crete roughly contemporary
with that in Pylos and was the same set of forces at work in both
cases? In plainer language were both disasters the work of the
Dorians?'

The first philological point to raise doubts about the current
archaeological picture has already been discussed. The tripod
cauldrons listed in the Pylian inventory (p. 160) are invariably
described as 'of Cretan workmanship'. How could this evidence
for imports of Cretan metal-work be squared with the idea of an
impoverished, stagnating Crete, without interest for the mainlander? No less disquieting were the facts which emerged from the
close study of the inscribed stirrup jars of the mainland. It is
fortunate that here we may follow Sir Arthur Evans's own
exposition.

In 1922 the Greek archaeologist A. D. Keramopoullos, while
exploring the Mycenaean palace, 'the House of Kadmos' at
Thebes, lit upon a store-room containing twenty-eight large
'stirrup vases' with inscriptions in the Linear B script on the
shoulders or body (fig. 27). Other inscribed fragments were known
from the German excavations at Tiryns and Mycenae, and yet
another complete stirrup-vase with a three word inscription in
two lines was unearthed by Professor Kourouniotis at Eleusis.
Evans was in a position to study all these inscriptions. He wrote:
'The correspondence of the signs on the vessels [with those of

Fig. 27. Linear B inscriptions on the Theban stirrup jars,
containing Knossian place names o-du-ru-wi-jo *and* wa-to.

Knossos] at once leaps to the eye. It is detailed in its manifesta-
tions and overwhelming in the proportion it bears to the number of
known mainland characters.' What was still more striking was that
many of the words on the vases recurred in the Knossos tablets.
As Evans pointed out, in view of the small amount of material
represented by these vessels, there is a remarkably high proportion
of word correspondences. It was not until the script had been
deciphered that the full significance of this fact could be seen.
Evans had taken the words in question to be personal names. We
can now see that the fullest Theban inscriptions have three words
in the pattern (1) personal name, (2) place name, (3) personal
name in the genitive or an adjective meaning 'royal'. What
deserves emphasis is the fact that the place-names (*O-du-ru-wi-jo*,
Wa-to) are Cretan; and not merely this, but the two which figure
most frequently on the jars actually occur adjacently on a Knossian tablet. Now on this same Linear B tablet there is another
place-name (*Pa₃-ko-we*); this word figures on the best example of

an inscribed stirrup-vase from Tiryns. Still more extraordinary is the specimen from Eleusis.

In the early thirties excavations were carried out on the site of Eleusis, the settlement to the west of Athens where in classical times the famous mysteries in honour of Demeter and Persephone were celebrated. Under the Hall of Initiation built by the Athenian tyrant Pisistratus foundations of a prehistoric structure were traced. On the floor a Mycenaean stirrup-jar was found bearing an inscription in the Linear B script (fig. 28). The pottery associated

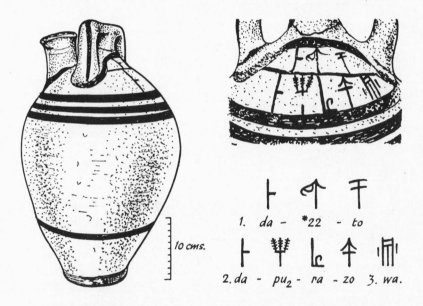

1. da – *22 – to

2. da – pu₂ – ra – zo   3. wa.

Fig. 28. Inscribed stirrup-jar from Eleusis. The inscription has a Knossos place-name (1), a personal name (2), and an abbreviation wa. for wa-na-ka-te-ro 'royal' (3).

with it enabled Professor Mylonas to date it to the latter half of Late Helladic III B. In absolute terms he suggested the end of the thirteenth and the beginning of the twelfth centuries as the upper chronological limit for the building and for the stirrup-jar, and went on to suggest that all the inscribed stirrup-jars of the mainland are roughly contemporary and belong to the closing years of the thirteenth century. In other words, they date from the last years of Mycenaean greatness, *c.* 1200 B.C.[1]

We can now see that the top word on the Eleusis jar is again a Cretan place of frequent occurrence, *da-22-to*; by an amazing chance it is coupled on one Knossian tablet with the place-name painted on the Tiryns jar (fig. 29). To cap it all another painted sherd from Mycenae also exhibited a Knossian place-name (*E-ra*).

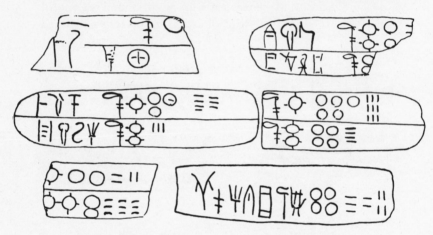

Fig. 29. Cattle inventories from Knossos. The middle tablet left links da-*22-to (*the place-name on the Eleusis jar*) *with* pa₃-ko-we (*the place-name on a Tiryns jar*).

We must realize that these few inscribed stirrup-jars represent a tiny, random sample preserved by the accident of fate at all these different centres. There is only one possible conclusion to be drawn from this high proportion of Cretan personal names and place-names: that this sample is representative of the total bulk of such vessels which existed on the mainland. For what purpose were these place-names painted on these vessels? If they were intended for export, then we should have to assume that the mainland centres all exported solely to Crete. It is more reasonable to suppose that these are marks of origin. We know also from the Linear B texts that such vessels were recorded in connexion with

[1] G. Mylonas unfortunately omits his own specimen from those reconsidered by him in a recent article. Important is the absolute identity of the spelling, *da-*22-to* with its rare and unread middle sign *22.

the manufacture of perfumed oil, which was used for ritual purposes. Professor S. Marinatos has pointed out to me that the Amarna correspondence shows that jars of oil were customary gifts between kings at that time, so that the machinery of export was presumably from palace to palace. But whether import or export, the inscribed mainland vessels are indisputable evidence for relationships with Crete. What was their date? Evans himself put them later than the fall of the Palace of Minos. Mylonas' evidence for Late Helladic III B seems clear. We may add that this elongated 'piriform' shape of stirrup-jar is said by some pottery experts to be typical of the Late Helladic III period.

Given this dating, it will be seen that a 'squatter' period at Knossos cannot be reconciled with the evidence presented by the inscribed jars at so many mainland sites. Their wide distribution suggests that Crete as late as 1200 B.C., so far from having no attractions for the mainlander, was in contact with the major Mycenaean centres.[1]

My doubts were further reinforced by the study of the arrangements for supervising slaves and the issue of rations (p. 121 ff). The virtual identity of the administrative arrangements and the close correspondence of the complex ration scales at both Pylos and Knossos made it difficult to believe in the alleged two hundred year gap.

The next step posed the question in a still more challenging form: were the Knossos tablets actually *later* than the Pylian archive? The point involved is one of great technicality. On the basis of the scattered forms in the dialects of classical Greece (*sātes*, *sētes*, *tētes*) the philologist K. Brugmann had argued that the parent Bronze Age form of the word for 'this year' was **kjāwetes*. Now the Mycenaean scribes, as they registered assessments and deliveries, had many occasions to use the expressions 'last year' and 'this year'. On one Pylian assessment document the scribe mentions first 'last year's deficit'. He then goes on to say 'What the bronze-smiths are not giving this year'. The last word is usually transcribed *za-we-te*. But in 1954–55[2] I had argued that

[1] For the evidence that Crete remained for some time unaffected by the disasters on the Mainland, see p. 318.

[2] A few months later, but quite independently, a Swiss scholar, H. Mühlestein put forward a similar view.

the first sign stood for *kja-*, and this theory was finally confirmed by new finds of tablets in 1957. Thus the Pylian word *kja-we-te* has precisely the form which K. Brugmann had predicted. General phonetic considerations suggested that a form *sjāwetes* had formed the bridge between *kjāwetes* of Pylos and the *sātes* of classical times. Now a tablet from Knossos likewise lists a deficit in an assessment. The word is written **85-u-te*. This was a particularly refractory problem. The value of the first sign was in some doubt; but in 1955 I had pointed out that a well-known place-name, *a-si-ja-ti-ja*, was also once spelt *a-*85-ta₂* and that this type of orthography reflected a general characteristic of the whole syllabary. This general theory, confirmed by tablets recovered in 1957, was formally embraced by Dr J. Chadwick at an international colloquium in 1958. What is relevant here is the value which emerged for the disputed sign with the inventory number **85: it was *sja*. Again thanks to the work of Dr Chadwick himself, it became clear that *we* could stand for *u*, and there were other indications that *u* could be read as a consonant followed by a vowel.[1] Thus the word on the Knossos tablet standing in a sentence referring, as all admit, to a deficit could be interpreted *sjawetes*.

That this Knossian form is linguistically later than the Pylian *kjawetes* is beyond all discussion. It is true, of course, that dialects differ in their rate of change and that isolated pockets may remain centuries behind the general development of the language. But this objection cannot be sustained here. In the first place all Mycenologists have remarked on the virtual identity of dialect in all the Linear B archives. Secondly Crete was certainly invaded from the Greek mainland. So it is hardly conceivable that the Knossians of 1400 B.C. used a dialect form linguistically more advanced than the parent mainland dialect as it appears in Pylos allegedly some two hundred years later.

Two other considerations reinforce the conclusion that the Knossos tablet in question is actually later than those of Pylos. The sentence recording the deficit contains the word for 'will be wanting'. It is in fact the verb 'go away' used in an idiomatic sense: the significant fact is that it is written in a more advanced

---

[1] A more recent example is the word *o-u-ka*. This, associated with a wool entry, may stand for *owika*, 'sheep's' (wool) as opposed to 'lamb's' (see above p. 117).

orthography than that of Pylos: *a-pe-i-si*. In Pylian conventions this would appear as *a-pe-si* since the *i* of the diphthong *ei* is ignored. Here we see Knossos on the way to the more accurate conventions of the Cypriot syllabary of post-Mycenaean times.

Finally, there was a point of morphology which suggested that the Greek of Knossos had reached a later stage of development than that of Pylos. In Homer we find traces of a case ending in *-phi*. The Pylos tablets presented evidence most gratifying to philologists: the ending in question was seen to have precisely the distribution postulated on comparative evidence. The ending appeared in the instrumental plural of noun classes except the second declension (corresponding to the Latin type *dominus*). Thus if the scribe had occasion to describe artefacts provided 'with ivory X . . .' he would write *e-re-pa-te-ja-pi* if the noun was feminine, but *c-re-pa-te-jo* if the noun was masculine or neuter. These spellings correspond to Mycenaean Greek words *elephantei-aphi* and *elephanteiois*, feminine and masculine instrumental plural respectively of *elephanteios* 'ivory'. Now by post-Mycenaean times this ending had spread to the nouns of this latter type. But Knossos shows some examples of *e-re-pa-te-jo-pi*: in other words it had advanced farther than the Pylian language towards the post-Mycenaean state.

More suggestive than these isolated and debatable points is the general picture afforded by the dialects of Crete in post-Mycenaean times. Above (p. 155) the statement was made that Crete was occupied by Dorians speakers. It has been observed, however, that these Doric dialects, particularly in Central Crete, are suffused with elements attributable to the Greek population subdued by the Dorian invaders. The handbooks of the ancient Greek dialects stress this fact and offer an historical interpretation. It is a reflection of the fusion of the two strata of Greek speakers in the island. This is reasonable, for linguistic elements do not hang about to infect new occupants of deserted sites. They are acquired by imitation in conditions of symbiosis.

The evidence for continuity between the Mycenaean and the Dorian occupation of Crete is supported by an observation made by ancient historians. Dorian communities were organized into three tribes — Hylleis, Dymanes, and Pamphyloi. Crete was no exception to this rule, but there we also find names attributed by historians to the pre-Dorian settlers. Tribes with such names are believed to have comprised elements of the Mycenaean population who were incorporated into the new Dorian states. One of these is the *Aithaleis*, and on this name the Pylos tablets offer an interesting gloss. One of the groups on coast watching duties was stationed in *Aithalewes* (later *Aithaleis*), and this may well be a district simply named after the people who inhabited it.

At all events, historians who believe in the incorporation of Mycenaean tribal organisations into the states of their Dorian conquerors cannot believe in a century-long gap between the expulsion of Mycenaeans from Knossos and the Dorian seizure of that part of Crete. In this they are at one with the philologists who have analysed the Doric dialects of Crete, and with the students of Homer who grant the essential accuracy of the epic picture of Mycenaean settlement at the time of Nestor of Pylos.

Such were the perplexities which gradually accumulated over the years after the decipherment of Linear B. Naturally, such points are open to criticism, and all manner of arguments can be devised to weaken their force. They may in fact be treated as purely autobiographical: they are the thoughts which suggested themselves to one scholar, who began to entertain doubts about the date of the tablets which he first put into print in 1956. In 1958, however, a leading Aegean archaeologist, C. W. Blegen voiced similar doubts from an archaeological point of view, and likewise suggested that the Linear B archives of Knossos reflect the closing months of a Mycenaean dynasty which was contemporary with the rulers of Mycenae, Tiryns and Pylos. Blegen's surmise or suggestion — he would call it no more than that — was prompted by technical considerations of archaeology. But this support of the general thesis from one with unrivalled experience, acquired in a lifetime of field archaeology, cannot be ignored or lightly dismissed. Philologists and archaeologists are both concerned with the history of human communities. But their material and the techniques of handling it are so different that no one scholar can hope to be a master in both fields. Yet no solution is acceptable which does not satisfy both sets of facts. It is thus all the more gratifying that the purely philological results should

agree with the general diagnosis of an eminent Aegean archaeologist. Blegen concluded his paper entitled 'A Chronological
Problem' with the words: 'A thorough examination of all evidence
available for the circumstances of discovery in each specific place
where tablets were found at Knossos is certainly needed to test
this suggestion.' At that time I had no idea of what evidence was
available bearing on the find-places of the Knossos tablets. In
1958 I had been working for six years in the Ashmolean Museum
at Oxford. It was not until 1960 that I ascertained that the
museum housed the records of the Knossos excavations. What
eventually led me to them was an attempt to probe more deeply
into the find circumstances of the stirrup-jar tablet: the one
already mentioned recording 1800 stirrup-jars.

5. THE ROOM OF THE STIRRUP-JARS

Evans had singled out this tablet and made it the central piece
of evidence in the elaborate stratigraphic picture which he
presented as providing a 'decisive' answer to the question of the
chronological placing of the tablets. The place concerned was a
small room in the northwest part of the palace (fig. 30). Its finely
measured stratigraphy, showing three floor levels, was first
published in the excavation report for 1903. Some eighty cm
below the surface Evans came on a clay floor on which were
standing some vessels of a late type, including stirrup-jars with
octopod decoration. Twenty cm below this clay floor was another
floor, of earlier date, made of plaster and clay. On this lower floor
Linear B tablets were said to be resting: evidently the tablets
belonged to the phase of the palace earlier than that represented
by the clay floor. Sixty cm still deeper than the second floor yet
another floor of plaster and clay was entered, and below this
were walls forming a sort of dungeon or 'prison', as Evans called
it, reaching down some seven metres. In 1935 Evans published the
fourth volume of his monumental *The Palace of Minos*. The
picture was now filled out. For the first time, thirty-five years
after their discovery, scholars learned which tablets had been
found in the room: they were a 'hoard of tablets referring to
painted clay stirrup-vases' from area above 'early keep'. In his

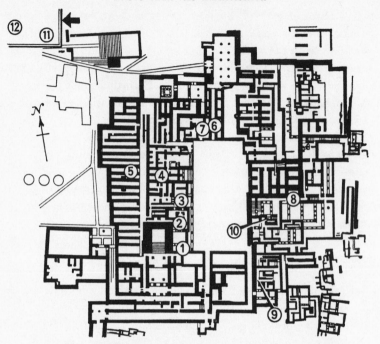

Fig. 30. Find-places of the Knossos tablets: (1) Clay Chest N.E. of South Propylaeum, (2) Room of the Chariot Tablets, (3) Room of the Column Bases, (4) Magazine of the Vase Tablets, (5) Western Magazines, (6) Northern Entrance Passage, (7) Room of the Stirrup-Jars, (8) East-West Corridor (Domestic Quarter), (9) Corridor of the Sword Tablets, (10) the Great Tablet S. of the Hall of Colonnades, (11) The Arsenal, (12) the Little Palace.

fig. 719, Evans reproduced 'one of the best preserved'. It is our fig. 32. In his next fig. 720, Evans supplied photographs of the 'Reoccupation pottery above deposit of tablets'. He summed up the whole section of his book with the words 'decisive evidence for relative dating of stirrup-vase tablets.' The documents to which I have referred were to show, step by step, that this elaborate stratigraphic picture was a total fabrication: there were no such three floors in that room; the tablet was the sole one and it had been found near the southwest entrance, while of the three pots in the picture the top two stirrup-jars had been found in 1901 on the

South Front, and the LM III B strainer at the bottom of the figure had been unearthed, also in 1901, in the west part of the site just south of the Throne Room, in the so-called Gallery of the Jewel Fresco (see below pp. 246 ff.). The emergence of these recorded facts may be set forth step by step.

I have already discussed the general problem of the stirrup-jars; but now we have a combination of archaeological peculiarities. The tablet records 1800 stirrup-jars, and stirrup-jars of the elongated type depicted on the tablet actually occur in the same room, separated (we are told) by a mere 20 cm (8 inches) of clay. According to Evans, some two hundred years separate the two layers and the tablets refer to stirrup-jars which he failed to find anywhere in the palace. Moreover, stirrup-jars actually found in the room had been sited above the tablet by sheer coincidence, for naturally the 'squatters' knew nothing of the archive of clay tablets below their floor. This coincidence is noted by Evans, who comments 'curiously enough, on the floor of the apartment built by the later occupants of the Palace site. . . .' The coincidence might well have prompted stronger expression.

Thus there were many disquieting features in Evans's 'decisive stratigraphy' from the Room of the Stirrup-Jars. Bewilderment was increased when the Knossos tablets were finally published. Evans had jealously guarded his secret during the whole of his lifetime, and a Finnish scholar, J. Sundwall, who had procured a sight of some of the tablets in the Museum at Heraklion, incurred Evans's severe displeasure and was obliged to break off his work. After Evans's death in 1941 the task of editing his *Handlist* of the tablets and seeing the work through the press devolved on Sir John Myres. *Scripta Minoa II* was published by the Oxford University Press in 1952. It is worth recording that eight years passed before a remarkable discrepancy was noticed by Linear B scholars. There was no 'hoard' of stirrup-jar tablets, as stated by Evans in 1935: the one he had illustrated was the sole one. Later, the combined searches of the foremost Aegean epigraphists in the stores of Heraklion and Knossos failed to bring any further fragment of such a tablet to light among the thousands of minor scraps that were recovered. What was worse was that Myres in *Scripta Minoa II* gave the location of Evans's tablet not as the

Room of the Stirrup-Jars in the northwest part of the palace, but as 'West Area: West Southwest Entrances', that is in a remote part of the palace. Here was a clear conflict of testimony, and further enquiry was necessary. But could Myres be relied upon? It must be stated that the book abounds in typographical errors, self-contradictions and wrong references. In fact, what the *Handlist* showed when it was finally tracked down was that Myres' version was a misreading for 'Nr. Southwest Entrance'. At all events, since the evident flaws in the book might be due to careless proof reading, I approached the Oxford University Press to ask whether the manuscript of *Scripta Minoa II* was still available. I was referred to the Ashmolean Museum. Informed that Myres' papers were stored in the basement, I asked whether the Museum possessed Evans's *Handlist* of the Linear B tablets, to which Myres refers. I was first shown Evans's own notebooks of the excavations, some of the papers which came to the Ashmolean after his death. They turned out to be interesting, but scrappy. They cannot be regarded as furnishing a satisfactory record for an important excavation. But in the same cupboard was a large number of notebooks. This was the 'Day Book of the Excavations at Knossos' kept by Duncan Mackenzie.

Mackenzie, we are told by Dr Joan Evans in her *Time and Chance*, 'was a Scot with an inaudible Highland voice, a brush of red hair, an uncertain temper, a great command of languages, and great experience in keeping the records of an excavation.' The last point is important. The Day Book is a most meticulous document. Day by day, after work was over, this experienced excavator recorded in the diary what had been done and found. The whole work is lavishly illustrated with sketch plans giving grid references and measurements in centimetres. A brief perusal was enough to show that here was the detailed information concerning the find-spots of the tablets which had long been desiderated.

It is the entry for Tuesday May 8, 1900 which records the data relating to the Room of the Stirrup-Jars. It reads as follows. 'In the centre of the threshing-floor area 46)1 [this is a reference to the accompanying sketch plan] large quantities of inscription tablets in a very soft and crumbling condition appear all over the floor near the W wall of the room. Near the NW corner of the same room was found on the floor a large false-necked amphora with bands in brown-black varnish on an ochre ground. In the S part of the room as many as five vases whole or in fragments of the amphora type but almost entirely plain were found lying on the floor which is covered with a tough deposit of clay above the real floor which seems to be of cement. The tough damp clay must have had a good deal to do with the bad preservation of the inscriptions many fragments of which continue to appear all day.'

Two points must be stressed. This record was written on the day the room was excavated. The vases and the tablets were removed. On the following day the floor of the room was completely freed of deposit down to the underlying cement floor. Thus no later information about their relative positions could have been obtained. The evidence was destroyed in the process of excavation. Secondly, Mackenzie makes no distinction in his entry between the floor on which the tablets were found ('all over the floor') and the floor on which the 'false-necked amphora' (=stirrup-jar) was resting. He again says simply 'on the floor'. He does not say that the tablets were on the cement floor and the vases on the clay floor. On the contrary, Mackenzie explicitly states in the first entry of his Day Book referring to this set of rooms (this was on 4 May 1900) that the tablets were found 'on the clay floor': 'In the same region and extending along what seems the W wall of the space many fragments of inscription tablets in a very crumbling condition were found on the clay floor.' The matter is made clear by Mackenzie's sketch plan (our fig. 31). Fortunately, there is no conflict with Evans's own notes: he also drew a plan of these rooms (our Plate 19) and entered 'Many tablets: much perished' along the west wall of the 'Room of Bügelkannes'. It is fortunate also that he entered 'some tablets' in the south part of the Room of the Flower Gatherer and wrote alongside '1 m. down, May 3', the sketch being dated May 4.

For our present purpose it suffices to note that the documents show clearly what was observed and recorded in 1900 when the rooms were excavated and the objects removed. In retrospect it now appears strange that this neat stratification was not challenged at an earlier date. It did not appear in the excavation report for 1900 but not until the end of the fourth season in 1903.

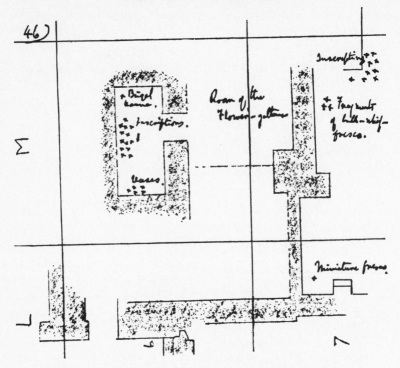

*Fig. 31. Sketch plan from Duncan Mackenzie's Day Book
of the Knossos Excavations recording finds of tablets in the
Room of the Stirrup-Jars.*

It is evident that there had been retrospective adjustment of the observed data. Could this be justified? Let us trace the further examination of this area in 1901.

In 1900 it was observed that the north wall of the Room of the Flower Gatherer had not been preserved and that this part of the site had been much disturbed by intruders.[1] In 1901 Mackenzie found that the floor itself had been removed in the northern part of the room. He took advantage of this to get below the level of the plaster floor uncovered in 1900. Forty cm below it he came across another floor again consisting of plaster but with a gypsum

[1] The excavation report makes the point that the north confines of the Room of the Saffron Gatherer had been deeply dug in search of stone; that there was a heap of debris; and that painted wall plaster had been thrown pell-mell into the adjoining portico.

slab embedded in it. Above, though not on, this floor were some
pieces of Linear B tablet. He concluded that this showed that
both floors (i.e. this and the upper one of 1900) were 'Mycenaean'.
Evans echoed the same conclusion in his own notes. The 1901
published report gives a somewhat confused version of the facts,
omitting the tablets found in the Room of the Flower Gatherer
altogether. But it does not state that the new finds indicated that
the published observations of 1900 had been faulty. The retrospective adjustment, as we have said, took place in the report for
1903. But further enquiry and the emergence of yet other
documents were to show that Mackenzie had been quite right in
his unreported conclusion of 1901: the lower floor was indeed
'Mycenaean'.[1] The plaster of which it was composed turned out to
be typical of the so-called 'reoccupation period'. This was
established in 1923 in another investigation which was not
disclosed. This will be discussed in the following chapter (pp.
223 ff.). Here a bald statement of the emergent excavation data will
suffice. The Room of the Stirrup-Jars had only two floors and not
three. The three floor levels were actually observed in the
neighbouring Room of the Saffron Gatherer (see figs. 33, 34), and
here all three levels had been occupied in the Late Minoan III
period. This is how Evans achieved his 'decisive stratigraphy'. He
transferred the three floors to the Room of the Stirrup-Jars. The
tablets observed and recorded 'on the clay floor' in both rooms
were moved down to the second floor. In 1935 he illustrated the
tablets allegedly found in this room by reproducing a fragment
from 'near the southwest entrance' and transforming it into a
'hoard'. This much was clear to me in 1960. But in 1961 another
document came to light which showed that the vases assigned by
Evans to the Room of the Stirrup-Jars were also not found there.
How Mackenzie's pottery notebooks came into the picture will be
told in the next chapter. Meanwhile it will suffice to say that the
facts are not in dispute and have been acknowledged in print by
Evans's defenders: the stirrup-jars were found on the South Front
and the strainer in the west wing, all in the 1901 campaign.

The prolonged search for the evidence asked for by Professor
Blegen had thus yielded facts which went far beyond his own

[1] That is Late Minoan III B.

217

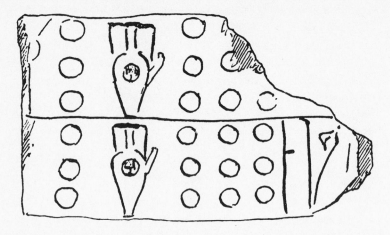

*Fig. 32. The Stirrup-Jar tablet recording 1800 such vessels.
Recorded as found 'West Area: Near South-west Entrance'.*

surmise. Not only had my doubts about the stratigraphy reported from the Room of the Stirrup-Jars been substantiated: but Mackenzie's later conclusions, as written down by him in 1923, suggested that there had been no fewer than three different floor levels, all attributable to the LM III period. The second had belonged to a set of rooms that represented a drastic rebuilding of the constructions to which the lowest LM III floor belonged. Thus the problem was transformed. The redating of the Linear B tablets some 200–250 years later was a comparatively minor matter. The problem now was rather how many architectural phases of the palace were to be assigned to the so-called 'squatter period'. In the next chapter we shall see how the same picture was gradually revealed in many parts of the palace. Constantly we shall unearth evidence, misreported or not disclosed, which indicates not merely that the great fire came at the time Blegen and I had deduced but that important parts of the building had actually been *constructed* at a much later date than Evans had supposed and Aegean archaeologists for sixty years had believed.

Finally, doubts are stimulated on a still more fundamental matter. Archaeologists draw minute distinctions between pottery styles. They have concluded that the palace was destroyed when

LM III A: 1 was in vogue,[1] and the post-destruction period at
Knossos began with the style LM III A: 2. Leading Aegean
archaeologists are now expressing doubts on this basic matter.
My own researches support them. If, for instance, *some* vessels
classified as LM I A and LM I B are actually later than *some*
classified as LM III B, then much of the current picture of Aegean
prehistory lies in ruins. As Professor Levi has written: we must
wipe the slate clean and start all over again from the very
beginning.

[1] On this modification of Evans's statement that the destruction took place 'at
the end of LM II', see below p. 305.

Chapter VII

Checking the Facts

In the preceding chapter I have described how growing doubts prompted both by archaeological and philological investigations stimulated an enquiry into the sole stratigraphic statement offered by Evans as evidence (which he deemed 'decisive') for the dating of the tablets. The Knossos documents which successively came to light showed that doubt attached to every item of this complex and minutely detailed picture. The actual excavation data from the Room of the Stirrup-Jars and the neighbouring rooms were totally different from those reported. In archaeology we are dependent almost entirely on the statements made by the excavator about the find positions, for the evidence is destroyed when the objects are removed from the ground. For the Room of the Stirrup-Jars this stage of destruction was reached on 9 May 1900, when the floor was cleared down to the underlying terrazza (concrete). The very least that can be said is that, in view of the documentary evidence, it would be unsafe to rely on Evans's stratigraphic key. Yet this is the sole one he proffered: the whole question of the date of the tablets, with all that implies for Aegean prehistory, was now in the melting pot. Moreover, the strange errors in the use of his own documents, such as the transformation of one tablet found near the southwest entrance into a 'hoard' found in the Room of the Stirrup-Jars, were bound to shake confidence in the trustworthiness of the main witness for the Knossos excavations.[1] It was now all the more necessary to

[1] That Evans did not rely on his memory when writing the account of his 'decisive stratigraphy' for the fourth volume of *The Palace of Minos* is shown by the comments in his *Handlist*. It is clear that he cut his drawing of the stirrup-jar tablet out and sent it to the publisher having marked it off with four crosses in red ink and written underneath the words 'same size'. I have taken a tracing of the figure in the book and it fits exactly over the drawing. There is no doubt that the drawing in the *Handlist* was thus used in compiling the book. Above the

carry out the fundamental scientific precaution of checking the facts, by which I mean the data obtained by excavation.[1]

1. AN EGYPTIAN OBJECT

By way of illustration of what is involved in verifying Evans's statements about the evidence he obtained in the Knossos excavations I choose an example which is considered of prime importance in Aegean prehistory. My choice is influenced by the fact that it has figured in recent publications by two eminent specialists in the field. It will be seen that no specialist knowledge or training is required to carry out the check.

In his contribution to the revised edition of the *Cambridge Ancient History*, the chapter entitled 'Minoan Civilization: Maturity and Zenith', the German scholar F. Matz writes: 'The absolute chronology of the Minoan periods is fixed by relations with Egypt and the Near East.' By this means Matz determines the date of Middle Minoan IIA and B pottery as 1850–1775 B.C. He goes on: 'This date is supported by the fact that MM II B sherds were associated at Cnossus with a diorite figure of the late Twelfth Dynasty, which places the beginnings of MM II B pottery as early as the eighteenth century B.C.' The same piece of evidence was adduced by another authority, Professor Paul Åström in a lecture to the Cretological Congress at Heraklion in September 1961. Apropos of the Egyptian statuette he wrote: 'It is said to have been found in the lower part of a stratum which contained only Middle Minoan II B pottery'. Åström gave the references to Evans's *The Palace of Minos*. This source we must now examine to check the accuracy of the stratigraphic statements.

Evans's account of the find place of the statuette with its hieroglyph inscription has all desirable precision. It was found 70 cm below the paving of the Central Court. Test pits sunk in 1913 had revealed a widespread Middle Minoan II B stratum on

drawing in the usual place for such indications Evans had written in 1900 the find spot: W. Area: nr. SW Entrance.

Even so the question of 'fraud' need not arise. The vital point is that he consulted his record and transformed a single tablet found near the southwest entrance into a hoard found in the Room of the Stirrup-Jars. We rely on this witness for our knowledge of the Knossos excavation data. Is he a reliable witness?

[1] On the question 'what is an archaeological fact?' see below p. 284.

Checking the Facts

which was directly superimposed a Late Minoan stratum. It was to this underlying MM II B stratum that the statuette belonged. Our check thus needs two simple operations. Was the statuette found 70 cm below the pavement of the court? Did the 1913 tests reveal a widespread Middle Minoan II B stratum below a LM stratum? The documents provide a no less clear answer. Mackenzie records the finding on 25 April 1900. In grid square K 7 there was an isolated patch of paving: 'The find was made just on the pavement about ·70 down.' In other words, the depth was 70 cm below the modern surface before excavation on the pavement and not 70 cm below the pavement. We now turn to the 1913 notebook of Evans to ascertain the results of the 1913 test pits. Again we are fortunate: Evans had drawn a sketch plan in the notebook of the tests in the Central Court, had numbered them and had given indications of the content of each pit, even sketching some of the sherds. It has been possible to identify most of the boxes in the Stratigraphical Museum. Certainly the deposit below the pavement contained MM II sherds but in the test pit closest to the find place of the statuette there were only a few, the bulk being Neolithic. But the test pit immediately east (no. 56) which went down to 50 cm below the pavement produced Late Minoan II, while the one west of this close to the Throne Room actually yielded a sherd which according to the prevalent system of classification is LM III A : 2, in other words 'post-destruction'.

Professor Åström, to whom I communicated the above facts, now agrees that 'the statuette will have to be excluded from close Cretan-Egyptian synchronisms in future.' Yet enshrined in the new edition of the *Cambridge Ancient History*, it will continue to mislead students for a long time to come.

The example is concerned with the Middle Minoan Period and so does not directly concern the date of the tablets apart from the evidence bearing on the date when the pavement of the Central Court was laid. It is quoted simply to illustrate the simplicity of the checking processes which will be attempted in the present chapter. All who can read and follow a simple plan and section may take a hand. What has emerged bears on the central question: how far can we rely on Evans's testimony for the experimental evidence secured during the Knossos excavations? The question

222

can no longer be evaded. Evans's factual statements are still the basis of authoritative works addressed to scholars and students by the most eminent authorities.

2. The Room of the Stirrup-Jars

In the previous chapter we have seen how doubts gradually arose about every detail of Evans's decisive stratigraphy which he assigned to this room, with its carefully measured three floor levels. The whole question was transformed with the discovery that in 1923 there had been an elaborate investigation in this set of rooms. It had been minutely recorded, with a plan, by Mackenzie in a notebook bearing that date. The results may be briefly summarized as Mackenzie interpreted them. They are best set forth in the form of diagrams (figs. 33 and 34). Mackenzie started in the room south of the Room of the Saffron Gatherer (see Plate 19), which was called the Room of the Lotus Lamp. The floor under examination he stated to be of gypsum slabs lying 80 cm below the paving of the Central Court. This is an exact datum point which enables us to verify his entries today. In 1903 Evans had published an elaborate section for the Room of the Lotus Lamp, which may be summarized thus:

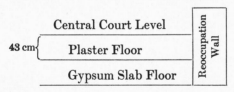

The first question is to decide which floor Mackenzie was referring to in 1923. It is identifiable in two ways: (1) composition (gypsum slabs); (2) level (80 cm below the Court). Is it the plaster floor at 43 cm depth? This may seem a strange question to put. Yet it is necessary because of a still stranger reaction. A professional archaeologist, J. Boardman, promptly assured his colleagues and the public that I had made a mistake: the floor examined in 1923 was the upper one of plaster uncovered in 1900. Fortunately, the floor in question is still *in situ*; when I visited Knossos in 1961 it was possible to verify the main details in Mackenzie's account.

The identification is beyond question and the new results must be faced. A summary follows:

The room was flanked on the west by a ramshackle wall built of re-used miscellaneous materials. Mackenzie diagnosed it as a work of the 'Reoccupation'. This was confirmed when he dug down alongside it: he found 32 cm below the level of the gypsum slabs the remains of a LM II B jar. He concluded that the wall had been built when this kind of pottery belonging to the end of the so-called 'Palace Style' had got stratified.

Mackenzie next examined the floor itself. The gypsum slabs had been extensively patched with plaster. This was of a composition identical with that found in 'reoccupied' parts of the site and also in the mainland Mycenaean palaces of the Late Helladic III B period. He examined it minutely: there were many layers, showing repeated repairs. Mackenzie now traced the course of the late plaster. It dipped down into the room to the north. This was

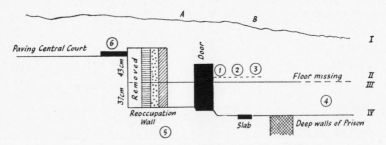

Fig. 33. Section S–N from Central Court to Room of Saffron Gatherer. I. Surface. II. Clay floor (1900). III. Plaster ('cement') floor (1900). IV. Gypsum slabs + plaster floor (1901, 1923).

A. Room of Lotus Lamp. Floor level IV examined in 1923. Floor patched with 'reoccupation' plaster; slanting west wall also 'reoccupation'. (5) LM II B sherds 32 cm below floor level. (6) South wall of latest phase built over steps descending to floor IV.

B. Room of Saffron Gatherer. Above floor II: (1) and (2) purple lamps, (3) Saffron Gatherer fresco, also tablets. Floor III: 'cement' found incomplete in northern half. Floor IV patched with 'reoccupation' plaster etc. (4) tablets (1901).

the Room of the Saffron Gatherer, and here the plaster joined on to another gypsum slab in the centre (fig. 33). It was evident that the late plaster had been used to reconstitute an earlier floor of gypsum slabs. At this point Mackenzie gives us some interesting information bearing on the important room to the west — the Room of the Stirrup-Jars. He tells us that the floor in that room was 30 cm higher than the late plaster in the adjoining Room of the Saffron Gatherer: see fig. 34. Not merely that, but he volunteers the information that the floor was of terrazza (concrete mixed with small pebbles) and that at the time of the original excavation in 1900 this floor had been complete all over. It had

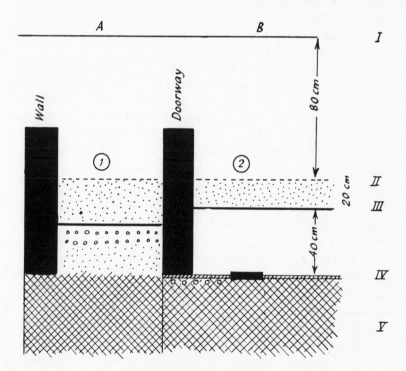

Fig. 34. Section W–E.

A. Room of Stirrup Jars. B. Room of Saffron Gatherer.
I. Modern threshing floor. II. Clay floor (1900) with (1) and
(2) late vessels and tablets. III. Plaster floor (1900). IV. Plaster
covering terrazza which is repeated 30 cm higher in A.
V. Deep walls of prison. For Evans' account see pp. 211 ff.

been dug away at the north and south ends of the room in later excavations (1901, 1903) leaving a strip in the middle. These later excavations had revealed the deep walls of the so-called 'prisons' underneath; they began 25–35 cm below the terrazza. This can still be observed on the site.

Mackenzie's notes on this undisclosed excavation thus yielded information that was catastrophic in its implications. In the first place the triple floor structure alleged by Evans for the Room of the Stirrup-Jars had not existed at all. But what was even more disturbing was the discovery that the third floor level down in the Room of the Saffron Gatherer (see fig. 34) had been patched with late plaster attributed by Mackenzie to the so-called 'squatter' period. In the room to the south at the corresponding floor level the room had been divided by the building of a ramshackle partition wall perched aslant on the underlying well-built 'prison' wall. If the third floor level down was in LM III B occupation, then evidently the top floor of clay was even later. And it was above this top floor that all the famous finds of 1900 had been recovered, including tablets (see below on the Saffron Gatherer Fresco). It was above this lowest LM III floor that the few tablets had been discovered in 1901 (fig. 33).

We shall never know Evans's 'interpretation' of the minute and complex data yielded by this important excavation of 1923. He never referred to it, and the results remained unknown until I published them in 1961. The sole reaction on the archaeological side was the unaccountable blunder noted above, which declared in effect that $80 = 43$ and gypsum slabs = plaster. The whole problem was transformed by the new data. The redating of the tablets was now a minor matter. The new question was: How many LM III phases were there in the architectural history of this part of the palace? Renewed investigations into the neighbouring Northern Entrance Passage were to reveal exactly the same state of affairs: the tablets were found above an earth LM III B floor, and deeper down was a paved floor which, as later tests revealed, also sealed in LM II–III sherds. In other words, here too we had a building with a number of different phases all attributable to Evans's 'squatter' period. But before we turn our attention to it, the last step in checking Evans's statements about the Room of the Stirrup-Jars must be told. The tale can be brief. Mackenzie's pottery notebooks showed that the vases attributed by Evans to this room were found in other parts of the Palace. The 'decisive stratigraphy' was revealed as a total fabrication.

3. THE NORTHERN ENTRANCE PASSAGE

Evans's concentration on the 'Room of the Stirrup-Jars' is all the more remarkable because only a few yards away to the East he had found a great mass of tablets with a clearly recognized pottery context. It was this find which occasioned the excited message to his father: 'With regard to prehistoric inscriptions "the cry is still they come".' The 'Great Deposit of Tablets', as it is called, was found closely clustered on the west side of the Northern Entrance Passage.

What is of the greatest importance is that the tablets were found intermingled with large quantities of pottery which leaves no doubt whatsoever about the ceramic context, and hence the dating, of this great hoard. The vessels in question were the so-called couple-amphorae, that is a pair of two-handled vessels joined like Siamese twins. Mackenzie wrote on Thursday May 10, 1900: 'The concurrence of these amphorae with the inscriptions makes excavation in this extensive deposit a matter of excessive difficulty and slowness.' It so happens that another specimen of these peculiar vessels had been found right at the beginning of the excavation in the south-west part of the site in a superficial stratum along with a stirrup-jar of a type marking the extreme period of the Reoccupation. It remains to add that in the same superficial stratum the first Linear B tablet was found on March 31, 1900. Thus from the very first discovery the tablets were found in deposit recognized as belonging to the 'Reoccupation'.

Evans himself in the *Palace of Minos* submits the evidence from the Northern Entrance Passage in the clearest form with a stratigraphical diagram (fig. 35)[1] which indicates the find-spot of the tablets on the 'clearly defined' LM III surface. He adds the remark, however, that they are LM II tablets. We repeat that tablets as archaeological objects can be dated only by their

[1] In this I have inserted the new evidence from later excavations (see below).

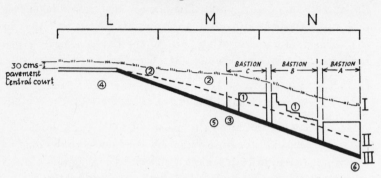

Fig. 35. Section through the Northern Entrance Passage
(cf. Palace of Minos *III, 171, Fig. 114).*

I. Original surface. II. LM III roadway. III. MM III paved
way. (1)–(1) 'Great Deposit' of tablets. (2)–(2) surface deposit
of tablets. (3) LM II–III sherds (1913). (4) LM III sherds
(19᠄). (5) LM II sherd (1929). (6) LM III sherds (1901).

ceramic context. However, let us again reconstruct the physical
history of these tablets on the assumption that they were written
and stored in their boxes *c.* 1400 B.C. In the first place the architectural history of the Northern Entrance Passage will repay a brief
glance. At first a gangway some seven metres broad, it was nar-
rowed in the Third Middle Minoan Period (*c.* 1700 B.C.) by the
construction of three 'bastions'. What is of the greatest interest in
the present connexion is that after the 'final' destruction of the
palace in LM II (*c.* 1400), in the early days of the 'reoccupation'
demolitions were undertaken on these bastions and the passage
was restored to two thirds of its original width.

With Evans's dating of the Great Deposit of Tablets we should
have to suppose that the tablets in their boxes survived the
destruction of 1400 B.C. and persisted throughout the demolitions
and remodellings of the Northern Entrance Passage only to
become involved in the later catastrophe of the twelfth century
B.C. By an unfortunate chain of physical accidents these boxes of
fifteenth century tablets somehow became intermingled with 'vast
quantities' of the later pottery, which impeded the work of the
archaeologist and complicated his interpretation. The clearest
possible ceramic context for a closely clustering mass of tablets

provided a dating which Evans felt bound to reject: these, he states, were LM II tablets on an LM III surface.

Now in view of the general doubts which had been roused, the next step was to check Evans's stratigraphic statements about the Great Deposit. They proved accurate in the main although the picture had been somewhat simplified. At all events, this great mass of tablets had been found above the latest earth floor, entangled with a large number of vessels undoubtedly belonging to the so-called 'squatter period'.

Evans's defenders thus faced some awkward excavation data. My archaeological collaborator began the task of devising hypotheses to explain the facts away. First he suggested that the boxes of tablets had been carried into the entrance passage by plunderers operating at the end of the Late Minoan period, some 200–250 years after the destruction of 1400 B.C. On breaking the boxes open they had been disappointed to find tablets and simply left them lying in the pottery store, where according to Evans's imaginative account, a squatter potter had exposed them for sale to persons passing up the entrance passage to what had been the central court of the palace. Here we have a neat example of a besetting sin of archaeology: the ready resort to complex *ad hoc* hypotheses of a kind we have already encountered in Woolley's story about the commercially minded potter at Alalakh. The proffered escape hypothesis had the further disadvantage that it did not explain the find data. Consequently yet another story had to be invented. This I propose to examine. As we shall see, each successive phase of the new hypothesis prompted further enquiry with the result that once again new evidence was disclosed. This revealed the same architectural story as in the Room of the Saffron Gatherer: there were several architectural phases in the Northern Entrance Passage all attributable to the Late Minoan III period.

I start with the primary evidence. Evans's sketch plan for this area (see Plate 19) enters 'Great Seal and tablets' at a point just south of the little passage opening west in which *inter alia* Evans records 'Arse of Bull Relief'. Mackenzie's Day Book provides the information that this deposit was found *from the surface* down to 90 cm (35·5 inches). Evans repeatedly adverted to this deposit in his publications, and in *The Palace of Minos* he reproduced the 'Great Seal' (*PoM* iv, 568, fig. 542 a). All his public statements are consistent and they agree with the notebooks. The tablets, with the sealing, and fragments of the container were found much higher than the adjacent Great Deposit: they were close to the original surface at this point. The tablets were listed by Evans in his *Handlist*. They contained a coherent group, those referring to ewes, lambs and wool (see p. 117). It will be evident that the plunderer story will not do: this would not explain the find position high above the LM III earth floor. Only Evans's own account is satisfactory: he concluded that they had fallen from a room overlooking the Northern Entrance Passage. He apparently did not realize that this implied that they had remained in the said room during the drastic rebuilding of the passage after his supposed destruction of LM II, when the east bastions had been torn down and the passage widened to five metres. They had not fallen until after the store of double-amphorae had been 'exposed for sale' by his supposed squatters. His defender was thus forced to devise a second story to replace that of the plunderers. He now declared that the tablets had been shovelled in to the passage by the 'reoccupation' folk to make up their earth floor. But this was not to explain the facts but to alter them: in other words it was proposed to readjust the observed data just as Evans had done in the Room of the Stirrup-Jars. But this move down encountered much the same difficulties: new evidence now came to light showing that the next floor level down had sealed in Late Minoan III pottery.

The evidence in question came from Evans's own notebook of 1913. The entrance passage at this point had been cleared down to the lowest paved floor by 1900 (see fig. 35), and by good fortune a photograph in the Ashmolean collection taken in 1902 showed the state of the passage at this very point together with the passage opening west (see Plate 19). Evans's notebook recorded three test pits in the passage at this point and inside the passage opening west. The entry was surprising: 'Large no. of fine pieces of Palace Style jars. Rest rather mixed', this below a paved floor ascribed by Evans to the Middle Minoan III A period! Still odder was the entry 'rest rather mixed', for surely a floor is dated by the *latest* class of pottery found below it. The suspicion crossed my mind that the 'mixture' might have contained Late Minoan III sherds besides the large number of Palace Style jar fragments. But how to find out?

At this point we must introduce the evidence of the so-called Stratigraphical Museum at Knossos. This was one of Evans's most laudable enterprises. Realizing that the primary evidence in archaeology is pottery, he had the sherds, whose find-places in various parts of the site had been carefully registered by Mackenzie, placed in labelled containers and housed in a makeshift 'museum' created by his partial reconstruction of the buildings. Eventually this collection comprised a few thousand boxes of sherds. At a later date they were examined by J. D. S. Pendlebury, who succeeded Mackenzie as Evans's assistant in 1928. His *Guide to the Stratigraphical Museum* was published by the British School of Archaeology at Athens in 1933–35. This work contains an important statement by Evans bearing on the problem I now faced: how to discover what sherds were contained in the 'mixture' obtained by Evans in his 1913 investigation. He tells us that in 1913 he had been alone at Knossos, where he had carried out close on a hundred test pits. He had entered the details on wooden labels, which he had placed in the boxes containing the sherds obtained from each test pit. Now, in his notebook he had given the numbers 77, 78 and 79 to the test pits with which we are concerned, ringing the numbers round. It turned out that there were corresponding boxes in the Museum, and they contained wooden labels bearing these numbers ringed round in exactly the same way. The boxes contained the fine pieces of Palace Style jars he had entered in his notebook: they also contained LM III sherds, as I had suspected. Not merely this, but the facts had already been printed by Pendlebury in his *Guide* under the reference numbers J II 5 and J II 10, which he sited correctly on the plans published with the *Guide*. These facts were established by a young French scholar, Mr J. Raison, to whom I had sent the extracts from Evans's 1913 notebook. Thus archaeological data that made nonsense of Evans's account of the Northern Entrance Passage had been obtained in 1913, and the results had been in print for thirty years but had passed unnoticed.

Checking the Facts

As we shall see in the next chapter on the 'Conflict of Scholars', an effort had now to be made to discredit this evidence. It was alleged that the 1913 sherds had been obtained from an earth baulk that had survived all the excavations between 1900 and 1913. However, it turned out that the *Guide* contained other information relating to more tests, this time in 1929. Throughout the entrance passage the evidence was completely consistent: LM II–III sherds had been recovered under and alongside the intrusive bastions which Evans dated to the beginning of Middle Minoan III A (eighteenth century B.C.).

It will be evident that no serious consideration can be given to the plea of 'intrusion' with sherds obtained from below foundations of bastions and a paved way. In his account of the history of the Northern Entrance Passage (1930, *PoM* iii, 160 ff.) Evans had evidently forgotten about the tests of 1913, 1928 and 1929. He begins his account with the statement: 'Very complete evidence is forthcoming for the date when this North Entrance Avenue was carried out.' But he makes no mention of the LM II and III sherds which were recovered at so many points. However, he does make it clear that the Great Deposit of tablets was found *above* the LM III earth floor, representing the third phase of the architectural history; and they were entangled with pots ascribed by Evans to LM III B, a classification doubted by no Aegean expert. Some hypothesis had to be devised to put asunder what had been found together. It runs as follows. The tablets must have been exposed to fire, otherwise they would not have been preserved. But the associated pots show no signs of fire damage. Thus they cannot date the tablets found with them. This piece of archaeological reasoning, widely acclaimed and repeated, is one of the strangest episodes in the whole controversy. This question will be examined in the next chapter. But even if we grant the validity of the dogma (and it is no more) on the supposed effects of fire, the find facts still remain to be explained. We have to devise some story to account for the fact that masses of tablets written and stored *c.* 1400 B.C. were found in an archaeological context datable about a quarter of millennium later. How had they survived the drastic reconstruction? By what means had they been transported into the later entrance passage and mixed up with the store of double jars in a room or lean-to, the north wall of which was a flimsy construction actually resting on the later earth floor? Above all, how had a coherent set of tablets together with a sealing come to be so close to the modern surface? Sherds and other archaeological fragments may drift about; but here we had pieces of clay, not intended to survive for more than a year as written, which allegedly had preserved their togetherness throughout the long 'squatter' period and had so remained until Mackenzie recorded them in A.D. 1900. Plunderers or, alternatively, roadmaking activities of the 'squatters' were hypotheses hardly deserving serious attention.

Evans, let it be repeated, offered no such far-fetched stories. He saw clearly that the tablets must have fallen from a room or rooms overlooking the Entrance Passage. Originally, he implied, they had been associated with LM II pottery. Once again we encounter this remarkable archaeological circumstance. Although the tablets and sealings, 'of all objects the most perishable', as Evans says, remained intact as a set so close to the surface in the most unfavourable survival conditions for over three thousand years, no LM II pottery was reported by the excavators. Yet, according to the story, the palace must have been largely stocked with pottery of this class, for there is no other meaning to a palace 'of LM II date' (revised after Evans's death to LM III A: 1). Again and again we shall encounter this strange archaeological circumstance in the Palace of Minos that the hand of chance has separated tablets from the pottery which *ex hypothesi* had been their companions at the time of the burning of the palace and brought them into bad company, for which embarrassed excuses had repeatedly to be found.

Yet the whole of our long investigation and elaborate argument, as we have seen, was made unnecessary by the results of the undisclosed investigations of 1913, which yielded LM II–III sherds from below the paved way at a point where the Great Deposit adjoins the higher level deposit of the 'Great Seal' (fig. 35). It is still more disappointing to have to disclose that after all this work had been done, further acquaintance with the documents and closer reading of *The Palace of Minos* showed that Evans had made many clear statements and even published a photograph that indicated the Late Minoan III B date of the fire. In extenuation I should plead that the facts had also escaped the notice of archaeologists, including Evans's main opponent Wace.

4. THE LAPIDARY'S WORKSHOP OF REOCCUPATION DATE

In 1901 Evans was excavating the eastern part of the South Front of the palace, when he came across two basement rooms in one of which a seal cutter had been busy. There were some unfinished seal stones and even some trial impressions on lumps of clay. Now burnt beans had been found in both these rooms,[1] while the floor of the northern of the two was found partly covered with a layer of charred wheat. In *The Palace of Minos* II, 762, fig. 490 Evans presented a plan of the area entering 'Lapidary's Workshop LM III' with 'Stores of Egyptian Beans' to the north. In IV, 594 a whole section of the book is headed 'Lapidary's Workshop of Reoccupation Date'. Now it will be hardly denied that burnt beans and charred wheat are evidence suggestive of fire, and it would be extravagant to assert that the 'squatter' lapidary had been making seal stones for his fellow squatters careless of the debris deposited on the floor some two hundred and fifty years before.

I drew attention to these facts at a discussion in London in February 1961. The reaction was immediate. It is thus recorded in the Minutes: 'Evans's dating accepted where convenient' (J. Boardman). This is a disguised way of saying 'I reject Evans's dating because it is inconvenient'. It is a curious method of defending Evans to reject his careful circumstantial accounts of the area in question. A few weeks later yet another odd coincidence was to put into my hands documentary evidence which revealed why Evans had so firmly dated his lapidary to the 'reoccupation' period (LM III B). I was lecturing at Cambridge, and in the subsequent discussion a member of the audience got up and said that Professor Palmer might be interested to know that there were still notebooks of Mackenzie kept in the Villa Ariadne (the house built by Evans at Knossos and later made over to the British School). I immediately applied to the Management Committee

---

[1] This is stated by Mackenzie.

and received permission to examine the notebooks with the proviso that there could be no question of priority since they were now under examination by members of the School. I arrived at Knossos in September 1961 and found that the books were Mackenzie's pottery notebooks. It was not until I returned home in October that I learned to my discomfiture that these books had been described some nine years before in a work of popular archaeology. An Oxford friend (a scientist) drew my attention to a passage from Mr Leonard Cottrell's *Bull of Minos*, a work with which I had no first hand acquaintance.

The passage ran: 'As I put back Evans's Presidential Address to the British Association I noticed a group of notebooks with faded covers resting on a lower shelf. I picked one out at random; it was filled with pencilled diagrams of pottery and notes in a careful handwriting. The signature was "D. Mackenzie" . . .'. This was the priceless document I began to study, in the company of resident members of the School, at Knossos in September 1961. It was a great disappointment to find that Mackenzie had begun his pottery notes in 1901. There was nothing for the important first year of the excavations. I opened the first notebook and almost immediately came to pages dealing with the area of the wheat and the beans. Much whole pottery had been found, and it clearly emerged from Mackenzie's detailed descriptions that it was all Late Minoan III B. This was the unreported evidence on which Evans had based his repeated declarations that these basement rooms had been used by the 'reoccupiers'. Burnt material had been found in the deposit from the surface (beans and tablets) right down to the floor covered with charred wheat at 2·60 metres. Evidently, the mass of whole vessels recorded must have been recovered below the surface and in all probability, in view of their condition, on the floor itself. The opposition were now in a quandary. There was now no question of rejecting Evans's date. Without hesitation the pots were moved up to a level and assigned to a floor not recorded by Evans or Mackenzie, high above the floor on which the wheat had been found. This not only went counter to Evans's explicit statement that a pot of beans had been found in an adjacent corner: it implied that the great quantity of whole Late Minoan III jars had sunk down into the fire debris, which had closed over them. For Evans had written of this very area that clay sealings and fragments of inscribed tablets had been found 'in the upper earth' (*PoM* II, 767), a statement corroborated by the day-to-day entries of D. Mackenzie. To get the pots above the tablets and the other burnt debris they would have to be placed above the surface.

The defenders of Evans had now been forced into total rejection of his own circumstantial account; they had devised an elaborate stratigraphy neither he nor Mackenzie had recorded or reported. But yet another victim had to be sacrificed. In 1960 the Oxford University Press had published a book on *Cretan Seals* by a leading expert in that field. Mr V. E. G. Kenna had discussed the seal stones in the Lapidary's Workshop and pronounced them (p. 77) to be of late date. He was induced to retract. It remains to add that Mackenzie's pottery notebooks revealed that the Stirrup-Jars assigned by Evans to the Room of the Stirrup-Jars in his elaborate 'decisive stratigraphy' were found on the South Front. On p. 79 of the same notebook he describes a strainer from the west part of the palace: it tallied exactly with that on the photograph published by Evans to illustrate the vessels from the same room. This we shall examine below (pp. 246 ff.).

5. THE SCHOOL ROOM

Such was the first impact of the new evidence brought to my notice by Mr R. W. Hutchinson. The result had been to turn Evans's supporters against the man they were defending. A still more wholesale rejection of Evans was to be occasioned by the strainer whose real find-place had also been disclosed by the pottery notebooks (see pp. 246 ff.). It was a further disappointment to find that all this search and labour had also been entirely unnecessary: Evans had long before published a photograph and given detailed information bearing on it which clearly indicated the date of the fire. Once again I urge in extenuation that the facts had also escaped the notice of the archaeologists concerned, including Wace, who had actually used the evidence from the rooms in question in an argument in support of his case that the *LM II palace* was occupied by Mainland dynasts.

Checking the Facts

We must return to Blegen's article 'A Chronological Problem' and the reception it received from his fellow archaeologists. One of the few scholars to advert to it in print was Miss D. H. F. Gray, Lecturer in Homeric Archaeology at Oxford. She dismissed Blegen's arguments with a single sentence: 'the general arguments for making the Knossos and Pylos tablets more nearly contemporary do not seem strong enough to convict Evans of so large an error.' By way of 'adequate' stratification adduced by Evans, the distinguished expert quoted the Room of the Stirrup-Jars and the so-called School Room. The first has proved to be a complete fabrication; the present state of the room is inconsistent with Evans's account. No such long investigation was required for the School Room. Evans's detailed treatment and copious illustration proved sufficient, without the aid of the documents, to demonstrate the late date of the fire. What had escaped general notice was that in his first volume Evans made a serious error in the diagnosis of the pottery found here, a mistake which he frankly rectified in the third volume of his great work. It was this recantation that had been missed. The School Room, thus singled out in rebuttal of Blegen, is certainly worth a visit and close scrutiny.

To take our bearings reference may be made to the general plan of the palace in fig. 30. We cross the Central Court from the Northern Entrance Passage (6) to the Domestic Quarter on the east side and descend the Grand Staircase. Passing along the East-West Corridor (8), we turn left just before the east staircase begins and continue along this north return of the corridor until we come out in the School Room, facing and giving on to the Court of the Stone Spout. Fig. 36 shows more detail. The chief point to be noted about the finds is that a rubble wall had blocked this north leg of the corridor turning it into a magazine, in which Evans found a store of whole pots of different kinds. The inner part of the School Room (so-called because it had benches along the walls) had likewise been used as a pottery store, where the pots were found on a stone bench. In Volume I of his great work Evans classified the pots as Middle Minoan III B, and he concluded that this part of the palace had been engulfed in that period and that reconstruction had taken place above the debris. It was not until 1930 that Evans realized that he had made a

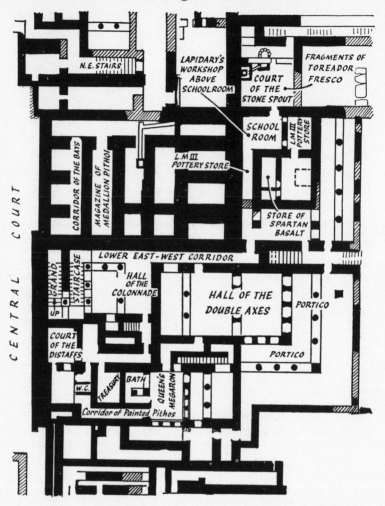

Fig. 36. The East Wing (Domestic Quarter) of the Palace of Knossos.

catastrophic blunder in diagnosing the pottery. He wrote (III, 265): 'It is necessary in this place to rectify an erroneous view, previously adopted, as to the date of the later arrangements in this part of the area ....' The pots were not Middle Minoan III B but Late Minoan III B! Not merely this, but further probes showed that the rooms had been largely rebuilt when the so-called 'squatter' period had far advanced. The evidence for this was obtained by lifting the great threshold block of the entrance into the Court of the Stone Spout. Underneath a series of LM III B sherds were found, including two or three bases of the latest class of pedestalled cup.

Evans now printed a correction referring to the plan of the area published in the first volume (p. 367, fig. 266), which ascribed the room to the Middle Minoan III period. He stated that this was now to be taken as 'showing the arrangement of this area in the Reoccupation period'. This is the arrangement shown in our fig. 36. Note the 'LM III pottery store', the pots from which were reproduced by Evans in the photograph already referred to, but there were wrongly dated. Evans also reproduced a photograph of this room taken from the Court of the Stone Spout and looking towards the west wall of the corridor which had been made into the pottery store. It shows the empty sockets in the wall, and Evans in his text comments that at the time of the excavation they had contained the charred remains of the wooden posts.

Here then we have direct evidence for the conflagration. How do archaeologists date such an event? By the pottery found in the room. We now know that the pots in the store alongside this wall with the charred wooden posts belonged to the end of the LM III B period — the very end of Evans's so-called 'Reoccupation'. We repeat Evans's words: the rebuilding 'was entirely the work of the "Reoccupation Period" — carried out indeed not earlier than its later phase.'

This evidence bearing on the date of the fire might be deemed sufficient to all who have the inclination to consider it. But examination of Evans's own notebooks was to show that he had obtained in 1905 evidence bearing on the late arrangements in this part of the site. In that year he had sunk a test pit in the most southerly of the suite of rooms — the Room of the Wooden Posts, which is the room space on our plan (fig. 36) which is occupied by the words 'Store of Spartan Basalt'. The room was excavated in 1901 and showed signs of exceptionally fierce fire. A block of the upper storey (marked black on our plan) had been kept in position by the fallen debris and below it Evans traced remnants of the wooden post which once had kept it in position — hence the name he gave to the room. The floor when reached proved to be of limestone slabs, but it was covered with powdered gypsum, the product of the fierce heat on the gypsum stone of the construction. Evidently the deposit had been undisturbed since the fall occasioned by the destructive fire. We now know from Evans's notebook that a test of 1905 in that room[1] produced *inter alia* LM I–III sherds. This proved that the floor had been paved when the latest type of sherds recovered from the pit had already got stratified. The test agreed with that made in 1928 when the adjacent blocking wall of the corridor was removed (see Fig. 36): there, too, LM III B sherds were found underneath the wall.

It now remains to survey what was found within these rooms (fig. 37). The results are disconcerting. Of the date of the fire there can now be little doubt. But in the Court of the Stone Spout, thus rebuilt and reoccupied late in the 'squatter period', Evans had found at a high level in the deposit the famous Toreador Fresco (Plate 10). Once again only complex *ad hoc* hypotheses can save the high dating of the fresco. The plain find data are as we have now elucidated. We now consider other important discoveries. The room immediately adjoining the School Room was one of those stated by Evans to have formed part of these late arrangements: it contained a store of Spartan basalt, partly worked. This stone, *lapis Lacedaemonius*, is obtainable only from a site near Sparta. Here was evidence for imports of a luxury material at a time when, according to the standard text books, Crete had long been a quiet backwater cut off from world commerce. Above this store of sculptor's material was another room. In this Evans had made one of his most remarkable finds. Within 25 cm (some ten inches) of the surface he had found two magnificent stone jars in an unfinished state. Evans rightly concluded that they represented work in progress in the last days before the conflagration. Yet they are dated stylistically to LM II and compared to the stone vessels found on the floor of the Throne Room.

Let us reconstruct their history on the current assumption that stylistic diagnoses can be translated into absolute chronology. In

[1] It bears the reference number 126A Q10; the test pit must have been below the limestone paving laid bare in 1901.

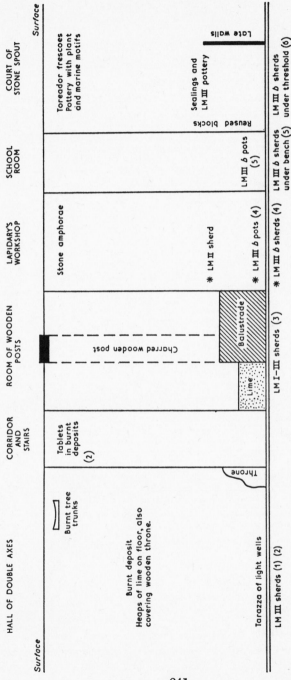

Fig. 37. Schematic Section in 'School Room' Area: Reconstructed in Late Minoan III B. Note the LM III sherds below the floors and walls overlaid with fire debris.

241

1400 B.C. the stone sculptors were interrupted in their work by the disaster to the palace. They ran away leaving their vessels on the floor, and the palace collapsed on them as a consequence of the fire, evidenced by the burnt gypsum on the floor of the neighbouring room. In the room below their workshop reposed the supply of Spartan basalt. Came the reoccupying squatters. They completely rebuilt this set of rooms, even lifting the threshold slab weighing nearly a ton. They formed a magazine by building a blocking wall but did not bother to repair the wall, which they left with the burnt wood in the sockets, laying their own pots alongside. Most remarkable, they ignored the store of Spartan basalt and were apparently also tunnelling underneath the room with the unfinished stone amphorae, which lay above their heads so close to the surface. A few feet away the top block of the Room of the Posts remained to be a landmark on the site when Evans came and dug in 1901 and found the stone jars, which the squatters had failed to detect even when they built the blocking wall at a much lower level.

We cannot exclude the possibility in the present inflamed state of opinion that some archaeologists may prefer this complex 'story' to a more straightforward reading of the excavation evidence, although I do not see how the undisclosed test of 1905 in the Room of the Posts can be explained away. What is strange is the argument of Wace, the opponent of Evans. As late as 1956 in his Foreword to Ventris and Chadwick's *Documents in Mycenaean Greek*, Wace seized on the store of Spartan basalt as evidence for trade relations *in LM II*. He had apparently not noticed Evans's recantation in the third volume and his attribution of the rooms in their latest arrangement to the LM III B period.

A similar blindness was shown by Evans's lieutenant Pendlebury. A Swedish scholar, N. Åberg, in a work on the chronology of the Bronze Age, had asserted 'that there is little true stratification at Knossos, that the accepted stratification has been invented in accordance with an analysis of the styles of pottery and that this analysis is unsound.' In refutation Pendlebury cited *inter alia* the Room of the Stone Pier (east of the Store of Spartan Basalt in fig. 36) as an example of MM III B immediately above MM III A. He gave a reference to the first volume of Evans's work: he also was apparently unaware of the recantation in the third volume, which changed MM III B into LM III B.

Other doubts about chronological deductions from stylistic analyses are prompted by another misfortune of the expert on Cretan seals, Mr V. E. G. Kenna (see above p. 236). In his work on *Cretan Seals* Mr Kenna assigned a well-known sealing showing a bull's head with a double axe between the horns to the Temple Repositories in the west wing of the palace and discussed it as an example of the Middle Minoan Transitional period. We now know from a drawing of the sealing in Evans's 1902 notebook that it was found in the reoccupation deposit of the Court of the Stone Spout in the east wing. All this has its bearing on a matter fundamental for prehistoric archaeology. As we shall see, some of the leading experts in this field have now expressed doubts whether stylistic distinctions in pottery and seals can be taken as valid evidence for chronological differences (see pp. 302 ff.).

6. THE DOMESTIC QUARTER

By now it was becoming increasingly clear to me that the great labour of studying the documents and collating the data with the published accounts had been entirely unnecessary. We have worked back from the School Room to a point where the corridor turns west to run as far as the Grand Staircase (fig. 34). It was along this corridor that Evans had found one of his most massive and concentrated deposits of tablets — the ones dealing with sheep (see p. 115). On the landing of the stairs was a mass of clay sealings, evidently fallen from above. Now both Evans and Pendlebury had made emphatic statements to the effect that the whole Domestic Quarter had been used during the 'Reoccupation' period. Evans in 1909, indeed, declared not only that there were signs of large scale reconstruction but that parts of the building may have been in continuous occupation. Pendlebury in 1939 stated bluntly that the whole Domestic Quarter had been completely cleared of debris and reinhabited with little or no alteration. Now if the LM II debris had thus been removed, it would need only a slight movement of thought to conclude that it was not there any more when Evans dug in 1901. Evidently the deposit actually found *in situ* must have belonged to the following period when this part of the building housed 'dynasts of diminished status' (Evans). What did the excavators find? First a layer of burnt rafters and other timber work covering a stone-hard deposit formed by the action of moisture on the 'plaster of Paris' created by the action of the heat on the gypsum stonework. This hard deposit, some three metres thick, overlay looser deposit extending some 4 metres down to the floors of the lower rooms. In this conflagration debris were embedded the masses of sealings and tablets we have already noted.

Once I had pointed out the implications of the statements by Evans and Pendlebury about the Domestic Quarter the reaction was inevitable. Their accounts were rejected in their own defence! But Pendlebury in 1939 had quoted his evidence: he had referred to the boxes of sherds from this area in the Stratigraphical Museum ('N. and O. *passim*'), a work he had published in 1933–35. This was embarrassing. It meant that evidence available for nearly thirty years had now to be re-examined and a case made out convicting Pendlebury, a man of unrivalled experience in Cretan archaeology, of ceramic incompetence.

Once again Mackenzie's pottery notebooks made a decisive intervention. One of Pendlebury's references concerned the LM III B reoccupation of the so-called Queen's Megaron (fig. 36). The box he referred to contained much late pottery (LM III A and B) assigned to the area of the 'Fish Fresco'. This is the famous work of art now known as the Dolphin Fresco. Closer investigation of the find circumstances in the light of all the available documents was to show Evans's methods of archaeological reporting in the gravest light. In the first place, the testimony of the Stratigraphical Museum, which Pendlebury had quoted in 1939 to support his conclusion that the Queen's Megaron had been in use during the so-called 'reoccupation' period, was vindicated in a striking way. A mysterious number inscribed on the boxes turned out to be a reference to Mackenzie's pottery notebooks. In this passage the excavator had described in great detail the mass of pots found along with the 'Fish Fresco'. They were almost entirely vessels of unmistakable LM III B character. The next step was to study Mackenzie's day-by-day account of the progress of the excavations in the Day Book for 1902. There was complete agreement: he had marked on his sketch plan the find place of the fresco (east wall of light well of Queens Megaron, see fig. 36) and remarked that just over the wall against its west face was a large heap of Mycenaean pottery. The circle of witnesses was made complete by an entry in Evans's own notebook, which I quote *verbatim*: 'In S. Portico of Hall near fish deposit fine piece of "Palace Ware". Smaller pieces of same but also many fragments of stirrup-vases of late style.' The find facts were plain: the Dolphin Fresco had been found with a mass of LM III B vases and a few fragments of 'Palace Style'. These are the words in which Evans later communicated the excavation evidence: 'Some sherds of LM II pottery were found among the latest elements of the stratum in which they [the fragments of the fresco] occurred' (*PoM* i, 330). He dated the fresco to Middle Minoan III. But worse was to follow.

The fresco lay above the floor of the light well (fig. 36), which was composed of a kind of concrete mixed with small pebbles which the excavators called *terrazza*. In 1913 a test pit was sunk below this concrete, and underneath was found 'an appreciable amount of LM II–III'. This indicated that the concrete floor had been laid after this kind of pottery had got stratified. The conclusion that this part of the palace had been constructed or reconstructed late in LM III was supported by other tests. On fig. 36 a staircase is shown north of the Queen's Megaron. A test was made in 1905 under the lower surface of the seventh step from the top: among the sherds was one of LM II. Again in 1928 a further probe under the top step yielded a few LM III sherds. Conclusion: the masonry dates to this period. It remains to add that late walls had been built west, east, and south of the Queen's Megaron. The evidence obtained throughout the excavations was thus consistent. It bore witness to the conclusion published by Evans himself in 1909: there had been large scale reconstruction in this part of the palace in the LM III B period, just as in the northern area discussed above, and also in the suite of rooms opening off the Court of the Stone Spout with its famous Toreador Fresco.

Checking the Facts

Pendlebury was undoubtedly right in the statement he had published in 1939, and the evidence he had quoted in support (Stratigraphical Museum) was corroborated by all the documentary sources including Evans's own notebook. The fire was equally evident in the Queen's Megaron area and especially in the area of the 'fish fresco'. Since tablets and sealings occurred at all levels in the destruction debris in the Domestic Quarter, there could be little doubt that they belonged to the very end of the LM III B period. Complex special pleading would be required to assign the frescoes found in the same environment to a much higher date, and the fact remained that Evans had mentioned only the few fragments of LM II pottery, keeping silent about the mass of LM III B pots. Yet Mackenzie's first entry reads: 'Basket 1. Reserved: fragments of about 9 Bügelkannes [stirrup-jars] late chiefly with octopus design. . . .

The consequences for so late a date for the Dolphin Fresco may be gauged from the fact that as recently as 1960 the so-called Marine Style of Knossos was being dated by the 'contemporary' Dolphin Fresco. Dr Theocharis, who had found a vessel of this class in an Attic tomb along with vessels of Late Helladic III A–B class, was consequently induced to hazard the guess that his 'marine style' vase was loot from the sack of Knossos. Once again we encounter an example of the *ad hoc* hypothesis already discussed apropos of Woolley's enterprising potter. The 'story' is invented simply because the environment does not fit into Evans's dating, which is accepted without question.

7. A MISPLACED STRAINER

It will now be abundantly clear that the greatest masses of tablets occurred in undisturbed conflagration debris characterized by great quantities of LM III B pottery. What is more, the floors themselves sealed in LM III sherds. In the Queen's Megaron we have also noted late sherds extracted from the masonry of the stairs. No further evidence is now needed, since study of the tablets reveals cross references to texts in other parts of the palace, while the associated sealings carry impressions which can be matched elsewhere. One such example is that of a 'collared bitch'. It remains to go to the heart of the matter and to examine Evans's account of the evidence from the Throne Room. But I propose to approach it by a devious route. Convergent lines of investigation will uncover the same state of affairs. The tablets were found in an LM III B (or LM III C!) environment, above pavements sealing in late sherds. Again we shall unearth information either distorted or undisclosed. Again we shall find Evans's defenders constrained to total rejection of his own elaborate accounts. It is a fitting and inevitable climax that this attack on Evans by his own defenders was supported by a piece of invented evidence.

The story, curiously enough, starts once more with the Room of the Stirrup-Jars. Evans, it will be recalled, had included among the vessels illustrated from that room a strainer decorated with a kind of 'Catherine wheel' at the centre. Mackenzie's pottery notebooks disclosed that it had not been found there. In 1900 Evans had left a strip of ground south of the Throne Room (fig. 30, 4) unexcavated because it was being used as a gangway for the wheelbarrows. In 1901 this was cleared with some most interesting finds. One was a fine piece of fresco relief showing a man putting a necklace round a woman's neck. This was unfortunately later destroyed when an earthquake wrecked the museum. Evans called the magazine the Gallery of the Jewel Fresco. At a high level in the deposit was found a coherent hoard of tablets and some sealings, including one of the 'collared bitch' which we have just mentioned. But among the vases in the magazine was our strainer and another like it but more fragmentary. This new item of information, as we have seen, showed the total falsity of Evans's 'decisive stratigraphy' from the Room of the Stirrup-Jars. But more important was the positive side: a 'collared bitch' sealing had been found with tablets along with a vase long presented to scholars as typically LM III B; and examples of the same seal were found in the area of the Lapidary's Workshop of 'reoccupation' date and also in the Domestic Quarter, which Evans himself had declared to be the home of 'diminished dynasts' during the period of decadence. All the evidence was consistent. We may now contemplate the reactions of Evans's defenders to the newly revealed piece of evidence.

Checking the Facts

8. EVANS AND HIS DEFENDERS

He was immediately accused by his defenders of ceramic
incompetence. He had written (*PoM* iv, 735 f.): 'Along with these
[the stirrup-jars actually found on the South Front!] were also
found the perforated disk-shaped utensil, fig. 720 c, with a low
rim, . . . showing a late form of the 'adder-mark' motive — and
five two-handled pots or 'amphoras' of pale plain clay.' Twenty-
eight years later his advocate declared in his defence that the
vessel is LM I–II. In other words, Evans was capable of such gross
errors in ceramic diagnosis and classification as would update his
findings from *c.* 1150 B.C. to 1500–1400 B.C. Yet Furumark, the
outstanding authority on Mycenaean pottery, had written that
the chronology of Late Minoan pottery 'was — and still is —
primarily based on the stratification at Knossos, and the only
more detailed discussions of the subject are to be found in *The
Palace of Minos*, espec. Vol. IV'. This is the volume now under fire
from Evans's main advocate. But this drastic updating was to
encounter still more serious difficulty: it made nonsense of
archaeology's main instrument in determining chronology. An
LM I–II vase now formed part of burnt debris deposited above a
pavement that had sealed in LM III B bowls. This led to a
further attack on Evans by his defender.

The hoard of tablets found with the strainer recorded vases
(actually offerings of jars of honey), and this deposit had been
scattered across the Long Corridor into Magazine VIII (see fig. 38).
This had been excavated in 1900 with the following results. A
burnt beam had been found 40–50 cm (16–20 inches) above the
pavement at the point of the corridor where the tablets occurred.
The corridor had been cleared in 1900 down to its pavement,
which consisted of 'finely compacted' stone slabs extending the
full width of the corridor. All this was duly described in the
excavation report of 1900. However, in 1903 Evans suspected from
experience in the adjoining magazines that the pavement might
conceal sunken containers belonging to an earlier phase of the
palace. So he lifted the slabs and reported a 'surprising result'.
Throughout the whole length of the corridor the pavement
overlaid a continuous series of sunken chests or cists. Now in

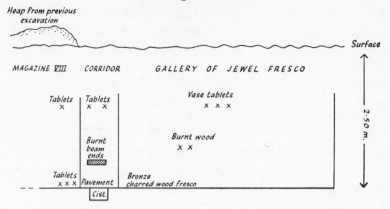

Fig. 38. Find circumstances of the Vase Tablets. The Gallery of the Jewel Fresco contained the LM III B strainer assigned by Evans to the Room of the Stirrup Jars. The pavement of the corridor, found complete in 1900, was lifted in 1903. The cists of a former phase which it was found to conceal contained LM III B bowls and other sherds, some burnt.

order to date the laying of the pavement, the archaeologist examines the debris filling these cists. The latest pottery found gives a *terminus post quem*. The archaeologist rightly reasons that such vessels had been made, used, broken and the bits incorporated in the earth used to fill the cist before the later pavement was laid. Evans found in the rubbish among other things some plain bowls, and later he was to give a more exact description. In the first volume of the *Palace of Minos* he made it known that the bowls were 'identical with' those from the School Room! At that time, of course, he believed that the latter were Middle Minoan III, and so he was not disturbed in his general conclusions. But by 1930, as we have seen above (p. 237), he had come to realize that he had been wholly mistaken about these School Room pots: they were LM III B of the latest phase. The result was catastrophic: the pavement of the Long Corridor had been laid when vessels of this very late class had already got stratified. Once again the evidence in various parts of the palace was consistent: it had been drastically rebuilt late in the so-called 'squatter period'.

Checking the Facts

Evans's advocate was now in a painful dilemma. Thanks to his rejection of Evans's date for the strainer, he had an unaccountable archaeological 'inversion'. One way out might have been the standard move of archaeologists faced with evidence too early for its environment: the strainer might have been an 'heirloom'. This course was rejected. Instead it was declared that in the *Palace of Minos* Evans had been guilty of a double error in addition to his misdating of the strainer. Nor was this enough. Pendlebury's *Guide to the Stratigraphical Museum* also recorded LM III sherds from the cists below the pavement. This supported Evans. Only one course remained: this was to play the trump card of the archaeologist — the sherds were 'intrusive'. But Evans in 1900 had said that the pavement was 'finely compacted', and this story he repeated in the first volume of *The Palace of Minos* twenty years later, when he also reaffirmed that in 1903 the discovery of the cists had come as a surprise to him. It was this situation that led to one of the most disquieting episodes in this embittered controversy.

Evans's advocate, already driven to question his ceramic competence and then faced with his circumstantial account of the excavations in the Long Corridor, was now forced to reject Evans's whole story. In particular he had to devise some way of getting the LM III B bowls and other sherds underneath the pavement as an 'intrusion'. He had to make out a case wholly contrary to Evans's own story: the pavement had to be breached. A hole or holes had to be made, contrived in far off times, long before Evans arrived on the scene, through which the late bowls and sherds, such awkward evidence, had 'intruded' into the debris underlying the pavement. To buttress this story a photograph was produced from the Ashmolean collection. This piece of evidence we must now examine for its authenticity.

The photograph[1] shows the Long Corridor looking south. The pavement has been broken through, and four or five deep holes have been made. The decisive question is: when was this photograph taken? Evans's advocate, who produced this 'hitherto unpublished photograph', declared that it was taken before the

[1] Published as Plate IX in *On the Knossos Tablets*, Part II 'The Date of the Knossos Tablets' by J. Boardman.

250

excavation of the cists covered in by the pavement commenced [p. 39]. His statement reads: 'the floor has been cleaned and the broken paving over the plundered cists uncovered.'

There are many puzzling things about this assertion. In the first place it goes counter to Evans's repeated statements that the pavement was 'finely compacted' and that the discovery of the cists came as a complete surprise to him. It was Evans who had the photograph taken, and we are invited to believe that the significance of these deep holes had escaped him. Moreover, these pits had been revealed in 1903 along the middle of the corridor simply as the result of cleaning the floor. For three seasons excavators and groups of archaeological tourists and visitors had unsuspectingly walked along the corridor unaware of their peril, although these pits were concealed by a covering so light that it had been dispelled simply by cleaning. . . . Yet another mystery surrounds the circumstances of the photograph. Although, we are told, it was taken before Evans had the rest of the paving lifted (that is the parts not already removed by the 'intruders'), the photograph shows two piles of paving slabs, one over half the height of the first great jar on the left, and the other behind the seventh jar.

There was yet another peculiar circumstance. At this very point of the corridor, as we have seen (fig. 38), burnt debris had been deposited at a high level, including some of the Vase Tablets. But there is a most significant detail: the ends of burnt beams from the ceiling were also found at this point outside the Eighth Magazine, 'fallen below their original level'. All this, according to Evans, was due to the great fire of *c.* 1400 B.C. Into these complex find data we must now fit the new 'escape' story. Evans's defender devises a sub-plot. After the great disaster 'intruders' had plundered the cists. To do this they naturally had had to lift the pavement slabs, and in so doing they had inserted the Late Minoan III bowls and other late sherds. Yet the observed facts could be explained only by a further assumption: since the intruders had left the tablets and other burnt material un-disturbed, they must have done their plundering by tunnelling along the corridor under the burnt beam and the tablets. Fortunately Mackenzie's entries enable us to give precisely the head room available for the 'intruders': the burnt beam lay a bare

40–50 cm (16–20 inches) above the pavement. When, working in such constricted conditions, the plunderers had torn up the pavement in several places and confused the archaeological record by inserting the LM III B bowls and other sherds below the pavement, the deposit settled down so satisfactorily that it entirely misled Evans to the end of his days. He continued to believe that the pavement had been complete and that he had been surprised to discover the underlying cists when he lifted the 'finely compacted' pavement in 1903. He had actually taken the photograph now produced to confound him. It was not until 1963 that the truth was revealed to an archaeologist embarrassed by Evans's circumstantial account of this part of the palace.

It was clear that the new 'evidence' had to be checked for its accuracy. The key point was the statement about the moment when the photograph had been taken. On the face of it, if we accepted Evans's own story, the photograph had been taken when some of the cists shown in the photograph had been opened and the paving slabs already removed had been piled up against the east wall of the corridor. I asked for permission to examine the boxes of photographs in the Ashmolean collection. On identifying the photograph on which the plate in the book was based, I looked for the indication justifying the statement that it had been taken before the uncovering of the cists. The photograph simply bears on the back the words '? 6th Magazine'. This was evidently a guess by an unknown person (perhaps the one responsible for filing the photographs), who had no familiarity with the site, for it evidently shows the Long Corridor looking south. At all events, there were no grounds for the statement, which alone might justify the story of 'intrusion', that the photograph had been taken before the lifting of the pavement in 1903. That statement was pure invention.

Further examination of the box of photographs disclosed other relevant evidence. There were several photographs that corroborated Evans's account of his excavations. They were taken from different view points and they all showed the pavement complete throughout its entire length. It was clear that the publication of one or all of these would suffice to justify Evans against this attack by his defender. It turned out that this was unnecessary.

Checking the Facts

No fewer than three of them had already been published. The best one figured, of all places, in Evans's own *Palace of Minos*. In the first volume, as we have seen, Evans had repeated his story about his 'surprise' at discovering the cists underlying the pavement in 1903. He had there told us that the bowls found in the fill of these cists, sealed in by the pavement, were 'identical with' the bowls from the School Room, the ones he recognised belatedly as very late LM III B. In supplementary Plate XI of the same volume Evans had reproduced the photograph justifying his 'surprise': it is a fine photograph taken looking south, which shows the 'finely compacted' pavement of the Long Corridor complete along its whole length. It was this illustration (apart from two other publications) that had escaped the notice of his defender, who produced the unpublished photograph to justify his total rejection of Evans's account. Such were the results of yet another detailed piece of investigation.

This episode represents the climax of the duel between Evans and his defending counsel. The facts and their interpretation are of such importance that I propose to make clear the nature of the confrontation between Evans and Boardman by a dialogue.

E. I found this strainer in the Room of the Stirrup-Jars.

B. No, Mackenzie's register shows that you found it in the Gallery of the Jewel Fresco along with the Vase Tablets.

E. It is typically LM III B.

B. No, it is LM I–II.

E. The Vase Tablets were found in a burnt deposit scattered across the Long Corridor into the Eighth Magazine. Burnt beams were found 16–20 inches above the pavement.

B. I quite agree. But add the strainer.

E. I cleared the pavement in 1900. It was finely compacted.

B. The pavement was not finely compacted. There were gaping holes in it, which you did not notice.

253

E. I lifted the pavement in 1903 and was surprised to discover that it concealed cists.

B. You ought not to have been surprised.

E. In the fill of the cists there were bowls identical with those from the School Room (LM III B).

B. You are mistaken. They were not identical with those from the School Room.

E. There were other late sherds in the fill. They are now in the Stratigraphical Museum. They got into the cists possibly when the pavement was lifted for repairs.[1]

B. I agree about the sherds. But if your hypothesis is right, then the repairs must have been effected when LM III sherds were stratified. This would mean that the palace was still occupied by the people who carried out the repairs.

E. How then do *you* imagine the sherds got under the pavement?

B. They were put there by plunderers.

E. but the cists had been filled in with rubbish, covered over with a layer of clay mortar and the pavement laid on top of that, hundreds of years before your supposed plunderers. What possessed them to tear up the pavement?

B. They were searching for treasure.

E. In any case how do you know that there were gaping holes in the pavement before I started to lift it? After all you weren't there in 1903.

B. I agree, but there is that photograph you never published. It shows the holes.

[1] PoM i, 453 f. The Stratigraphical Museum shows that the sherds included LM III: boxes D. iv. 5, 6, 8, 9.

E. Yes, but I took it, and if you will look there are several others which show the pavement complete. In any case, the one you rely on shows two piles of paving slabs. And by the way, how do you know at which stage of the excavation the photograph was taken?

B. On the back are written the words '? 6th Magazine' by some unknown hand.

E. So all those years there were those deep holes down the middle of the Long Corridor. They were revealed when I had it swept?

B. Yes.

E. And just above the pavement in 1900 lay the burnt ceiling beams? They were the relics of the 1400 fire, like the tablets at the same point?

B. Yes.

E. And the plunderers who tore up the pavement and put the LM III sherds underneath had been working underneath the burnt beam?

B. Yes.

E. And then they had gone away leaving the pavement slabs lying about. These escaped the notice of Mackenzie, the architect Fyffe and myself.

B. No, you replaced them and then took a photograph across the Corridor showing the pavement complete.

E. So my statement that I found only the two northerly cists open was knowingly false?

B. Well, I have to explain the late pots and sherds in the cists.

255

Checking the Facts

The total rejection of Evans's story by Boardman will now be patent. The excavation evidence, as set forth by Evans, but completed by the insertion of the misplaced strainer, is represented in our diagram fig. 38. A coherent hoard of tablets had been found in a burnt deposit above a pavement that sealed in LM III B pots and sherds. Once again the same constellation of excavation data had been obtained as in other parts of the palace. The tablets represent the final actions in rooms actually constructed or reconstructed when LM III B pottery had already got stratified. The bowls and sherds had been part of the earth and rubble with which the cists had been filled preparatory to laying the pavement above them. All this Evans had made clear.

9. THE THRONE ROOM

The conflict between Evans and his main defender had thus again been fruitful in disclosing precise excavation data. It led by a strange inevitability to an attack on one of Evans's chief collaborators by the same scholar: its object was no less a person than Pendlebury. When I intervened in the latter's defence, this produced a reaction which once again provoked research that uncovered significant evidence. This time it concerned the very heart of the matter — the Throne Room.

In his article of 1958 C. W. Blegen had pointed out that some parts of the palace had been 'reoccupied' and that tablets had been found in these places. He singled out the Eighth Magazine, which has entered into the facts discussed in the previous section. I recall what was said on p. 54: on the pavement of this magazine Evans had found just inside the door a whole set of Linear B tablets, evidently in their original order and very imperfectly baked. At a higher level at this very point some of the Vase Tablets had been found, the extreme westward point of the scatter from the main focus to the east (fig. 38). Pendlebury quoted his evidence for his statement that the magazine had been 'reoccupied': a box of mainly LM III sherds. As Blegen pointed out, this meant that the tablets must have got into their positions at the end of this 'reoccupation'. The defence reacted: Pendlebury was mistaken. He had no right to draw any such conclusion: the

256

sherds in the box were collected from the 'surface' and so were not
admissible as evidence. I pointed out that the date given in the
Guide was 1904, whereas the magazine had been completely
cleared in 1900. Promptly Pendlebury was saddled with a further
error: the printed date was wrong and should have been 1900. A
few months later a piece of evidence was reported from Knossos:
the box contained a wooden label bearing the inscription 'K 00',
which appeared to mean Knossos 1900.

Evans himself had given a detailed account of these wooden
labels, and they are of prime importance as indicators of the time,
place and circumstances of the sherds contained in the boxes of
the Stratigraphical Museum. Evans's remarks on this subject may
be recalled at this point. He had been alone at Knossos in 1913
and had carried out nearly one hundred test pits in various parts
of the Palace. He tells us that he wrote summary references to
these test pits on wooden labels. We have already used their
evidence in the discussion of the Northern Entrance Passage
(pp. 230 ff.), where Evans sank three test pits in 1913. It was yet
another wooden label that was brought to light by investigations
prompted by the production of the wooden label to uphold the
attack on Pendlebury's account of the Eighth Magazine.

Evidently malicious Truth was having her sport with Evans's
advocates. She had another wooden label up her sleeve and it
concerned of all places the Throne Room area. Here we are at the
very heart of the matter, and it is here that we shall see in the
clearest light not only Evans's strange use of evidence but also the
scientific methods of his defenders. We begin with Evans's most
elaborate account of the Throne Room, that in the final volume of
The Palace of Minos (IV, 900 ff.). The direct question we put to
the key witness is, 'What evidence did you obtain for dating the
building of the Throne Room to Late Minoan II and its destruction
to *c.* 1400 B.C. ?' Here is the testimony:

'For the ceremonial suite and its dependencies to which we are
now drawn there is no parallel within the Palace area. The structures that here rose in the North-West Palace Section during the
last period of the building represent a revolutionary intrusion,
effacing all previous remains. It was not here a question of en-
grafting on to an existing system or of raising a new structure

over its remains. What we here encounter is a *tabula rasa*, with a
wholesale invasion of new elements.'

* * *

'It was in vain that a series of tests were made under my super-
intendence beneath the floors of the intrusive block. The whole
sub-soil proved to belong to the same sub-neolithic stratum that
immediately underlies the greater part of the Central Court as
first laid out, after the whole of the upper deposits had been
cleared away for its formation.

'It was only in the course of the supplementary Excavations of
1913 that some data bearing on the chronological place of the new
structure were at last extracted. Underlying the threshold of the
first doorway left of the line of entrances to the Ante-room of the
"Room of the Throne" from the pavement level of the Central
Court ... was found a sherd illustrating the best period of the
"Palace Style". Again under the threshold of the entrance immediately north of this, there occurred some LM I and LM II
fragments, in the latter case not so distinctive.'

Now this clear statement of the sole evidence bearing on the
date of the Throne Room must be read in conjunction with another which bears on its interpretation. In 1913 Evans sank
test pits in the West Court. He found that all the periods were
represented up to the pavement of the court laid down in LM I.
'Above this point the deposit was of a more unstratified nature
containing remains of LM II and LM III periods.'

He then went on to stress the difficulty of drawing clear
dividing lines.

'All such stratigraphical demarcations are of their nature
somewhat arbitrary. ... All is in fact transition ... One form
merges into another by imperceptible gradations and where, as is
the case with a large part of the material, an object is derived
from an unstratified deposit, it is at times difficult, in default of
direct evidence, to decide on which side of a more or less artificial
dividing line it should be placed.'

Let us assume, however, that the evidence of the sherds is more
clear-cut than Evans himself would have approved. The picture of
the creation of the 'revolutionary' Throne Room block presents

itself as follows. Gangs of workmen in the employ of the New
Dynasty set to work clearing the site of its centuries-long ac
cumulation of débris. They perform their work so thoroughly that
the soil is laid bare down to the sub-neolithic level. Of all the
countless sherds doubtless present in this overburden they leave
only a few fragments of different periods. One of these is attributable to the mature 'Palace Style'. On top of this they proceed to
lay the threshold block.

Now the basic principle in the interpretation of stratigraphic
evidence is the common sense 'upper is later'. We might then have
expected Evans to say 'the threshold block of the revolutionary
intrusion is above, and therefore later than, the Palace Style
sherd underneath it.' In other words, this vital piece of evidence is
a *terminus post quem* for the construction of the Throne Room
block.

Now it so happens that Evans had contradicted himself on this
vital matter of interpretation. In the previous volume (III, 5) he
had written that the sherds found under the thresholds were a
terminus a quo, in other words the pots in question had been made,
used, got broken and the pieces had found their way into the
ground *at some time before* the threshold blocks were put into
position. This in fact is accepted archaeological doctrine, though
on occasion such evidence may be explained away by assuming
that at some date repairs may have been carried out involving
lifting the blocks in question (see below p. 264 on Evans's use of
this device against his adversary Wace). The interpretation of the
evidence in Volume IV was different. Now Evans takes the sherds
underneath the threshold as more or less contemporary with the
construction of the Throne Room block. 'The general conclusion
resulting from these finds is that the structures with which we are
dealing date from the early part of LM II, when the Palace Style
first reached maturity.'

Whatever be the truth of the matter, what is not in doubt is the
slightness of the evidence proffered (one sherd) bearing on the
date of this unexampled architectural revolution and the aggressive
New Dynasty whose creation it was.

In the first edition of this work I wrote that no archaeologist
whom I had consulted could give me any information about this

historic sherd, the single one on which Evans had relied to date the Throne Room, and repeated enquiry had failed to disclose its whereabouts. Soon after the appearance of the book it was run to earth, and an astounding picture of the course of events presented itself. It became apparent that in composing the definitive account of the Throne Room in 1935 Evans, on consulting his notebook, had read his own sketch plan upside down and omitted much of the evidence.

The evidence was presented in Evans's own notebook for 1913. In it he had drawn a sketch plan of the Anteroom to the Throne Room and the part of the Central Court on which it faced. The test pits sunk by him were sited and numbered, the numbers being ringed round (55, 56, 57, 58, 59 and 60). On a later page of the same notebook Evans gave a summary description of the sherds found in each pit, and actually drew some of them. The next step was to try and find the actual boxes of sherds in the Stratigraphical Museum. This was also successful thanks once again to the researches of Mr J. Raison, who established that the boxes assigned to the Throne Room area had inscriptions and wooden labels with the same series of numbers as in the notebook and ringed round in exactly the same way. Still more satisfactory was that it was even possible to identify some of the sherds drawn by Evans. Thus there could be no shadow of doubt about the authenticity of the evidence.

The evidence may be simply stated. Certainly Evans had found a Late Minoan II sherd when he lifted the threshold block of the Anteroom. So far so good. But this was not the only evidence brought to light in this crucial test for dating the Throne Room block. Evans drew another sherd in his notebook and commented '? Palace Style'. This sherd was found in the box by J. Raison, who classified it as LM III A: 2, in other words, by present standards 'post-destruction'. But still more evidence was revealed which was consistent with this. Here too we may set forth the successive reactions of Evans's defenders.

I pointed out that the Stratigraphical Museum located a test under a slab in the south part of the pavement of the Anteroom. Pendlebury had classified one of the sherds as LM III. This indicated that the pavement had been laid after this type of pottery had got stratified. The test was ascribed to the year 1913. Immediately the witness of the Stratigraphical Museum, in print for thirty years, was challenged. It could be conclusively proved, said the defence, that no such test had taken place in 1913. Again J. Raison's researches in the museum gave the answer. He identified the box and the sherd. It was the foot of a 'champagne cup', that is typical of LM III: Pendlebury's classification was correct.[1] But what of the date? There was a wooden label inside the box giving the date as 1903, and the same date was inscribed on the box itself together with the location inside the Anteroom! The defenders were now in a painful dilemma. They had just rejected Pendlebury's printed date 1904 and corrected it to 1900 on the evidence of a wooden label. They now faced exactly the same situation in the Throne Room. The label revealed that the printed date was a misprint or simple error (of which there are many, as is only to be expected in a work of this kind). But now the argument against the location of the test in the Throne Room had failed; it could no longer have any relevance to say that there was no such test in 1913. Without a moment's hesitation the reply came that this time Pendlebury had been justified in ignoring the evidence of the wooden label: he had 'reasonably corrected' it to 1913. By this it was hoped to carry the offending evidence out into the Central Court and identify it with one of the tests there. But now a new embarrassment arises. All the 1913 tests are numbered and located, and the wooden label has no number. Nor does any of the tests entered by Evans in his notebook correspond in content: there is no test of 1913 which records the foot of a LM III 'champagne cup'.

Thus the 'reasonable correction' foisted on Pendlebury had failed. The evidence must be left in the position assigned to it by the wooden label in the box: under the pavement of the Anteroom. But yet other evidence not disclosed by Evans was to prove quite consistent with so late a date for the construction of the Throne Room. In 1900, to be precise on 27 April, Mackenzie records the finding of a remarkable vessel in the Throne Room corridor. It was a type of vase of a new shape not met with until Evans's

---

[1] By LM III Pendlebury meant 'post-palatial'. It will not help now to declare that it is LM III A: 1.

'post-destruction' period: a so-called 'pilgrim's bottle or flask'. As late as 1939 Pendlebury, in his survey of Late Minoan III pottery, had included the 'pilgrim's bottles' among the new shapes that make their appearance at this time. The great authority A. Furumark also gives the shape a range LM III A: 2–III C: 2. Despite this, on Mackenzie's description alone, the new evidence was countered by the statement that a vessel of this type could not be dated. Once again, it was necessary to institute a search in the Heraklion Museum to see if the vessel could be identified. It was fortunate that Mackenzie had given a very close description of the 'pilgrim's wine bottle': it was of flat shape and had loop-handles all round for holding the suspending cord in position. Its decoration consisted of concentric circles in brown-black varnish applied on the usual ochre slip.

In September 1961 I entered the Heraklion Museum with the intention of asking the Curator for permission to search for the vase. It proved unnecessary. While passing through the exhibition rooms I identified the bottle on display in a case devoted to the 'Post-palatial period'. The museum catalogue listed it among a number of other vessels typical of this late period and 'having a clear Mycenaean character' (see Plate 16). It had been found immediately alongside of the stone basin or font that tourists now see placed in the Anteroom at Knossos. By a strange coincidence the bottle is displayed in the show-case of the Museum alongside the stirrup-jar attributed by Evans to the Room of the Stirrup-Jars, but actually found on the South Front in the area of the burnt wheat etc. Thus this vessel, displayed by the museum authorities as typical of post-palatial Knossos, turns out to be from the Throne Room area. Most important is that it was discovered alongside the burnt doorposts in the Corridor. It was found in the company of the famous stone 'font' which still greets the tourists who enter the Throne Room. As they contemplate it, they may be mindful that the pavement they stand on once sealed in, below a slab on the south side, another late sherd that might have demonstrated to Evans in 1903 that the pavement had been laid at a time when he believed the site had been the haunt of 'squatters'.

We are still not at an end of our documentary explorations

affecting the Throne Room. Once again we encounter the testimony of Mackenzie's notebooks for 1923, to learn that yet another unreported examination took place in that year in the palace quarter lying to the north of the Throne Room Corridor, where the late pilgrim's bottle was lying. Mackenzie makes it plain that there had been considerable alterations to these magazines in the so-called 'reoccupation' period. This completed the cycle of evidence relating to the Throne Room area. It had proved wholly consistent with that affecting other parts of the palace. The tablets were found in rooms where a very late vessel had been found, but not disclosed. The paved floor had sealed in LM III pottery, which indicated that the rooms had been constructed in the so-called post-palatial period. Once again we had discovered evidence that had not been included in Evans's public accounts.

10. EVANS AND WACE

We must now pay closer attention to the date of so many of these unreported excavations which yielded data, that, on Mackenzie's own written testimony, were catastrophic for Evans's version of history. These supplementary excavations were carried out in 1923. It was in 1923 that the dispute between Evans and Wace came to a head and Wace ceased to be Director of the British School at Athens. As Mr Chadwick has written, 'Only a few archaeologists dared to question the orthodox doctrine, and the most courageous, the late A. J. B. Wace . . . paid dearly for his heretical views; he was excluded from digging in Greece for a considerable period.' Some idea of the heat engendered by this controversy may be gathered from an article written by the late Professor J. P. Droop in 1926 entitled 'Legitimate and Illegitimate Criticism'. I quote some key passages. 'The sheep are being led astray: Messrs Wace and Blegen are a scandal and it were better that a millstone had been tied about their necks. . . . The Fathers are already in arms to crush heresy. . . .' What was this heresy? Wace believed that the famous 'Treasury of Atreus' at Mycenae was much later in date than had been supposed. To test this he obtained permission to explore underneath the great threshold blocks and underneath the walls of the *dromos* or entrance passage. Underneath the threshold in circumstances that precluded 'intrusion' he found a late sherd which has convinced scholars that the famous tomb was built in the thirteenth century B.C. Evans's date was far earlier — he believed it to be of Middle Minoan III date (in the early seventeenth century B.C.). Evans first tried to discredit the evidence of the late sherd. What had happened, he surmised, was that at some date repairs had been made to the threshold in the course of which it had been lifted; and it was then that the tell-tale sherd had 'intruded'. On this move Professor Droop commented with an asperity which now seems quite incomprehensible: it was a crime. 'Our crime — for such an attempt to discredit our mystery is a crime not only against common-sense, but also against good manners — is without profit. There are more throats to be cut before we can feel sure that the guilty secret is safe.'

Evans acted vigorously and eventually he produced positive evidence for his contention that the tomb was a construction of the Middle Minoan III period. He published a lavishly illustrated paper entitled *Shaft Graves and Beehive Tombs of Mycenae*. The show pieces produced were certain pieces of carved stone found at Knossos. In particular great prominence was given to some carved rosettes, which Evans subjected to a detailed stylistic examination. They were virtually identical in technique with those from the façade of the Treasury of Atreus and, he argued, there could be not the slightest doubt that both were contemporary work. It was at this point that Evans produced his trump stratigraphic card: the stone rosette had been found 70 cm below the Middle Minoan concrete floor of the South Propylaeum. This indicated a Middle Minoan III A date, and so, in view of the evident stylistic identity, the Treasury of Atreus must likewise be of this early date, some four centuries earlier than Wace had suggested.

It is curious to observe Wace's reaction to this attack. It was open to him to argue that, granted the stylistic equation, since he felt sure of his own stratification, Evans's stratigraphic statement might be open to doubt. Now Wace in fact did not take this line. He argued instead that the stylistic identity was not proved; but that he had found another piece of carved stone in the citadel itself at Mycenae with a closer resemblance to Evans's specimen but in unstratified conditions. So, he went on, Sir Arthur's stratification suggested that there had been an earlier phase to the palace at Mycenae. But Wace at this point lapsed from accuracy. In giving the references to Evans's pieces of carved stone he committed a double error. If he had got the reference right, he might have observed a curious discrepancy: the photograph used in Evans's above quoted paper had already been published in the first excavation report in 1900. Moreover, Evans had stated that in that year the South Propylaeum had been dug down to the *Late Minoan III* terrazza floor. How then could he have found the rosettes 70 cm below the *Middle Minoan III B* terrazza floor? Once this strange flaw in the case as presented was noted, it was necessary once again to consult the documents to find out what had been recorded on the day of the discovery. Fortunately, both Mackenzie and Evans had made notes and they were in agreement.

The stone rosettes had in fact been found right at the beginning of the excavation proper. Mackenzie began to strip off the surface of what proved to be the South Propylaeum on 29 March 1900, and a few centimetres down he uncovered the rims of a group of Late Minoan III B ('reoccupation') jars. They stood on a *terrazza* floor which was at a depth of 90 cm. On April 2, that is on the fourth day of the excavation proper, Mackenzie records the finding of the carved rosettes 'on or near the floor level indicated by the bases of the pithoi [jars]'. Better still, Evans also drew a sketch plan on which he marked the position just east of the jars and wrote against it '70 cm down'. In other words the carved rosettes were found 20 cm *above the Late Minoan III B terrazza floor* and not 70 cm below the Middle Minoan III B terrazza floor.

Now that the true stratigraphic facts have been ascertained, we can use Evans's stylistic equation to argue a thirteenth century date for the palace. This is important since the pots and tablets give witness only to the last months of the occupation of the palace. The elaborate decorative stonework may be taken as evidence bearing on the date of construction. We may end with Evans's recorded words on first viewing the piece: 'the under-cutting and fineness of sculpture surpass anything I remember at

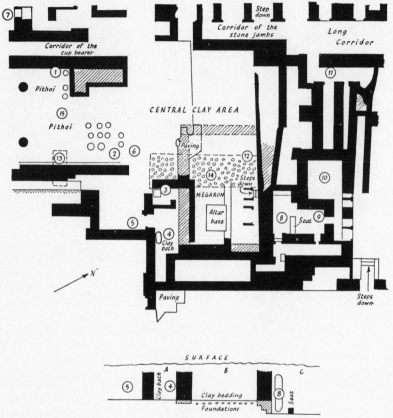

The section shows the stratigraphy of the Clay Bath containing tablets with Pithos 6 (4) alongside, between 'Reoccupation' walls, and the 'tea service' (5) to the south. Note also the Chariot Tablets (8) alongside the 'Mycenaean' wall of the 'Megaron'.

Fig. 39. The first finds at Knossos, 1900.

266

The black walls are the actual walls of the palace system found *in situ* as surveyed by Evans's architect Theodore Fyffe.

(1) and (2) are the first LM III B jars (pithoi), with the first tablet (6).

(3) is a bronze statuette found between walls constructed at an advanced stage of the 'Reoccupation'. Evans said it had been found in a Middle Minoan environment. These late walls of the 'bath-room' and its inner recess represent the last of three architectural phases. The north wall rested on the foundation of the 'megaron' discovered in 1907. The 'megaron' overlay the foundations of the former stair bastion (14).

The clay bath was filled with Linear B tablets in a burnt deposit starting 30 cm below the surface. Next to the bath was a jar (pithos) (4), unreported by Evans. Just to the south a 'tea set' (5) was found in a burnt deposit at a level above the base of the jar. Evans removed all the late walls and restored the palace in the form represented by the stair bastion; he sited the bath and tablets in this earlier phase.

The first Chariot Tablets (8) were found in a burnt deposit, again above the bases of the LM III B jars. Immediately south was the 'Mycenaean' cross-wall which cut the palace into two. Evans restored the former phase represented by the disused door-jambs with steps leading down. The cross-wall was removed and the Room of the Chariot Tablets swept away. The Chariot Tablets were now cited in a cupboard under a stair to the east which Evans constructed. (9) is the north limit of the Chariot Tablets.

(10) is the Room of the Stone Vases, including the famous lioness-head rhyton. These vases were scattered as far as (12) where a steatite lamp overlay the clay bedding of the latest phase.

(11) is the Corridor of the 'House Tablets'.

(13) is a concealed cist (discovered in 1925) underlying the wall of the latest phase. The east side of the cist contained LM III sherds.

(15) is the piece of carved rosettes found between the LM III B jars 20 cm above the LM III B terrazza floor. In his attack on Wace Evans stated that it had been found 70 cm beneath the Middle Minoan III B terrazza floor.

(7) is a doorway giving a datum level, south of which tablets were found above the level of the bases of the adjoining LM III B jars.

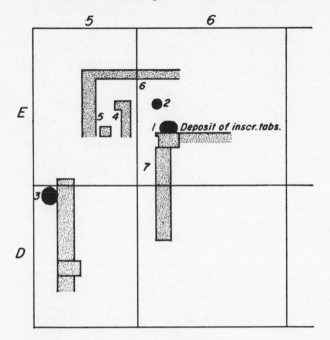

Fig. 39a. The first hoard of tablets at Knossos (after D. Mackenzie).

(1) The Clay Bath containing a set of tablets in a carbon ash deposit. The floor of the bath was at a depth of 70 cm ($27\frac{1}{2}''$) below the surface. The burnt deposit extended to within 30 cm ($11\frac{3}{4}''$) of the surface. (2) Jar no. 6, unreported by Evans. (3) Jar no. 2 of LM III B type. Just south of this in 1925 the wall was found to overlie a concealed cist belonging to an earlier phase of the palace. On the east side of the wall the fill of the cist contained LM III sherds. (4) The partition wall of the bath-room. Its construction belonged to 'a very late period of re-occupation' (D. Mackenzie). (5) The west wall of the bath-room belonging to the same late period. When removed it was found to overlie the foundations of the former stair bastion. Between 4 and 5 a bronze statuette was found. (6) The north wall of the bath-room. It rested on the foundations of the south wall of the 'megaron'. (7) Here was found a 'tea service' in a carbon ash deposit within 40 cm ($15\frac{3}{4}''$) of the surface above the level of the base of jar 6 inside the bath-room.

Evans restored the palace in the form represented by the stair bastion, removing all the late walls enclosing the bath. He assigned the bath tub with its tablets and burnt deposit to this earlier palace. The wall underlying the north wall 6 he regarded as part of a Greek temple, whose 'deep foundations' were laid within one metre of jar 6.

Mycenae.' The clear find circumstances as recorded in his own hand suggest a date contemporary with the building of the Treasury of Atreus, i.e. the thirteenth century B.C.

11. The Mycenaean Megaron

Evans's sketch plan, to which we have just referred, yielded yet another piece of information again undisclosed. It revealed that Evans had obtained on the third day of the excavation, March 31, 1900, the first clear association of late pottery with an undisturbed hoard of Linear B tablets. His plan shows a 'pithos' (i.e. jar) in the position where a few days later a clay bath tub was unearthed packed with Linear B tablets in a deposit of carbon ash starting a bare 30 cm (12 inches) below the surface. As already stated, two such jars came to light on the first day, nos. 3, 4, and 5 on 30 March; and no. 6, the one just mentioned, appeared on 31 March. Pithos no. 6, the first clear association of a datable pot with an undisturbed hoard of Linear B tablets in a burnt deposit, was never reported.

Such was the information bearing on the date of the tablets and the fire obtained in the first week at Knossos. In this south part of the site, which Evans agreed had been 'reoccupied', he had found 16 jars. Fifteen of these he entered carefully on the published plan. Only the key one, no. 6 standing on the north side of the clay bath with its tablets in a burnt wood deposit, was missing. Evidently the late date of the tablets and the fire could be saved only by *assuming* that no. 6, unpublished as it was, was earlier than the other 15, assigned by Evans himself to the 'reoccupation'.

Evans's defenders now found themselves compelled to assert that the undisclosed jar was in fact of LM II class. But now a new dilemma arose. Mackenzie tells us that the west wall of the little bath-room was built at 'a very late period of reoccupation' (see fig. 39). This new fact forced the defenders to another assertion: the admittedly late walls belonged, they said, to a floor above the burnt layer containing the bath and the tablets. Now, since the burnt layer started at about 12 inches from the surface, then the alleged new floor must have been within the first 11 inches. The excavators had missed it, for Evans wrote in the 1900 excavation report: 'Owing to the small depth of the soil whatever cover the bath may have had in this case was lost. . . .' How deep were the late walls of the bath-room? In 1907 the north wall, about a yard away from pithos 6, was found to be resting on the 'deep foundations' of a rectangular building that was diagnosed as a mainland megaron; the wall went down well below the floor of the bath-room. The flimsy west wall of the chamber (fig. 39a, 5) was demolished in 1922, when the deep foundations of the former stair bastion were being traced. Thus there was no evidence at all for the higher floor alleged to have been above the bath and its tablets. This was another piece of stratification invented by Evans's defenders to counter the new evidence which Evans had not disclosed.

Evans reported his discovery of the mainland megaron (entered on our fig. 39) in *The Times* for July 15, 1907. On its south side was the bath-room we have just discussed with its bath and water jar. On the north side of the rectangular hall directly adjoining its wall the great deposit of Chariot Tablets had been found in 1900, the first specimens being observed in carbon ash deposit above the bases of the pithoi. The wall of the megaron itself had been closely described in 1900: it was of typically Mycenaean masonry. In 1928 Evans was to give a wholly different account. Now he said that the building was a Greek Temple, built by the Dorians eight or more centuries after the supposed destruction of the 'Minoan' building. This implied an archaeological miracle which emerges from our fig. 39. This minutely attested picture of the environment of the first concentrated hoards of tablets enables us to pose the general problem in the clearest form. We distinguish firmly, as always, between observed data and interpretative 'stories'. The essential factors in the excavation evidence are (1) the deposit of tablets close to the surface in a burnt deposit; (2) the clay bath with the jar alongside; (3) Mackenzie's description of the late character of the west wall of the room and the fact that, like the west wall of the neighbouring room, it concealed the foundations of the former stair bastion; (4) the north wall of the bath-room rested on part of the south wall of the 'megaron' with its deep foundations' well below the floor on which the bath rested.

Checking the Facts

We may now scrutinize Evans's final version of his interpretative 'story', as it appears in *The Palace of Minos*. In 1400 B.C. a great fire had deposited a hoard of Linear B tablets, all dealing with the same subject, in a Minoan bath tub (with, we may add, a jar only a pace away). Around this bath tub and jar in their carbon ash deposit a 'little chamber' had been subsequently built with masonry belonging to a very late period of the 'reoccupation'. Some five or more centuries after the 'squatters' had passed on, a new set of Greek invaders who had come to Knossos built a temple. They laid the foundations a step away from the jar *at a lower level than the base*. Still more mysteriously they had left a wall, of characteristic Mycenaean construction, above their foundations. For some unknown period, but at least until the fifth century, these Dorians had worshipped their god in his (or her) temple bringing their offerings and votives. Then came the time of their own destruction. Still later unknown forces of interference and disturbance removed every trace of Greek masonry, every column, every votive, and every sherd of this date from within the temple area. They deposited instead a fine Minoan lamp with a carved spiral base (entered in Evans's notebook) inside the rectangle close to the north wall, which was of typical Mycenaean masonry. Through all this long period of 'squatterdom' and of Dorian occupation and later destruction, the Minoan bath tub filled with its Linear B tablets and the jar alongside remained strangely inviolable until Evans found it a bare twelve inches below the grass still in its carbon ash deposit in A.D. 1900.

Evans's main advocate, J. Boardman, first suggested that the undisclosed jar beside the bath tub may have been of earlier date than the other 15 unearthed during the same few days. Then the evidence bearing on the late character of the bath-room walls was produced. His reaction was once again to invent a piece of stratigraphy: there was evidence, he said, that the late walls must have been connected with a floor *above* the clay bath with its tablets in a burnt deposit. Both Evans and Mackenzie had remained unaware of the existence of this floor. Evans, indeed, in the excavation report for 1900 had commented on the shallowness of the earth deposit above the bath (it was less than 12 inches) and had suggested this as a reason for the absence of any kind of lid.

271

Moreover, the late walls in question went down, as we have seen, below the level of the floor on which the bath tub rested. Thus the supposed 'reoccupiers' must have built the little room around the pile of burnt debris in full unawareness of its existence, laying their floor within 12 inches of the modern surface. Subsequently erosion or denudation removed this floor but spared the walls. But what of the wall of the adjoining 'megaron', forming the north wall of the bath-room within one yard of the jar? In a communication to the Cretological Congress in 1961 Boardman informed his audience that the 'megaron' was built 'high over the Palace floors and debris.' This is one more instance of an 'explanation', which simply alters the facts. Mackenzie speaks of the 'deep foundations' of the megaron.[1] The first Chariot Tablets were found in a carbon ash deposit alongside the north wall of the 'megaron' considerably above its foundation course. Once the 'megaron' is restored to its observed position with its 'deep foundations' well below the floor of the bath room, the same absurdities appear. What we are invited to believe is that this elaborate building with its typical Mycenaean masonry is an 'intrusion': its south wall was laid within one yard of the jar standing next to the clay bath tub. I prefer to believe that the bath-room was built before the tub was put in it and not built round the tub several centuries later.

If we take the complex of find facts simply as they present themselves, a less complicated reading of the evidence would be this. The Mycenaean Greeks built one of their typical megarons on the south part of the former 'Minoan' palace just as they inserted the 'revolutionary intrusion', the Throne Room block, in the north part of the west wing. A massive cross wall cut the west wing into two (see fig. 39). The little bath-room was an annexe, and it is of interest to note that in the little bath-room at Pylos a water jar likewise stood next to the tub. Evans himself in 1900 thought that the room may well have been a bath-room, and he pointed out that there was a terracotta drain in the next room. As for the hoard of tablets found in its carbon ash deposit, we may adopt the explanation which Evans everywhere offered to explain

---

[1] Note the two disused steps on the north side of the Megaron in fig. 39. They *descend* to the base of the 'Mycenaean wall', which was preserved to a height of 40 cm.

their find positions. The tablets had originally been stored in an upper storey. When the palace burnt, a box fell into the bath tub, where they remained until Evans dug them up close to the surface in 1900. The tablets formed a coherent set dealing with offerings to gods. Evans began his *Handlist* with this deposit. In fact the tablet to which he gave the inventory number 1 began 'To Dictaean Zeus', an appropriate invocation for the discoverer of a Mycenaean palace. Its find place, too, was appropriate: alongside the wall of a Mycenaean megaron. At last we have the piece of architectural evidence desiderated by archaeologists at Knossos during the period of occupation by Mycenaean potentates. It matches the contemporary megaron at Hagia Triada, to say nothing of that traced at Tylissos only a few miles to the west of Knossos.

12. The 'Vindication' of Evans

Examination of the excavation notebooks had now yielded data, from all parts of the site, of high precision and great abundance, that had been distorted or suppressed in the published accounts. Yet close study of the work published by Evans and his lieutenants had shown that enough information had long been available to prove the late date of the conflagration (see above pp. 237 f.). Pendlebury's statement about the complete clearance and re-occupation of the whole Domestic Quarter was alone sufficient, to say nothing of the published photograph of the burnt wall of the School Room. The resulting picture of the history of Knossos vindicated Homer against Evans. There had been a Mycenaean king of Knossos at the time when Nestor was ruling in Pylos. It is at this stage of the investigation that we must consider a factor that has throughout bedevilled what should have been a dispassionate scrutiny of the evidence: the excavation data. This distorting factor is the general public. From the time of Schliemann's famous telegram to the King of Greece that he had gazed upon the face of Agamemnon archaeologists have been at pains to convey news of their discoveries at the first opportunity through the channels of the daily press and the weekly illustrated papers. Popular works on archaeological topics pour from the press and find eager readers. Tours to Greek sites are accompanied by guest lecturers who are archaeologists of the first rank. All this is laudable, but this enmeshment with the public carries its own dangers. Professor Levi has made specific reference to the difficulties which the immense literature of 'vulgarization' creates for a scholar who demands a fundamental reassessment — in his case for a clean sweep to be made of all that has been believed and taught hitherto in Cretan archaeology and for a completely new start to be made. Levi's revolutionary findings at Phaestos, as we have seen, encountered public silence and private obloquy.

It will be no disservice to scholarship to survey the public reactions to my own communications. Let it be stated for the record that my first communications were to audiences of scholars. In the Trinity Term of 1960 (April–June) at Oxford I gave a course of lectures in the Ashmolean Museum during which I showed slides of the Knossos documents prepared by the photographic department of the Museum. On 1 June 1960 I read a paper[1] to the Mycenaean Seminar of the Institute of Classical Studies, London, at which I chose the most objective possible method of presenting the evidence. I had arranged with the Director to have two projectors. On one I showed the published evidence, on the other the recorded evidence. The Minutes of the meeting reproduce my actual comment: 'This cannot be reconciled with the entry in Duncan Mackenzie's Day Book for 8th May 1900. . . .' Despite this cautious formulation the reaction was immediate and violent: 'The accusation of deliberate misrepresentation cannot be assessed without access to the notebooks. . . . Dishonesty supposes a motive.' To this outburst we quietly insist that the proffered evidence must be checked for its accuracy and completeness. Above all, there must be renewed excavation. It was a great piece of good fortune that excavations at Knossos were being conducted by the British School under the Director Mr Sinclair Hood at the time when the date of the tablets was brought into question.

The Sword Tablets and the Arsenal

Mr Hood has publicly stated that he is prepared to believe that some of the Linear B tablets may be of later date; and he also concedes that the building retained something of its palatial character

[1] 'The Knossos Tablets and Aegean Prehistory'.

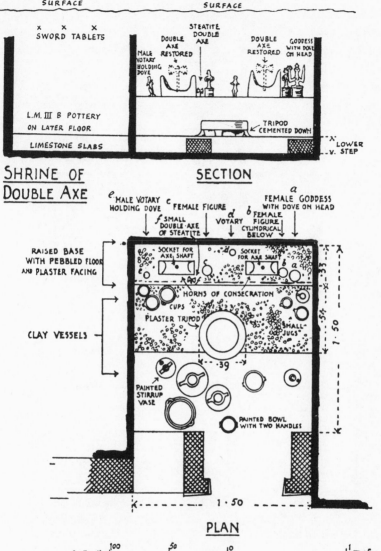

CORRIDOR
SURFACE

SHRINE
SURFACE

x   x   x
SWORD TABLETS

STEATITE
DOUBLE
AXE

DOUBLE
AXE
RESTORED

DOUBLE
AXE
RESTORED

GODDESS
WITH DOVE
ON HEAD

MALE
VOTARY
HOLDING
DOVE

L.M. III B POTTERY
ON LATER FLOOR

LIMESTONE SLABS

TRIPOD
CEMENTED DOWN

LOWER
V. STEP

SHRINE OF DOUBLE AXE

SECTION

e MALE VOTARY
HOLDING DOVE

c FEMALE FIGURE

a
FEMALE GODDESS
WITH DOVE ON HEAD

f SMALL
DOUBLE AXE
OF STEATITE

d
VOTARY

b FEMALE
FIGURE
CYLINDRICAL
BELOW

RAISED BASE
WITH PEBBLED FLOOR
AND PLASTER FACING

SOCKET FOR
AXE SHAFT

SOCKET
FOR
AXE SHAFT

·33

·54

1·50

HORNS OF CONSECRATION

CUPS

CLAY VESSELS

PLASTER TRIPOD

SMALL
JUGS

·39

PAINTED
STIRRUP
VASE

PAINTED BOWL
WITH TWO HANDLES

1·50

PLAN

Centimetres 100   50   0   1 metre.

Fig. 40. Find circumstances of the Sword Tablets. The floor level in the shrine and the corridor had risen 25–30 cm. The Sword Tablets were found in the 'upper strata' of the corridor; they were dated by Evans to the 'period of decadence'. A clay sealing was found with them. Impressions from the same seal were found in the Armoury (see fig. 42).

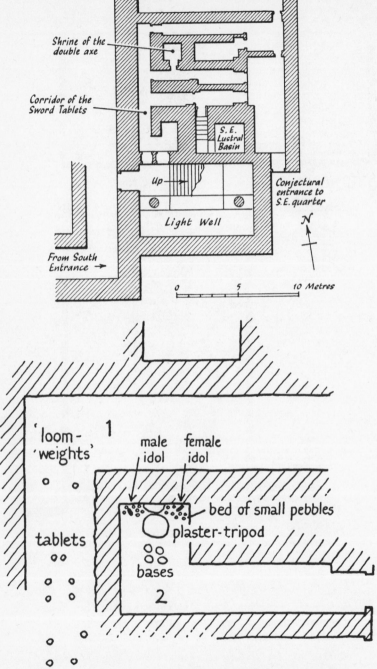

Shrine of the double axe

Corridor of the Sword Tablets

S. E. Lustral Basin

Up →

Conjectural entrance to S.E. quarter

N

Light Well

From South Entrance →

0   5   10 Metres

'loom-weights'

1

male idol   female idol

bed of small pebbles

plaster-tripod

tablets

bases

2

Fig. 41. *The Shrine of the Double Axes and the Corridor of the Sword Tablets: top figure after Sir Arthur Evans, lower figure after D. Mackenzie.*

during the so-called 'squatter' period. This, we may recall, was Evans's own opinion: 'dynasts of the old stock still maintained a diminished state on the Palace site.' Among the tablets of this late date Hood, like Evans, singled out the Sword Tablets (see above p. 201). When I was residing at the British School in 1959, Mr Hood asked me to examine the handwriting of these admittedly later tablets to see if I could detect any lateness in the script. This no Mycenaean epigrapher had commented on, and I was able to report that in my opinion there were no adequate grounds for separating this group of tablets from the rest on the score of the script.

Evans had given a clear account of the find circumstances of the Sword Tablets in the excavation report of 1902. They are set out in diagrammatic form in our figs. 40, 41. They were found in the 'upper strata' of a passage, above the higher of two floor levels on which rested late Mycenaean pots (these are described in Evans's notebook for 1902). In 1909 Evans, after long pondering on his finds, firmly pronounced the tablets to belong to the 'period of decadence'.[1] As we have seen, the swords depicted on the tablets are of a type both Evans and Pendlebury assigned to a period verging on the Iron Age. Now Evans also reported fragments of actual swords in the same deposit. Still better, there was an inscribed clay sealing which bore the impress of a seal. This proved to be a valuable cross-link.

Two years later, in 1904, Evans excavated what turned out to be the Arsenal just outside the palace (see fig. 30). In the burnt deposit were charred boxes containing bronze arrow heads, and alongside were again a number of inscribed sealings (fig. 42). More significantly, they bore the impress of the same seal as that found with the late Sword Tablets in the south-east part of the palace. Evidently the official in charge of armaments had been active in both parts of the site. If we accepted, as Hood did, Evans's firm dating of the Sword Tablets to the 'period of decadence', the same must be true of the Arsenal. Again, the chariots depicted had been of a type assigned by Evans to the Late Helladic III period. All the evidence was consistent. Hood's admission of the

---

[1] In *The Palace of Minos* IV (1935) he tried to go back on this and offered a rearranged stratigraphy.

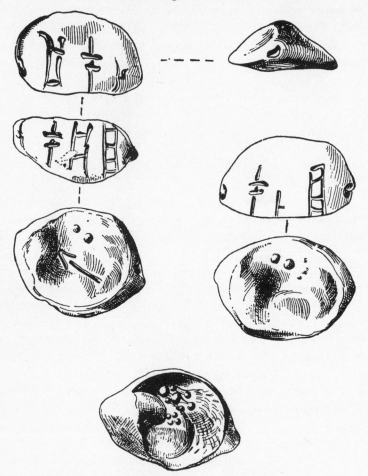

Fig. 42. Inscribed sealings with arrow ideogram from the Arsenal (Knossos).

late date of the Sword Tablets had involved him in a painful dilemma, for he was actually excavating at a point adjacent to the Arsenal.

Six days after the appearance of my article in *The Observer* on Sunday 3 July 1960 a report appeared from Hood in *The Times* for Saturday 9 July 1960. It was headed: 'Findings by Sir A. Evans at Knossos supported'. The Director of the British School at Athens announced that he had discovered tablets in 'pure deposits with great quantities' of Late Minoan II pottery: 'This new evidence is in complete agreement with what Evans says about the discovery of the Armoury tablets.' The report, despatched in haste to counter my *Observer* article, was to prove premature and had to be retracted later. But almost immediately after its publication another extraordinary coincidence put some more documentary evidence into my hands which had a direct bearing on Hood's excavations. The week following Hood's article a London colleague, Professor W. S. Maguinness of King's College, sent me the catalogue of an Italian bookseller and drew my attention to an interesting item: it offered for sale some excavation notebooks belonging to Duncan Mackenzie. These were acquired by the Ashmolean Museum and put at my disposal. They proved to contain details of excavations in the Arsenal area of 1905. It emerged with all clarity that Evans in that year had found a fair quantity of tablets scattered in a deposit that had been deeply disturbed by later intruders. 'That the disturbance had been considerable was apparent from the fact that though the occurrence of the tablets was only occasional, the sum total of fragments found was in the circumstances considerable.' The same tale was repeated when excavation was renewed in 1922, but this was not reported.

It was now evident that Hood had all unaware been excavating for years in an area where deep disturbance had been established over fifty years ago. He was now digging still farther away from the Arsenal than Evans's digs of 1905 and 1922. How then had he obtained tablets in a pure Late Minoan II medium? 'Only an earthquake can upset these results', wrote Mr Hood. I awaited with curiosity his Annual Report to the British School of Archaeology at Athens.

On 6 February 1961 Hood had to confess that he had been mistaken in his preliminary report to *The Times*. He had had the same experience as Evans in his undisclosed excavation: the scraps of tablet had after all not been found in a pure LM II medium, but in a deposit plentifully permeated by much later elements. *The Times* carried a leader entitled 'Still in the Labyrinth'.

Mr Hood continued, however, to dig in the Arsenal area, and in

1961 I visited the site and by his courtesy was able to examine the scraps of tablet he had found. All had again turned up in disturbed deposit which contained pottery of widely differing date, some as late as I could have wished. This was the last of Hood's digs in the area.

Years of effort had failed to confirm Evans's date. Not that this surprised me in view of the evidence of the sealings linking the Arsenal deposit with the late deposit of the Sword Tablets, whose late date Hood had accepted. I again awaited with interest his annual report but was unable myself to attend the meeting. Early on Wednesday morning 7 February 1962 I was rung up by the correspondent of a London newspaper, who invited my comments on the sensational annual report presented by Hood to the British School at Athens the day before. *The Times* heading read 'Sir Arthur Evans Vindicated', and the next day Hood figured as 'The man in the news' and the vindicator of Evans. On February 17 an illustrated version appeared in *The Illustrated London News* again entitled 'Sir Arthur Evans vindicated.'

A glance at the report was sufficient to convince me that the matter had nothing to do with the date of the Linear B tablets. It concerned a minor point of pottery classification. Evans had distinguished a style Late Minoan I A, which was characterized by decoration with naturalistic plant designs. This was followed, in his system, by Late Minoan I B, the so-called Marine Style featuring creatures and plants of the sea. Late Minoan I A was considered to end about 1510 B.C., while Late Minoan I B lasted until about 1450 B.C. But other archaeologists had disputed this succession of the two styles: they maintained that they were both in use at the same time. Now Hood had discovered specimens of both styles on one and the same floor. In other words, on a point of pottery style and dating he had vindicated Evans's critics, and the matter had, in any case, nothing at all to do with the great controversy that had engaged public attention. Normally so trivial a matter would have been discussed quietly in the technical journals. Instead, the vindication of Evans's critics had been twisted into a vindication of Evans. This was not likely to impress the professional archaeologists concerned. In fact, Professor D. Levi, against whom the attack was really directed, soon made short work of Hood's claims. But the 'vindication' had been launched on to the public by careful press preparation. What loomed large in the public mind was the 'great Knossos row', with which Hood's announcement had nothing to do. A colleague who had attended the Annual Meeting wrote to me that there was great danger of the public's being misled. It was necessary to take action. It so happened that only a few weeks before I had become acquainted with a document which threw a searching light on much more fundamental questions. These were (1) the excavation methods used at Knossos; (2) Evans's knowledge of his own results; and (3) the accuracy of his reporting.

13. EVANS AND MACKENZIE

The document in question was a long letter from Mackenzie concerning the excavations of 1904 and 1905. I had come upon it quite accidentally while engaged in a search for a photograph. Above I have described how Mackenzie records a very late vessel, the pilgrim's wine bottle from the Throne Room Corridor. In September 1961 I had identified it in the Heraklion museum and I had also read Mackenzie's pottery notebooks in the Villa Ariadne. In these books Mackenzie often comments 'see photograph'. On my return to Oxford I obtained permission to look through the boxes of Evans's photographs in the hope that I might find a photograph of the pilgrim's bottle. I searched in vain, but right at the end I came across a box that contained not photographs but letters. Among the most interesting were a number from Mackenzie. But my attention was especially attracted to one eight pages long. It threw a flood of light on a number of questions of key importance for the understanding of Evans's methods of archaeological excavation and reporting.

The occasion was as follows. A certain Captain Tupper had offered his services in smuggling some antiquities out of Crete to Evans. Mackenzie used the opportunity to send out the few Early Minoan sherds which had been found. When the consignment reached Evans, he seems to have been angry to discover how meagre they were, and he administered what Mackenzie calls a 'reprimand'. In defending himself the excavator explained to his

281

employer precisely how the few sherds had been obtained and the inconclusive nature of the evidence. Evans's dismay is understandable. In the excavation report for 1904 he had published an elaborate stratigraphic diagram showing three superimposed and minutely measured Early Minoan layers labelled thus:

	MIDDLE MINOAN II
44 cm	EARLY MINOAN III
56 cm	EARLY MINOAN II
32 cm	EARLY MINOAN I

I pose a number of basic questions which Mackenzie's letter now enables us to answer. How was the material obtained? The workmen had been left to themselves and had missed the floor levels. 'The floor-levels were largely made out with the help of Manolaki [the foreman] through actual examination of the sections left by the excavators.' This meant that the sherds had been not distinguished according to floor level or depth.

What material was obtained? It was so scanty that the very notion of a 'division of the spoils' excited Mackenzie's derision: 'Few as the EM fragments were, had they gone by way of the Museum [DM was smuggling them out to Evans] they would have been kept if recognized, for Hazidakis [the Curator of the Museum], who knows nothing about the scarcity or otherwise of the finds in this connexion, is quite as anxious for an EM series from Knossos as you are. Fancy then a division of the EM spoils at our disposal!'

What was the stratification? 'The circumstances are simply that the Early Minoan Series which you imagine was never found at Knossos either in the W. Square section or anywhere else.' . . . 'As regards an EM series I cannot understand how you came to imagine such a series either from the W. Square section or anywhere else at Knossos.' A subsequent discovery 'reduced the amount of Early Minoan deposit in the W. Square section to that occupying about *one cubic metre* and in this one cubic metre none of the scanty pottery was floor deposit and all of it was fragmentary. Where then does our series of Early Minoan fragments marked according to metres come in? And where are our metres?' Mackenzie concludes his letter with the words: 'The thing is simply impossible.'

What emerges clearly from the letter is that Evans as late as September 1905 had no inkling of what had been found in the way of Early Minoan pottery at Knossos. Mackenzie was at a loss to understand how his employer had come to imagine his carefully distinguished strata. Yet in the spring of that year (1905) Evans had communicated to an international congress his famous 'Système de Classification', which was to remain canonical and is still defended. He was now in a painful situation. It was necessary to confess that there was no excavation evidence for the triple Early Minoan stratification; that he had now been informed of the true state of affairs by his excavator; and that he had made his communication without first-hand knowledge of his own excavation data. A strange trick played by fortune gave him his chance. I quote Evans's own words. 'Unfortunately, indeed, owing to the incompetent hands to which the editing of the *Comptes rendus* of the Congress was entrusted, the abstract supplied by me of the above communication appeared not only in a mutilated but in a wholly misleading form. The order of periods was inverted, and I was made, for instance, to ascribe the chief masterpieces of Minoan Art to the last epoch of its decadence!' So Evans published his corrected version in 1906. He now had received Mackenzie's letter. But there was no change, and the whole diagram was repeated fifteen years later in the first volume of *The Palace of Minos* p. 33. It continued to mislead even his own lieutenants. Thus when Pendlebury was replying to Åberg's charge that the stratification at Knossos had been invented, his first examples read: 'EM I, deposit on a floor level in the West Court at Knossos; EM II, deposit on a floor level above the preceding; EM III, deposit on a floor level above the preceding...'.

14. THE SAFFRON GATHERER FRESCO

Fate had in fact played Evans an ironical trick in making the incompetent editor of the *Comptes rendus* ascribe the chief masterpieces of Minoan art to the 'squatter' period. Evans had in fact done precisely the opposite with a famous work of art. In 1900 he had discovered the Saffron Gatherer Fresco. In his sketch plan (our Plate 19) Evans entered this as found above the floor uncovered in 1900. As we have seen (p. 215), a layer of clay covered a plaster floor about 1 metre down. Along with the fresco were a number of other objects including a 'large black steatite vase with spirals'. In *The Palace of Minos* III, 20 Evans moved the vase down on to an earlier floor uncovered some 40 cm deeper in 1901. This third floor down was the one patched with the typical 'reoccupation' plaster (see above p. 223 f.). In his definitive account Evans says nothing of the 1923 investigations, and he dates the lowest floor to MM II B. On page 22 he goes on to say that it was on this same floor that he found the Saffron Gatherer Fresco. He even suggests a still earlier date: 'Nor indeed does the fact that it was found in apparent connexion with a M.M. II B floor by any means exclude the possibility that it was executed at an earlier date.'

Thus a fresco found above the latest of three Late Minoan III floors is dated perhaps as early as the eighteenth century B.C. although its find place suggests what Evans called the extreme limits of reoccupation by his imagined 'squatters'. Pendlebury hesitated for stylistic reasons between MM II and MM III, but he failed to detect Evans's radical adjustment of the find position, and he knew nothing, of course, about the undisclosed excavations of 1923 in that room.

15. What is an Archaeological Fact?

This final example will help us to focus the issue first raised by accounts of the stratigraphy in this room and the neighbouring Room of the Stirrup-Jars. Is it considered permissible in archaeological circles to make such adjustments in the recorded find positions? Is it normal to present as *actually observed* stratifications which in fact are 'reconstructed' and achieved by retrospective adjustments of the recorded data in the light of later conclusions? This is what Evans did to achieve the 'decisive stratigraphy' in the 1903 report. I was surprised to find that some prominent archaeologists defended Evans's practice. In fact I was publicly reproached at a Congress for my inexperience in this matter: Day Book entries are constantly revised, I was assured. The point must be clarified. I am not saying that later observations may not throw doubt on the accuracy of earlier ones. The question is: is it permissible to adjust the earlier observations and to publish them in the adjusted form *as observed*, just as a scientist might touch up a botched experiment and publish results not actually obtained in the laboratory?

Some pages were devoted to this theme by Dr. G. Daniel, editor of the journal *Antiquity* in March 1962. Dr Daniel rebuked me for my insistence on facts: 'Professor Palmer is like Mr Gradgrind in *Hard Times*, who said "What I want is Facts" '. He then went on to elucidate what an archaeological 'fact' is: 'The facts of Knossos are the *interpretation* by Evans and Mackenzie of what they found and dug, *not* entries in day-books.' By all means let us apply this doctrine to the present case. Mackenzie in 1923 not only made a careful record and plan of his dig, he also *interpreted* it. He concluded that the *lowest floor*[1] in the Room of the Saffron Gatherer and the room to the south had been patched with plaster on repeated occasions by the same 'Reoccupation' people who had deposited the late vases in the Room of the Stirrup-Jars. How Evans interpreted the new data we do not know since he maintained a complete silence about these supplementary excavations, and nothing was known until I published the results in 1961. Thus Dr Daniel's admonition to trust the excavator leads precisely to the drastic revolution argued in this book.

However, although the doctrine favours me, I continue to prefer the more natural view propounded by Professor Wace in another number of *Antiquity*: 'It would be wise to distinguish between excavation reports, which should be factual, and what we may term "synthetic" works, which are all too often diluted with theory.' Elsewhere Wace had defined a 'fact' as evidence obtained by excavation. This definition I embrace.

In the present work, as in my book *The Find Places of the Knossos Tablets*, I have been concerned primarily with checking statements of such evidence. What has emerged throughout the palace and the course of its excavation is a picture of adjustment, suppression and invention of archaeological data. This began on the third day with the non-disclosure of the first ceramic indicator for the date of the tablets and the fire: pithos no. 6 alongside an

---

[1] On the identification of this floor see p. 223 f. and fig. 33.

undisturbed hoard of tablets in a bath tub in wood ash deposit. It culminated 28 years later with the publication of Evans's *Shaft Graves and Beehive Tombs of Mycenae.* As we have seen, in his attack on Wace he adduced the evidence of the carved stone rosettes. To prove their MM III A date he said he had found them 70 cm below a Middle Minoan III B terrazza floor. All the records including his own notebook, show that they were found 20 cm above a Late Minoan III B terrazza floor. Such are archaeological 'facts' as I understand the term.

Chapter VIII

The Conflict of Scholars

The announcement that the statements made by Sir Arthur
Evans apropos of the finds in the Room of the Stirrup-Jars,
which he presented as his 'decisive' key to the stratigraphy
and dating of the tablets, were discrepant with the corresponding
entry in the Day Book kept by his official recorder Duncan
Mackenzie, provoked a storm of protest in the public press. My
own comment on the two conflicting statements of fact was simply
that they could not be reconciled. In the press version of my
article this assumed the ambiguous form that Evans had 'mis-
represented' the facts, and I took immediate steps over the radio
the same evening and the following morning in the leading
newspapers to correct this impression. Despite this the steps to
'an accusation of deliberate misrepresentation' and 'archaeological
Piltdown' were swiftly taken by the critics and defenders. But the
question of '*deliberate* misrepresentation' is irrelevant to scholarship. What we are concerned with is to establish what evidence
was really obtained by the long continuing excavations at Knossos.
To carry out a careful check on the facts is all the more necessary
because of the overriding importance of Knossos in prehistory.
We have to cast a critical eye on the excavation reports and the
monumental work which Evans published, so long after the main
excavation, between 1921–35, the work being completed with the
Index volume in 1936, when Evans was eighty-six years old.

1. THE CRITIQUE OF EXCAVATION REPORTS

By good fortune, when the controversy was at its height, a work
was published on this fundamental theme of archaeological
scholarship by a man who had had first-hand experience of both
disciplines — archaeology and philology. *Archaeology, Place-*

The Conflict of Scholars

names, and History by F. T. Wainright is a work which should be pondered by all who have engaged in the Knossos discussions. There is one distorting factor which Wainright stresses and we must firmly face in order to counteract its influence by clear awareness. This is what one may term 'demarcation' resentment. Wainright comments (p. 97): 'However much one may play it down, there seems to be an inherent antagonism between scholars trained in different disciplines. . . . Among historians, archaeologists and place-name scholars it seldom breaks out into denunciations and violent abuse, but it lies behind many a caustic comment, many an artless question, many a genial thrust.' Such academic antagonism is naturally stimulated when archaeologists and philologists are addressing themselves to the same groups of undergraduates with totally different accounts not merely of the historical conclusions but of the evidence itself. It may well be that each side has a part of the truth and that progress towards full truth will be hastened by exchanges even in the heated form known as controversy. But there are rules which must not be broken; they are rules of evidence and its presentation and treatment. On this subject, too, Wainright has some forceful and salutary things to say.

After reminding archaeologists that their work inevitably involves the destruction of evidence he goes on to consider the nature of excavation reports. He insists that these are not archaeological 'evidence' at all. They have to be treated as historical documents. 'If they seem to have the character of historical evidence, that is not surprising, for they are historical evidence, though of a rather specialized kind. They are not archaeological evidence at all. They pose the same questions of trustworthiness as other historical sources. . . . An author's state of mind is involved, and therefore the reliability of all these written accounts is open to debate and suspicion in a way that archaeological evidence proper can never be. Questions of honesty and competence arise. . . . One archaeologist has said in print that he keeps a mental list of excavators on whose reports he can rely, and every one who tries to use excavation reports must do the same. . . . the same questions of reliability must be raised against all excavation reports whether they come from contemporaries or from an earlier generation. One must apply to them much the same tests as a historian applies to his sources, using whatever internal or external checks present themselves, taking into account other works by the same author, and even bearing in mind that an obsession or blind spot may or may not colour the whole of a report.'

Such source criticism is so fundamental to our theme that it will be well to focus the issue on a concrete case. As Wainright says, 'Ideally an excavation is a deliberate and planned piece of research designed to provide answers to certain specific questions.' I choose one such piece of excavation which excludes Mackenzie: as we have seen, in 1913 Evans told us that he was alone at Knossos and carried out nearly one hundred test pits. Three of these we can site exactly. We have discussed them above: those under the pavement of the Northern Entrance Passage half-way up, opposite the passage opening west and inside the passage itself. What archaeological question had Evans in mind in making these tests? Evidently he wished to obtain data bearing on the date when the pavement was laid, just as when he lifted the threshold block of the Anteroom in that same year. As we have shown in detail above, the sherds obtained included LM II–III. The same result was obtained after Pendlebury had joined him in 1928: this time LM II–III sherds were found actually below the foundations of the east and the west bastions (above p. 231). Such was the archaeological evidence. How was it reported? Evans himself entirely ignored it in the account he published in 1930. This presumably went to press the year before, when he and Pendlebury had made their tests under the bastions. As we have said, his account of the history of the Entrance Passage begins with the words: 'Very complete evidence is forthcoming for the date when this North Entrance Avenue was carried out.' Yet there is complete silence about all the test pits which had yielded consistently late evidence throughout the length of the passage below its lowest paved floor. Evans got Piet de Jong to draw his imaginative reconstructed picture of the passage looking south up towards the Central Court (*Palace of Minos* III, 163, fig. 107). The donkey half-way up has its hind legs on the spot when test pits 77, 78 and 79 were sunk in 1913. The passage opening west is at this point.

We now apply Wainright's canon. The *Palace of Minos* is to be treated as a secondary source and tested for its reliability. I quote again: 'A statement in any of these sources [i.e. historical sources] may be true or false, an accurate summary by someone who knew the facts, an ill-formed assumption by someone who did not, an official or censored version a piece of propaganda, an imaginative fiction, or even a deliberate attempt to deceive.' In the present case I limit myself to the simple question on which I have insisted throughout this enquiry: did Evans report fully and accurately the evidence he had obtained by his excavations? The answer plainly is in the present case that in his definitive account in the *ᴾalace of Minos* he made no mention at all of it. Yet in fairness it ‸ust be stated that he caused the Stratigraphical Museum to be organized and had the *Guide* published by Pendlebury and his assistants. The paramount question remains the establishment of the facts. The primary source in the present instance is Evans's 1913 notebook, and the 'evidence' is the sherds in the boxes containing his wooden labels, which Pendlebury classified and published and which have since been rechecked by J. Raison. All the rest is 'interpretation'.

2. EVIDENCE AND INTERPRETATION

A leading archaeologist has declared, as we have seen, that in archaeology the facts are the interpretations. But what is it that is interpreted? Let us say that what is interpreted is the *evidence*, and that this consists, in our chosen case, of a structure with different floor levels and various archaeological objects in recorded positions and levels. In the last resort all the archaeological 'stories' published about this set of observed data are simply attempts to account for the find positions. Such accounts must be examined for their plausibility. But one thing we shall rule out of court firmly from the beginning. No 'story' will be accepted which attempts to alter the facts. We have seen one such: it is the assertion that the tablets were shovelled in to make up the LM III earth floor. On the other hand, the imaginative picture of the disappointed plunderers is admissible for scrutiny. We shall simply say that it does not explain all the facts: a coherent batch of tablets was found near the modern surface above the said earth floor. Evans's own story was the simplest: the tablets had fallen from above on to the LM III B pots and the surface on which they had been stored. But this, as we saw, involved assuming that the boxes of tablets had survived for centuries throughout the post-destruction 'squatter period'. In the end Evans's defenders gave up the attempt to account for the primary evidence and concentrated on a purely defensive strategy. This is the now notorious 'fire-escape'.

3. CONFLAGRATION: EFFECTS AND DATE

We now approach a fundamental archaeological question which has assumed major significance in the Knossos debate. It is in fact the last resource of the defenders of orthodoxy. They cannot deny that massed deposits of tablets were found inextricably associated with great quantities of whole LM III B pots above an earth surface laid in LM III times in a part of the palace drastically rebuilt after the supposed destruction of 1400 B.C. Some hypothesis had to be devised of putting asunder what was found together. This dogma relates to the expected effects of fire on tablets and pots stored with them in the palace at the time it was consumed. Since it is the last defensive position and manned by many leading archaeologists, the doctrine deserves close scrutiny. Fortunately, the effects of fire in a complex building are a matter of ordinary experience and common-sense. It does not require the expertise of the trained archaeologist. Every firewatcher of the wartime period may presume to proffer his opinion, to say nothing of the local fire-brigade. It is one of the strangest aspects of this controversy that archaeologists the world over hailed and acclaimed a doctrine of fire that goes counter not only to common-sense but also to the plain statements of Evans himself.

Combustion, it will not be denied, depends on the supply of oxygen, and in a complex building consisting of basements and cellars, with upper stories consisting of sun-dried brick within a wooden framework, the ventilation conditions will be infinitely varied with different degrees of fire intensity. Now Evans himself makes a detailed statement on this very matter. He wrote (*Palace of Minos* IV, 944): 'The conflagration itself does not seem to have barely extended to the basement stories, where the carbonization of the columns was in many cases the result of gradual chemical action rather than actual burning. In such areas as, in the Domestic Quarter, the lower part of the Hall of the Colonnades, and the Grand Staircase, and in the sections of the great Megarons there, as within the Little Palace, they seem long to have preserved their supporting function. In the West Quarter again, the shafts of the columns that flanked the "Lustral Basin" opposite the throne were found largely existent, though here as elsewhere reduced to charcoal, which broke up in the course of excavation.'

That the fire affected the basement spaces less than the upper floors should surprise no one. The point is of importance because of Evans's statements about the storage places of the tablets. He tells us, what is evident from their find positions, that they had been originally stored in upper rooms and that they had fallen into the basements at the time of the destruction. The pots on the other hand, had largely been stored in the ground floors and basements. What should we expect to observe? In the first place we must bear in mind not only the different storage places of tablets and pots, but also their different composition. Tablets were made of clay which had been merely sun-dried. They were not intended for long keeping. The pots, for their part, were not only made of carefully prepared clay, but they had been fired in a kiln up to a temperature of perhaps 800–1000° centigrade. The tablets, because of their position, had been exposed to heat of greater intensity than the pots in the sheltered basement spaces. It is fortunate again that Evans makes a detailed statement on the general condition of the Linear B tablets (*Palace of Minos* IV, 884): 'the great bulk of the tablets had a light brown sun-baked appearance'. Evans expressly excepted from this statement 'the tablets which had suffered from the burning of the structure that had contained them'. But quite a number of the tablets had not been baked at all and so were in a very friable condition. Evans describes how he had inadvertently left out over night some of the first tablets he found, along with a very interesting sealing showing a chariot team. A rain storm came on that dissolved these merely sun-baked pieces of clay. Yet in the very room where these unburnt tablets were found Evans reported charred boxes of wood. This very room provides a striking illustration of the capricious effects of fire. One tablet had been broken: one half was of the light brown kind, and the other half was charred. Evans commented: 'broken before conflagration'. He did not say: 'The fire must have had identical effects, therefore the two halves belong to different epochs.'

Evans had been particularly explicit on the effects of conflagration in the upper stories. In *Scripta Minoa* I, 41, apropos of the sheep tablets found in the corridor of the Domestic Quarter (see p. 116), he wrote: 'The gallery in which these tablets, or rather the series of coffers that contained them, were originally deposited had here been on the third story, apparently immediately under the roof. One result of this lofty position was that they had been more affected by the conflagration of the building than those belonging to other hoards, some specimens indeed having been charred to such an extent as to obliterate the inscriptions (fig. 18).'

Such were the effects of fire as described by Evans. They will surprise few who have observed a burnt out building. Upper floors may collapse and smother ground floors or basements before the fire reaches them. Conditions will vary even from one part of a room to another. Such are the *arcana incendii*. If the bulk of the tablets, sun-dried as they were, stored in the upper rooms showed little signs of fire, the same will *a fortiori* be true of kiln-fired pots stored at a lower level in basements, which on Evans's testimony had barely been affected by the blaze.

After these preliminaries we may now examine the fire doctrine brought to bear on the finds in the Northern Entrance Passage. The doctrine has been enunciated in order to invalidate, to explain away, the association of tablets with LM III B double jars. The actual words are as follows. 'The tablets, of unfired clay, are preserved by a conflagration which baked them. Some are blackened, almost vitrified. There are good scorched examples from the Northern Entrance Passage in Oxford. What happened to tablets must have happened to any pots stored with them *at the time of the fire*. This is why we have no whole LM II pots beside tablets! And why the intact and unburnt pots beside the broken and burnt tablets do not afford a dating context. It is utterly naïve to imagine that objects found together were manufactured at the same time, especially when their conditions are so different' (J. Boardman).

The argument is in two parts. The first is concerned with the absence of positive ceramic evidence: it is admitted that no whole LM II pots were found with any hoard of tablets. The second part contrives to *explain away* the presence of unwelcome pottery associations — the great store of LM III B double jars. It will be expedient to examine separately the two parts of the double excuse. I take first the absence of positive evidence.

The fire is made responsible for the disappearance of the pots *assumed* to have been stored with the tablets. An assumption is not a statement of evidence. As we have stressed, the evidence for dating contexts must take the form 'These pots with these tablets', and it will be satisfactory if such statements can be made and justified in different parts of the palace. Now what has been admitted is that no such statements can be made for any hoard of tablets: there are no whole LM II pots beside tablets anywhere throughout the palace. We are told by way of excuse that the fire destroyed them all. Now, fire may certainly reduce pots to fragments and even cause extreme damage and distortion. But it is difficult to believe that there was total annihilation of the resulting sherds. This in fact is not implied in the above excuse. Seeing that this is by hypothesis an 'LM II palace', which means that the palace was largely stocked with LM II pots, if the fire so largely destroyed them, then there must be enormous quantities of burnt LM II sherds in the palace stores. Moreover, since tablets were found virtually in every room during the first season's dig, we should expect to find a similar distribution of burnt LM II sherds.

This was implied in the review of the first edition of this book in a broadcast by the B.B.C. Mr J. Boardman said: 'The tablets, to survive, had to be accidentally burnt; they are dated by the smashed and burnt pottery and other objects found with them.' This is a statement of evidence. It is implied that burnt LM II sherds were found with the tablets. The broadcast was made a few months after the reviewer had paid a visit to Knossos and had heard the report of his pupil, who had been sent to search the pottery stores for burnt sherds. The result surprised the investigator.

The Conflict of Scholars

In scientific terms what had been undertaken was the 'verification' of a hypothesis. The hypothesis had two parts: (1) LM II pots had been stored with the tablets and (2) the fire had destroyed them.[1] The 'expectation' or deduction from the hypothesis takes the form of great quantities of burnt LM II sherds. The experimental verification is simple: it consists in an examination of the boxes of sherds in the museum. It is fortunate that this was undertaken by a scholar already deeply committed to the defence of Evans.

Mr M. R. Popham reported his surprising results. 'I found fewer burnt sherds than I had expected.' This was an understatement. He found no burnt sherds at all which could be unequivocally assigned to LM II. Moreover, not a single one could be attributed to the extensive area covered by the 1900 excavations. In other words, nothing in the boxes of the Stratigraphical Museum contradicts Mackenzie's statement that no Palace Style sherds were found in the 1900 season except for those in the disturbed Eighth Magazine (see pp. 189 f.). But there was a further oddity about the few burnt sherds picked out from so many hundreds of boxes: they were of different ceramic classes or 'dates'. This bears on a still more fundamental question — the validity of chronological deductions from pottery styles. This will be discussed below (pp. 302 ff.).

Further investigation disclosed that there had been no need for the Oxford archaeologist to wait for the report of his pupil from Knossos. There was plenty of evidence available in the Ashmolean Museum itself. I recall the curious circumstance (see pp. 187 ff.) that although the 'LM II palace' *ex hypothesi* had been stocked with this class of pottery at the time of its supposed destruction, yet the most prolific sources had been the disturbed west magazines and a dump in the southwest quarter outside the limit of the palace proper. The pottery expert A. Furumark stressed this fact in his book *The Chronology of Mycenaean Pottery*, p. 83: 'The

---

[1] This is a purely empirical question to be answered by those with experience of excavating burnt buildings. Thus the palace at Pylos was destroyed in a particularly fierce fire. Yet thousands of complete pots were found. Blegen dismissed the above argument; 'in any event the argument that all pottery which has gone through a fire is without exception indelibly marked by it, is not valid. Many have come through without a sign of burning'.

richest deposits from the last palace period at Knossos are those found at the S.W. angle . . .' It turned out that Evans had presented to the Ashmolean a rich assortment of sherds from this quarter. On inspecting them I found that not a single one bore any traces of fire. Some in fact were remarkably bright and new looking. In Oxford, too, the verification of the hypothetical 'LM II fire' had been wholly negative.

We now turn to the other part of the excuse: it does not seek to account for the absence of evidence, but tries to *explain away* the evidence actually found in the shape of great quantities of whole LM III B double jars. The argument may be stated thus, bringing out its hypothetical nature. (1) If the said pots had been stored along with the tablets, and (2) if all the tablets are marked by fire, then (3) all the pots *would be bound to show* the same effects of fire *in the state in which they were examined in 1961.*

We first examine the assumptions. Where were the tablets stored? It is agreed by all that they were not stored where they were found. Evans opined that they had fallen from upper rooms overlooking the entrance passage; his defenders reject this and propose as alternatives: either that they were dragged there by plunderers, or that they were shovelled in to make up the earth floor laid by the people who used the LM III B double jars. At all events both sides agree that they were not stored with the LM III B pots.

We must now recall the materials of which the tablets and the pots were made: the tablets of unbaked, merely sun-dried clay and the pots which had been fired to a high temperature. The pots were stored in a little room or lean-to against a massive external wall deep down in the entrance passage (see fig. 35). Another important factor is the direction of the wind at the time of the fire: Evans tells us with much circumstantial detail that a very strong south wind was blowing, and the entrance passage sloped steeply to the north. Now that we have reconstructed the physical positions and circumstances of the tablets and the pots, we can approach the main question: the attempt to assign the objects found together to different epochs. We have to pronounce common-sense judgement on the doctrine offered by the defence against accepting the primary evidence: 'what happened to the tablets *must have happened* to any pots stored with them. . . .' In the B.B.C. broadcast review this was put into a vivid form. 'It is like finding fresh potatoes beside potato-crisps and pretending that their histories had been exactly the same since they left the soil.' In this comparison the fresh potatoes are the kiln-fired pots; the crisps are the sun-dried tablets. It would be more apt to use the combination of pie-crust and pie-dish: 'the dish would be bound to show the same effects of the oven as the crust.' However, it will be better to examine first the phrase 'what happened to the tablets. . . .' What did happen? Evans has told us: the great bulk of the tablets were of a light brown and sun-dried appearance. The varying effects of fire are illustrated by the state of the hundreds of unpublished fragments examined in 1955 in the museum. The editors group them according to colour: red, buff, grey. These distinctions reflect degrees of firing. The buff ones fall into Evans's light brown category; on the darker red pieces the editors note that they are in a particularly fragile and crumbly condition.

We are, however, particularly concerned with the Northern Entrance Passage. It is in connexion with the Great Deposit, entangled with the late jars, that the fire doctrine has been advanced in order to effect a separation of two sets of clay objects found together. The advocate for the defence published a statement that there are good scorched examples from this palace quarter in the Ashmolean Museum. The jury will wish to know whether this is a complete statement of the evidence from this region available in Oxford. The same show-case also contains tablet E 777, and we have particularly accurate information about its find circumstances. It formed part of the surface deposit of the Great Seal (see pp. 229 f.), which occurred immediately south of the Great Deposit (see Plate 19). The tablet is a light terra cotta colour and shows virtually no signs of fire damage. It contrasts with the badly scorched specimens singled out for public mention by the Oxford archaeologist. The tablet is of interest because it records monthly rations of wheat for the women of Knossos, the women of Amnisos and the women of Phaestos; there is an endorsement on the back of the tablet describing them by a word which recurs in cloth contexts (see fig. 18). Thus a tablet, showing little sign if any of fire, found at a high level above the LM III earth floor, gives evidence that the administration it reflects was in close control of Phaestos. But it is with the visible effects of fire on tablets that we are at the moment more closely concerned. The show-case in the Ashmolean offers a fine example of the varying effects of fire on different parts of one and the same tablet. Ra 1540 is a summation of swords (see fig. 25, tablet top left). The fracture runs through the last sign of the word *pa-ka-na = phasgana* 'swords'. The left part of the tablet is black and its thin end is charred. The right part of the tablet by contrast is terracotta in colour, and though it too shows the effect of baking, there is nothing which could be described as distortion or charring. It is a striking illustration of the capricious effects of fire. I recall that these tablets were found close to the surface above a late floor with LM III B pots on it; that they illustrate a type of sword which Evans classed as late; that he assigned them to tablets from the Age of Decadence; and that M. S. F. Hood singled out these tablets for me as those whose late date he accepted (see pp. 274 ff. with figs. 40, 41).

We may now put the question to the jury: they have to pronounce common-sense judgement on the doctrine offered by the defence. A great revolution in Aegean prehistory depends on the answer. The defence has failed to bring any positive evidence to support their contention that the fire took place when LM II pottery was largely in use. Not one burnt sherd has been found of this class either in the Northern Entrance Passage or indeed in any part of the palace where the first thousand or so tablets were found (on the Domestic Quarter, where the great bulk of the rest were found, Evans and Pendlebury themselves admitted the reoccupation in the 'Period of Decadence', see pp. 243 ff.). Consequently what remains to us is to decide the strength of the last redoubt whose sole defensive work is a handful of mixed burnt sherds. This is the assertion to be pondered: 'what happened to the tablets *must have happened* to any pots stored with them. . . . This is why the intact and unburnt pots beside the broken and burnt tablets do not afford a dating context.' Were all the tablets broken and burnt? We have seen that they were not. Were they stored with the pots? They were not. Is it absolutely certain that pots stored in this low position would be bound to show the effects observable only on some of the tablets, stored higher and made of a different and more delicate material? Professor Blegen has observed that kiln-fired pottery may get red-hot and still show no traces of fire. If then tablets (pie-crust) showed such little effects of the fire, can we *assume* that the fire would indelibly mark the pots (pie-dish) stored in a lower and more sheltered position? The jury may be reminded that the words on which its verdict is sought are '... *would be bound to show.* ...' What is being sought is a certificate for putting asunder what was found together. Not only are tablets more delicate than pots. Consider the frescoes found in the burnt rooms. Are they all marked indelibly by the fire?

Now let us assume that the verdict of the jury, despite the affidavit of the professional archaeologist who excavated Pylos and the evidence from Mycenae, decides that the mass of LM III B pots are part of a different destruction debris, which was not accompanied by fire; and that we must assign tablets and pots to different periods. We still have not proved that the tablets are LM II: that can be settled only by producing positive ceramic evidence. In fact what results from such a verdict is the possibility that the tablets are still *later* than the LM III B pots.

In archaeology, as in other sciences, the evidence is supreme: all explanations must account for the observed data. Now let us grant for the sake of argument that pie-dishes stored in the basements will show the same fire-effects as pie-crust stored in the upper floors. We still have to account for the actual find positions. We must note not merely the Great Deposit on the LM III earth floor but also the adjacent Deposit of the Great Seal (see Plate 19), found close to the modern surface along with the sealing. We now scrutinize the explanations offered for the said find positions. So far only Evans's explanation pays due heed to the observed phenomena. He said that the tablets and sealings had fallen on to the LM III B pots in the passage after it had been drastically reconstructed after the supposed destruction of 1400 B.C. This implied that the boxes of tablets had survived for some centuries undetected in rooms rebuilt and reoccupied. This was so self-evidently absurd that, once I had pointed it out, the explanation was tacitly abandoned by Evans's defenders. Instead they offered a choice of two explanations. The first was that plunderers at the end of LM III B times had rummaged in the ruins and dragged the boxes into the entrance passage. They had broken them open, but disappointed to find tablets instead of treasure, left them lying with the LM III B pots, to the confusion of the archaeologist. However, while recognizing the ingenuity and recalling that the Pylos tablets had also once been accounted for as loot from Knossos, I feel bound to point out that while this may account for the Great Deposit on the earth floor, it ignores the surface deposit high above the LM III earth floor. For these yet another explanation must be devised.

The same weakness is inherent in the second attempt at an explanation. I quote again from the broadcast review. 'If we have to guess how the tablets got there I would suggest that they were shovelled in to make up the floor.' This does not explain, but alters the facts. Evans clearly states, and represents in his stratigraphic diagram, that the tablets were found *on* a clearly defined LM III floor on which the flanking wall of the pot-room had been constructed. No less firmly does he locate the Deposit of the Great Seal in the upper earth of the deposit, a fact given precision by Mackenzie's entry: 0· — ·90 m. To 'shovel in' the tablets is to interfere with the facts. It is fascinating to watch how Evans's defender is forced along exactly the same path of fact adjustment as Evans himself. Evans moved the small deposit in the Room of the Stirrup-Jars, recorded as 'on the clay floor', down into the clay floor without being able to produce any corresponding LM II sherds. But the deposits in the entrance passage he allowed to remain in their recorded positions. It is this primary evidence which the defence now proposes to adjust by moving the Deposit of the Great Seal down from its find position close to the surface and incorporating it in the earth floor.

But here too history repeated itself. Just as the move down in the Room of the Saffron Gatherer encountered the evidence found for LM III occupation on the next floor down (see above pp. 223 ff.), so the investigations of 1913 and 1929 produced late sherds from below the paved way which underlay the late earth floor in the entrance passage. This has already been discussed in detail. Precisely at the point where the Deposit of the Great Seal adjoined

the lower lying Great Deposit Evans probed in 1913 and found
LM II–LM III sherds below the paved way. In 1929 he dug under
the foundations of the bastion immediately east of this point and
found an LM II sherd. The probe under the foundations of the
most northerly bastion on the west side in the same year yielded
LM III sherds. These results, which were paralleled in various parts
of the palace, transformed the whole question. It made the 'potato
crisp argument' pointless, if the bastions and the paved way,
representing an earlier architectural phase, had been built when
LM II–III pottery had got stratified. This enquiry has, however,
been worth while since it concerns a fundamental point of
archaeology on which there were profound differences between the
experts. On the one hand, C. W. Blegen, who may be regarded as
uniquely qualified to pronounce on the comparative effects of fire
on Linear B tablets and contemporary pottery, declared that the
above doctrine, *a priori* as it is, is invalid. Many pots stored in the
Pylos palace at the same time as the tablets came through
unscathed. On the other hand British experts, with remarkable
unanimity, hailed and acclaimed the 'fire-escape', which was
widely repeated as offering a sure proof of the date of the Linear B
tablets. The 'proof' we may repeat, was a negative one: it aimed at
the chronological separation of tablets and pots. It did not bring
the tablets into association with burnt LM II pots or indeed with
any LM II pottery whatsoever. We may now summon the B.B.C.
reviewer for re-examination. His audience was offered by implication the following statements of archaeological evidence: (1) the
tablets were incorporated in the earth floor and (2) they are dated
by the burnt pottery and other objects found with them. Neither
part of the statement is true. No burnt LM II pottery was found
associated; the tablets were not in the earth floor.

4. The Dilemma of Archaeology

The emergence of so much undisclosed evidence bearing on the
archaeological history of Knossos has led to a strange situation.
Prehistoric archaeology is essentially a search for well stratified
pottery. This is the primary evidence on which the historical
reconstructions are based. Now leading archaeologists are insisting

vehemently that the historical conclusions they drew before the decipherment of the Linear B tablets from the ceramic evidence were erroneous. Not merely this, but the whole distribution of pottery styles at Knossos itself and throughout the island of Crete conflicts with the witness of the tablets. I find myself in the peculiar position of defending the claims of sherd-based history against the attacks of its chief practitioners. In the following pages I propose to examine what has been said by the leading figures in Aegean archaeology, starting with the fundamental matter of the pottery. I shall try to show that all is well if only we accept the primary evidence as it stands without complex adjustments and 'escape' hypotheses.

Pottery

I take first the odd ceramic picture presented by what archaeologists call 'Late Minoan II Knossos'. First the stirrup-jars. Evans insisted repeatedly, as we saw, that he found not a single one of LM II date in the palace precincts, although there was an abundance of specimens from the 'reoccupation period'. The tablets record thousands. This means that all the right ones have disappeared and have been replaced by large quantities of later date. But stirrup-jars are not the only puzzling blank in the archaeological record. Not a single whole LM II pot was found along with the tablets. Yet tablets were found in virtually every area of the palace. Evans comments on another mysterious fact, to which we have referred above (p. 191): there was also a dearth of smaller vessels contemporary with the 'palatial fabrics'. The 'excuse' offered is the wealth of the inhabitants, who used bronze vessels which plunderers had wrested from the grasp of the archaeologist. At all events, the picture presented by the excavator is an 'LM II palace', abundantly provided with tablets and sealings but with no LM II pots to go with them, no LM II stirrup-jars and no LM II small pottery.

Nor were excavators any more fortunate at other Cretan sites. The distribution map of LM II pottery in the island bears no resemblance to that which has emerged from the Linear B tablets. Phaestos, as we have seen, was in the firm grip of its Knossian overlords, 'during LM II' (if the tablets are of that 'date'). Even the food rations were controlled by palace bureaucrats, while shepherds kept their flocks and delivered up their wool under the watchful eyes of the king's representatives. Where was the residence of the Mycenaean governor of Phaestos 'in LM II times'? How is this reflected in the pottery styles? Is it conceivable that his residence had different styles from those of Knossos? Did a royal representative proceeding to his post pass from one ceramic area to another? If so, how can we ever reconstruct historical communities and political complexes on the evidence of pottery? If on the other hand we leave the 'date' of the tablets open and simply look in the area of Phaestos for a Mycenaean residence, our eyes fall upon the megaron at Hagia Triada. True, it offers no Linear B tablets. But nor does Tiryns a short distance away from Mycenae and one of the most powerful fortresses in the Mycenaean world.

Let us turn our eyes to the west, for this region of Crete has been the subject of comment in the most recent archaeological work on the Mycenaean age. In his book *The Last Mycenaeans and their Successors* (Oxford, 1964), Desborough reaffirms Pendlebury's statement that the west of Crete was not opened up until 'after the disaster of LM II'. Yet, as we have seen, the tablets list men and beasts at Aptara and Cydonia, places not built until LM III 'times', and then on commanding sites so characteristic of this later period in Cretan settlement. What could the scribes of 'LM II Knossos' have been doing? I have deliberately put 'LM II Knossos' between quotes because we have now reached the most fundamental point. How well founded is sherd-based history? What good grounds are there for chronological distinctions and more or less precise absolute dates like 1400 B.C.? How can archaeologists be so certain that Knossos was destroyed at the transition of style LM III A: 1 to LM III A: 2? It is fortunate that the very bases of Cretan prehistory have been recently questioned by two of the leading authorities in this field of study.

H. van Effenterre, the French excavator of Mallia has written: 'One may now say, by a sort of paradox, the more carefully one analyses pottery, the decorative motives of seals or any kind of archaeological objects whatsoever, subdividing them into classes at will, the less one feels justified in attributing to these distinctions any clear-cut chronological significance.' Effenterre speaks of the deplorable tendency (fâcheuse tendance) in modern archaeology to attach chronological significance to considerations of 'stylistic evolution'. It has been shown, he says, that pottery styles believed to form a chronological series were in fact in contemporary use.

It was Professor Doro Levi, head of the Italian school of archaeology at Athens, who incurred obloquy by enunciating this great heresy. I propose to take one clear example and then apply it to Mr. Desborough's book. Levi excavated a Minoan villa at Gortyna, a little distance north of Phaestos. In it he found much typical Late Minoan I pottery. But in the same destruction debris (the house had been fired) were idols of a very late date. More interesting was a striped stirrup-jar very like those from Wace's House of the Oil Merchant at Mycenae: in other words its classification according to the accepted canons is LH III B. Yet jars of the same shape were found on the floors of the palaces at Phaestos and Hagia Triada. The decoration of the Gortyna specimen had the rudimentary octopus tentacles which the experts assign to the late period Late Helladic (Late Minoan) III B. For an authoritative opinion on the point we may cite A. Furumark, who calls this design 'curtailed cuttlefish', equivalent to Evans's 'degenerate octopus'.

Levi does not shrink from the archaeological consequences which the given association of 'early' and 'late' pottery styles imposes. He insists, on the contrary, that the implications must be faced. We should not be deterred by objections of a face-saving kind. Of course it is true that if we abandon the canonical ceramic scale with its fine stylistic-chronological gradations, then archaeologists will no longer be able to date objects from Late Minoan palaces otherwise than by a vague reference to the two centuries assigned to this 'period'. The Gortyna stirrup-jar will focus the issue on a particular example. If we give it its Furumark classification and date, then we might conclude that the villa was burnt at much the same time as Wace's House of the Oil Merchant i.e. at the end of the 'Late Helladic III B period', *c.* 1200 B.C. If with Levi we abandon the chronological implications of Furumark's classifications and allow such stirrup-jars to float within the two centuries; if we accept instead the dating of the associated Late Minoan I

304

pottery, then we should date the stirrup-jar to *c.* 1400 B.C. But more recently, at the Congress held at Heraklion in September 1961, Levi has confessed that date 1400 B.C. which he gave as the end of the Minoan palaces must also be considered provisional.

Observations at the Palace of Minos and other Cretan sites reinforce these doubts. It remains to add that the recent examination of the sherds in the Stratigraphical Museum at Knossos disclosed some evidence which might be taken as support for Levi's experience at Gortyna. I recall that M. R. Popham looked for burnt LM II sherds to verify the contention that the fire must have affected all the LM II pots stored with the tablets. In one and the same box from the Little Palace Popham reported burnt sherds which he classed as LM II/III A: 1 and LM III B. Still more peculiar was the yield from the box relating to a house to the north-east of the palace (box Q II 2), for here the burnt sherds were assigned by Popham to LM II/III A: 1, LM III A: 2, and LM III A(?). LM III A: 2, according to present orthodoxy, is a 'post-destruction' style. As we saw, the pottery expert, faced with these 'surprising' results of his expectant search, did not venture to conclude that the differently classed sherds were evidence for fires of different dates. Instead, he commented that the earlier ones were such as could have survived into the later period. Thus one and the same fire appears to have affected specimens of pottery styles that were pre-destruction, destruction, and post-destruction, according to the accepted ceramic scale. Evans, of course, had firmly stated that the Little Palace was fired at the end of the 'squatter period' and he denied a fire altogether for the LM II period in this building. Yet another odd example of ceramic co-existence may be recalled. In the East Wing two pots, one LM I A and the other LM III B were found side by side in the Queen's Megaron (p. 244), both in use as lime receptacles, this being a part of the building which all admit was in use during the LM III B style. In view of such contemporary use of different pottery classes, how is it possible to determine the date of the final conflagration on the basis of minute stylistic differentiations? It was the expert Furumark who revised Evans's date by determining the last 'predestruction' pottery style as LM III A: 1. What has Popham to say on this determination? 'The archaeological evidence available to and cited by him hardly seems to justify the certainty with which he [Furumark] fixes the limits of the stylistic phase when the palace was destroyed.'

Sealings

Effenterre included the stylistic dating of seals and sealings (i.e. the pieces of clay with seal impressions) among the dubious indicators of chronology. In the preceding pages we have noted the misfortunes of a leading English expert in this field. The famous sealing showing a bull's head with a double axe between the horns and dated to Middle Minoan III transitional turned out to be from the deposit[1] of a court (see p. 236) actually rebuilt at a late stage of the Late Minoan III B period. On the other hand, the seals found on the floor of the Lapidary's Workshop and dated by him to the Reoccupation Period had to be reclassified because of the burnt wheat and beans found in those rooms. The Great Seal found near the surface in the Northern Entrance along with a coherent group of tablets was also awkwardly placed (see p. 229). It is apropos of the Little Palace that the data are most massively documented and publicly acknowledged by Evans himself.

It was in the campaign of 1905 that Evans had located the 'Little Palace' a few hundred yards northwest of the main palace (see fig. 30). A seal impression from this building has already been mentioned apropos of the horse (fig. 22), for Evans stressed 'the exact correspondence between the dressing of the mane here shown and that of the horses on the fragmentary frescoes found in the Megaron of the Palace at Mycenae'. As for the contents of the house itself, Evans noted that although a decline of wealth was noticeable, there was no real break in the continuity. His next observations are of such vital importance that they must be quoted verbatim.

'In nothing is this [continuity] more perceptible so far as regards the present building, than in the heaps of more or less fragmentary clay sealings, *found on the later floors*, attesting the survival of similar usages as regards securing documents and possessions and presenting in a somewhat degraded style the same artistic types

---

[1] It will not help to say that the sealing came from the late walls, since LM III sherds were also found embedded in these walls.

as those of the preceding age. But what is still more interesting is
the evidence, now for the first time supplied by some fragmentary
clay tablets found in connexion with these sealings, that the fully
developed linear script of Minoan Crete continued to be at least
partially in use during the later period. It appears that the fall of
the palace did not bring with it the absolute extinction of letters,
and the true dark ages of Crete were not yet.'

The archaeological information and the conclusions based on it
are clear and unambiguous. The report (1905) was written when
the facts and their impact were fresh in the excavator's mind. In
later years Evans retracted. In the *Palace of Minos* (II 343) we
read apropos of these same tablets found in the Little Palace: 'In
Scripta Minoa I I had suggested the possibility of some of these
having belonged to the period of the Reoccupation. That the use
of the Linear Script B survived the overthrow of the Palace is
probable, but the squatters who at a later date introduced their
crude fetish worship into the "Little Palace" were surely *anal-
fabeti.*' In other words, the archaeological facts must accommodate
themselves to a preconception.

We must ask a plain and simple question. Were the seals found
on the later floors as stated in the excavation report? If this is so,
and yet, for non-archaeological afterthoughts, we deny them to
these later occupants and ascribe them to a previous phase of the
palace, then we are again required to believe that the sealings and
the associated tablets remained in being for centuries throughout
the 'squatter' occupation and were not precipitated on to these
later floors until the final catastrophe which put an end to this
upper and later culture. This involves a further difficulty. Evans
notes that there was no catastrophic break in the history of the
Little Palace such as characterizes the major building. On the
contrary there was no conflagration, with the result that the fluted
wooden pillars of the LM II building left their imprint on the
later plaster and rubble, thus providing us with invaluable architectural evidence. But if there was no fire until the end of LM III
(c. 1150), how could the sealings have survived unbaked for something like a quarter of a millennium and then have deposited
themselves in heaps on the floors and staircase, in all cases along
with pottery of the latest 'squatter' type? The excavation

documents when consulted on this point provided an unequivocal answer. Mackenzie had drawn a careful sketch plan on which he had entered the positions of the sealings. Evans had drawn a rougher plan but the details agreed, and he also drew some of the tablets found along with them. Sealings and fetishes had been found in one and the same deposit. Mackenzie had written a careful account of the state of the deposit. He noted the rich tawny-red earth characteristic of the Minoan stratum. This, he wrote, was produced by the action of fire on the earthy constituents of rubble walls and the plaster and brick materials. The sealings had fallen from the upper floors. And the fetishes? They too bore the marks of fire: the stone was considerably burnt and found in the tawny deposit. As for the seals found in abundance, 'the pottery found was also invariably of the same Late Minoan III character as elsewhere in the house.' It is evident that Evans's account in the excavation report and in *Scripta Minoa* I four years later was perfectly correct. The presumed illiteracy of 'fetish worshippers' was no more than a rationalist's prejudice. People who bow down to wood and stone may also be able to write.

Now that the Late Minoan III B environment of the Little Palace sealings has been established, we turn once again to the stylistic analysis and diagnosis. Kenna (*Cretan Seals*) draws no distinction between the Little Palace sealings and the other deposits. In fact he notes the resemblance of one sealing from this building to another from the Tenth Magazine in the west wing of the palace. The equation is significant. Since it is now established that Evans's early account of his finds in the Little Palace was correct, two conclusions follow. Either the stylistic equation is valid, and in that case we have an LM III B date for the magazines; or the stylistic equation is without chronological significance. We may leave the choice to the expert.

Stone Vases

Here we are on uncertain ground. Pendlebury stressed the chronological dangers involved. The index to his *Archaeology of Crete* has an entry: 'Stone vases, dangerous for dating.' The reason is evident: stone vases may be used for hundreds of years after their manufacture. Fortunately we have two famous vases

The Conflict of Scholars

found in an unfinished state *in situ* in the School Room area (see above p. 240), and they were equated by Evans himself with the ritual vessels found on the floor of the Throne Room. But I propose to examine the find circumstances of the famous lioness head rhyton, which Evans compared with the gold lion's head rhyton from the Fourth Shaft Grave at Mycenae. Evans goes so far as to say that the dependence of the Knossian vessel on a metal original is so close that 'it might almost have been copied from the Shaft Grave specimen.' We now ask the key archaeological question: where and in what circumstances was it found? We can give the answer with great precision thanks to the reports and their supplementation by the documents. The Room of the Stone Vases immediately adjoins on the west side the Room of the Chariot Tablets (see fig. 39). In other words it lay immediately to the north of the great cross wall of typical Mycenaean construction which cut the palace in two (see p. 267). But there were other stone vessels in a kind of annexe. Moreover, closely associated was an unpublished object: a lamp of grey steatite with a spirally fluted pedestal and base. Fortunately Evans not only drew this in his notebook of 1900 but entered its exact find position: it was found within the rectangle of the 'mainland megaron' (see fig. 39) just to the south of the Mycenaean cross wall which was the north wall of this 'megaron'.

Bronzes

It was in the 1903 report that Evans, as we saw, acted on his belief that it was admissible to readjust observed data in the light of later interpretation. There is another section of the same report which makes it clear that the excavators had arrived at a conception of the nature of the 'reoccupiers' which was leading them to disregard the facts of the stratification. This is to be found in their account of the discovery of the famous bronze vessels in a building just outside the west wall of the palace. They called it the Northwest House. On Monday April 6, 1903 Mackenzie excavated a room in this area and found at about one metre from the surface a column base marking a late Mycenaean floor, as was evident from the common Mycenaean sherds. Over two metres below the surface he found another column base, this lower floor

309

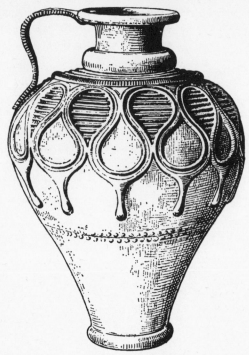

*Fig. 43. Bronze Ewer from Northwest Treasure House,
Knossos.*

being dated by Palace Style pottery. The twofold stratification
was in harmony with that established at other parts of the site.

The next day, Tuesday April 7, excavation shifted to the room
lying adjacently to the south. Mackenzie had begun to think that
it was hardly worth while carrying on in this area. Then in the
superficial stratum some loose earth fell away and revealed a find
of unique importance: four bronze basins, one inside the other, and
a bronze ewer. Evans enlarged on the 'boldness and simplicity' of
the decoration, its 'consummate finish, surpassing any examples of
the kind that have hitherto come to light either in Minoan Crete
or at Mycenae.' While the excavation report notes that these
magnificent objects lay at a depth of only about one metre below
the surface, it does not communicate the important fact that in
the adjoining room at this level there was a floor of the Reoccupation period with a column base *in situ*. Both Mackenzie

310

and Evans in fact immediately rejected the possibility that these objects belonged to the late period indicated by the stratification. They belonged, in their view, without any doubt to the second period of the palace. Their high position was doubtless due to their having been originally on an upper floor.

Again we reconstruct the physical history of these objects on the hypothesis of their having been left on an upper floor when the destruction came in 1400 B.C. It is odd that the basins were still *in rouleau*, despite their fall. We are told that they had probably got fixed together through rusting before the floor fell in. At all events the deposit was now sealed until the year A.D. 1903, when the ewer and basins were unearthed still in their 1400 B.C. positions. But meanwhile the Reoccupiers had come and actually built a room adjoining this now sealed off ruin, by sheer chance laying their floor and setting up the columns on the same level as these magnificent bronzes, which lay unsuspected and undiscovered in the next room. This is what is implied by the Evans-Mackenzie account of the matter.

Now, however, that we know of tripods 'of Cretan workmanship' in LH III B Pylos, we shall no longer be surprised by the discovery of good bronze work in the Knossos of the same date. This will enable us to accept the facts of the stratification in all their simplicity without recourse to complex *ad hoc* hypotheses. We may also embrace an observation made by Evans in the excavation report of 1903. 'It is a noteworthy fact that on the remaining part of a clay inventory from the 'Room of the Chariot Tablets' undoubtedly referring to the Royal Treasures, an ewer of the same general outline . . . is seen placed in a basin with the rounded

Fig. 44. Service of bronze vessels on Linear B tablet, Knossos.

handle presenting the characteristic contour of the present hoard.'
This is most satisfactory. The LM III stratification of the tablet
is in perfect accord with the LM III level of the vessels which it so
faithfully portrays.

I have discussed this important find at length for the light it
throws on the mentality of the excavators in 1903. We recall again
Wainright's admonition to be on the look-out for obsessions which
may colour archaeological reporting. Once again we return to this
vexed question because it is fundamental to our whole enquiry.
Mackenzie carefully enters the two floor levels each with its
column base. In *The Palace of Minos* II, 618, fig. 387, Evans offers
a plan of the 'North-West Treasure House'. The lower column
base is entered. The upper one is omitted. Yet it was at the upper
level that the bronzes were found. Again we ask: is this permissible
archaeological reporting?

5. HISTORICAL HYPOTHESES

The difficulties now facing Aegean archaeologists need no
further stressing. It will be evident that historical sequences
deduced from minute gradations and series of pottery styles will
not be tenable if those experts should be proved right who maintain
that it is merely a 'deplorable tendency of modern science' to
attach chronological values to such pottery classifications. Moreover, those who insist on the 'LM II date' of the Knossos tablets
involve themselves in self-contradictions precisely in the matter of
the distribution of pottery styles in Crete at a time when it was
dominated by Mycenaean Knossos. Nor is it possible to deduce
from the pottery when the Greeks came to Crete.

To take the last point first, Professor Matz, the leading German
authority, has confessed that the revelation that the Linear B
tablets were written in Greek was wholly contrary to the witness
of archaeology: 'The realisation [that the Linear B tablets were
Greek] was all the more surprising because the Cretan finds for
this period show an unbroken continuity.' We have already seen
that the galaxy of scholars who contributed to the so-called
'Mid-Century Report (above pp. 178 ff.) were virtually unanimous
on this point. The same emerges from a paper, written in 1947 by

H. Kantor, which is justly regarded as a judicious summing up of the debate which had so long been raging between Aegean scholars of the first rank about the relations of Crete and the mainland in the Late Minoan period.

No large-scale Minoan immigration and conquest of Greece is implied by the archaeological data. On the contrary the great wealth of the Shaft Graves at Mycenae with their chariot scenes suggests that the mainland rulers must have possessed formidable power. It was during the LH I and II periods that the Minoan traders seem to have been completely displaced by their mainland competitors so that they had lost the hegemony they had exercised in the Aegean during Middle Minoan times. On the other hand, Late Minoan I and II were 'still flourishing phases of Minoan culture' . . . 'a peaceful relationship prevailed between Crete and the mainland'. After the destruction of the Cretan capital in 1400 B.C. there was a tremendous increase in Late Helladic trading.

Miss Kantor, the author of the article, adds: 'Unfortunately it is not possible to reconstruct the complex political situation reflected by the archaeological data without the aid of other types of evidence which still remain absent.'

But for an authoritative statement of what we may call pure, sherd-based history it would be right and proper to attend to the testimony of the acknowledged authority in the field of Mycenaean pottery. It is fortunate that Professor A. Furumark was moved to write a much lauded historical synthesis on these lines just before the decipherment. Our summary will throw into high relief the discrepancy between the 'sherd-based' and the text-based historical pictures. Furumark decides firmly against a Greek occupation at Knossos associated with the pottery style LM II–LM III A. Consequently his present acceptance of this high date for the Greek-written tablets involves a total rejection of his own archaeological history, published in 1950, two years before the decipherment. My own low date, on the other hand, is consistent with his purely archaeological deductions. The philologist is thus defending the archaeologist against self-immolation. Here then is briefly Furumark's historical synthesis (see p. 171).

In Crete a 'new era' began about 1700 B.C. This was the time when the palaces assumed their definitive form. This was a period of great prosperity and productiveness. Gradually Knossos took the lead until by Late Minoan I A (1550–1500) it dominated most of the island. Phaestos became the seat of a vassal king. Roads with forts and guard stations linked the different centres, a main artery being the north-south road linking Knossos to the south coast of the island. A minor earthquake occurred at Knossos, but this was not a crippling blow. On the contrary, there followed the great LM II period with its characteristic 'Palace Style' pottery virtually confined to Knossos. This is the palace that was finally destroyed at the end of LM II *c.* 1400 B.C.

We now turn to the relations of this Minoan culture and power with the mainland of Greece.

We find that during the greater course of the Middle Helladic period (1900–1550) there are practically no signs of a connexion between Crete and the mainland. From late in that period, however, a gradual process of minoization sets in, but at no stage does this justify the theory of a Minoan conquest. On the contrary, the increase and spread of Minoan cultural influences are bound up with the rise of the royal power of Mycenae and the Argolis in Late Helladic I.

Even in Late Helladic II A (1500–1450) the minoizing tendencies, evidenced in the new style based on the Knossian LM I B, show that Argolis was the chief agency. In other words, Knossos was the Cretan centre and Mycenae the mainland centre. The primary channel of the cultural exchange ran between the 'paramount kings' of the island and the receptive mainland respectively. It was the increasing wealth of the kings of the Argolis that created a luxury demand for the superior products of the Cretan craftsmen, and these stimulated the Helladic artisans, who, however, retained much of their native Helladic traditions. It is Furumark's thesis that during this first century of the Late Bronze Age (1550–1450), though there were now two political powers in the Aegean, their relations were peaceful, despite some signs of the inevitable conflict of interests.

It is apropos of the Late Minoan II (1450–1400) phase at Knossos that Furumark's account is in head-on collision with the testimony provided by the Linear B tablets. He vigorously denied the connexion of the LM II style of pottery with the mainland. In other words, he rejected the case argued by Wace: on the contrary, the connexions at this time may actually have been severed. Cretan pottery was rarely seen on the mainland. It is this uncompromising dismissal of Wace's thesis that Ventris's decipherment seemed to have invalidated. I should defend Furumark against his self-condemnation: his case stands as printed in 1950 if the late date for the tablets is accepted. In other words, the great expert on pottery is simply invited to accept the evidence of the pottery found with the tablets. I focus the issue on a single key point. A 'pilgrim's bottle' was found in the Throne Room corridor alongside a burnt doorway. Furumark dates the shape itself to the post-destruction period, and this flatter (lentoid) form is later: it may even be LM III C. In order to insist on the rejection of his whole picture as submitted in 1950 Furumark would have to devise some special pleading to explain the 'pilgrim's bottle' away as an 'intrusion'. Simple acceptance of this piece of evidence, which (let it be stressed) Evans failed to disclose, removes the explosive charge from under the great pottery expert's carefully elaborated historical construction.

Now the same is true if we examine Furumark's picture of what we may call the colonial struggle between the Minoans and the Mycenaeans in the island of Rhodes. It was in the phase called LH II B (1450–1425) that the Mycenaean colonization of Rhodes began. There had been an earlier Minoan settlement at the place called Trianda. First there was a period of peaceful coexistence between the two, but then the Minoan settlement was suddenly destroyed. Furumark describes this LH II B period as the calm before the storm. These events in Rhodes were the prelude to the destruction of Knossos at the end of LM II or shortly afterwards at the end of the pottery phase which Furumark called LM III A: 1, i.e. *c.* 1400 B.C. or 1375. The cumulative archaeological evidence available in 1950 left Furumark no room for doubt: this disaster at Knossos was due to an attack on Crete from the Greek mainland. It is to Furumark's great credit and honour that he was among the very first to welcome with unstinted praise the decipherment which had apparently made complete nonsense of his closely argued archaeological history.

The Conflict of Scholars

By a still better piece of good fortune a distinguished English authority in the same field followed up Furumark's paper with one based on his own examination of Mycenaean pottery in the Levant. This was Dr F. H. Stubbings of Cambridge. In 1951 he confirmed Furumark's chief points. Apropos of the evidence from Rhodes Dr Stubbings drew his conclusions from the study of the Mycenaean settlement at Ialysos and the neighbouring Minoan settlement at Trianda: 'this must mean that after the fall of the Minoan central power [at Knossos] the Rhodian outpost underwent the same fate.' The Greeks attacked and burnt Knossos before moving on to Rhodes, where the Minoan colony was wiped out. Now again we observe the same strange phenomenon. Like Furumark, Stubbings accepts the decipherment and the revelation that what he had believed to be the 'Minoan central power' was in fact Mycenaean Greek. We now make the necessary verbal substitutions in his statements of 1951, bearing in mind that this was the year before the decipherment and that the author was purveying the pure milk of archaeological deduction without the adventitious aid of philology. 'The Minoan site of Trianda was suddenly deserted shortly after the fall of the Mycenaean palace at Knossos. The neighbouring Mycenaean colony continued to flourish down to the end of the Mycenaean age. This must mean that after the fall of the Mycenaean central power of Knossos the Rhodian outpost of Minoan culture underwent the same fate.' This is now complete nonsense. Sense is restored if the given LM III B associations of the tablets are accepted and the previous phase restored to the Minoans. Yet here too we encounter the same strange resistance. Masochistically Stubbings insists that his 1951 account was nonsensical. To achieve this self-destruction he also has to deny the ceramic findings of his own book. He, too, has much to say about 'pilgrim's bottles': the lentoid form is the later development of this shape. He must insist on the strange archaeological doctrine that all pots found associated with tablets must bear indelible traces of fire. The LM III B pottery found under paved floors and concrete courts, and even embedded in stair masonry all has to be discounted by variations of the 'intrusion' argument. Pendlebury has to be rebuked for his statement about the complete 'reoccupation' of the Domestic Quarter. His edition of the Stratigraphical Museum has to be challenged thirty years after its publication. All these challenges to, and adjustments of the evidence are required in order that Furumark and Stubbings may insist that the careful deductions they drew from a study of the archaeological evidence were wholly erroneous. My own case is simple: accept the ceramic associations established (and not contested) for the tablets; refrain from *ad hoc* 'escape hypotheses'; and your deductions may stand. In a word, I propose to save the distinguished archaeologists from themselves.

In 1964 another English expert published what we may call the sequel to Furumark and Stubbings. This is the book to which we have already referred: *The Last Mycenaeans and their Successors* by M. R. d'A. Desborough. The work is purely archaeological: it seeks to elicit the history of the late Mycenaean period and the following 'Sub-Mycenaean' from the examination of pottery styles and their distribution. The chapter on Crete deserves our special attention since we can now control the results of archaeological investigation by reference to the Knossos tablets. One point will suffice. Desborough follows Pendlebury's account of the progress of settlement in Crete after the supposed disaster of LM II. It was then that 'some attempt was made to open up the western part of the island'. Desborough refers to this as one of 'the main points made by Pendlebury, and they are of importance in virtue of his very extensive knowledge, although much of his evidence may be from surface finds only. Excavation since 1945 has tended, on the whole to confirm his general picture, though not all his points of detail.' It will be recalled that this was the view of Kirsten at the First Cretological Congress in 1961 (see above p. 184). Reference may now be made to Pendlebury's maps giving the distribution of Late LM II and LM III sites respectively. The latter includes Phaestos and Cydonia, the former excludes these places. We may put the same question to Desborough: how can LM II tablets record men and beasts at Cydonia,[1] which was not founded until the following archaeological period? Sense and harmony are restored simply by accepting the observed ceramic associations of the tablets.

To encourage the highest degree of precision I take one such

[1] This is Canea in north-west Crete,

317

tablet. No. 59 records bulls at places including Cydonia and Tylissos. The tablet was found in the Room of the Chariot Tablets. This room was flanked to the south by the north wall of the mainland megaron (see above fig. 39). The content of the tablet shows that Cydonia was now in existence. Therefore in Desborough's view the tablet must be LM III B. Its archaeological environment includes a megaron. What of Tylissos, which also figures on the tablet? Above we have seen that N. Platon has traced the outline of a fine megaron there. Here is an archaeological puzzle: what was the relation of the occupants of the Tylissos megaron to the supposed squatters of Knossos?

All these facts have long been available to Desborough. What answers does he suggest for these puzzles? It is strange that a book published in 1964 should remain so unaffected by the discussions which have been raging round these very points for the last four years, including the mention of Cydonia. The author is, of course, well aware of them. 'It is realised that controversy still surrounds the date of the Linear B tablets found at Knossos, but no attempt will be made to discuss the matter.'

The decipherment is accepted. It makes nonsense of the archaeological picture offered by the author. Yet the disputed date will not be discussed. Here too I find myself defending the validity of the ceramic evidence. Some of Desborough's deductions and historical readings are in striking agreement with the evidence of the tablets, if their archaeological environment is simply accepted. There is no difficulty about dynasts of LM III B date referring to Cydonia, for it had now been founded (*sic* Desborough). But agreement goes far beyond this item. I have argued above that life at Knossos went on after the destruction of the mainland palaces. This is Desborough's own conclusion: 'In Crete it would seem that the troubles of the mainland had no immediate effect.' The same was true of the Central and South Aegean; there was no disturbance at Rhodes and Cos. There is one important archaeological symptom for communication over a wide area: we observe a wide distribution of the stirrup-jars with octopus decoration. Here philology and archaeology make physical contact: the tablets are associated precisely with such vessels.

There is thus the most satisfactory harmony and concord

The Conflict of Scholars

between the deductions from both types of evidence — the pottery and the tablets. All that is necessary is for archaeologists to observe the ceramic associations of the tablets at Knossos and to refrain from *ad hoc* escape stories that allege 'intrusion'. There can be no better end to this chapter about the conflict of scholars than to quote Pendlebury's own words on the relationship between archaeological and philological evidence. In the Introduction to his standard work *The Archaeology of Crete* we may read some words that are particularly apposite today. 'As to theory, archaeology, as the late Professor T. E. Peet said, is not an exact science. In the absence of documents which we can read and believe, we are bound to progress by means of theories. Any theory is justifiable which agrees with the greatest number of facts known at the time and neither contradicts a vital fact nor human nature and reason.' Now we have such documents, and Furumark, Stubbings, and Desborough accept them. They know, as Pendlebury did not, that the Linear B tablets were the records of Mycenaean kings who were in control of Phaestos and Cydonia, besides much else. It contradicts human reason to suppose that these kings had records relating to a place not yet founded. Thanks to the Knossos excavation documents we also know much purely archaeological evidence not available to earlier archaeologists. No theory is justifiable which contradicts these new facts. With A. J. B. Wace we can declare: 'We must guard against the facile assumptions of the past and look at everything afresh from the new point of view.' With D. Levi we can affirm that in Cretan archaeology we must wipe the slate clean and start all over again from the very beginning. One fundamental principle must be reaffirmed. We are concerned with evidence and its assessment. 'To be swayed by the convenience or inconvenience of the results or the conclusions is to lose our intellectual integrity' (H. Chadwick, in another connexion).

Yet if sentiment be allowed a place, what end could be more satisfactory than that modern science should confirm Homer's picture of Mycenaean Crete at the time of Nestor of Pylos? 'And spear-renowned Idomeneus was captain of the Cretans that held Knossos and wall-girt Gortys, Lyctus and Miletus and chalk-white Lycastus, and Phaestus and Rhytium, well peopled cities, and

319

yet other peoples who dwell in Crete with its hundred cities. Of them all was spear-renowned Idomeneus captain and Meriones, the peer of Enyalius, slayer of men. With them followed eighty black ships.' It was the Palace of Idomeneus and his descendants that Evans excavated in 1900.

Postscript

In a lecture given in London on 30 September 1964 Mr. Sinclair Hood, who has been one of Evans's main defenders, made the following admissions.

(1) The 'reoccupation' at Knossos is a myth invented by Evans and Mackenzie.

(2) The Linear B tablets and associated sealings were found in the same horizon of destruction as the so-called 'reoccupation' pottery, 'as Professor Palmer has emphasized'.

(3) Pottery of the styles LM II, LM III A and LM III B occurred in one and the same destruction deposit.

(4) As far as he could see, there was no evidence for A. Furumark's chronology of Late Minoan pottery.

(5) He was uncertain about the chronological gap between the destructions of Knossos and Pylos: 'there was still a lot of work to be done on the dating of the pottery.'

This concedes the main theses of this book. Mr. Hood proposes a drastic updating of LM III B pottery. Thus his present position is this: Evans was wrong in his facts, but also wrong in his pottery dating. By this double error he arrived at approximately the right chronology.

Chapter IX

The Coming of the Greeks

1. THE ARCHAEOLOGICAL EVIDENCE

For the prehistorian of Greece the question 'Who were the Greeks?' represents the pinnacle of his endeavour. Archaeological opinion on this question is strangely undivided. What may be called the orthodox view, which has long remained without effective challenge, has recently and cogently been stated by the late Professor A. J. B. Wace.

It will be recalled that the Late Helladic culture (often called 'Mycenaean'), with its well-established three main divisions LH I, II, and III, was preceded by that of Middle Helladic. This MH culture had lasted for a considerable time, assessed at some three and a half centuries. But evidence for stratification is insufficient to establish securely its internal divisions, and Professor Blegen has stated 'it is premature, and going beyond the evidence yet available, to use the terms Middle Helladic I, II and III as if they were established general concepts with validity for the whole Greek mainland.' There is, however, impressive evidence that Middle Helladic represents an intrusive people. Architecture, burials and, above all, a distinctive style of pottery, the so-called Grey Minyan ware, mark it off from the preceding Early Helladic. Many of the Early Helladic sites show a burnt stratum, and a large number were abandoned and never reoccupied.

These archaeological facts are virtually unchallenged, and it is on them that Professor Wace based his arguments in stating the common opinion that the people who brought the Middle Helladic culture are to be identified with the Greek invaders.

'With the beginning of the Middle Bronze Age on the mainland of Greece in the nineteenth century B.C. a new element appears . . .

321

The Coming of the Greeks

It is clear that a new factor at this time came into Greece; and since the material signs of its culture, pottery (which was made on the wheel), house plans, tombs, and in general all artefacts, differ markedly from those of the preceding Early Bronze Age, we assume that these differences mean a difference of race. This new racial element presumably in its turn also overran and amalgamated with the survivors of the Early Helladic inhabitants. From this time onwards there is no similar sign of any cultural break: the Middle Bronze Age develops slowly and naturally into the Late Bronze Age. . . . Thus by a process of elimination we deduce that since neither the Neolithic nor the Early Helladic people were Indo-Europeans, that is Greeks, then the Middle Helladic people who introduced into Greece the mysterious pottery called Minyan ware (the characteristic pottery of the Middle Bronze Age) were probably the first Greeks to enter Hellas. So far no sign of their presence in the north of the Balkan peninsula can be found, and apart from Troy we have no indications of the their presence in Asia Minor. The original home of the Greeks still remains a problem awaiting solution.'

This diagnosis of the experienced archaeologist is commendably cautious. In his reference to Troy Wace has in mind the culture known as Troy VI. This famous site, first discovered by Schliemann, had been the scene of meticulous re-exploration during the thirties of this century by an American expedition headed by C. W. Blegen, whose monumental report could hardly be bettered. There appears to be little doubt about the affinity of this culture with that of Middle Helladic. But Blegen, too, prefers to regard the significance of this affinity as one of the unsolved problems of Middle Helladic. His formulation takes the form of unanswered questions. 'What is the meaning of the homogeneous culture in Troy VI? How did it establish its supremacy over the mainland and some islands of the Cyclades? . . . Was it brought by a people of Indo-European — possibly early Greek — stock? . . . Many of these questions may long remain in the field of surmise and speculation.'

Blegen expressed himself in similarly guarded terms in the excavation report. More recently Professor D. L. Page has reviewed the evidence; he is bolder in expression than the professional archaeologists. 'It is now as certain as such things can be' that the Middle Helladic invaders and the people of related culture at Troy VI were Greeks. In this contention he has received powerful support from Mr James Mellaart, a scholar who has especially distinguished himself in the field of Anatolian archaeology. The 'Grey Minyan' ware of Middle Helladic, he believes, must be derived from Western Asia, and his summing up leaves little room for doubt. 'This interpretation of the conquest of Greece by the first Greek-speaking elements from N.W. Anatolia, based mainly on the archaeological evidence will, we hope, supersede the old concept of savages from Central Europe introducing bits of Schnurkeramik, battleaxes, Indo-European speech and widespread destruction.'

In these forthright statements the pattern of facts is clear, the principles of interpretation simple, and the conclusion unambiguous. A Greek-speaking people established itself in the Trojan area at the beginning of the second millennium, and remained there for some six hundred years. It was from this area that the invasion of Greece was launched which brought the Middle Helladic culture and also Greek speech, which has persisted there until our own day. Now we should note that here a *philological* conclusion has been drawn from *archaeological* data. What is being affirmed is that the makers of Minyan pottery spoke Greek, and the reason given by Wace is this: there is no cultural break discernible between the admittedly Greek-speaking Mycenaean culture of the Late Bronze Age and the preceding Middle Helladic culture. Thus the argument takes the classical form of (1) observation of facts (the distribution of the pottery type), (2) an hypothesis ('no break — no new intrusion'), and (3) the deduction (Greeks in the Troad for six hundred years from c. 2000 B.C.).

What is peculiar is that once having drawn this *philological* conclusion, not one of the numerous reasserters of this doctrine has thought it worth while to take the next scientific step. This is to make observations to see whether the *linguistic* conclusion is verifiable. If Greek was spoken for six hundred years in the Troad, surely some signs of this must be discernible, for instance in the place-names. It must be said that there is no shred of confirmatory evidence. Where is there even a single place-name in this area of

Anatolia recognizable as characteristically Greek? What should give pause is that during the whole of the second millennium B.C. Anatolia was dominated by Indo-European languages of a type wholly different from Greek.

2. THE LANGUAGES OF ASIA MINOR

One of the greatest advances in the study of the Indo-European languages during this century has been the discovery of an entirely new group known as the Anatolian languages. The best known of these is Hittite. During the German excavations, which began in 1906, at the site of Boghaz Keui, some two hundred kilometres east of Ankara within the bend of the Halys river, clay tablets inscribed in a cuneiform script were found in large numbers. The language was deciphered by the Czech scholar Hrozný during the first World War, and it turned out to be of the Indo-European type. The speakers of this language called it 'Nesian'.[1] But Hittite was not the only language used in the records. As early as 1919 the German scholar E. Forrer was able to distinguish no fewer than eight different languages in the archives of the Hittite capital. Of these languages two are clearly also Indo-European and are close cousins of Hittite. Palaic appears to have been used in the Pontus region on the Black sea coast. Much more important and extensive was Luvian, which was the language of the powerful Arzawa countries, eventually brought under Hittite sway. Anatolian scholars agree that Luvian was used in the regions occupying roughly the southern half of Asia Minor including the coastal areas.

But long before the discoveries at the Hittite capital the attention of scholars had been drawn to the monumental inscriptions in a hieroglyphic script (fig. 45) which were found scattered over Asia Minor, with a main concentration in the southeast. Since this area was known to the Assyrians as the 'Land of the Hatti', the unknown language was attributed to the 'Hittites'. The task of deciphering the script was long and laborious, but it had been virtually completed by 1939. The discovery in 1946, of a bilingual text at Karatepe, a site in the foothills of the Taurus,

[1] It has recently been suggested that this is identical with 'Kanisian', so called after the town on the Halys river the ancient Kanesh (modern Kültepe).

Fig. 45. A Hieroglyph Hittite inscription from Carchemish. The language is closely related to Luvian.

upstream of Adana, brought confirmation and greatly furthered the work of interpretation. It is now clear that the language, though it is called 'Hieroglyph Hittite', is in fact so closely related to the Luvian of the cuneiform tablets that it has been regarded as a dialect of Luvian. Some scholars even refer to it as 'East Luvian'. It is now also clear that the language of Lycia, which we know from inscriptions of classical times, is a descendant of a Luvian dialect. The position of Lydian to the north is less clear, but there is little doubt that it also belongs to the same

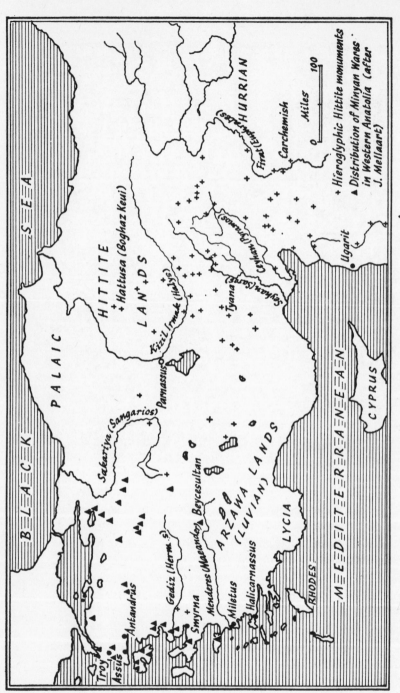

Fig. 46. The languages of Asia Minor in Hittite times. Hittite, Palaic, Luvian and Hieroglyph Hittite belong to the Anatolian group of Indo-European languages. There is a gap in the Troad region but this region is linked to the Luvian area to the south by the occurrence of 'Minyan' pottery.

language group.[1] The language distribution in Asia Minor is set out in fig. 46, which also shows the sites where Hieroglyphic Hittite inscriptions have been found. It will be clear that there is nothing here which should give the slightest encouragement to those who believe, on archaeological grounds alone, that Greek was spoken for some six hundred years in the north-west.

The position has been made still more untenable by progress in the archaeology of Anatolia, for which we have a valuable survey article by Mr James Mellaart. From this it appears that *c.* 1900 B.C. there was widespread destruction of sites in Anatolia, which leaves no doubt that some kind of upheaval took place throughout the country. The destroyed or deserted sites lie along the natural route leading from the Caucasus to the Northern Aegean.

Now at Troy linked with the new culture distinguished by 'Minyan ware' (see above) we have a most important fact: this is the first appearance of the horse, which at least is an indicative 'symptom' of Indo-European intrusion. But new discoveries and studies have shown that this type of Minyan ware had a wider distribution in western Anatolia than had been suspected. Outside the Troad it occurs all along the west coast as far as Smyrna. Most significant, closely related types have been added from the important excavation by the British Institute at Ankara on the site of Beycesultan in the upper Maeander valley (fig. 46). What is important for our theme is that this site lies within the Luvian area and is believed by the excavators to be the capital of the Arzawa countries. The presumed linguistic link is thus with Luvian, and since the culture is brought by Mellaart into relation with that of the 'Minyan' Troad, the attribution of the latter to 'Greeks' becomes even more suspect.

3. LUVIAN AND LINEAR A

A wholly unexpected possibility was opened up during my own enquiries into the languages of Anatolia and especially Hieroglyph Hittite. I recall again that analysis of the religious texts from Pylos had established with reasonable certainty that *Wanassa* 'Queen' was the Mycenaean cult title of a goddess corresponding

[1] Recently a case has been made out for including Carian in this family of languages.

to the Earth Mother of Western Asia and that confirmation had come for our further deduction that *Wanax* 'King, Ruler', was in all probability the title of the 'Young God', who is the son and consort of the Mother Goddess. In Hieroglyphic Hittite we find reflexions of analogous divine titles. An inscription from Carchemish on the Euphrates contains an ideographic reference to 'EARTH-GOD GREAT-QUEEN', and we know from other evidence that the corresponding word was *hassu-saras*, where *hassu* is the word for 'king' and *-sara-* is the feminine suffix with a function like the English suffix *-ess*. Thus the word for 'queen' is really 'king-ess', with a structure like *princ-ess*. In the same language the Wine God is called *Taparas* 'the Ruler'.

If we now turn to cuneiform Hittite, we find that the Babylonian Ishtar, who became the foremost of the Hittite goddesses, is commonly dignified by the title 'My Lady'. This is usually written ideographically GAŠAN-*YA*. Fortunately we also know the Hittite expression which lies hidden behind the ideogram. 'Lady' is *isha-ssara-* where *isha-* is the word for 'lord' and again *-sara* the feminine suffix, the whole word being analysable as 'lord-ess'. Furthermore, in the Anatolian languages as a whole the possessive 'my' is expressed by attaching *-mi/me-* as an 'enclitic' to the end of the noun. Thus 'My Lady' in Hittite is *isha-ssaras-mis*,='Lord-ess-my', a most complex and easily identifiable word. It is also worth noting that *Ishassara-* occurs independently as a divine name exactly equivalent to the Mycenaean *Potnia*.

Now the corresponding Luvian form is not attested in its full phonetic form, but there is a way round this difficulty. It is well established that to Hittite words beginning with *i-* there correspond in Luvian words beginning with *a-*. A case in point is the word 'make, do'; in Hittite it is *ija-*, but in Luvian *aia-*. Again the 'City of the Sun' (*ištanuš*) appears in two forms Hittite: *Istanuwa* and Luvian *Astanuwa*. Thus there are good grounds for believing that the Luvian title of 'My Lady' would have been *Asha-saras-mes*.

It was at this point that my researches backfired in a wholly unexpected way at a problem which I had given up as hopeless. This was the language lying behind the Linear A script, which was used in Crete before the Linear B of the Greek occupation. In this attitude I had been influenced by the discussions conducted early in April 1956. A 'colloquium' of Mycenologists was held under the auspices of the *Centre national de la recherche scientifique* at Gif-sur-Yvette near Paris. During the session devoted to Linear A Michael Ventris was asked his opinion. He considered that the available material was too limited to admit of a cryptographic solution. It remained open simply to apply the values of Linear B and resort to the discredited 'etymological' method. I preferred to concentrate my efforts on the more promising field of the Anatolian languages especially those of the western and southern areas with which the Mycenaeans were most closely concerned.

Now the resemblance of Linear A to the later script is so close that less weight attaches to the general doubts justifiably expressed about the advisability of attributing values to the signs merely on the basis of their resemblance to signs of another system. In any case the researches of the Swedish scholar A. Furumark had shown that pairs of signs like *ja* and *a*, which alternate in the B-script, were similarly interchangeable in the A-script. This proved that the same relations held good within the two scripts, and this was strong encouragement to those who believed that it was permissible to tackle the problem of the A-language by giving the signs the same phonetic values as their B-counterparts. Unfortunately the material thus obtained does not permit a clear solution. Most of the words in Linear A texts are proper names, while the ordinary words most securely identified are names of pots and the like. The spelling rules in any case allow great play to the interpreter. If, for instance, we take a Semitic language and give heed only to the consonantal structure, it would be possible to identify words as dissimilar as *pottery* and *bottle*, both being represented as *p-t-r* in these orthographic conventions. Moreover, even if we admitted the equation, say, of our *pottery* with the French *bouteille*, we still could not conclude that English is identical with French or even related to it. The fact is that such words tend to be borrowed from one language into another and this is peculiarly so in the Aegean. In Greek the majority of the words for such vessels are loan-words. In general it is an established principle that vocabulary alone can never be a safe guide for conclusions about linguistic relationship. The comparative philologist attaches most

*Fig. 47. Recurrent word in Linear A, believed to be the
name of a divinity. Note the alternation of the signs a and
ja in the first syllable and the addition of a final sign
(-me) in the 2nd, 6th and 8th examples (after N. Platon).
but these are now doubled.*

weight to facts of morphology. Grammatical structures are not
exported or borrowed. It was precisely such a fact of grammar
that our Anatolian *Ishassarasmis/*Ashassarasmes* unexpectedly
brought to light.

Excavations in Crete had gradually assembled a variety of cult objects such as altars, 'ladles' (believed in fact to be lamps) and the like bearing inscriptions in the Linear A script. One word recurred no fewer than six times, (fig. 47) and Evans concluded

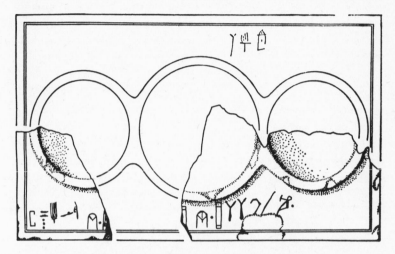

Fig. 48. The Linear A inscription on the altar from the Dictaean cave. The last word reads Ja-sa-sa-ra-me '*My Lady' (Luvian). (After J. Boardman.)*

that this must be the name of the deity to whom these objects were dedicated (fig. 48). In view of its recurrence at so many different places he thought it likely that the word was the name of the most prominent divinity, and this was the Mother Goddess. If we now apply Ventris's values to the name, we find that it reads *A-sa-sa-ra*, with a variant spelling *Ja-sa-sa-ra*. This is extra-ordinarily like the Anatolian title[1] we have just discussed. But something much more significant was to come. In three of the Linear A examples there is an extra syllable, and the word reads *A-sa-sa-ra-me*! What is clear is that we have a detachable suffix, and that this is exactly the Anatolian enclitic possessive pronoun *-me*. In other words the divine title diagnosed by Evans, and other scholars after him, as the title of the Mother Goddess reads clearly in Luvian '(My) Lady'.

At this point we must summon all our reserves of caution.

[1] Note that in Luvian *-sh-* becomes *-ss-*.

Certainly Luvian was the language of the parts of Asia Minor nearest to Crete, and it survived in the form of Lycian down to classical times. But could not this title merely be a religious loan-word and imply nothing more than a religious movement from Asia Minor into Crete, such as students of religion had already suggested? The name would then be of interest as giving some indication of the immediate source of this religious movement. It might reflect the arrival of Luvian missionaries. A title of the type *Madonna* could easily be borrowed. The philologist could reasonably object that *Madonna* is a term of art history in English and does not belong to the religious vocabulary; we do not ring the changes between *Donna* and *Madonna* and thus inscribe our religious dedications. However, let us by way of preliminary say no more than that the equation opens up the possibility that Luvian may be the language of the Linear A inscriptions.

4. A FURTHER TEST

Epigraphical research after the appearance of the first edition of this work made it doubtful whether there were in fact any examples of the name *A-sa-sa-ra* without the attached *-me*. This did not affect the diagnosis of the whole word as a divine name, on which scholars had long been agreed. However, it did weaken the argument from morphology. It is quite possible for a whole word like *Madonna* to pass into another language, and the presence of such a loan word could not offer any clue to the nature of the debtor language. This is true of loan words in general. A case in point is the Greek *kuanos* (*cyanus*), a word for dark blue enamel which occurs in the description of Homeric armour. This word figures in descriptions of furniture in the Linear B tablets (see above p. 163), while from Mycenae we have references to 'cyanos workers' in tablets found in the burnt acropolis house. *kuanos* is now known to be a loan word from Luvian, and its presence in Mycenaean Greek is not surprising in view of the close contacts of the Mycenaean world with Asia Minor. Loan words are thus evidence only for cultural connexions, direct and indirect.

For a cogent diagnosis of the language we must insist on grammatical phenomena. But if the material is too scanty to permit of a true decipherment, then we are moving in a circle. The sole method at the moment is to use the decipherment of Linear B as a working hypothesis. We apply these phonetic values to the Linear A texts and see what emerges. From the outset we must be clear that isolated word resemblances with vocabulary items from other languages have little cogency. What we require are whole sentences exhibiting grammatical machinery and yielding a meaning appropriate to the context. Here lies the main difficulty: most of the available texts are counting-house dockets containing little more than names of persons and places. This is why it will be better to start with the texts inscribed on cult artefacts, for here the object itself delimits to some extent the likely context. The divine name with which we started is a case in point. What is attempted in this section is the interpretation of a text on an altar. Once the interpretation is elucidated on the said hypothetical basis, I propose to go to the other extreme and take a wholly sceptical attitude to the result. We shall say that it is illusory and due entirely to chance. The decipherment of Linear B will be denied; further, even if the decipherment is admitted, then the values do not necessarily apply to Linear A; and finally, to take care of possibly uncertain readings and sign identifications, we shall declare that *all the readings are wrong.* This will forestall all possible types of objection: the text studied will be declared wholly illusory and as a consequence the 'intelligible text' will have emerged as a purely random process. This will enable us to give a mathematical expression to 'scepticism', and the gullibility of scholars can be measured by statisticians.

The text chosen comes from Knossos. Its discovery is described by Evans in *The Palace of Minos* II, 438 f. In 1923 renewed excavation to the northwest of the palace brought to light the famous 'House of the Frescoes', the decoration of which included the scene with a blue monkey in a rocky landscape (see *PoM* II, 447). In one of the rooms Evans found a large part of a libation table. Two of the faces which were preserved bore an inscription in Linear A. It comprised eighteen signs with marks of word division. Evans noted the presence of the word which I transcribe *Ja-sa-sa-ra,* and he drew attention to its recurrence on other cult objects. What is of the greatest significance in the present context, with our insistence on grammatical features, is his comment on the last sign on the first face of the altar: 'The small "feline head" No. 9 is of special interest, as it may refer to the Minoan Lion Goddess'. In the first 'hypothetical' treatment of the inscription I shall give this sign the value of its Linear B equivalent, i.e. *ma*. The inscription has been recently re-edited by W. C. Brice, and I propose in the first instance to accept his readings and sign identifications as correct. This is part of the 'hypothesis'. In the second 'sceptical' part I shall assume that all his readings are wrong. The essence of the experiment is that we are testing an extremely complex hypothesis: the language is closely related to Luvian; it is 'Luvoid'. This involves us in a severe linguistic examination. What results from our hypothetical application of Ventris's values is an 'unseen translation' in which we are required to satisfy the examiners, these being the acknowledged experts in that branch of philological studies. Our knowledge of 'Luvian', as has been stressed, comes from three sources: the cuneiform tablets of Boghaz Kevi, the Hieroglyph Hittite inscriptions, and the Lycian texts of classical times, for this last language has been proved beyond all doubt to be 'Luvoid' in character. I now set the unseen, simply by giving Ventris's values to Brice's text. The two sides are rendered in two separate lines A and B:

A. *ta-nu-a̞-ti ja-sa-sa-ra-*[*ma*]
B. *na da-wa-*[] *du-wa-na i-ja*

Textual note: Evans read the 'cat sign' *ma* in the final position of A.

Translation: *ta-nu-a̞-ti* is a clear Luvian verbal form meaning 'he erects'. The word is attested from 'hieroglyph' sources in a number of grammatical forms. It is the third person singular of the verb *tanu-*, characterized by the third person singular ending of present tense *-ti*. In Hieroglyph Hittite we get such sentences as 'I erected this *stele* for Ba'alat', the verb being in the past tense *tanuwaha*. We also have examples of the first singular present, the imperative, and the passive participle.

An important grammatical consequence flows from this first

result: the divine name which follows must be in the dative case. What form is expected? In later Hittite *ishassarasmis* would have the dative *ishassari-mi*, but in the old language the form would have been *ishassara-ma*. Examples are lacking from the other Anatolian languages although in Hieroglyphic Hittite the expression 'Sun-my' meaning 'His Majesty' once occurs as *istanas-mias*, showing that *-mis* has been incorporated in a different declensional class. At this point we can utilize Evans's reading of the final sign: can it be an accident that the form which emerges from this reading is precisely the expected old Anatolian dative form of the divine title 'Lady-my'? Doubtless the name of the donor stood on the missing side of the altar, and examples from Hieroglyph Hittite suggest that the inscription would have had the following lay-out: '[This altar X] sets up for My Lady'.

Despite this encouragement we remain firmly hypothetical and now tackle the translation of the second line of the unseen. The first word is *na*, which is easy, for it occurs frequently in Hieroglyph Hittite in the meaning 'not', and it can also be used with imperatives. This enables us to diagnose this part of the inscription as the usual formula protecting the religious object and its offerings. The next word is broken but it begins *da-* and this is a verb attested in all branches of Anatolian in the sense 'take'. A good example is from Carchemish: 'Should anyone take the bread or the libations away', where the verb is *ta-ti-a*, the root being *ta-* 'take'. The next full word is *du-wa-na* and again easily recognizable in its root form: *duwa* (*tuwa*) occurs in all three 'Luvian' sources, cuneiform *duwa-*, Hieroglyph *tuwa-*, Lycian *tuwe-* meaning 'to put'. Further, we know that nouns are derived from verbs by the suffix *-na*: e.g. *upana-* from the verb *upa-*. Thus the word will mean 'things put', probably in the sense of 'offerings' rather like the Greek *anathema*. This brings us to the final word *i-ja*. In Hieroglyph Hittite one of the most frequent words is the demonstrative pronoun stem *i-*. It invariably refers to the object on which the inscription is written: e.g. '*This* tablet . . .'. As for the case form, there appear to be two possibilities. *iā* is the neuter plural form, but this would involve an abnormal word order 'offerings these'. So it might be better to take it as a dative 'from it' or even adverbial 'from here'. In Lycian there is a corresponding enclitic form *ije*, also meaning 'to him, to it, or here'. It can be seen in the following sentence:

se	ije	ti	eseri	tadi	tice	kupa	ebehi
'and	from it	who	away	takes	anyone	tomb	his'.

Here we may also point out the verb 'he takes' *ta-di* corresponding to the Hieroglyph Hittite *ta-ti*.

Thus the whole translation of our 'unseen' as a Luvian text is as follows: '[This altar X] erects to My Lady. No one shall take the offerings from it (or here)'. The first line is reasonably clear, for the verb form is morphologically transparent and the divine name was long ago diagnosed as such by Evans himself. The main difficulty in the second line was the broken word *da-wa-*[. This makes its morphological diagnosis difficult, and we may use it to illustrate the sort of difficulty facing scholars in this branch of studies. We might expect the indefinite pronoun 'anyone', which could be appended to an accented word as an 'enclitic'. The pronominal stem in question is related to the Latin *quis*, which occurs in cuneiform Hittite transparently as *kuis*, and in Lycian as *ti* (see above example). But unfortunately the value of the relative pronoun sign is not securely established for the hieroglyph script. However, if those scholars are right who have suggested *hu* or *hwa*, then the pronoun might be *hwasa* or *hwasha*.[1] This would be rendered in the Linear A script (on the analogy of B!) as *wa-sa*. The boldness of 'restoring' *da-wa-*[*sa*] in an undeciphered text needs no emphasizing, and the time has now come for complete scepticism over the results of our 'unseen'.

I now yield unresistingly to objections of every kind. Experimentally I declare that the Ventris decipherment is a delusion. To those who admit the decipherment but deny that it can be properly applied to Linear A texts no objection is offered. Finally, to less radical critics who admit both decipherment and its applicability to Linear A but query the readings and sign identifications, unconditional surrender is made which goes

---

[1] The postulated *na ... hwasha* 'not anyone' can be supported from a hieroglyph inscription likewise containing a warning against interference with the monument on which it is inscribed: *i-pa-wa-ta na* HWA-*a-s-ha sa-na-ti* 'this (stele) not anyone shall overturn'.

beyond all possible criticism: we say that the text of our unseen is in fact one hundred per cent faulty. Our position now is that the examiners have set a text simply by taking a typewriter with some 75 blind keys and typing a passage of eighteen syllabic signs. This means that what emerged was a random choice of 1 in 75^{18} phonetic values. They added a further hazard by making it unclear whether there was a word break half way, that is between the last sign on side A and the first sign on side B. It would have been bad enough if they had now invited the candidate to treat it as a specimen of *any language* known to him. Instead they had the additional fun of prescribing it as a text from one branch of the Anatolian languages, the one used in the part of Asia Minor nearest to Crete. The examiners now have the candidate's effort before them, and since we have agreed to join in the fun, we can measure our own scepticism. First let us mark the paper.

Certainly *tanu-* means 'put up, erect', and the dialect is also correct for the verbal ending *-ti* is preserved in Luvian, whereas in cuneiform Hittite it is changed to *-zi*. As against this, *Jasasara* is not directly known from Luvian sources: it has been reconstructed by a sound law from the Hittite *ishassara-*. On the other hand the dative inflection of the appended personal pronoun corresponds with old Hittite. The examiners' text, thus randomly arrived at, can be construed as Luvian and the sense is appropriate to the object on which it is inscribed. The 'sceptical' examiners have succeeded in a chance of one in 75^{9}.

The second sentence is less satisfactory. We have the negative *na*, certainly appropriate to a text of this kind; then a broken word which begins with the syllable giving the verbal root 'take'; a word *du-wa-na*, not actually attested in any text but starting with two syllables known to have the meaning 'put'; and finally a word *i-ja* which begins with the syllable known from Hieroglyph Hittite as the demonstrative stem 'this'. Verdict: too many unknowns except for the word 'not'. The choice between 'credulity' and 'scepticism' thus concerns primarily the first side of the altar. Scholars will divide into sheep and goats: those who live their lives on the cheerful acceptance of chances of one in 75^{9} and the others.

The 'others' may care to consider the dialect implications.

This is what emerges from approval of the test translation. The Linear A language is a *-ti* dialect not a *-zi* dialect. Moreover, the verb *tanu-* is known only from Hieroglyph Hittite, though this may be due to accident. However, those who find some plausibility in the proposed version of line B will note that the prohibitive *na* points in the same direction, since it is only in Hieroglyph Hittite that the negative has the same form both for denial and prohibition. Luvian contrasts prohibitive *nis* with the negative *nauwa*, and Lycian shows a similar distinction between *ni* and *ne*, while Hittite has a different particle altogether for the prohibitive: *le*. The same pattern is revealed for the last word, if this is really some form of the demonstrative pronominal stem. Here too *i-* is the form which appears in Hieroglyph Hittite, whereas Luvian has *za-* and Hittite *ki-*. Thus the preliminary diagnosis of the Linear A language as Luvoid made be given further precision if the above 'unseen translation' should survive scrutiny. It would be possible to say not merely that the 'Minoan' language forms part of the Anatolian group of Indo-European languages but also shows closer affinities with the 'East Luvian' revealed to us in the Hieroglyph Hittite inscriptions.

There has been growing support in recent years for such a diagnosis. The Russian scholar V. V. Shevoroshkin for instance in a communication dated 1 July 1963 wrote: 'it is noteworthy that the ancestors of Karian and Lycian (which also seems to have many features in common with Minoan) form a link between Minoan and the languages of Asia Minor geographically as well perhaps one may speak therefore of a "Hittite-Minoan" linguistic community.' A similar conclusion has recently been reached by the Swedish scholar A. Furumark, who now specifies the Linear A language as possibly Luvian. In his previous analytical study he has left the question of the language open. Then he had suggested that certain words ending in *-ti* are third person singular verbs: our own example *ta-nu-a-ti* gives a precise instance. On the other hand pa_2-*ti-da*, which he diagnosed as a case form of the place-name pa_2-*ti* is no longer directly equatable with Hieroglyph Hittite ablative *-da* since Bossert's value for the 'foot' sign has proved to be inaccurate and Laroche has shown that the Luvian ablative case ending is *-ati*. However, recent research has given new cogency to another morphological phenomenon discussed in the first edition of this work.

Like other scholars before him Furumark drew attention to the name of the Cretan goddess Dictynna, which he regarded (as I do) as a derivative of the mountain name Dicte (*Dikta*), meaning 'She of Dicte'. Now such a derivational form cannot be explained within the morphological framework of Greek. If on the other hand we simply ask which language in this part of the world makes derivatives from place names (the technical name for such adjectives is 'ethnics') by means of a suffix -*una*, the answer is again Luvian. An important paper has recently been devoted to this subject by the eminent authority in Anatolian studies E. Laroche of the University of Strasbourg. In the earliest stage of Anatolian there was a suffix -*uwan* which appeared in the northern branch as -*umana* with progressive reduction to -*umna*, -*umma*, -*uma*- and -*ma*. It is the development in the southern branch that interests us in the present connexion, for here the development was -*uwanni* and -*unni*. We can conveniently contrast the north and south developments by the derivatives from the town name *Halpa* (Aleppo): *Halpumma*- is the Hittite word for 'of Aleppo', while in Hieroglyph Hittite we have the form *Halpa-wanna*-. It is the suffix -*wanna*- which is reduced to the contracted form — -*unna*-. A man from Adana will be called *Adana-wanna*-, and this is what we find in the contracted form in Egyptian sources *Danuna*. *Dictynna* thus fits perfectly into the framework of known Luvian morphology: a person from *Dikta* will have been called *Dikta-wanna*-, and this was regularly reduced to *Diktunna*. Evidently the people who coined this name from the name of the holy mountain Dicte could only have been those whose language contained this morphological resource. In other words they were Luvians. As we shall see, another study by Laroche of the important place-names in -*assos* like *Parnassos* points in the same direction (see below).

We now again turn to the archaeologists to ask whether they have information bearing on a possible migration from the Luvian areas into Crete. Our question will be addressed in the first instance to the excavators of Beycesultan, for they believe that this was an important Luvian centre. The discoveries made during the

Fig. 49. A religious shrine from Beycesultan.

season of 1957 are especially relevant to our first religious clue. The excavation report reads as follows:

'This year's most outstanding discoveries were related to the evolution of religious life in western Anatolia during the fifteen or so centuries of the Bronze Age — a subject on which we have hitherto remained in almost total ignorance ... At the very end of the 1956 season ... traces were found of something resembling a religious shrine. .... It was a structure consisting of two upright clay *stelae*, originally perhaps 5 ft high, the gap being emphasized in front by clay "horns" resembling Minoan symbols of a much later period.' (fig. 44).

The 1957 season established that a type of sanctuary consisting of a pair of shrines, one of a 'male' and the other of a 'female' character, had existed from the Early down to the Later Bronze Age on this site. 'In front of the shrine a low curb enclosed a semicircular space of some special significance. Some shrines had two concentric curbs of this sort and the "male's" shrine was usually distinguished by a stout wooden post or pillar set axially on the perimeter of the outer circle. The "female" shrine seemed usually to be furnished with a small clay platform built against a neighbouring wall. This has been described as a "blood altar". . . . Flat marble figurines of the "mother-goddess" type were also found exclusively in the "female" shrine.'

The Minoan affinities of Beycesultan had already been evident from the results of previous seasons. 'In previous reports of our finds it has been made abundantly clear that the orientation of this south-western culture is towards the Aegean; and if in default of any familiarity with the mainland architecture of this period we turn, for instance towards Crete, an entirely different picture presents itself. In fact the most superficial comparison of the Beycesultan remains with those of the Cretan palaces at Knossos, Phaestos and more particularly, Mallia is sufficient to convince us immediately of some striking and significant relationship . . . (the evidence) suggests that the Beycesultan palace must already have been in ruins when the Cretan palaces acquired this definite form in 1700 B.C.'

The architectural resemblances as set forth by the excavators are so complex that little doubt was left in their minds about the connectedness of the two cultures. The only question which remained was this: 'Which of these two cultural milieu — Crete or the mainland — is likely to have exerted sufficient influence on the other to result in the assimilation of architectural practices? In this respect the first consideration must be chronology. We must again remind ourselves that in Crete we are considering the palaces in the form which they had newly taken during the Third Middle Minoan period in about 1700 B.C., with only slight modifications added in the first Late Minoan period. The lifetime of the Beycesultan palace is a shade less closely dated, but its foundation has been shown archaeologically to have been at least a century and a half earlier. As for its destruction, there are reasons for attributing this to the Hittite king Labarnas, the first conqueror of Arzawa; and if we follow the dating which is archaeologically the most acceptable for this period in Anatolia, such an event would have occurred during the second half of the eighteenth century B.C. All of this suggests that the Beycesultan palace must already have been in ruins when the Cretan palaces acquired their definitive form in 1700 B.C.'

The excavators' findings and their conclusions are clear-cut. They bring the palaces of the Minoan 'new era' (c. 1700 B.C.) into connexion with the finds from the Luvian area. Now it is with the first palaces that the Linear A script takes its rise: it is inseparable from this epoch of Cretan history. We resume the stages of discovery. Evans had diagnosed a word in this script as a religious title of the Mother Goddess; Ventris had provided the phonetic key to the name; Furumark had detected certain linguistic phenomena in the Linear A texts; students of religion had connected the religion of Minoan Crete with western Asia; and the Beycesultan shrines provided the first known parallel to the 'horns' which so often characterize the appurtenances of Minoan shrines. The Palace of Minos was architecturally derivable from Beycesultan, in Luvian territory. We emphasize that all this had been established before my researches provided a possible key to the language. We say no more than that the Luvian key turns easily in this complex lock constructed by earlier investigations.

If there now appears to be some reason for believing that another Indo-European people, the Luvians, preceded the Greeks in Crete, attention is drawn to the Greek mainland. We have seen that here, too, the archaeological pointers suggest a conclusion 'which is as certain as such things can be': this is that an invasion of Greece took place c. 1900 B.C. from north-western Asia Minor. All the linguistic evidence goes, however, as we have seen, contrary to the commonly accepted view that these people spoke Greek. Let us now, while not venturing to doubt the validity of the archaeological picture, marry the archaeological to the philological facts at the point of departure. This time we shall say that the invaders are likely to have spoken a language akin to Luvian. If this is so, then we must expect to find traces of this language on Greek soil. These are the observations which will verify, or fail to verify, the hypothesis.

The Coming of the Greeks

It is especially to place-names that the philologist turns for evidence of earlier ethnic occupation of a given country. The Celtic place-names of England are a case in point. Now since the days of my own teacher, Paul Kretschmer, who in 1896 published his famous book *Introduction to the History of the Greek Language*, the place-names in *-assos* such as *Parnassos* have been a showpiece of pre-Greek, 'Aegean' linguistics. As is well known, they are found extensively in Greek lands and in Asia Minor. As such they appear in every treatise on the prehistory of Greece as indubitable evidence for a movement of 'Pre-Greek peoples' from Asia Minor into Greece and the Aegean islands. Since Middle Helladic was assigned to the Greek invaders, it was taken for granted that the *-assos* names had been brought by the bearers of the Early Helladic culture. Recent research has again thrown an altogether different light on these facts.

In the first place it will be evident that if names merely distinguished by the suffix are regarded as belonging to the same class and language, *a fortiori* will this be true of names which are identical both for the root and the suffix. Such a one is *Parnassos*. It occurs not only as the name of the Greek mountain on whose flanks Delphi stands; a town *Parnassos* is also known from central Anatolia. We now make the experiment of siting the Asiatic *Parnassos* on a map showing the distribution of Hieroglyphic Hittite inscriptions (fig. 41). The town falls within this area; and it is also true that names exhibiting the suffix *-assos* are densest in the Luvian area. We now proceed to analyse the name *Parnassos*. This is perfectly transparent; in Luvian *parna-* means 'house', but in the 'East Luvian' (Hieroglyph Hittite) texts it seems possible to read the special sense '(divine) house, temple'. Not merely this, but the suffix *-assa-* is especially characteristic of this language in the sense 'belonging to'. The place-name occurring in the Luvian area thus transparently means in Luvian '(place) of the temple'.

New evidence was now forthcoming. From cuneiform sources there was testimony for yet another *Parnassa-*: this time the indications were that it was situated in the south-east, that is to say the area where there is the densest concentration of Hieroglyph Hittite inscriptions. Not merely this, but Professor E. Laroche showed that there was an earlier form of the suffix

343

-*asjas*. This was powerful support for a theory put forward in 1939 that the Luvian suffix was connected with the inherited Indo-European genitive ending -*osjo*, which would have become -*asja* in Luvian. Thus the 'belonging' adjective in -*asjas* was clearly a derivative from the old genitive, much as the Latin adjective *cuius* is inseparable from the genitive *cuius*. Both noun *parna*- and the ending -*as(j)a*- could be regarded as purely Indo-European.

This new finding made it still more certain that the Asianic forms were connected with the Aegean ones, if any doubt existed. It was now clear that the suffix possessed a 'palatalized' -*s*-, which we have transcribed as -*sj*-. Now the Greek names of this suffix are spelt, according to dialect, either with a double sigma as in *Parnassos* or with a double tau as in *Hymettos*. Classical philologists have long agreed that the sound represented in this way was once a palatalized sound. Thus the two sets of names characterized by this suffix were even more closely resemblant than had been previously supposed. All doubts about identity could be set at rest.

We now turn to the Greek *Parnassos*. Place-names can, of course, be transported by peoples who no longer understand their former significance. Welsh *Bryn Mawr* may figure as the site of an American ladies' college. But what are the chances that it will be applied to a 'Big Hill' (the meaning of the Welsh) by people who do not understand its meaning? This is the problem which faces us here. The meaning of the name in Luvian where it originated is 'place of the temple'. It is applied to the mountain which dominates the most important religious centre of Greece. Is the appropriateness of the name due to mere chance? This appropriateness is the vital fact. Would it be more 'cautious' to assert or deny this possibility of 'accident'? Those who follow me in preferring the latter must conclude that *Parnassos* was named by Luvian speakers who lived there and worshipped at a shrine important enough to be called '*the* temple', a temple important enough to survive a new ethnic invasion and to remain a religious centre of the Greeks.

We return briefly to Troy, where Professor Page has confidently installed the Greeks and permitted them to remain undisturbed for six hundred years. Professor Page is no less convinced that the *Iliad* has preserved accurate memories of Bronze Age cities. It will be fair to let him state his own case.

'The Catalogue, it is very noticeable, has nothing to say about the south coast of the Troad; but the *Iliad* preserved the memory of two raids by Achilles into that area. First he captures Thebe, the town of Eetion, father of Andromache, in the land of the Kilikes, a people unknown to the Catalogue. At the same time he sacked Lyrnessus, and took Briseis captive. Secondly he chased Aeneas down from Mount Ida and destroyed Lyrnessus and Pedasus. Where are these two places? There is not, I think, any dispute about the site of Pedasus ... it is the place known to the later world as Assos ... as for Lyrnessus ... it is probably the other chief settlement on this coast Antandros. ... Now let us ask the explanation of this fact: the *Iliad* knows of two places in this region, Lyrnessus and Pedasus; but it does not know the only two names of any importance in the same region in historical times, Assos and Antandros. An Ionian poet who wished to introduce prominent place-names into his work from this narrow strip of coast has no choice but to take Assos and Antandros. No other name is worth mentioning or generally known. But the Greek Epic, his own Epic, chose Pedasus and Lyrnessus, of which nobody knew anything at all from the earliest historical period onwards. The answer is the same as before: these names were never known to the Ionians except through the *Iliad* ... Pedasus and Lyrnessus, like Alybe and Mount Phthires, have been inherited from the Mycenaean past and have survived through the continuous tradition of oral poetry.'

The argument is conducted with all Professor Page's admirable force and clarity. No less forcibly does he argue and conclude that Greeks had been established in the Trojan area since *c.* 1900. We may now pause to ponder on the significance of the place-names whose antiquity he has so convincingly upheld. *Lyrnessus* is self-evidently of the same type as *Halicarnassus*, the echo of which we detect in *Karnessopolis*, the earlier name for *Lyktos* in Crete, as has been noted long ago. In fact what Professor Page has proved to us is that there was a name of the Luvian -*assos* type in Mycenaean times in the Trojan area. Since archaeologists had already stressed the affinities of this region with the west coast areas to the south

which are Luvian in speech, this is most welcome confirma
tion that the Troad area was *not* occupied by men of Greek
speech.

One more argument relating to the *-assos* names must be
clarified. The most fundamental study of the distribution of these
names noted that it coincided with the distribution of *Early
Helladic sites*, many of which as we have seen, were abandoned in
the subsequent Middle Helladic period. Now this coincidence of
distribution is regarded as 'significant' and the conclusion drawn
that the names were bestowed by the Early Helladic people. There
is a curious flaw in this argument from distribution. Names, like
all linguistic elements, are transmitted from generation to generation by word of mouth. Thus if they were bestowed in the Early
Helladic period and survived into Hellenic times, this means that
they must have been also on the lips of men during the intervening
Middle Helladic generations. What significance can there be
therefore in the apparent coincidence of distribution with Early
Helladic sites? Once such sites had been abandoned, how would
Middle Helladic men have found occasion to refer to them and
perpetuate the names for after generations? In other words even
if the names had been bestowed by the EH people, the only ones
which could have survived would refer to the sites which remained
in occupation later. Thus we should also observe a no less significant correlation with Middle Helladic sites, and of course with
Late Helladic sites, because in their turn the Mycenaean people
relayed these ancient place-names and passed them on, to be
eventually recorded in the documents of Hellenic and even
Byzantine times. One must therefore reject the distribution
argument as having any bearing on the attribution of the names
to this people or that.

The significance of the *-assos* names for the prehistory of Greece
has been further reinforced by an important observation made
before the decipherment of Linear B. In his book *Asia* (1946)
Professor Bossert, the discoverer of the bilingual inscription of
Karatepe, drew attention to another place-name suffix which had
previously escaped attention. This was *-wa*, which figures for
instance in *Arzawa* and *Tuwanuwa*, *Adanawa*. Transparent examples are *Wattarwa* 'Water-town', *Istanuwa* 'City of the Sun

(*istanus*)'. Now Bossert pointed out that the distribution of these -*wa* names coincides to a great extent with that of the -*assa*-names. He concluded that they belong to the same ethnic group. 'The -*uwa* names must in future be taken into consideration by all who concern themselves with problems of Indo-European migrations.' Unexpected echoes were to come from the Linear B tablets. One of the most puzzling features of the place-names in these texts has been the frequency of names of wholly un-Greek appearance ending in -*wa*: e.g. *Ro-o-wa*, A_2-*ra-tu-wa*, *A-pa-ta-wa*, *Ri-so-wa* etc. The coincidence of the formation with that studied by Bossert may now add its weight to the long established -*assos* names in support of the Luvian hypothesis we are trying out.

We return to Delphi. Apollo, according to the well-known myth, when on his way to Delphi, found his way barred by a female dragon, which he killed with his arrows. This myth has been interpreted historically. Apollo, it is said, succeeded to a shrine which was originally an oracle of the earth, and the serpent is a figure of the earth-religion. However, our concern is with another dragon, half serpent and half woman, which later accounts connect with Delphi. The name is *Delphyna*. While it is true that we know of the existence of this name only from Hellenistic authors, it would be preposterous to deny the connexion of the name with *Delphi*. Here we are faced with the same problem as with Dictynna. Greek procedures of word formation cannot account for the connexion of place-name and derivative. The suffix is again -*una*, and again Luvian accounts for the procedure of derivation. The fact may add its slight weight to the already impressive evidence of Parnassos. But what of the god himself? What are the origins of Apollo? We quote again from one of the most level-headed summaries of the discussion.

Professor Guthrie, in his book *The Greeks and their Gods*, while giving due weight and consideration to the arguments of those who would ascribe a northern origin to Apollo, nevertheless finds that 'the cumulative effect in the matter of an Anatolian origin for Apollo seems to me to be strong.' Thus 'Lycian' Apollo takes us once again to Asia Minor. We emphasize that these are three separate enquiries, yet they related to a coherent complex Par-

The Coming of the Greeks

nassos-Apollo-Delphyna. All three roads of enquiry lead to Asia
Minor and to the Luvian areas in particular.

We may review the long history of investigation into the affinities of the pre-Greek population and their speech. For over sixty
years the significance of the place-names in *-assos* has been an unchallenged part of scholarly thinking on this question. *Parnassos*
has been singled out and given pride of place because here we have
identity of a whole name and not merely the suffix. Now we know
that the holy mountain of Greece was named *appropriately* in
Luvian, shall we shy away and abandon the equation? It is curious
to observe how scholars for generations accepted the evidence
when it was vaguely diagnosed as 'pre-Greek', but now that it is
brought into sharp focus and Parnassos assigned to an actual
language spoken in Anatolia throughout the second millennium,
many feel alarm and disquiet.

In the last resort the verdict must rest with the experts in the
field of Anatolian linguistics, and it is encouraging that one of the
most eminent scholars in this branch of studies has recently
propounded a Luvian theory similar to that presented in the first
edition of this book. Laroche also postulates, on the basis of his
studies of Anatolian place-names, a Luvian invasion of the
Aegean about 2000 B.C., with a second wave of Indo-Europeans,
the Greeks, about 1500 B.C. This emerges from the following
tabulation as it has been published by Laroche.

DATE	GREECE-AEGEAN	DATE	ANATOLIA
–2000	'Mediterranean' language: place-name types *Thebae*, *Athenae*	–2000	Pre-Hittite 'Asianic': place-name types *Hattusa, Arinna, Zipla(n)ta.*
2000–1500	Indo-European I ('pre-Hellenic'): place-name types *Parnassos*, *Erymanthos*	2000–1200	Hittite-Luvian: place-name types *Parnassa* *Wijanawanda*[1]

[1] Made up of wijana- 'wine' and the suffix meaning 'possessing' -want- equivalent to the Greek -went-. Thus *Wijanwanda* is the correspondent of the Greek
form *Oino-wessa*.

348

The Coming of the Greeks

DATE	GREECE-AEGEAN	DATE	ANATOLIA
1500–	Greek (Mycenaean and other dialects): place-name types *Oenowessae, Oenoussae, Megara.*	after 1200	(a) Phrygian (b) survivors of Hittite-Luvian, i.e. Lycian etc.: place-name types *Oenoanda, Termessos.*

If a *prima facie* case for the presence of Luvians in Greece and Crete has been established, we should now return to re-examine the arguments of Wace and others which have led to the philological impasse of bringing Greeks from Asia Minor in the decisive invasion which marked the beginning of Middle Helladic. The flaw lies in the tacit assumption that because there is no decided interruption in the cultural development after the major catastrophe of Middle Helladic, this means that no new group of invaders could have established themselves. Again and again in the archaeological literature we meet this principle of interpretation, and it is open to grave doubts. We saw how constantly Sir Arthur Evans used it in Crete. Professor Wace even insisted that there was no major break after the collapse of the Mycenaean power. He and other archaeologists for this reason have denied the reality of the Dorian invasion although the linguistic map of post-Mycenaean Greece can be explained in no other way, to say nothing of Greek folk-memory. Mellaart observes, apropos of the invasion of the Hittites, that not a single weapon, pot or other object can be ascribed to them. 'The complete absence of any material culture attributable to the newcomers inevitably suggests that they were culturally far inferior to the people among whom they settled and whose civilisation they adopted.' Schachermeyr stated the principle with all frankness. Since they are apposite, we quote his words again: 'It is a great mistake to assume that historical events are always reflected in the archaeological record of stylistic phases. Many historical upheavals occurred without leaving such traces behind them.' Thus if the 'no break' fact is upheld, then the corollary of our equation of Luvian with the Middle Helladic invaders is that the Greek invaders of Late

Helladic times were culturally so inferior or so similar to the Luvians that their intrusion caused no discernible break in the archaeological record. If that were the case, the 'original home' of the Greeks would remain for ever a mystery insoluble by archaeological means.

It is not to be expected that this thought will be warmly embraced by Aegean archaeologists without close inspection. But in fact the views given authoritative expression by Wace that the Greeks arrived at the onset of the MH period have not gone unchallenged. M. P. Nilsson had postulated an arrival of the Greeks at the beginning of Late Helladic, early in the sixteenth century B.C. One of the greatest names in prehistoric science, the late Professor V. G. Childe, in a discussion of 1955 likewise insisted that there is a break between MH and LH, which he deduced from the sharp contrast in burial rites — individual burials in cists or jars within the settlement in MH, whereas in LH we have collective burials in cemeteries or tholos tombs and rock-cut chambers. 'These family vaults would surely indicate the arrival of a new stratum.'

We may add some significant pointers culled from Professor Mylonas's *Ancient Mycenae*. 'Perhaps the earliest primitive palace was built on top of the Citadel' in the time of Schliemann's Grave Circle A (1600–1500). The building of the Cyclopean wall and the first construction of the south-west wing of the palace is dated to *c.* 1350, and Professor Wace would not trace the first palace to earlier than the beginning of Late Helladic I (p. 66). As for the chamber tombs and the tholos tombs 'neither . . . could have developed from the types used at Mycenae toward the end of the Middle Helladic period.' If then the building of the palace and the new types of tombs may be taken as symptomatic of new residents at Mycenae, the low dating would square with Professor Blegen's findings at Pylos. These suggest strongly that the builders of the Palace of Nestor arrived there at the beginning of LH III B and played out their parts entirely within the limits of that archaeological period (1300–1200 B.C.).

We submit, therefore, that the views of the archaeologists may be harmonized satisfactorily with the philological analyses we have presented. We can equate the Middle Helladic invaders from

The Coming of the Greeks

Asia Minor with the Luvian speakers. Some two hundred years were to elapse before, in their further advance, other contingents from the south-west areas occupied Crete and began that 'new era' of Middle Minoan III B whose architecture reminded the excavators so forcibly of the palace at Beycesultan.

Here we may anticipate an archaeological objection. The Luvian penetration of Asia Minor appears to have embraced ultimately the coastal areas from the Troad southwards and then eastwards as far as Cilicia, bringing to the extreme south-east the name of the tribe, the Kilikes, which Homer attests for the Troad area. This does not rule out, of course, land movements through the Konya plain, where there is much evidence of destruction of Early Bronze Age sites. But kingdoms established in new cultural areas during this great movement of a conquering people could quite easily have different cultural reflexions in the archaeological records. It may well be that the Luvians established in the extreme south-east, in the Syrian area, became culturally quite distinct from their forebears in the Troad. It would not be difficult to find historical analogies. We may recall that our own island in the space of a few centuries was invaded first by Norsemen based in Scandinavia and then from France by their later kinsmen, who now spoke a variety of the Latin tongue which had already seduced their still more distant Germanic cousins, the Franks. At least the language situation was less complex with the Luvians. They and their more potent Hittite cousins dominated Anatolia throughout the second millennium.

This brings us to our final assessment in this play of probabilities. How does the invasion of Greece and Crete by Luvians early in the second millennium square with the general geopolitical situation sketched for this period by specialists in the history of Anatolia? According to the masterly survey by Professor A. Goetze, who has combined the archaeological and the philological evidence, Asia Minor in pre-Hittite times was clearly divided into a western and an eastern half each with its characteristic culture. Both halves were ethnically and linguistically different. The western cultural area, with which we are most concerned, was eventually to be occupied by the Luvians. Before the beginning of the second millennium we can observe a displacement

351

to the east. We may suppose that it was then that the Luvians came to Cilicia. Whether the date be right or not, there can be no disputing the eventual distribution of this form of Anatolian speech. Such a distribution and expansion of the Luvians, which accords with the use of the 'East Luvian' of the hieroglyphic monuments long after the fall of the Hittite Empire (c. 1200), could hardly have been carried out without a far-reaching command of the sea. Within this framework an invasion of Crete is easily accommodated. One may even claim that it is inherently probable. Thus we can account for the striking affinities noted by the excavators of Beycesultan.

In conclusion, the philological cobbler would be wise to return to the last from which he has perhaps rashly absented himself. His excuse has been that philological conclusions have been drawn from archaeological observations. To encourage incisiveness of debate the two arguments may be starkly contrasted. Both take the form of (1) observation of the facts (2) hypothesis (3) deduction from hypothesis (4) verificatory observations. The Wace theory marries the archaeological data of Late Helladic (Mycenaean) Greece to the now demonstrable Greekness of that culture. Then, on the 'no break — no intrusive people' hypothesis, it deduces from the archaeological record the conclusion that the West Anatolian culture was Greek-speaking. But no verificatory observations were attempted. Once made, they are seen to be clearly negative.

My own theory follows Mellaart in linking the West Anatolian culture, particularly of Beycesultan, with the Luvian language, which Anatolian specialists have unanimously sited in this area of Asia Minor. Again following the archaeological current to Middle Helladic Greece and eventually to Middle Minoan Crete, we now expect to make confirmatory philological observations in these regions. This time the evidence is positive to a striking degree. Above all, the most important type of pre-Greek place-name is firmly linked with Luvian. Whatever hypotheses in future may be erected to account for the cultural patterns and sequences observed in the areas under investigation, (J)A-sa-sa-ra-me 'My Lady' and the appropriateness of the mountain name Parnassos '(place) of the temple' together with its recurrence in the regions of Luvian speech, must play their part in the calculus of resemblances which are the primary data on which both philologists and archaeologists must found their conclusions.

5. The Alleged Gap between Linear A and Linear B at Knossos

From Asia Minor we must return to Knossos, for another question of stratigraphy is now posed in an acute form. If the Greeks are to be identified with the LM III phase (1400–1150), then we must perforce conclude that the preceding phase was still the habitat of their predecessors, the Luvians. In other words we ought to find in this stratum evidence for the use of Linear A. This point was made in an early criticism of my thesis: 'Was Knossos illiterate for nearly 400 years between the latest Linear A and the earliest Linear B tablets?' There is a minor error of arithmetic here, for the latest Linear A evidence is in fact dated to 1450 B.C. and the end of LM III is *ca.* 1150 B.C. However, three hundred years is still a long gap, and the point must be met.

In the first place tablets survive only if accidentally baked in a destructive conflagration. Consequently, all we can reasonably expect to find is documents from the very end of a given period. Archaeologists assign no fewer than 250 years to the two phases of LM III. Thus if the whole LM III B period is regarded as Mycenaean Greek, the alleged gap is reduced to some 75 years. Now a quarter of a millennium is a very long time, and if the palace was in full occupation for this period, then we ought to be able to detect signs of repair, adaptation, rebuilding and so on. Crete will not have been immune from those destructive earthquakes and other natural disturbances which figure so prominently in the archeological discussions of the earlier periods of Knossos. Here we are up against an almost insuperable difficulty. Sir Arthur Evans was not interested in the 'squatters'. His great work ends with the LM II period *ca.* 1400. Moreover, as always, we are dependent for this long LM III period on the distribution and analysis of pottery. On enquiry I found that there has never been a systematic publication of Late Minoan III pottery from Knossos.[1] Nevertheless, closer scrutiny of the sources revealed things of importance which

[1] Such a survey is now in progress.

had escaped notice. Most significant are the facts concerning the Room of the Saffron Gatherer Fresco. This lies to the west of the northern Entrance Passage and gives access to the Room of the Stirrup-Jar. Tablets were found there in 1900 at the same time as the rest of this great deposit, and there can be no doubt that all these tablets in this northern area belong together. Now it is made perfectly clear that in 1900 all the tablets in the Saffron Gatherer Room, as in the Stirrup-Vase Room, were found '*on the clay floor*', on which the late reoccupation pottery stood. But in the following year part of this floor was removed, and another floor was revealed about 40 cm lower. Above, but not on this floor, a few fragments of tablets were collected in a very bad condition. No pottery was reported which could serve to characterize the earlier floor level. In his *Handlist* Evans assigns all the tablets found in 1900 to the Room of the Saffron Gatherer, and we do not know which texts were found in the Room of the Stirrup-Jars. In the first edition of this book I wrote that it was not possible to single out which were the tablets found in 1901 at the lower level. But once the *Handlist* was made available after it had been retrieved from the basement of the Ashmolean Museum, analysis showed that the texts from 1901 were written on different paper from those of 1900 and also bore numbers higher than 917. It thus proved possible to identify the few texts found above the lower floor in 1901. They were of the usual type and in Greek. In subject, too, they linked up with those found the previous year. Unfortunately, though this new precision had been secured, the stratigraphic circumstances of the find remained obscure. Certainly the tablets had been secured *above* the lower floor, but at a point where the upper floor had not been found preserved. This meant that these pieces of clay could easily have worked down to their find positions. In any case, the lower floor above which they were found was re-examined in 1923 and proved to have been repatched with typical LM III B plaster (see above p. 224). If despite these obscurities, we insist that the tablets were of an earlier date than those found in 1900, then this would give us welcome evidence for the Greek occupation at an earlier date within the long LM III B period. Mackenzie does not record any sherds along with this small batch of tablets.

The Coming of the Greeks

If there were in fact Linear B tablets at two different occupation levels, both LM III B, this would give us a welcome archaeological parallelism with the facts brought out in our discussion of the School Room in the Domestic Quarter (p. 236), where we saw clear evidence, acknowledged by Evans, for some work of reconstruction during the 'Reoccupation Period', pottery of the latest date being found underneath the blocking wall and the threshold. Similar facts appear in the western magazines.

Thus if LM III B pottery is found under such late structures, we should not be surprised to find LM III B tablets in similar circumstances. It is a pity that the 1901 tablets from the Room of the Saffron Gatherer never appeared in the archaeological communications or discussions despite Mackenzie's unambiguous entries.[1] On the contrary, Evans simply published a statement about tablets found to the north of the Room of the Stirrup Jars without ceramic context, beneath the late pottery on the overlying clay floor. This, as we saw, (pp. 223 ff.) conflicts with primary sources.

So much for signs of adaptation and rebuilding during the LM III period, which is assigned a length five times that of LM II (1450–1400). We now turn to another question. What evidence have we met for the latest use of Linear A? Again we encounter disquieting facts. In 1901, while excavations were being carried out on the south front of the Palace, basements were found containing much late Reoccupation pottery. In this area a vase was found bearing an incised inscription, which Evans believed to be in Linear B. It lay along with others in a layer of burnt wood, and just above the floor on which it lay were the foundations of rubble walls belonging to the latest period of re-occupation. Later Evans realized that the inscription was in fact in Linear A. This is precisely the stratification we expect: LM III B, to which we have assigned the Linear B tablets (some of which were found at this level in this very area), immediately overlies a stratum with a Linear A inscription. Later, when he had come to realize that he had made a mistake about the script, Evans repented of the stratification. He wrote (*Scripta Minoa* I, p. 29): '... the stratigraphic conditions of this discovery were not rightly appreciated

---

[1] 'The conclusion is that the earlier floor as well as the later is Mycenaean.' (Entry for 8 April 1901).

when the preliminary account was written'. To this we must add
that the writing was not appreciated either. To state the facts in
the most objective way, we observe that Evans's second thoughts
about the stratigraphic conditions are concomitant with the
realization that the script is A and not B.

Now we make a precisely similar observation in Evans's treatment of other inscribed pottery from the south-east part of the
site. There the walls showed a triple stratification. On the topmost
floor level there was a jar 'apparently belonging to the Latest
Palace Period. In this stratum were also found fragments of good
painted pottery of the Palace Style and the two ink-written
inscriptions described in the preceding report.' These are Evans's
own words, published in 1903. The two plain cups with ink-
written inscriptions belonging to the same deposit had been reproduced in the report for 1902. There we note that Evans believed
that the script was of the B type; and he transcribes the texts into
normalized Linear B characters. But again he later came to
realize that he had made the same mistake; the script was in fact
Linear A. This is how the find circumstances were subsequently
reported: 'Here . . . was a floor level upon which were found
several characteristic vessels of the Third Middle Minoan class.
Among these were two cups exhibiting round their inner surface
ink-written inscriptions of this same [i.e. A] class.' Once again
we state objectively that the revision of the find data is concomitant with the realization that the script is A and not B, as he
had previously supposed. The associated 'good painted pottery of
the Palace Style' has turned into 'characteristic vessels of the
Third Middle Minoan class'. Now all we say is that the facts of the
primary communication[1] harmonize more with our findings than
the second thoughts, where non-archaeological considerations of
the script have intervened. Middle Minoan III pottery could
hardly be confused by a competent archaeologist with good
painted pottery of the Palace Style. If it was so confused by
Evans, then we cannot escape the conclusion that doubt attaches
to much of his archaeological reporting and to the division into
periods characterized by particular styles of pottery. We remind

---

[1] Now confirmed by an entry in Evans's private notebook for 1902: 'In a
distinct Mycenaean stratum with pottery of good Palace period.'

ourselves that as late as 1925 the author of *The Palace of Minos* was confusing MM III B pottery with LM III B. We now have added a key instance where he was apparently in doubt as between MM III and 'good painted pottery of the Palace Style'. It is in the light of these instances of ceramic uncertainty that we must assess the fact that the dating of the Throne Room depended on a statement made by a man of eighty-five in the year 1935 about a sherd which he had found in 1913 and believed to be of Palace Style. The fall of Knossos is a cardinal date in the prehistory of Europe.

6. Epilogue: Philology and Archaeology

We conclude with some general reflexions. The disciplines of archaeology and philology in this field of endeavour are both concerned with the same ultimate purpose, which is to illuminate the prehistory of Anatolia and the Aegean. The truth will not be clearly established until the two images coincide. It remains to say that the techniques of the two sister disciplines are so diverse that each group of scholars would do well to advance to the frontiers of its competence and then ask questions. Nothing is gained by mutual defiance. In the above analysis we have accepted without question the archaeological findings and the conclusions based on them and have limited ourselves merely to examining the philological implications. In so doing a possible way of bringing the archaeological and the linguistic images together has been suggested. Briefly the thesis is that the archaeological 'Grey Minyan folk' from Asia Minor are to be identified with the philological 'Parnassos folk' from the same region.

Chronological Table

CHRONOLOGICAL TABLE

	CRETE			MAINLAND
2000	Middle Minoan I–IIIA. First palaces at Knossos and Mallia. Use of the Hieroglyph and Linear A scripts.			
1900				
1800				Middle Helladic. LUVIANS ARRIVE IN GREECE ('Grey Minyan Folk' = 'Parnassos Folk'). Connexions with Crete only via Cyclades until very end of period.
1700	Middle Minoan IIIB. The 'New Era'. ARRIVAL OF LUVIANS. Appearance of Linear A script. Rise of second palaces. Knossos and Phaestos royal abodes.			
1600	Late Minoan IA. Dominance of Knossos. Mallia destroyed (Furumark). Phaestos now seat of vassal king.		······→	Late Helladic I. COMING OF THE GREEKS. Rise of Royal Power in Argolis. Start of Minoization.
1500	Late Minoan IB. Artistic hegemony of Knossos. Phaestos, Hagia Triada etc. destroyed (Furumark)?		······→ ······→ ······→	Late Helladic IIA. Culmination of Minoization. Trade with Aegean opened up at expense of Crete. Rise of Tholos tombs.
1450	Late Minoan II (Knossos only): the 'Palace Period'. Connexions with Mainland interrupted (Furumark). Destruction of Knossos (and all Cretan cities?). Last Linear A texts.			Late Helladic IIB. Connexions with Crete interrupted. 'The calm before the storm'. Increased penetration of Aegean. Colony established in Rhodes (Ialysos). 'Destruction of Minoan colony at Trianda.
1400	Late Minoan III. ARRIVAL OF THE GREEKS, who dominate whole island. Phaestos and Hagia Triada reoccupied. New settlements under control of Knossos in Western Crete. Knossian pottery 'democratized' and new style influences Mainland. Use of Linear B script.		←————	Late Helladic IIIA. Expedition launched against Crete.
1300				Late Helladic IIIB. Acme of Mycenaean power and expansion. New dynasty in Pylos. Building of Palace of Nestor. Use of Linear B script. Destruction of Pylos and houses outside palace at Mycenae.
1200	Continuance of Mycenaean power in Central and South Aegean under Cretan influence. Destruction of Knossos by the Dorians.			Late Helladic IIIC. Destruction of Mycenae by the Dorians.
1100				

NOTE: The absolute dates are rough approximations, but the dates for Middle Minoan may be 200–300 years too high (Astrom and Levi). Late Minoan IA and IB are probably contemporary.

	TROY	EGYPT	
		Dynasties XII–XIII	2000
	TROY V		1900
From W. Asia Minor ←	TROY VI Probably occupied by Anatolian people speaking a language akin to the Luvian of the 'Parnassos Folk'		1800
		Hyksos in Egypt	1700
			1600
		Dynasty XVIII	
			1500
			1450
			1400
			1300
	TROY VIIA Destroyed by Mycenean Greek expedition.	Dynasty XIX	
			1200
	TROY VIIB	Dynasty XX	
			1100

The status of Late Minoan II (Palace style) is contested. ·······→ denotes 'cultural influence', ———→ denotes 'invasion'.

Index I:
Names and Subjects

Index

Index

Index

Index

Index

Index II:
Linear B Words

369

A NOTE ABOUT THE AUTHOR

LEONARD R. PALMER, born in 1906, holds a Ph.D. from the University of Vienna (1931), and from Trinity College, Cambridge (1932). He was Professor of Greek and Head of the Classics Department, King's College, London, from 1945 to 1952, and has been Professor of Comparative Philology at Oxford since 1952. Among his publications are An Introduction to Modern Linguistics *(1936),* A Grammar of the Post-Ptolemaic Papyri *(1945),* The Latin Language *(1954),* The Interpretation of Mycenaean Greek Texts *(1963), and* The Find Places of the Knossos Tablets *(1963). Professor Palmer lives with his wife and daughter in Oxford, England.*

July 1965

A NOTE ON THE TYPE

The text of this book is set on the Monotype in a type called SCOTCH. *Though there is a divergence of opinion regarding its exact origin, a cutting of such a face was undertaken and recorded by Messrs. Miller and Richard, of Edinburgh, in 1808. Their specimen sheet of 1812 shows the undeniable features of the face. It is the "Scotch" version of a general renewal of style, the change-over from the pen-derived "Old Style" to the tectonically conceived "Modern" initiated by the Didot-Bodoni revolution of the late eighteenth century. Its essential characteristics are sturdy capitals, full-rounded lower-case letters, the graceful fillet of the serifs, and a general effect of crispness through sharply contrasting "thicks and thins."*